Prince George County, Virginia

Order Book

1714/5–1720/1

Wesley E. Pippenger

HERITAGE BOOKS
2022

HERITAGE BOOKS
AN IMPRINT OF HERITAGE BOOKS, INC.

Books, CDs, and more—Worldwide

For our listing of thousands of titles see our website
at
www.HeritageBooks.com

Published 2022 by
HERITAGE BOOKS, INC.
Publishing Division
5810 Ruatan Street
Berwyn Heights, Md. 20740

Cover photo: Merchants Hope Church, Prince George County, Virginia

International Standard Book Number
Paperbound: 978-0-7884-2609-4

INTRODUCTION

This work presents a verbatim transcript of the original record book that runs from the court term March 1714/5 through March 1720/1, with a few pages at the end for executions over multiple years.

The order book contains the usual variety of items that occur during the daily business of the county court. Entries include: adjudgements for age of Negroes; appointment of officials (including constable, guardian of an orphan, sheriff, road overseer, or vestryman, etc.); appointment of estate administrators; apprenticeships; exemptions from levy; ordinary licenses; periodic county expenses for buildings, roads, repairs, salaries, etc.; presentment by churchwardens of women claimed to have produced a bastard child; probate of wills; status of court cases (civil and criminal); tithables; and more. There is much activity about suits for debt, as the absence of banks left the court as the arena for settlement of many financial disputes.

Images of the original record are found in more than one place, including the Library of Virginia and online at *FamilySearch.org*. The original is found copied on the Library's Miscellaneous Reel 7 as a positive print, while it also appears on Miscellaneous Reel 31 as a negative print that was presumably taken from a photostat. The latter offers a better reproduction of disbound pages and shows page edges that are often obscured from view on the earlier microfilm product. Reel 7 is missing pages 299-300, while Reel 31 contains a duplicate image sequenced as both page 117 and page 147.

Wesley E. Pippenger
Little Egypt
Tappahannock, Virginia
February 2022

ABBREVIATIONS AND TERMS

&c	Etcetera, indicating further information may have been given earlier and not repeated
accot.	Account
Admr.	Administrator
als exec.	Execution has been performed
complt.	Complaint or complainant
Deced:	Deceased, with variants
deft.	defendant
demurrer	An allegation of a defendant who admits matters of fact in the complaint to be true but states they are insufficient for the plaintiff to proceed or to oblige the defendant to answer
detinue	Action for recovery in specie of personal chattels from one who acquired them lawfully but retains without right
Exor.	Executor
Exrx.	Executrix
imparlance	Given time to either party to answer the pleading of another.
nil debit	He owes nothing.
non detinet	Plea that indicates one does not detain the goods at issue.
non est inventus	He is not found; the Sheriff's return to process results in the person not being found in the jurisdiction.
plt.	plaintiff
plene administravit	The administrator pleas all assets of the deceased's estate have been exhausted.
retraxit	Latin for he has withdrawn.
scire facias	a writ that requires the person against whom it is brought to show why the party bringing it should not have advantage of such record
sd.	said
Sherr:	Sheriff
Sterl:	Pounds Sterling
trover	For the recovery of damages against a person who had found another's goods and wrongfuly converted them to his own use.
wch.	which
wth.	with
ye	the

[Note: Pages 1 and 2 are missing, as is the date of the beginning court term that is likely April Term 1714/5.]

[page 3]

The Action on the Case Entd. by William Wheatley against Edward Goodrich neither party appearing is Dismisst.

The action of accot. render between William Wheatley and Edward Goodrich is Continued till next Court by Consent.

In the Action of Debt between Jean Steagall plt. and James Loftin Deft. for Six hundred pounds of Sweet Scented Tobacco and Caske Due by Bill Dated the twelveth of March One thousand Seaven hundred and ten, Eleaven, the Deft. being returned *non est Inventus* and failing to appear on the motion of the plts. Attorney an Attachment is granted her agst. the Estate of the said Deft. for the aforesaid Sum with Costs returnable to the next Court for Judgement.

In the action on the Case between William Mathews plt. and Elizabeth Lim[brey] Executrix &c of John Limbrey Deced. Deft. for One pound Sixteen Shillings and one penny half penny Current money Due by accot. &c the Deft. appears an[d] prays Oyer of the plts. accot. wch. is granted and time till the next Cout to Consider the Same.

Whereas by Virtue of an Attachment granted (by One of his Majestys Justi[ces] of the peace for this County) to Nathl. Harrison Eqr. Attorney of *John Grove and Company*, Merchants in Barbadose, against the Estate of ffrancis Clement who had withdrawn himselfe so that the Ordinary process at Law could not be Served against him which said Attachment at the Last Court being re[turned] Executed on a part of the Estate of the sd. ffrancis and he failing to app[ear] to replevy the same, Judgement was granted the sd. Nathaniel Attorney as aforesaid against the said ffrancis for the Sum of One hundred ninety nine pounds, thirteen Shillings and five pence farthing Sterl: and the said Estate att[ached] as aforesaid Ordered to be Appraised according to Law, and Delivered the said Nathaniel and toward the payment and satisfaction thereof, and that a Report of the appraisement of the same be made to this Court so that Execution might for the residue of the aforesaid Sum, and the Sherriff accordingly now reports the said Estate to be appraised to the sum of One hundred fifty two pounds One Shilling and Six pence, which is Ordered to be recorded, and that the Nathaniell have Execution for the residue of the aforesaid Sum of One hundred Ninety Nine pounds thirteen Shillings and five pence farthing Sterl: being forty seaven pounds Eleaven Shillings and Eleaven pence farthing due with Costs.

On the motion of Sampson Merredeth [Sherr] for the allowance of his f[...] in Attaching the Estate of ffrancis Clements as above mentioned, It's Ordered be allowed for the Same as for an Execution.

[page 4]

In the action of Debt Depending between John Doby plt. and Elizabeth L[imbrey] Executrix of the Last Will and Testament of John Limbrey Deced: Deft. for four hundred Ninety Seaven pounds of Tobacco Due by Bill Dated Sixteenth Day of January One thousand Seaven hundred and Six, the plt. made Oath that he never reced: any Satisfaction for the Same, whereupon by Consent of the sd. Deft. Judgement is granted the plt. against her for the Sum of four hundred Ninety Seaven pounds of Tobacco wth. Costs. Als. Exec.

In the Action of Tressprass [sic] on the Case between John Ellis Junr. plt. and Randall Platt Deft. at the Last Court the Deft. pleaded and demurred, the plts. Declaration who had time till this Court to Consider the Sa[me] now appearing Joins in the Demurrer aforesaid, which is referred to the next Court to be Argued.

The Attachment awarded Charles Goodrich plt. against the Estate of Daniell Higdon Deft. is Continued till the next Court.

The action on the Case between Elizabeth Epes Exrx. &c. of Wm. Epes [deced:] plt. and Richard Hamelin Deft. is referred till next Court.

The Suit in Chancery between John and Samuell Vaughn, Complts. James Sevecar Deft. is referred till next Court.

The Order that ffrancis Clements Yeo: give Security for George Bleighton Deced. his Estate is Continued till next Court.

In the Suit in Chancery between Joshua Irby and John Melone [McCone] the respondent appears and files a Demurrer to ye Complaints. replication at whose prayer time is granted till the next Court to Consider the Same.

In the action on the Case between John Cargill and Sarah his wife plts. and Bryan Farrell Deft. for three thousand One hundred pounds of Tobacco Due by accot. &c at the former Court the Deft. pleaded that he [...] Detained not the aforesaid Sum of Tobo. and the plts. Joining in the same -- -- -- was referred to this Court for Tryall and the said partys now appearing and a Jury being Impannelled and Sworne to trye [the] matter in Issue by Name, Thomas Simmons, John Wilkins, John Lett, James Bell, Hugh Golightly, Wm. Cuerton, Thos. Booth, ffrancis Poythres, Wm. Harrison, Samuel Vaughn, William Wells and Wm. Standb[ack] Junr. who haveing heard the Evidence and received their Charge were sent out.

1

The Suit in Chancery between John Williams & Uxor. and J[ohn] Owen is referred till next Court.

[page 5]
In the Action on the Case between Isham Epes plt. and William Wheatley Deft. the plt. by Robt. Blawes and Edward Goodrich his Attorneys Setts forth that on the tenth Day of November Last past in the Parrish of Varina in the County of Henrico the sd. plt. did lend & Deliver to the Deft. one Sadle and furniture belonging to this plt. of the Value of five pounds Current money which he hath not as yet redelivered but the Same doth refuse to the plts. Damage Seaven pounds Current money, and the Deft. being called and not appearing, On the motion of the plts. Attorneys Judgement is granted him against Robert Rogers returned Security for the Deft. for the said Sum of Seaven pounds Current money and Costs, unless the Deft. appears at the next Court and answers the said Action.

Judgement being this Day granted unto Isham Epes against Robert Rog[ers] for the Sum of Seaven pounds Current money and Costs by reason of the nonappearance of William Wheatley in an Action on the Case at the suit of the sd. Isham, On the motion of the said Robert an attachment is granted him against the Estate of the said William Wheatley for the aforesaid Sum and Costs, returnable to the next Court for Judgement.

The action of Debt between William Browne Assignee of John Hatch, plt. and Richard Wallpoole Deft. neither party appearing is Dismisd.

John Woodson plt. against ffrancis Clements and Lydia his wife Admrx. of the Estate of George Bleighton Decd. Defts. per [*scire facias*] [and] wherein the plt. setts forth that at a Court held for this County the thirt[...] Day of May one thousand Seaven hundred and twelve, Judgement was gran[ted] him against the said Defendts. for the Sum of four pounds five Shillings with Costs, and that Execution thereof yet remains to be Done, and said Defts. being Summoned to appear before this Court to show cause why the said plt. ought not to have Execution against them of the Debt and Damages aforesaid according to fforme force and Effect of the said Judgement, and they failing to appear to do the Same, Therefore it is Considered by the Court that the said plt. have Execution against the said Defts. for his Debt and Damages aforesaid according to the forme Tenor and Effect of the sd. Judgemt. wth. present Costs.

In the action on the Case between Edward Goodrich plt. and ffrancis Clements Deft. the plt. setts forth that on or about the first Day of J[une?] Last past in the County of Surry, the sd. Deft. did promise and Assume and with the plt. that if he'ed accept and take the Sum of One thousand poun[ds] of good Dress pork for and in Consideration of the Sum of One thousand pounds of Tobacco then Due and Owing to this plt. from ffrancis Clements the young son of this Deft. that then he the said Deft. would pay and Deliver the same to this plt. at Some Convenient Landing in Martins brandon in the County within ten days next ensueing, and the said Deft. being returned *Non*

[page 6]
Est Invent[us] and not appearing, on the motion of the plt. an Attach[ment] is granted him agst. the Estate of the sd. Deft. for the aforesaid Sum & Costs returnable to the next Court for Judgement.

In the action on the Case between James Bell and Martha his wife Administratrix of the Estate of Edward Marks Deced. plts. and ffrancis Clements Deft. the plts. Set forth that in the year of our Lord One thousand Seaven hundred and Eleaven, the Church Wardens of Martins Brandon Parrish in this County were Justly Indebted to them the Sum of four hundred fifty nine pds. of Tobacco for Services done for the use of the said Parrish, and pr. the said ffrancis on or abt. the tenth Day of December in the year aforesaid and Parrish aforesaid did [&] promise and Assume to the plts. that in Consideration they would release and Discharge the said Church Wardens from the Debt afroesaid, that he the said ffrancis would Satisfie and pay to the sd. plts. the sd. Sum of Tobacco and Demand, and the said Deft. being returned *non est Inventus* and not appearing on the motion of the plts. an Attachment is granted them against the Estate of the said Deft. for the aforesaid Sum wth. Costs, returnable to the next Court for Judgement.

In the Action of Debt between James Bell and Martha his wife Admrx. of the Estate of Edward Marks Deced: plats. and ffrancis Clements Executor of the Last Will and Testament of Wm. Barto[n] Deced: Deft. for five hundred and Nineteen pounds of Tobacco in Cask Due by Bills Dated One thousand Seaven hundred and Ten, the Deft. being returned *non est Inventus* and not appearing, on the motion of the plts. an Attachment awarded them against the Estate of the Sd. Deft. Barton in the hands and possession of the sd. Deft. Executor as aforesaid for the sd. Sum & Costs, returnable to the next Court for Judgement.

In the action on the Case brought by Richard Hamelin plt. against ffrancis Clements Deft., the plt. Setts forth that on or about the tenth Day of October Last past in the Parrish of Martins Brandon in this County the said Deft. did promise and Assume to and with the sd. plt. that in Consideration he the said Richard would pay to Issau Lowry the Sum of Six hundred and Seaventy pounds of Tobacco and five Shillings & Seaven pence halfe penny Current money which the said ffrancis stood Justly Indebted to the said Issau, that he the said ffrancis would Satisfie and repay to the sd. plt. the aforesaid Sums of Tobo. and money on Demand on the plts: motion an Attachment is awarded him against the said Defts. Estate for the aforesaid Sums, and Costs returnable to the next Court for Judgment.

[page 7 pencil]
fformer Court being returned *non est Inventus* and not appearing at the plts. prayer an Attachment was awarded him against the Defts. Estate returnable to the next Court for Judgemt., which being now returned Executed on a part of the sd. Defts. Estate, he the sd. Defendt. appears and vacates the same and on the motion of John Hatch he is Entred. Special Baile for the said Deft., who failing further to plead or to offer any thing in barr or preclusion of the plts: said Action, It's therefore Considered by the Court yt. the plt. recover against the sd. Defendt. the aforesaid Sum of Nineteen pounds seaventeen Shillings and Nine pence half penny, unless the Deft. appears at the next Court and answers the said Action.

Daniel Higdon in Open Court acknowledges that he has Confirmed and made Over to John Hatch One Negro man Slave named Tom wth. Condition that if the said Daniel shall Indemnifie the said John from the payment of any money or other Damage which shall be awarded Charles Goodrich in an Action of Debt now Depending in this Court between the sd. Charles and the said Daniell and in which at the request of the said Daniell the said John Hatch became Speciall Baile that then this present recognizance to be Void and of None Effect otherways to remain in full power force and Vertue.

Richard Harrison having attended One Day as an Evidence for Arthur Biggins in the Action of Tresspass on the Case brot. by the said Arthur against William Short, Ordered the said Arthur pay him forty pounds of Tobacco for the Same wth. Costs: Als. Exec.

Richard Harrison haveing attended One Day as an Evidence in the Suit Depending between Arthur Biggins and William Short, Ordered that the said William pay him forty pounds of Tobacco for the Same wth. Costs: Als. Exec.

John Brockwell haveing attended one Day as an Evidence in the action of Tresspass on the Case between Arthur Biggins plt. and William Short Deft. before Issue Joined, therefore Order'd that the sd. plt. pay him forty pounds of Tobacco for the Same wth. costs: Als: Exec:

John Brockwell haveing Attended one Day as an Evidence in the Action of Tresspass on the Case Depending between Arthur Biggins plt. and William Short Deft., order'd the said Deft. pay him forty pounds of Tobacco for the Same, wth. Costs. Als: Exec:

[page 8 pencil]
pay all costs and Damages that Shall be awarded the Deft. against the plt. in this Suit, and thereupon the Same is referred by Consent till next Court.

In the Action of Debt brought by Joan Steagall plt. agst. [...] Loftin Deft. the said Deft. at the Last Court being returned *non est Inventus* and failing to appear an Attachment was awarded the plt. against his the said Defts. Estate returnable to this Court for Judgment and the said Deft. now appearing Vacates the Same and files a demurrer to the plts. Declaration who has time till the next Court to Consider the Same.

In the action on the case between William Mathews plt. and Eliz[a] Limbrey Exrx. &c of John Limbrey Deced: Deft. for One pound Sixteen [shillings] and one penny half penny Currt. money Due by accot. &c. at the Last Court Oyer of the said accot. was granted the Deft. and time to Consider the Same this Court, and the sd. plt. faileing to file the sd. accot. till this day, therefore on the Deft. motion time is granted her till the next Court to C[onsider] the said accot. as aforesaid.

John Ellis junr. plt. vs. Randall Platt Deft., in an action of Tr[...] on the Case, Damage thirty pounds Sterl:, wherein at a former Court [...] Deft. pleaded and Demurred to the plts. Declaration, who Joining in [the] said Demurrer the Same was referred to this Court to be argued [...] Attorneys of the said partys Now appearing and the Demurrer aforesaid be sufficiently argued is Adjudged Insufficient, whereupon the plt. filed Demurrer to the Defts. plea abovemention'd who Joins in the Same, and is thereupon referred till the next Court to be Argued.

Elizabeth Epes Exrx. &c. of Wm. Epes Deced. plt. against Richd. Ha[melin] Deft. in an action on the case for twenty three Shillings and ten pence Due by accot. Dated 1704 to which at a former Court the Deft. having pleaded *nil debit* and the plt. Joining in the Issue the Same was referred Randall Platt Gent. to Determine and to make report of his proceeding to this Court, who faileing therein, and the said partys now appearing and putting themselves on the Court for Tryall of the Issue aforesaid and [the] plt. faileing to prove her said accot. at the Defts. motion the suit thereupon Dismist.

In the action of Debt Depending between Charles Goodrich plt. Daniell Higdon Deft. for Nineteen pounds, Seaventeen Shillings and [...] pence half penny Due by Bill Dated Jany. the 24th 1710, the Deft. at [...]

[page 9 pencil]
Rebecca Harrison Administratrix of Hannah Harrison Deced. retu[rned] a further Inventory of the said Deceds. Estate, Ordered it be recorded.

Pursuant to the Direction of an Act of Assembly Entitled an Act Concerning Jurys, Ordered that the Sheriff Summon twenty four freeholders of this County to appear at the next Court, out of which to be Impannelled a Grand Jury to make Enquiry into the breach of the penall Laws &c.

James Thweatt in Open Court acknowledges his Deeds of Lease and Release (of Land) (Indented and Sealed) bearing Date the Eighth and Ninth Days of April 1715 to John Cureton and his heirs for ever on whose prayer the same are Ordered to be recorded.

Littlebury Epes plt. vrs. John Peterson Deft. [on] an Action of Tress[pass] on the case Damage Ten pds. &c to which the Deft. haveing pleaded and Demurred and the plt. Joining in the said Demurrer the Same was referred [to] this Court to be Argued and the sd. partys now appearing and the Demurrer aforesaid being Sufficiently Argued by the Attorneys of both (the sd.) partys is Adjudg[ed] Good and the Suit thereupon Ordered to be Dismist.

John Cargill & Uxor. vrs. Bryan ffarrell for three thousand One hundred pounds of Tobacco Due by accot. Dated 1704 wherein at a fformer Court the Deft. pleaded that he Detained not the aforesaid Sum of Tobo. and the [plt.] Joining in the Issue it thereupon was referred to the Last Court for Tryall when a Jury was Impannelled and Sworn to trye the Same, who after haveing heard the Evidence and reced. their Charge were Ordered to [...] and agree on and return their Verdict and not haveing time then to do the Same are now again Ordered to retire for that purpose, and after Some time spent therein at being made appear to the Court that the said Jury cannot agree on a Genrall Verdict they thereupon are Directed and Ordered to find the Same Specially and to Deliver their said Verdict ([...]up) to the Sherriff to be by him Returned to the next Court.

Majr. Robt. Munford, Present

The Attachment awarded Colo. Diggs against the Estate of ffra[n]: Mallory is Continued in full force till next Court.

In the Suit Depending between Charles Anderson Surviveing Exr. &c. plt. [vrs] Samuel Sentall Deft. the Deft. appears and files a plea to the plts. Declaratoin who has time till the next Court to Consider the same.

[page 10]
In the action of Debt Depending between Robert Nicholson plt. and Rich[ard] Jones junr. Deft. for two thousand three hundred and Sixty pounds of Tobacco D[ue] by Bond Dated the twelveth Day of January 1713, at the Last Court oyer of the sd. Bond was granted the Deft. and time to Consider the Same till this Court and being now called and faileing to appear and to Offer anything [in] barr or preclusion of the plts. Action. Therefore it is Considered by this Court that the said plt. do recover against the sd. Deft. the aforesaid Sum of two thousand three hundred and Sixty pounds of Tobacco, unless he appears at the next Court and answers the said Action.

In the action of Tresspass on the Case brought by Arthur Biggins plt. against Wm. Short Deft. the plt. Setts forth that on the Sixth Day of January 1714 in the Parrish of Wyanoake in this County he the sd. plt. was possess[ed] of One Grey Gelding of the Value of ten pds. Sterl: with a Sadle and Bridle of the Value of fifty Shillings Sterl: on the said Gelding being, and that the sd. Deft. at the time and place aforesaid did cutt, mangle and Disfigure the said Gelding by dying and shareing [shearing] his main and Tail and the Sadle and bridle on the sd. Gelding did cutt, spoill and render utterly useless to the plts. Damage twenty pounds Sterl: to which the Deft. at the Last Court pleaded Not Quity and the plt. Joining in the Issue the same was referred to this Court for Tryall, and the said partys now appearing and the Jury being Impannelled and Sworn to Trye the Issue aforesaid by the name Edmond Irby, Robert Poythress, Gilbert Hay, Roger Taylor, Edward Epes, Richard Kirkland, Roger Rease, James Grenan, William Reves, John Lewis, Paul Jones, and Charles Williams who haveing heard the Evidence and reced. their Charge, are Ordered to withdraw, and after Some time Spent therein return their Verdict in these words vizt. we find for the plt. forty Shillings Sterl: Damage, Edmond Irby, foreman) [sic], which at the plts. prayer is Ordered to be recorded and Judgement is granted him against the said Deft. for the aforesd. Sum of forty Sterl: wth. Costs. Als: Exec.

In the action of the case Depending between Elizabeth Epes Exrx. &c of Wm. Epes Deced. plt. and Peter Wynne Admr. &c of Joshua Wynne Deced. Deft. the Judgement of the Last Court is Continued in full force and Effect till the next Court.

In the acton of accot. Render brought by William Wheatly agt. Edward Goodrich, Robert Rogers, Enters Himselfe Security for the sd. plt.

[pages 11-12 are missing]

4

[page 13 pencil]

James Chappell in Open Court acknowledges a Discharge to James Jones junr. for all his the said James Chappells part of his Deced. father's Thos. Chappells Estate, in the hands and pos[session] of the sd. Jones, Ordered the said Discharge be recorded.

Jean Dewell Admrx. of the Estate of Job Dewell Deced. returned a further Inventory and an accot. of the appraismt. of the sd. Deceds. Estate, Ordered the Same be recorded.

On the Petition of William Plains Senr., Ordered that he be County Leavy free for the future.

Pursuant to the Direction of an Act of Assembly Entituled an Act Concerning Jurys, at the Last Court it was Ordered that the Sherriff Shou'd Sumon a Lawfull Grand Jury to this Court to make Enquiry into the Breaches of the penall Laws of this Collony, who accordingly brings to the Barr John Evans, Thomas Lewis, John Hobbs, William Rease, John Arnall, Richard Scoggin, Danl. Higdon, Thomas Addison, Nicholas Robertson, Richard Smith, John Ellis junr., John Vaughn, Wm. Adams, John Ledbetter & Robert Birchell who being first sworn and haveing their Charge withdraw, and after Some time Spent, return their presentments as follows Vizt. Elizabeth Bristoll in the Parrish of Martins Brandon for haveing a Bastard Child. John Evans foreman.

Ordered that Elizabeth Bristoll be Sumoned to appear at the next Court to answer the presentment of the Grand jury.

On the motion of Wm. Browne, of Surry County, Robt. Rogers is Entred. his Attorney, all Causes and matters that may be at any time hereafter Depending in this County Court.

John Butler and Elizabeth Woodleif in Open Court acknowledge their Deeds of Lease and Release of Lands (Indented and Sealed) bearing Date the Eleeventh and twelveth Days of April 1715 to Richard Tomkins and Michall Rosser and their heirs for ever, Ordered the said Deeds be recorded, and then also did Mary the wife of the sd. John Butler freely relinquish her right of Dower of in and to the said Lands she being first privily Examined according to Law, Ordered the Same be recorded.

On the motion of the Churchwardens of Westopher Parrish it's ordered that Margaret Sloan be Summoned to the next Court to answer the presentment of the Grand jury.

On the Petition of Edward Denton, he is Exempted from paying the County Leavy for the future.

[page 14 pencil]

William Wynne haveing attended One Day as an Evidence in the Tresspass on the Case brot. by Arthur Biggins against William Short [...] the said Short pay him forty pounds of Tobacco for the Same wth. Costs &c

Ordered that Robert Wynne the Son of Major Joshua Wynne Deced. be an apprentice to John Hamelin untill he the said Robert shall attain the age of twenty one years, and that the said Hamelin use his [...] to Learn the sd. Robert to Read and to write, and also the Occupation of a Ship carpenter.

And then the Court Adjourn'd till Court in Course. Test. Wm. Hamelin, Cl. Cur. John Hamelin.

Att a Court held for the County of Pr. Geo: the Second Tues.
in May 1715 being the tenth Day of the said Month

Present	John Hamelin	Randall Platt	Robt. Hall
	John Peterson	& John Hardyman	Gent. Justices

John Price in Open Court acknowledges his Deeds of Lease and [Release] of Land (Indented and Sealed) to Samuell Lee and his heirs forever, Ordered said Deeds be recorded.

Ann Kemp, Widow and relict of John Kemp of this County, Late Deced. Comes into Court and makes Oath that the sd. John Kemp [died] Intestate as farr as she knows or believes, and upon her giveing [security] for her just and faithfull administration of the said Deceds. Estate, it is Ordered that a Certificate be granted her for Obtaining Letters of [Adm]istration in Due forme, where upon Joshua Irby becomes her [surety] and together is [for] the sd. Ann Enter's into Bond in the Sum of forty pounds wth. Condition accordong to Law.

Instance Hall, Richard Hudson and Wm. Mayes or any two of [them] are Ordered to Appraise the Estate of John Kemp Deced. they being first Sworn by Some Justice of this County for that purpose, and that they [may] report of their proceedings therein to the next Court, when Ann Kemp Admrx. of the sd. Estate is to return the Inventory thererof.

Robt. Munford and James Thweatt present

Thomas Griffith a Servt. of Mr. Randall Platt, is Adjudged to have been Eighteen years of age at Christmast Last.

[page 15]

The suit in Chancery Depending between John and Saml. Vaughn and James Sevecar is referred till the next Court.

In the Suit in Chancery Depending between Joshua Irby and John Melone [McCone] at the Complaints. prayer time is granted him till the next Court to amend his repl[ication] to the Responds. answer.

In the Suit in Chancery Depending between John Williams and Rebecca his Wife Executrix of the Last Will and Testament of Robert [Minnett] Mercht. in Barbadoes, Lately Deced. Complainants, and John Owen, Respondent, the Coplts. set forth that in or about the year of Our Lord one thousand Seaven hundred and four the said Robert Minnett did Constitute the sd. John Owen to be his Correspond. and ffacter to receive and Dispose of Such Goods and Merchandises as shou'd be Sent him by the aforesd. Robt. upon the proper accot. risque and to the use of the sd. Robt. and one accot. thereof and Due payment of the proceeds of the said Goods was to be rendered and made to him the said Robert his Executors &c when he the said Owen shou'd be thereunto required, and accordingly in or abt. the year aforesaid the sd. Owen did receive one Negro Boy from the said Minnett which the said Owen sold for thirty pounds, yet did never pay unto the said Robert in his Life time any part or penny of the sd. Sum nor to the sd. Executtrix nor to Either of the sd. Complaints. Since their intermarriage altho' Often thereunto required, And forasmuch as by reason of the Death of the said Minnett and the Clandestine Actions of the said Owen the Complts. bring remidiless at Common Law in the premises, Her Late Majestys writ[...] of Supena was Directed to the said Owen Commanding him per penalty to appear before this Court and upon his Corporall Oath to answer the premises who accordingly appearing Confesses the recept. of the sd. Negro and that he sold the same for thirty pounds, and that pursuant to the sd. Minnett's Directions the sd. Respondt. on [...] Corporall Oath Declares that for ye real proceeds of sd. Negro he remitted Bills of Exchange for England for the use of the sd. Minnett payable to Robert Chester Mercht. of London, and according to the best of his Judgement and Skill he the sd. Owen Discharged the trust and Confidence reposed in him by the sd. Minnetts, the said partys by their Attorneys agreeing to proceed to Tryall on Bill and Answer and the Court after haveing heard and Comsidered the Arguements of Each of the sd. Attorneys do approve and allow the sd. respond. answer and Adjudge that he hath Discharged the Trust and Confidence reposed in him by the sd. Minnett and thereupon Order yt. the said Suit be Dismist. wth. Costs.

[page 16]

John Davis of this County haveing unlawfully Departed the Same being Indebted to William Wallice the Sum of two thousand five hundred and Eighty pounds of Tobacco, who (by Virtue of an Attachment granted the sd. Wm. and Executed on a part of the sd. Davis's Estate) obtained Judgment for the aforesaid Sums wch. an order that the sd. Estate shou'd be appraised and Delivered the said Wm. for Discharge thereof, and that a report of the appraisement of the Same shou'd be made to this Court, and the said Wm. accordingly returns an acct. of the sd. appraisement under the hands of the Severall persons appointed for that purpose. Ordered the Same be recorded.

In the Suit Depending between Isham Epes and William Wheatley for &c at the Last Court the Deft. failing to appear, Judgment was granted the plt. agst. Robert Rogers returnd. Security for the sd. Deft. & upon Condition that if the said Deft. shou'd appear at this Court and answer to this Court that then the said Judgment to be void, and he now appearing (by Robt. Rogers his Attorney) vacates the same, and on the Demand of the sd. plt. the said Rogers Enters himselfe Speciall Baile for the said Deft. and being permitted to plead Doubly accordingly files a plea & Demurrer to the plts. Declaration who Joins in the Same and is thereupon referred for Tryall to the next Court.

The Attachment awarded Robert Rogers against the Estate of Wm. Wheatly is Continued till the next Court.

The Suit Depending between Edward Goodrich and ffrancis Clements is Dismist.

The Suit Depending between James Bell and Martha his wife Admrx. of Edward Marks and ffrancis Clements, as appearance, is Dismist.

The Suit Depending between James Bell and Martha his wife Admrx. of Edward Markes and ffrancis Clements Exr. of Wm. Barton Deced. (neither party appearing) is Dismist.

In the action of the case Depending between Richard Hamlin and ffrancis Clements for Six hundred Seaventy five pounds of Tobacco and five Shillings and Seaven pence halfe penny Current money Due by assumption &c 8ber the 10th 1714 at the Last Court the Deft. being returned [...] and faileing to appear at the plts. prayer an Attachment was awarded him against the said Defts. Estate

[page 17]

returnable to this Court for Judgemt. which being returned Executed on sufficient in the hands of Paul Jones to Discharge the Same, and the said Deft. faileing to appear to replevye and Vacate the said Attachmt. and the sd. Jones being Summoned and Sworn to Declare what part of the sd. Defts. Estate he hath in his possession, accordingly

Confessed to have in Tobacco, sufficient to Satisfie and pay the aforesaid Sums, which the plt. proveing by his Oath to be justly Due to him, Therefore it is Considered by the Court that the plt. have judgmt. 2/1 for Seaven hundred thirty One pounds of Tobacco against the said Paul Jones, Instead of the aforesaid Sum of Six hundred Seaventy five pounds of Tobacco and five Shlilings and Seaven pence halfe penny Current money, goether wth. Costs. Als. Exec. if the same be not paid and Discharged by the 30th Day of November next.

Robert Bolling Admr. of Edward Bolling Deced. returns a further Inventory of the said Decedts. Estate, Ordered it be recorded.

The Suit Depending between John Butler Executor of Mutas Butler Deced. and Hugh Dayly (neither party appearing) is Dismist.

The Attachmt. awarded Sampson Merredeth Sherr. against the Estate of Hugh Dayly is Dismist.

In the action of Debt Depending between John Smith and John Smith junr. for three hundred pds. of Tobacco Due by Bill &c the Deft. haveing pleaded payment and the plt. now Joining in the Issue the Same thereupon is referred for Tryall to the next Court.

In the Suit Depending between William Short and Richard Pidgeon for three hundred pounds of Tobacco Due by assumpsit &c the Deft. appearing and offering a Discount, it is therefore Ordered that the accts. of the said Partys be referred to ffrancis Mallory and Richard Hamlin to Adjust who are to meat at the Court house on Tuesday next for that purpose, and to make report of their proceedings therein to the next Court.

In the suit Depending between John Cargill et uxor and Bryan ffarrell &c the Jury at a former Court Impannelled and Sworn to Trye the Issue Joined therein make report that they cannot agree on a Verdict, whereupon by Consent of the said partys the said Jury is Dismist. and the accounts of [ye] aforesaid partys referred to Colo. Nathl. Harrison to adjust, they in Open Court promising and agreeing Equally to pay the Charge of this Suit.

[page 18]

John Willborn a Lad under the Care of Arthur Biggins is Adjudged fourteen years of age.

In the action Depending between John Hobbs and John Let[t] Damage One thousand pounds of Tobacco, at the Last Court an Imparlance was granted the Deft. till this Court and [but] now faileing to appear and plead or to offer any thing in Barr or preclusion of the plts. accon. therefore it is Considered by the Court that the plt. ought to recover against the sd. Deft. his Damages by means of the non payment aforesaid, but because it is unknown to the Court what Damages the sd. plt. in that part hath sustained, Therefore it is Commanded that the Sherr: cause to come before his Majestys Justices at the next Court twelve good and Lawfull men of his Balywick by whose Oaths Diligent inquiry may be made of the said Damage.

In the action of Debt Depending between Richard Hamelin and Adam Tapley, the Deft. Offering a Discount to the plts Bill it is therefore Ordered that the same be referred to Edmond Irby and Gilbert Hays who are to meet at the Court house on Tuesday next to Settle and adjust the Same and make report of their proceedings to the next Court.

In an action of Debt Depending between John Nicholls and John Sherrly, no appearance is Dismist.

The Attachment awarded Sampson Merredeth Sherr: against the Estate of John Sherley, is Dismist.

On the motion of John Hardyman, Ordered that Thomas Eldridge and Robert Blaws be Entred the said Hardyman's Attorneys in all causes that may hereafter be Depending for or against him.

And then the Court adjourn'd till Court in Course. John Hamelin. Test. W. Hamelin, Cl. Cur.

[page 19]

At a Court held for the County of Prince George on the Second
Tuesday in June Anno Domini 1715, being the fourteenth day of
the said Month

Present, Gent. Justices

		Randall Platt
John Poythres	Robert Munford	Robt. Hall
James Thweatt	Lewis Green	John Peterson

On the petition of Peter Jones, he is permitted to turn the Road that Leads through his plantation, Provided he make the Same Convenient.

James Thweatt in Open Court acknowledges his Deeds of Lease and Release of Land (Indented and Sealed) bearing Date the thirteenth and fourteenth Days of June Anno Dom: 1715 to Edward Mitchell and his heirs for ever, And then also did Judith the Wife of the said James, Acknowledge the Same to be her act and Deed and relinquish her right of Dower therein, she being first privily Examined according to Law, and on the motion of the sd. Edward the said Deeds &c are Admitted to Record.

Judith Thweatt the wife of James Thweatt (being first privily Examined) in Open Court relinquishes her right of Dower in and to Certain Lands mentioned in Deeds of Lease and release for the Same, and acknowledges by the said James Thweatt at the Last Court to John Cureton, Ordered the Same be recorded.

On the petition of Rebecca Harrison and Thomas Harrison, Exrx. of Wm. Harrison Deced. and Wm. Adams, it's Ordered that John Tiller be Summoned to the next Court to answer the Same.

Mathew Markes haveing petitioned this Court that his house be entred a publick meeting house for those persons called Annabaptists, it's Ordered the Same be done Accordingly.

On the petition of Hugh Lee a Surveyor of the highways of the County it is Ordered that Math: Anderson, ffra: Coleman, Thos. Clay, ffra: Norten, Edward Birchet, Danl. and Samuell Vaughan, wth. the male Labouring Tithables of their familys assist in Clearing and repairing the highways of which the sd. Lee is Surveyor.

The petition of John Womack that he be Leavy free is Dismist.

The petition of Xpher Davis that he be Leavy free is Dismist.

On the petition of Nathl. Tatum it's Ordered that he be hereafter Exempted from paying the County Leavy.

The action on the Case between Robert Hunnicutt and Robert Acock (neither party appearing) is Dismist.

[page 20]

In the action of Tresspass on the Case Depending between Randall Platt and John Hardyman on the motion of the Deft. an Imparlance is granted him till the next Court.

In the action of Debt between Thomas Lewis and William Worsham, for twenty Shillings to be paid in some Convenient Store in this County Due by Bill &c the Deft. being called and not appearing, on the motion of the plt. Judgmt. is granted agst. ffrancis Coleman returned Security for the said Deft. for the said Sum, to be paid as aforesaid, wth. Costs, unless the Deft. appears at the next Court and answers the said Action.

In the action of Debt between Thomas Harrison and Henry Duke for Seaven hundred and Sixty pounds of Tobacco, Due by bill Dated the 23d of December 1714, the Deft. being returned *non est inventus* and not appearing on the motion of the plts. Attorney an Attachmt. is granted him against the Estate of the said Deft. for the aforesaid Sum and Costs, returnable to the next Court for Judgmt.

Robert Norden an Annabaptist preacher Appears in Court and takes the Oaths and Subscribes the Declarations mentioned in an Act of Parliament of the 4th of William & Mary &c Entituled an Act for Exempting their Majestys Protestant Subjects Dissenting from the Church of England from the penaltys of Certain Lands, Ordered the sd. Declarations be recorded.

The action on the Case between John Hughs and Henry Duke (neither party appearing) is Dismist.

The action of Debt between Robert Burbridge and Henry Duke (neither party appearing) is Dismist.

In the action of Debt Depending between Elizabeth Harrison Admrx. of Benjamin Harrison Deced. and Charles Goodrich for four pounds Sixteen Shillings and three pence three farthings Sterl: Due by a Protested Bill of Exchange &c the Deft. being returned *non est inventus* and not appearing on the motion of the plts. Attorney an Attachmt. is granted her against the Estate of the said Deft. for the aforesaid Sum and Costs, returnable to the next Court for Judgmt.

The Attachmt. awarded John Simmons agst. the Estate of William Spiller (neither party appearing) is Dismist.

In the action on the Case between John Lett and Stephen Haven for Nine pounds Six Shillings and one penny Current money Due by acct. Dated 1714/15 the Deft. being returned *non est inventus* and nor appearing, on the motion of the plts. Attorney an Attachmt. is awarded him against the Estate of the said Deft. for the aforesaid Sum & Costs returnable to the next Court for Judgemt.

[page 21]

The action on the Case between Thomas Harrison and John Wall (neither party appearing) is Dismist.

In the action Depending between Charles Anderson Surviveing Exr. &c of Sarah Boisseau, and Saml. Sentall, the plt. files a replication and Demurrer to the Defts. plea who has time till the next Court to Consider ye same.

The action of Debt between Robert Nicholson and Richard Jones junr. (neither party appearing) is Dismist.

In the action on the Case Depending between Elizabeth Epes Exrx. &c of Wm. Epes Deced. and Peter Wynne Admr. of Joshua Wynne Deced. for Six hundred forty five pounds of Tobacco and One pound Sixteen Shillings and three pence Currt. money Due by acct. &c at a former Court the Deft. being called and failing to appear on the motion of the plt. Judgemt. was granted against John Woodleif returned Security for the sd. Deft. for the sd. Sums and Costs, unless he shou'd appear at this Court and answer the said action and he now appearing Vacates the Same, and pleads *plene administravit* whereupon the plt. has time till the next Court to Consider the same, and the Deft. ordered them to return an acct. Current of the Estate of the said Joshua Wynne Deced.

The action acct. render Depending between William Wheatley and Edward Goodrich is Continued till next Court.

In the Action of Debt Depending between Jean Steagall and James Loftin, the plt. files a Demurrer to the Defts. plea, who has time till next Court to Consider the Same.

In the action on the Case Depending between Wm. Mathews and Eliza. Limbrey, Exrx. of Jno. Limbrey Deced. the Deft. (being permitted to plead Doubly) files a plea and Demurrer to the plts. Declaration who has time till next Court to Consider the Same.

In the action of Debt Depending between Charles Goodrich and Danl. Higdon for Nineteen pounds Seventeen Shillings and Nine pence halfe penny Due by Bill Dated the 24 of January 1710 at the Last Court the Deft. failing to Offer any thing in barr or preclusion of the sd. Action Judgment was granted the plt. agst. the sd. Deft. for the said Sum and Costs unless he shou'd appear at this Court and Answer the said Action, and he Now appearing Vacates the Same and pleads *Nil Debit*, and the plt. on his motion has time till the next Court to Consider the Same.

The action on the Case Depending between Randall Platt and John Owen (neither party appearing) is Dismist.

The action on the Case Depending between Elizabeth Epes Exrx. &c of Wm. Epes deced. and Adam Tapley (neither party appearing) is Dismist.

[page 22]

In the action of Debt Depending between Richard Pidgeon and Samuell L[ucy] for Seaven hundred thirty three pounds of Tobacco Due by Bill Dated the twenty Seaventh Day of July 1713, the Deft. Came personally into Court and Confessed Judgment to the plt. for the same [words removed] whereupon it is Considered by the Court that the Deft. pay unto the plt. the aforesd. Sum of Seaven hundred thirty three pounds of Tobacco and Costs. Als. Exec.

In the action of Tresspass on the Case Depending between John Ellis Junr. and Randall Platt Sherriff of Prince George County for a nonfeasance in his office as Sherriff, to the plts. D[...] thirty pounds Sterl: the Deft. pleading not Guilty, and the plt. Demurring thereto and the same being argued by the Attorneys of the sd. partys it appears to the Court that the plea aforesaid of the Deft. in manner and form aforesaid pleaded is sufficient in Law to preclude the said plt. from maintaining his action aforesaid, upon which and on the plts. motion it is Ordered the sd. suit be Dismist wth. Costs.

The action on the Case Depending between Edward Goodrich and Wm. Spiller (the plt. failing to prosecute) is Dismist.

The action on the Case Depending between Edwd. Goodrich and Wm. Spiller (the plt. faililng to prosecute) is Dismist.

The action on the Case Depending between Elizabeth Limbrey and Wm. Spiller (neither party appearing) is Dismist.

In the action of Debt Depending between Henry Gill and Timothy Bridges for five pounds eight shillings Currt. money Due by Bill dated the third of January 1714/15 the Deft. being called and not appearing on the motion of the plts. Attorney Judgement is granted him for the said Sum and Costs, against the said Deft. and Thomas Loyd returned Security for him the said Deft. unless he appears at the next court and answers the said Action.

A Letter of Attorney from Benjamin Braine of Lond. Merchant to John Willcox Marriner was in Open Court proved to be the act and Deed of the said Braines by the Oaths of John Morren and John Harriss, Witnesses thereto, and on the motion of the said Wilcox the Same is Ordered to be recorded.

Elizabeth Woodleife in Open Court acknowledges a Deed of Release of Land (Indented and Sealed) bearing Date the fourteenth day of June 1715 to Joshua Renn and his heirs for ever, and on his motion the Same is Ordered to be recorded.

[page 23]

Elizabeth Woodleif and John Butler and Mary his Wife in Open Court acknowledged their Deeds of Lease and release of Land (Indented and Sealed) bearing Date the thirteenth and fourteenth days of June 1715 to William Cureton and his heirs for ever the said Mary being first privily Examined according to Law is freely Consenting thereto and relinquishes her right of Dower therin, and on the motion of the said Cureton the said Deeds & are ordered to be recorded.

The Order that Ann Kemp Admrx. of John Kemp Deced. return an Inventory of the said Deceds. Estate is continued till next Court.

The order that Eliza. Briscoll be Summoned to this Court to answer the presentment of the Grand=jury is Dismist.

The Order that Margaret Shaw be sumoned to answer the presentment of the Grand=jury and Information of the Churchwardens of Westopher Parrish is Continued till next Court.

The Suit in Chancery Between John and Saml. Vaughn and James Sevecar is refered till next Court.

The Suit in Chancery between Joshua Irby and John Melone [McCone] is referred till the next Court.

In the Action of Trespass on the Case Depending between Isham Epes and Wm. Wheatley for the Detaining of One Sadle and furniture belonging to the sd. plt. of the Value of Seaven pounds Current money the Deft. haveing pleaded & Demurred to the plts. Declaration who Joining therein and the Demurrer aforesaid being Sufficiently argued it appears to the Court that the said Declaration is insufficient and hath not sufficient matter therein Contained for the plt. to have and maintain his action aforesaid, whereupon and on the Defts. motion the suit is Ordered to be Dismist.

The Attachment awarded Robert Rogers against the Estate of William Wheatley is Dismist.

The action of Debt between John Smith and John Smith junr. (the plt. faileing to prosecute) is Dismist.

The action of Debt between Colo. Diggs and ffrancis Mallory (the plt. faileing to prosecute) is Dismist.

In the action on the Case brot. by William Short against Richard Pidgeon for three hundred pounds of Tobacco Due for a years Rent &c at the last Court the Deft. offering a Discount the accots. of the sd. partys was then referred to Auditors to adjust, who now report their proceedings therein by wch. it appears that ther is nothing Due to the plt., whereupon the suit is Dismist.

The action on the Case between John Cargill et uxor. and Bryan ffarrell, is Continued till next Court.

[page 24]

In the action Depending between John Hobbs and John Lett for three hundred pounds of Tobacco Due by assumpsit &c the Deft. appears andn pleads he Did not assume in manner and form as in the plts. Declaration is Set forth whereupon the plt. on his motion has time till the next Court to Consider the Same.

In the action of Debt Depending between Richard Hamelin and Adam Tapley, the Auditors appointed Last Court make report that there is Due to the plt. on Ballance of his ye sd. plts. bills ye Sum of ten Shillings and five pence, &c is thereupon Considered by the Court that the sd. Deft. pay to the said plt. the aforesaid Sum of ten Shillings and five pence wth. Costs. Als: Exed.

John Peterson and William Battee complain against Richard fflint in a plea of Debt for that the said Deft. Stands Indebted to them the sd. plts. by a Bill Dated the fourteenth of March 1714/15 in the Sum of thirty pounds Sterl: and haveing unlawfuly Departed this County that the Ordinary process at Law cou'd not be served against him, and the said plts. haveing Obtained an Attachment under under [sic] the hand of James Thweatt one of his Majestys Justices for this County, against the Estate of the sd. Deft. returnable to this Court for Judgement, which accordingly being returned Executed on a horse belonging to the said fflint, who being now called and faileing to appear and replevye the Same due the plts. proveing the said Sum of thirty pounds Sterl: to be Justly Due to them, thereupon Judgement for the Same and Costs is granted the sd. plts. against the said Deft. and the Sherr: Ordered to cause the saud horse to be Duly appraised by John Ellis junr., James Gresion and Gilbert Hay (they being first Sworn by Some Magistrate for that purpose) and Delivered the plts. for and toward the payment and Satisfaction of the above mentioned Sum, and that he make report of his proceedings therein to the next court, so that the said plts. may have Execution for the residue of the aforesaid Sum of thirty pounds Sterl: and Costs.

The action of Trespass on the Case Depending betweeen Littlebury Epes and John Peterson (neither party appearing) is Dismist.

In the action of Debt Depending between Edmond Brewer and James Loftin for three hundred pounds of Tobacco Due by Bill Dated 1712/13 the Deft. being returned *non est inventus* and not appearing, on the motion of the plts. Attorney an Attachment is awarded him against the said Defts. Estate for the aforesaid Sum and Costs, returnable to the next Court for Judgmt.

In the action on the Case Depending between William Robertson and James Loftin for two hundred and forty pounds of Tobacco Due by accot. Dated 1713, the Deft. being returned *non est Inventus* and faileing to appear on the motion of the

[page 25]

plts. Attorney an Attachment is awarded him against the said Defts. Estate for the aforesaid Sum and Costs, returnable to the next Court for Judgement.

The action of Debt between Joseph Pleasant and Abraham Quin is Continued till next Court.

The action Depending between John and Robert Bolling Exrs. of Robert Bolling Deced. and Olive Poxon, is Continued till next Court.

The writt of *De partitione farienda* brot. by Stith Bolling against Robert and Thomas Bolling is Continued till next Court.

Ordered that the Severall Surveyors of the highways, Rivers and Creeks in this County, Appointed in the year Last past, Continue in their said Offices and proved therein according to Law.

And then the Court adjourn'd till Court in Course. Randll. Platt. Test: Wm. Hamelin, Cl. Cur.

Att a Court held for the County of Prince George on the Second Tuesday in July
Anno Dominini 1715 being the twelfth Day of the said Months

Present   John Hamelin   John Poythres   Randall Platt
        Robert Hall   Lewis Green   Gent. Justices

The Last Will and Testament of Susanna Barton Late of this County Deced. was presented into Court by James Niblett and Thomas Bilbro, Executors therein Named, who made Oath thereto, and it being proved by the Oaths of Thomas Daniell and William Hoggwood the witnesses thereto, is admitted to record, and upon the sd. Executors giveing Security for their Due Executorship of the sd. Will it is ordered that a Certificate thereof be granted them for Obtaining a Probate thereof in Due form, whereupon Paul Jones and John Cooper became Securitys for the said Executors and with them enter into Bond according to Law.

Nicholas Jarrett, Richard Cotten, John Smith and Edward Scott or any three of them are Ordered to appraise the Estate of Susanna Barton Deced: they being first Sworn by Some Justice of the peace from this County for that purpose, and that a report of their proceedings therein be made to the next Court when the Executors are to return the Inventory thereof.

On the motion of Nicholas Robertson it's Ordered that his house be recorded as publick meeting house for the Sext of Annabaptists.

[page 26]

Nathaniel Tatum comes into Court and makes Oath that Samuel Tatum Late of this County Deced: dyed Without makeing any will as farr as he knows or Believes and upon his giveing Security for his just and faithfull Administration of the sd. Deceds. Estate it is Ordered that a Certificate be granted him for Obtaining Letters of Administration in Due forme, where upon Richard Carlile and Thos. Mitchell became his Security and together wth. him enter into Bond according to Law.

John Golightly, Hugh Golightly, Henry Chamblis and Thomas Addison or any three of them are Ordered to Appraise the Estate of Samuell Tatum Deced: they being first Sworn (by Some Justice of the peace for this County) for that purpose and that a report of their proceedings therein be made to the next Court wh[...] the Administrator thereof is to return the Inventory.

On the motion of Thomas Harrison it is Ordered that his bond for the Care and payment (of the Estates) of two Of the Orphans of Roger Drayton Deced: be Delivered him out of the Clerks Office, the sd. Estates being committed to the care of ffrancis & Peter Poythres Guardians to the said Orphans.

On the petition of Rebecca and Thomas Harrison Exrs. of Wm. Harrison Deced: and Wm. Adams, Securitys for Susanna Smith's Decent maintaining of Eliza. and Mary Smith Daughters of Wm. Smith Deced: and Due payment of their parts of their Deced: fathers Estate John Tiller who Intermarryed wth. the sd. Susan, was Summoned to give new Security for the Same, and accordingly appearing, on the Motion of John Wall and Adam Ivey they are Entred his the sd. Tillers Security [&] Ordered they enter into Bond accordingly and that the former Securitys be Discharged therefrom.

Pursuant to an Order of the Last Court, John Peterson returns an acct. of the Appraisement of the Goods Attacht. of the Estate of Richard fflint, Ordered the same be recorded, Vizt. Wee the Subscribers being first Sworn have in Obedience to an Order of Court appraised one gray horse belonging to Richd. fflint Attached by Mr. John Peterson &c at fifty Shillings, Witness our hands. Signed Gilbert Hay, John Ellis & James Gression, ver: rec: Test. Wm. Hamelin, Cl. Cur.

Sampson Merredeth haveing produced a Commission from the honble. the Lieut. Governor to be Sherriff of this County, is accordingly Admitted and Sworn he haveing Given Bond and Security according to Law, Ordered the said Bond be recorded, Vizt.

Know all men by these presents that wee Sampson Merredeth, Robert Hall and Richard Hamelin of the County of Prince George are holden and Stand firmly bound unto our Soveraign Lord the King in the Sum of One thousand pounds Sterling for the honest and true payment whereof to our said Soveraign his heirs and Successors, we bind our Selves, our heirs, Executors, and Admintrs.

[page 27]

Jointly and Severally firmly by these presents. Witness our hands and Seales this 12th Day of July 1715.

The Condition of the above Obligation is such that whereas the above bounden Sampson Merredeth by Virtue of a Commission from the honble. the Lieut. Governr. is this Day admitted and Sworn Sherriff of Prince George County. Now if the said Sampson Merredeth shall well and truely Execute the said Office of Sherriff and faitnfully do and perform all and every act and Acts thing and things relateing to and enjoined him in the said Office of Sherriff Dureing his [Sherrivalty] by Virtue of the Commission aforesaid that then this Obligation to be Void and of None Effect otherwise to be and remain infull force and Vertue.

Samson Merredeth sealed wth. a wafer
R. Hall sealed wth. Do.
Richard Hamelin sealed wth. Do.

Ver: rec: Test Wm. Hamelin, Cl. Cur.

Francis Poythres in Open Court acknowledges a Deed for Land (Indented and Sealed) bearing Date the twelfth Day of June 1715 to Peter Grammer and his heirs &c on whose motion the same is Admitted to record.

Pursuant to a Commission of the peace from the Honble. the Lieut. Governor bearing Date the 1st Day of May 1714, Richard Hamelin appears in Court ahd takes the usuall Oaths of Allegiance &c by Law enjoined, Signes the Test and is Sworn a Justice of the peace for this County.

William Rains in Open Court acknowledges his Deeds of Lease and release of Land (Sealed) bearing Date the fifth and Sixth Days of July 1715 to his Son Thomas Rains and his heirs &c on whose motion the same are admitted to record.

A Deed of Land from James Salmon to Wm. Raines was presented into Court by the said William with an Endorsement thereon of the Assignment of the Lands therein Mentioned to Richard and Thomas Raines, and acknowledged the Same to be his act and Deed, and on the motion of the said Richard the said Deed wth. the Endorsement thereon is Ordered to be recorded.

The Court Adjourn'd till Court in course. Jno. Hamelin. Test: Wm. Hamelin, Cl. Cur.

[page 28]

Att a Court held in the County of Prince George on Tuesday the 26th day
of July Anno Dom: 1715 for receiving and Certyfying to [words removed]
the Generall Assembly the Propositions and Grievances and Publick Claims of the
Inhabitants of the County aforesaid.

Present:	John Hamelin	John Poythres	Randall Platt	
	Robert Hall	James Thweatt	Richard Hamelin,	Gent. Justices

Sundry Propositions and Grievances (written on one Sheet of paper) were presented into Court by Mr. Wm. Harrison and others, ffreeholders of this County, and the Same Ordered to be Certified to the next Session of the Genrall Assembly.

Wm. Hamelin Clerk of this County Court presents into Court a Claim for forty pounds of Tobacco for Certifying to the Last Session of the Genrall Assembly the Publick Claims of Peter Jones Lieut. of the Rangers of this County, and of Thos. Smith (each of the Same being then and there allowed) Ordered the said Claim be Certified to the next Session to the Genrall Assembly for Allowance.

And then the Court Adjourn'd. Jno. Hamelin. Test Wm. Hamelin, Cl. Cur.

Att a Court held for the County of Prince George on the Second Tuesday in
August Anno Dom: 1715, being the Ninth Day of the said Month

Present	John Poythres	Randall Platt	Robert Munford	
	Lewis Green	& John Peterson	Gent. Justices	

Pursuant to the Direction of an act of Assembly Entituled an Act for Setting the Tithes and bounds of Lands and for presenting, unlawfull Shooting and rangeing thereupon It's Ordered that the Vestrys of the Severall Parishes within this County respectively Divide their Parrishes into so many Precincts as to then shall Seem most Convenient for processioning every particular persons Land in their Severall Parrishes respectively, and appoint the particular times between the Last day of September and the Last day of March next Comeing when Such processioning Shall be made in every precinct, and also appoint at Least two Intelligent Honest ffreeholders of every precinct to See Such processioning performed and take and return to the Vestry an acct. of every persons Land they shall procession, and of the persons present at the Same, and of what Lands in their precincts they shall faile to procession and of the particular reasons of such failure.

James Niblett and Thomas Bilbro Exrs. of the Last Will and Testamt. of Susanna Barton Deced: return an Inventory and an accot. of the Appraisement of the Estate of the said Decedt. upon Oath Ordered it be recorded.

[page 29]

A Power of Attorney from Dominick Skerretts to John Hatch was presented into Court by the said Hatch and the same haveing been proved to be the act and Deed of the said Skerrett, by the Oath of Robert Hall and Thomas Harrison the Witnesses thereto, is thereupon Admitted to record.

In the action of Tresspass on the Case Depending between Randall Platt and John Hardyman for the Detaining one Negro man Slave Named Robin of the Value of forty pounds Sterl: and to the plts: Damage fifty pounds Sterl: the Deft. haveing had time given him till this Court to plead and being now called to do the same did not appear nor after any thing in barr or preclusion of the plts: Action. Therefore it is Considered by the Court that the said plt. Ought to recover [a]gainst the sd. Deft. his Damages by means of the Detaind. aforesaid, but because it is unknown to the Court what Damages the said plt. in tthat part hath sustained, therefore it is Commanded that the Sheriff cause to Come before his Majestys Justices at the Next Court twelve good and Lawfull men of his Bailywick by whose Oaths Diligent Enquiry may be made of the said Damage.

The action of Debt Depending between Thomas Lewis and William Worsham on the plts. motion is Continued till the next Court he paying the charge of this Continuance.

The action of Debt Depending between Thomas Harrison and Henry Duke is Continued till the next Court.

The action of Debt Depending between Elizabeth Harrison Admrx. &c of Benja. Harrison Deced: and Charles Goodrich (neither party appearing) is Dismist.

In the action on the Case Depending between John Lett and Stephen Haven at a former Court the Deft. faileing to appear an attachmt. was awarded the plt. agst. the sd. Defts. Estate which being now returned Executed in the hand of James Jones who being Sumoned to Declare what he hath belonging to the sd. Deft. appears and being sworn confesses to have in his possession the Sum of four Shillings and two pence three farthings and the Deft. faileing to appear to replevye the Same, and the plt. proveing by his Oath the Sum of three pounds Eleaven Shillings and Seaven pence to be justly Due, Judgement is thereupon (granted) him agst. the said James Jones for the aforesaid Sum of four Shillings and two pence three farthings, and also Judgement agst. the sd. Deft. for three pounds Seaven Shillings and four pence one farthing, being the residue of the aforesaid sum of three pounds Eleaven Shillings and Seaven pence three farthings together wth. costs. Als. Exec.

In the Suit Depending between Charles Anderson Surviveing Executor &c of Sarah Boisseau and Samuel Sentall the Deft. appears by his attorney and Joins in the plts. Demurrer and plea, and the Issue referred for Tryall till the next Court.

The action on the case Depending between Eliza. Epes Admx. &c of Wm. Epes and Peter Wynne Admr. &c of Joshua Wynne Deced: is Continued till the next Court.

The Order that Peter Wynne Admr. &c of Joshua Wynne Deced: returned an accot. current of the said Deceds. Estate, is Continued till the next Court.

[page 30]

The action of accot. render Depending between William Wheatley and Edward Goodrich is Continued till the next Court.

The action of Debt Depending between Jean Steagall and James Loftin neither party appearing is Dismist.

The action on the Case Depending between Wm. Mathews and Elizabeth Limbrey Exrs. &c of John Limbrey Deced: neither party appearing is Dismist.

In the action of (Debt) Depending between Charles Goodrich and Daniell Higdon the plt. not appearing to prosecute, It's Ordered that he be nonsuited and that he pay the Deft. Damage according to Law with Costs. Als: Esec:

The action Depending between Henry Gill and Timothy Bridges neither party appearing is Dismist.

The order that Ann Kemp Admrx. &c of John Kemp Deced: return an Inventory of the said Deceds. Estate is Continued till the next Court.

Margarett Shaw a White Servant Woman belonging to John Hardyman haveing been presented by the Grand jury for haveing a Mulatto Bastard Child and being Summoned to answer the Same appears and makes no Defence or Objection why Judgement Ought not to pass against her according to the Direction of an Act of Assembly Entituled an act Concerning Servants & Slaves. It's thereupon Ordered that she Serve her said Master the term of one whole year from and after her time of Service by Indenture is Expired, and then and theereafter to pay to the Church Wardens of Westopher Parrish for the use of the said Parrish the Sum of fifteen pounds Current money, or be by them sold for the Term of five years to the use aforesaid, according to the Direction of the aforerecited act of Assembly.

The Suit in Chancery Depending Between John and Saml. Vaughn and James Sevecar is Continued till next Court.

In the Suit in Chancery Depending between Joshua Irby and John Melone [McCone] the Complaint. appears and files a repluation and the respondt. on his motion has time till the next Court to Consider the Same.

In the action on the Case Depending between John Cargill and Sarah his wife and Bryan ffarrell, for three thousand One hundred pounds of Tobacco Due by accot. Dated 1704, at a former Court the Deft. makeing many Objections at the sd. accot. the Same was then referred to Nathl. Harrison Esqr. to audit an setle, and the plts. now Exhibiting into Court the following report thereof Vizt. In the Difference Depending between Mr. John Cargill and Sarah his Wife plts. and Bryan ffarrell Deft. in Prince George County Court, the said Partys haveing by Consent Defered me to audit and setle the accots. between them, have in Complyance thereunto Examined and Setled the Same, and it appears to me that there is

[page 31]
justly Due from the said ffarrell unto the plts. the Sum of fifteen hundred Seaventy four pounds of Tobacco exclusive of any Costs and Charges of the said suit Given under my hand this 16th Day of June 1715. Nathll. Harrison, and the Deft. faileing to appear or make any Objection why the plts: ought not to have judgement against him for the aforesaid Sum of fifteen hundred Seaventy four pounds of Tobacco, it is thereupon Considered by the Court the Deft. pay to the sd. plts. the aforesaid Sum of fifteen hundred Seaventy four pounds of Tobacco, together with one Equall halfe of the Costs of this Suit. Als: Esec:

The action Depending between John Hobbs and John Lett is Continued till next Court.

The action of Debt Depending between Edmond Brewer and James Loftin neither party appearing is Dismist.

The action Depending between William Robertson and James Loftin neither party appearing is Dismist.

The action Depending between Joseph Pleasant and Abraham Odium neither party appearing is Dismist.

The action of Debt Depending between John & Robert Bolling Exr. &c of Robt. Bolling Deced: and Olive Poxom, is Continued till the next Court.

The Writt of Partition Depending between Stith Bolling and Robert and Thomas Bolling, is Continued till the next Court.

The action on the case Depending between Samll. Lucy and Robert Rogers, on the plts. motion is Continued till the next Court, he paying the costs of this Continuance.

The action of Debt Depending between Joshua Irby and Richard Pidgeon neither party appearing, is Dismist.

The order that Nathl. Tatum Admr. &c of Saml. Tatum Deced: return an Inventory &c of the said Deceds. Estate, is Continued till the next Court.

In the action of Trespass Depending between William Caleb and John Leonard, Benjamin ffoster Enters himselfe Speciall Baile for the Deft. on whose motion and Imparlance is granted him till the next Court.

The action of Debt Depending between John Smith and James Hobbs, neither party appearing is Dismist.

The action on the case Depending between Joshua Irby and Ann Kemp Admx. &c of John Kemp Deced: is continued till the next Court.

The action Depending between John Smith and William Hobbs, neither party appearing, is Dismist.

The action Depending between Robt. Jones and Richard Womack, neither party appearing, is Dismist.

In the action on the case Depending between Eliza. Epes Exrx. &c and Wm. Mayes on the motion of Robert Rogers Attorney for the Deft. a Special Imparlance is granted him til lthe next Court.

On the Petition of Michael Talbut it's Ordered that he be added to the List of Tithables.

And then the Court Adjourn'd till Court in Course. Jno. Poythres. Test Wm. Hamelin, Cl. Cur.

[page 32]

Att a Court held for the County of Prince George on the Second Tuesday in September Anno Domini 1715, being the thirteenth Day of the said month

| Present | John Poythres | Randall Platt | Robt. Munford |
| | Robert Hall | & Richard Hamelin | Gent. Justices |

John Mason in Open Court acknowledges his Deeds of Lease and release of Land (Indented and Sealed) bearing Date the Ninth Day of Sept. 1715, to Hannah Gee &c on whose motion they are admitted to record.

In the action of Debt Depending between Thomas Lewis and William Worsham for twenty Shillings & due by Bill &c the Deft. appears and pleads *Nil Debit* and the plt. Joining in the Issue the Same is thereupon referred for Tryall to the next Court.

On the motion of Sampson Merredeth Corroner it's Ordered that Randall Platt allow him the sd. Corroner the fee usually allowed the Sherr: for arresting Sundry persons at the suit of the said Randall whilst he was Sherr: of this County.

In the action of Trespass on the case Depending between Randall Platt and John Hardyman the Deft. files a plea to the plts. Declaration who has time till the next Court to Consider the same.

On the motion of Richard Pidgeon it's Ordered that a Lycense be granted him for keeping an Ordinary at the usuall place near the Court house of this County he haveing given Bond and Security according to Law.

Nathaniel Tatum Admr. of Saml. Tatum Deced: returns an Inventory &c of the said Deceds. Estate upon Oath, Ordered it be recorded.

Ann Kemp Admx. of John Kemp Deced: returns an Inventory &c of the said Deceds. Estate upon Oath, Ordered it be recorded.

Present Jno. Hamelin & John Peterson, Gent. Justices

In the action of Debt Depending between Charles Anderson Surviveing Executor of the Last Will and Testament of Sarah Boisseau Deced: who was Executrix of the Last Will and Testament of James Boisseau Deced: plt. and Samuel Sentall Deft. for Nine pounds thirteen Shillings Due by Bill &c for Sundry Apparrell or the said apparrell in kind, the Deft. haveing pleaded to the plts. Declaration and he replying and Demurring thereto and the sd. Deft. Joining with said [application] and Demurrer the Same was Submitted tothe Court for Tryall and the Deft. Exhibitting into Court a Discount (upon Oath) of four pounds five Shillings, and also Delivering to the plt. Sundry of the sd. Apparrell abovementioned amounting to the Sum of four pounds, Judgement is thereupon granted the plt. against the said Deft. for the residue of the aforesaid Sum of Nine pounds thirteen Shillings, the Same being One pound Eight Shillings, together with Costs. Als: Exec.

[page 33]

The action on the Case Depending between Eliza Epes Exrx. of Wm. Epes Deced: and Peter Wynne Admr. of Joshua Wynne Deced: is Continued till the next Court.

The Order that Peter Wynne Administrator of Joshua Wynne Deced: return an acct. Current of the said Deced's. Estate is Continued till the next Court.

The action of accot. render Depending between William Wheatley and Edward Goodrich is by Consent of the said partys Dismist.

In the Suit in Chancery Depending between Joshua Irby and John Melone [McCone] the Complt. haveing filed a replication at the Last Court when time was granted the respondt. till this Court to Consider the same and he now faileing to appear, it's thereupon Ordered that he be Summoned to appear at the next Court to rejoin in the said replication or Join with the plt. in Commission or [Elec] that the said plt. may have a Commission for Examining of Evidence &c.

The action Depending between John Hobbs and John Lett (neither party appearing) is Dismist.

In the Suit in Chancery Depending between John and Saml. Vaughn and James Sevecar who Intermarryed with Sarah Vaughn Executrix &c of Wm. Vaughn Deced: the respondt. in his answer alledges to have paid Sundry Debts against the said Estate amounting to the Sum of five thousand Eight hundred thirty Nine pounds of Tobacco and the Complts: proveing that three thousand Six hundred and twenty Eight pounds of the sd. Tobacco was part of the sd. Deced's. Estate, they thereupon file a replication wherein they charge the respondt. with Sundry other particulars than are Confest. in his said answer which he still Denys, it's therefore Ordered that the sd. Complts. bring their Evidence to the next Court to prove the same.

In the action of Debt between John and Robert Bolling Executors of the Last Will and Testament of Robert Bolling Deced: and Olive Poxon Administrator of James Proux Deced: for One thousand three hundred and thirty Six pounds of Tobacco Due by Bill &c the Deft. appears in Court and Confesses the same to be Justly Due; whereupon Judgement is granted the plts: against the sd. Deft. in the Capacity aforesaid for the said Sum of thirteen hundred and thirty Six pounds of Tobacco to be paid out of the said Decedt's. Estate with Costs. Als: Exec.

In the action on the case Depending between John Bolling and Olive Poxon Admx. &c of James [Pr]oux for Nine hundred fifty Six and a half pounds of Tobacco Due by acct. &c the Deft. appear in Court and pray the plt. may prove his acct. which he accordingly does whereupon Judgement is granted him against the sd. Deft. in the Capacity aforesaid for the sd. sum to be paid out of the said Deced's. Estate with Costs. Als. Exec.

On the motion of Stith Bolling it is Ordered and Appointed that Major John Bolling be [assigned] Guardian to Thomas Bolling who is an Infant, to Defend a Suit of Partition brought by the said Stith Bolling against Robert Bolling and the said Thomas Bolling.

[page 34]

The Writt of Partition brot. by Stith Bolling against Robert and Thomas Bolling is Continued till the next Court.

In the action on the case Depending between Samuel Lucy and Robert Rogers the plt. faileing to present his suit it's thereupon Ordered that he be nonsuited and pay the Deft. five Shillings with Costs. Als: Exec.

In the action of Trespass Depending between William Caleb and John Leonard the Deft. appears and pleads Not Guilty and the plt. Joining in the Issue the Same is thereupon referred to the next Court for Tryall.

In the action on the case Depending between Joshua Irby and Ann Kemp Admx. &c of John Kemp Deced: for Eleaven Pounds ten Shillings and three pence Due by Accot. &c the Deft appearing and makeing no Defence and the plt. proveing his said accot. to be justly Due Judgement is thereupon granted him against the said Deft. in the capacity aforesaid for the said Sum to be paid out of the said Deced's. Estate with Costs. Als: Exec.

In the action on the case Depending between Eliza Epes Exrx. &c of Wm. Epes Deced: and Wm. Moyes for two hundred Eighty three pounds and a half of Tobacco Due by accot. &c. at the Last Court a Speciall Imparlance was granted the Deft. till this Court and being now called did not appear or offer any thing in Barr or preclusion of the plts: action therefore it is Considered by the Court that the plt. recover against the said Deft. the aforesaid Sum & Costs unless the Deft. appears at the next Court and answers the said action.

The action Depending between John Gunter and John Lett (neither party appearing) is Dismist.

In the action Depending between Benjamin ffoster and John Tiller for One thousand five hundred pds. of Tobacco in Cassecks the Deft. being returned *non est Inventus* and faileing to appear on the motion of the plts. Attorney an Attachmt. is awarded him against the said Defts. Estate for so much thereof as will be of Value Sufficient to Sattisfie and pay the abovementioned Sum & Costs returnable to the next Court for Judgement.

In the action of Debt Depending between David Parker and John Tiller for Nine hundred forty Nine pounds of Tobacco Due by Bill &c the Deft. being returned *non est Inventus* and not appearing on the motion of the plt. an Attachment is awarded him against the said Defts. Estate for so much thereof as will be of Value Sufficient to Sattisfie and pay the sd. Sum and Costs returnable to the next Court for Judgement.

In the action on the case Depending between Charles Williams and Wm. Dickason for three pounds ten Shillings Due by Accot. &c the Deft. being returned *non est Inventus* and not appearing on the motion of the plts: Attorney

[page 35]

an Attachment is awarded him against the said Defts. Estate for so much thereof as will be of Value Sufficient to Sattisfie and pay the above Sum and Costs returnable to the next Court for Judgement.

Ordered that the Road be cleared from the Eastward Road to the Chappell and that Wm. Standback Overseer of the Highways in Jordans See the same performed.

Ordered that Wm. Short the Overseer of the Highway from Willkasons Brickhouse to Warthen's Mill and that he proceed in his said Office according to Law.

And then the Court Adjourn'd till Court in Course. Jno. Hamelin. Test: Wm. Hamelin, Cl. Cur.

Att a Court held for the County of Prince George on the Second
Tuesday in October Anno Dom: 1715, being the Eleaventh day of the said month

Present			
	John Hamelin	Randall Platt	Robert Munford
	Robt. Hall	James Thweatt	John Hardyman
	Lewis Green	& Richard Hamelin	Gent. Justices

John Hill in Open Court acknowledged his Deed for Land (Seald) bearing Date the [blank] Day of October Anno Dom: 1715 to John Pooke and his heirs &c and then also did Mary the Wife of the said Hill freely relinquish her right of Dower in and to the said Land she being first privately Examined according to Law and on the motion of the sd. Pooke the said Deed with ye Livery and Seizin endorst. thereon and then did Relilnquishment of Dower are ordered to be recorded.

A proclamation from the Honbles. the Lieut. Governor concerning the signing and Certifying Propositions and Grievances &c was read, and (according to the command therein) admitted to record.

In the action of Debt Depending between Thomas Lewis and William Worsham for twenty Shillings & Due by Bill Dated the 10th Day of Sept. 1711, at the Last Court the Deft. pleaded *nill Debit* and the plt. Joining in the Issue the suit was referred for Tryall to this Court and they now submitting themselves to the Court for Tyall and the Deft. Exhibitting a Discount of Seaven Shillings and Six pence, Judgement is thereupon granted the plt. against the sd. Deft. for the Sum of twelve Shillings and Six pence with Costs. Als: Exec:

The petition of William Temple and Hugh Lee agst. Nathl. Tatum is referred to the next Court.

In the action of Trespass on the Case Depending between Randall Platt & John Hardyman the plt. files a replication to the Defts. plea who has time till the next Court to Consider the Same.

[page 36]

In the Suit in Chancery Depending between Joshua Irby ahd John Melone [McCone] it's Ordered that the Last Court Order be Continued till the next Court.

In the suit in Chancery Depending between John and Samuell Vaughn and James Sevecar at the Last Court the plts. filed a replication to the Defts. answer wherein they charged the Deft. with Sundry particulars more than were confest in the said answer and were then Ordered to bring their Evidence to this Court to prove the Same and they faileing therein, it's Ordered that John Coleman, Instance Hall, and Mathew Anderson Appraise in Tobacco his sev[erall] Goods mentioned and confest in the said answer, they being first sworn by Some Justice for that purpose, and that a report of their proceedings be made to the next Court.

The suit of Partition Depending between Stith Bolling and Robt. and Thomas Bolling is Continued till next Court.

The action Depending between Elizabeth Epes Exrx. &c and Peter Wynne Admr. &c is Continued till the next Court.

The Order that Peter Wynne Admr. &c of Joshua Wynne Deced: return an accot. Currt. of the said Deceds. Estate is Continued till the next Court.

In the action of Debt Depending between Thomas Harrison and Henry Duke for Seaven hundred and Sixty pds: of Tobacco Due by Bill &c the Deft. appears in Court and Confesses the same to be Due, whereupon the plts. motion Judgemt. is granted him afst. the said Deft. for the said Sum and Costs. Als: Exec.

The Action of Trespass Depending between William Caleb and John Leonard (neither party appearing) is Dismist.

In the action on the Case Depending between Elizabeth Epes Exrx. &c and Wm. Mayes, the Deft. files a plea to the plts. Declaration who has time till the next Court to Consider the same.

The attachmt. awarded Benjamin ffoster agst. the Estate of John Tiller is Continued till next Court.

The attachmt. awarded David Parker against the Estate of John Tiller is Dismist. by the plts. Order.

The attachmt. awarded Charles Williams against the estate of William Dickason is Dismst.

In the Suit in Chancery Depending between William Smith and John Shirley the Deft. appears and on his motion has time till the next Court to answer the plts. Bills.

In an action Depending between Randall Platt and Olive Poxom (neither party appears) is thereupon Dismist.

[page 37]

In the action of Debt Depending between Joseph Pleasant and Abraham Odium for four pounds five Shillings Currt. money Due by Bill Dated the 9 Day of November 1713, the Deft. being called and not appearing on the motion of the plts. Attorney Judgement is granted agst. ffrancis Mallory returned security for the Deft. for the said Sum and Costs unless the Deft. appears at the next Court and answers the said Action.

In the suit in Chancery Depending Thomas Harrison and Thomas Smith the Deft. appears and on his motion has time till the next Court to answer the plts. Bills.

In the action on the Case Depending between Charles Williams and Wm. Dickason for three pds: ten Shillings Currt. money Due by accot. Dated 1690, the Deft. being called and not appearing on the motion of the plts. Attorney Judgmt. is granted him agst. John Hardyman returned Security for the Deft. for the said Sum and Costs unless the said Deft. appears at the next Court and answers the said Action.

In the action of Case Depending between Charles and William Williams Administrators of Charles Williams Deced: and William Dickason for One thousand pds: of Tobacco Due by Accot. Dated 1691, the Deft. being called and not appearing on the motion of the plts. attorney Judgement is granted them against Edward Goodrich returned Security for the Deft. for the aforesaid Sum and Costs, unless the said Deft. appears at the next Court and answers the said Action.

Mary Jones the Wife of Richard Jones appears in Court and (being Examined according to Law) freely relinquishes her right of Dower in and to Certain Lands mentioned in Deeds of Lease and release for the same made by the said Richard Jones and acknowledged in this Court in December Last to William Blaikeley &c on whose motion the said relinquishmt. of Dower is Ordered to be recorded.

17

John Willcox attorney of Benjamin [Braine?] of London Mercht. enters Robt. Rogers his Attorney in all Causes wherein the said John is or may be Concerned.

John Willcox appears in Court and Enters himself Security to pay all Costs and Damages that shall be awarded Peter Wynne Admr. &c of Josh. Wynne Deced: in a suit in Chancery brot. agst. him by Benjamin Braine of London.

In the suit in Chancery Depending between Benjamin Braine of Londo. and Peter Wynne Admr. &c of Josh. Wynne Deced: the Deft. appears and on his motion has time till the next Court to answer the plts. Bill.

In the action on the Case Depending between Richard Littlepage and Henry Duke, on the motion of the Deft. an Imparlance is granted them till the next Court.

In the action of Debt Depending between Charles Goodrich and Daniell Higdon, the plt. faileing to file his Declaration in time, on the motion of the Deft. he is thereupon Nonsuited, and Ordered to pay the said Deft. five Shillings with Costs. Als. Exec.

[page 38]

In the action on the Case Depending between Samuel Lucy and Robt. Rogers the plt. faileing to presente his is thereupon Nonsuited, and Ordered to pay the Deft. five Shlilings with Costs. Als. Exec.

In the action of Debt Depending between Robert Jones and Richard Womack, Robt. Rogers enters himself Speciall Baile for the Deft. whereupon & on his motion an Imparlance is granted him till the next Court.

The action Depending between Thomas Jackson and John Brooks (neither party appearing) is Dismist.

The action Depending between John Brooks and Thomas Jackson (neither party appearing) is Dismist.

Henry Tally and Mary his Wife in Open Court acknowledge their Deeds of Lease and release of Land (Indented and Sealed) bearing Date the 10 & 11 Day of this Instant, to Jeffery Hawks &c, also the said Mary being first Examined according to Law freely relinquishes her right of Dower in & to the said Land. Ordered the said Deeds &c be recorded.

Henry Tally and Mary his wife in Open Court acknowledge their Deeds of Lease and release of Land (Indented and Sealed) Dated the 10 & 11 Days of this Instant to Henry Tally Junr. &c, also the said Mary being first privately Examined freely relinquishes her right of Dower in and to the said Land. Ordered the said Deeds &c be recorded.

And then the Court Adjourn'd till Court in Course. Jno. Hamelin. Test Wm. Hamelin, Cl. Cur.

Att a Court held for the County of Prince George on the Second Tuesday
in November Anno Dom: 1715, being the eighth Day of the sd. Month

Present	John Hamelin	Robt. Hall	James Thweatt
	John Hardyman	& John Peterson	Gent. Justices

The Last Will and Testament of Susanna Jackson Deced: was presented into Court by Thomas Collup the Executor therein Naed who made Oath thereto, and it being proved by the Oaths of the severall Witnesses thereto, is Admitted to record and Certificate [words removed] granted the said Executor for Obtaining a Probate &c.

Present Randall Platt

Ordered that Thomas Collup Executor of the Last Will and Testament of Susanna Jackson Deced: return an Inventory of the said Decedts. Estate to the next Court.

[page 39]

Henry Baites in Open Court acknowledge his Deed for Land (Indented and Sealed) bearing Date the Eighth Day of November 1715, to Robert Davis and to his heirs &c and then also did Elizabeth the Wife of the said Henry freely relinquish her right of Dower of, in and to the said Lands and premises, she being first privately Examined according to Law, and on the motion of the said Robert the said Deed with the Livery and Seizin endorst. thereon and the said relinquishmt. of Dower are Admitted to record.

Present Major Robt. Bolling

The Last Will and Testament of Thomas Blackman Deced: was presented into Court by Ann his relict and Executrix therein Named who made Oath thereto and it being proved by the Oaths of George Tillman and John Brooks two of the Witnesses thereto was Admitted to record, and upon her (giveing) Security According to Law, It's Ordered that a Certificate be granted her for Obtaining a probate in Due form, whereupon John Brooks b'comes her Security and with her enters into Bond &c.

Ordered that Thomas Parram, George Tillman, Richard Vaughn and James Williams or any three of them appraise the Estate of Thomas Blackman Deced: they being first Sworn by Some Majistrate for that purpose, and that a report of their proceedings be made to the next Court, when the Executrix is to return the Inventory.

The Suit Depending between Randall Platt and John Hardyman is referred till the next Court, the Deft. paying the Charge of this Continuance.

Pursuant to the Direction of the Act concerning Jurys and Grandjury was Impannelled and Sworn Vizt. Thomas Lewis, Wm. Temple, Thomas Harrison, John Hobbs, Richard Harrison, Valentine Williamson, Nicholas Overby, Nicholas Vaughn, William Reves, George Tillman, Nathl. Tatum, John Shirley, Henry Baites, Wm. Mayes & Richard Hudson, and haveing their Charge were Ordered to Withdraw, and after sometime spent make return that they find no breach of the penall Laws, Thomas Lewis foreman.

The Petition of Hugh Lee and Wm. Temple agst. Nathl. Tatum is referred till the next Court.

The suit in Chancery Depending between Joshua Irby and John Melone is referd. till the next Court.

The suit in Chancery Depending between John and Saml. Vaughn and James Sevecar is Continued till the next Court.

The Writt of Partition brot. by Stith Bolling against Robert and Thomas Bolling is Continued till the next Court.

In the action on the case Depending between Elizabeth Epes Executrix of the Last Will &c of Wm. Epes Deced: and Peter Wynne Administrator &c of Joshua Wynne Deced: for Six hundred forty five pounds of Tobacco, and One pound Sixteen Shillings & three pence Currt. money Due by accot. &c the Deft. haveing pleaded [...] Administration the plt. appears by ffrancis Epes her Son and makes Oath the said Sums are Justly Due whereupon Judgemt. is

[page 40]

granted the plt. in her said Capacity against the said Deft. admr. &x as aforesaid for the sd. Sums & to be paid out of the said Decedent's Estate, when assetts thereof Shall come to hand.

Peter Wynne Administrator &c of Joshua Wynne Deced: returns an accot. Current of the Estate of the said Decedt. upon Oath. Ordered to be recorded.

The action on the Case Depending between Elizabeth Epes Exrx. &c and Wm. Mayes is Continued till the next Court.

In the suit in Chancery Depending between William Smith and John Sherley, the respondt. appears and files his answer upon Oath to the Complaints. Bill who has time till the next Court to consider the same.

The suit Depending between Joseph Pleasant and Abraham Odium is Continued till the next Court.

The suit in Chancery Depending between Thomas Harrison and Thomas Smith (neither party appearing) is Dismist.

In the action on the case Depending between Charles Williams and William Dickason for three pounds ten Shillings (Currt. money) & Due by accot. Dated 1690 at the Last Court the Deft. faileing to appear Judgemt. was granted against John Hardyman returned Security the appearance of the sd. Deft. unless he should appear at this Court and answer the sd. action, and he now also failing to appear and the plt. proveing the Sum of two pounds Nineteen Shillings &c Six pence to be Justly Due, Judgemt. is thereupon granted and Confirmed to the sd. plt. agst. the said John Hardyman for the said Sum and Costs. Als. Exec.

The action on the Case Depending between Charles Williams and William Williams Admrs. &c of Charles Williams Deced: and William Dickason is Continued till the next Court.

In the suit in Chancery Depending between Benjamin Braine of London and Peter Wynne Admr. &c of Joshua Wynne Deced: it's Ordered that the Deft. file his answer to the Defts. Bill within fifteen Days next comeing at [farthest].

The action Depending between Richard Littlepage and Henry Duke is Continued till the next Court.

The action of Debt Depending between Robert Jones and Richard Womack (the plt. faileing to prosecute) is Dismist.

In the action Depending between Benjamin Foster and John Tiller for One thousand five hundred pounds of Tobacco in Caske Due by accot. &c for rent &c at the Last Court the Deft. being returned *non est Inventus* and when appearing on the motion of the plt. an Attachmt. was granted him against the Defts. Estate returnable to this Court for Judgemt. which being now returned Executed on two Cows, two Heifers, two Calves, a parcell of Tobacco, abt. three bushells of Indian Corn, two Tubbs, one Table, one bear Cask and one bread Tray, of the said Defts. Estate and he faileing to appear to replevye the same, and the plt. proveing the Sum of Eight hundred and Eighty pounds of Tobacco to be justly Due, Judgemt.

[page 41]

is thereupon granted him for the said Sum and Costs to be Levyed on the Goods Attacht. Ordered that the Sherr: cause the said Goods &c to be Duly appraised by John Smith, Thomas Potts and Phillip Burrow, they being first Sworn by Some Majistrate for that purpose and that a report of their proceedings be made to the next Court.

In the action Depending between Dominick Skerrett and John Simmons for forty Six bushells and one halfe of wheat and fifty Shillings Currt. money, the Deft. being called and not appearing nor any Security returned for him, on the motion of the plts. Attorney Judgemt. is granted him against Sampson Merredeth Sherr: of this County for the said Sums and Costs, unless the Deft. appears at the next Court and answers the said Action.

Judgement being this Day past unto Dominick Skerrett against Sampson Merredeth, Sherriff of this County for forty six Bushells and an half of wheat and fifty Shillings Curt. money by reason of the non appearance of John Simmons in an action on the case at the suit of the said Dominick Skerrett on the motion of the said Sampson Merredeth an Attachmt. is granted him against the Estate of the said John Simmons for the aforesaid Sums & Costs returnable to the next Court for Judgemt.

In the action of Debt Depending between Charles Goodrich and Daniell Higdon an Imparlance is granted the Deft. till next Court.

The action Depending between Joseph Pleasant and Thomas Huckaby is Continued till the next Court.

In the action on the Case Depending between Thomas House and John Hines & ffrancis his Wife, Damage Ten pounds Sterl: the said John being returned *non est Inventus* and not appearing on the motion of the plts. Attorney an Attachmt. is granted him against the Defts. Estate for the aforesaid Sum and Costs returnable to the next Court for Judgement.

On the petition of William Burge, it's Ordered that he be added to the List of Tithables.

And then the Court Adjourn'd till Court in Course. John Hamelin. Test Wm. Hamelin, Cl. Cur.

Att a Court held for the County of Prince George of the Second Tuesday in December
Anno Dom: 1715, being the 13th Day of the said Month

Present	John Hamelin	Robert Hall	James Thweatt
	Lewis Green	& John Peterson	Gent. Justices

Tom, a Negro (Boy) belonging to Mr. Robert Hall is adjudged Nine Years Old.

[page 42]

Batt: Crowder in Open Court acknowledged his Deeds of Lease and release of Land (Indented and Sealed) bearing Date the twelfth and thirteenth days of this Instant, to Robert Munford &c on whose motion they are admitted to record, And then also appeared in court Elizabeth the Wife of the said Batt: and freely relinquisht. to the said Robert her right & Dower of in and to the Lands and premises in the said Deeds mentioned, she being first privately Examined according to Law. Ordered the same also be recorded.

Mathew Mayes in Open Court acknowledged his Deeds of Lease and release of Land (Indented and Sealed) bearing Date the Twelfth and thirteenth Days of this Instant, to Robert Munford &c on whose motion they are Admitted to record, And also did Elizabeth the wife of the said Mathew then appear in Court and freely relinquish her right of dower of in and to the Lands and premises in the said Deeds mentioned to the said Robert, the said Elizabeth being first privately Examined according to Law. Ordered it be recorded.

Present Majr. Robt. Bolling

The Last Will and Testament of Richard Nowlin Deced: (was presented into Court) by Elizabeth his relictt and Executrix therein Named who made Oath thereto, and it being proved by the Severall Wittnesses thereto is Admitted to record, and upon her gieveing Security according to Law, it was Ordered that a Certificate be granted her for Obtaining a probate in Due form, whereupon Nicholas Jarrard and Robert Rivers become her Security and accordingly entered into Bond.

Edward Wyatt, Benjamin Rix, Richard Cotten & James Niblett or any three of them are Ordered to appraise the Estate of Richard Nowlin Deced: they being first Sworn for that purpose by Some Justice of this County, and that a report of their proceedings be made to the next Court when the Executrix is to return the Inventory.

William Short and Elizabeth his Wife in Open Court acknowledged their deed of Land (Sealed) within Livery and Seizin Endorst. thereon to Travis Morris &c, of whose motion it is admitted to record, then then also did the said Elizabeth freely relinquish to the said Travis her right of Inheritance of in & to the Lands &c in the said Deed mentioned she being first privately Examined according to Law. Ordered it be recorded.

Majr. Robert Munford Present

The Order that Thos. Collup Exr. &c of [Su] Jackson Deced: return an Inventory of the said Decedts. Estate is Continued till next Court.

The order that Ann Blackman Exrx. &c of Thos. Blackman Deced: return an Inventory &c of the said Decedts. Estate is Continued till next Court.

[page 43]

On the petition of Hugh Lee and William Temple it's Ordered that Nathaniell Tatum Admr. &c of Samuel Tatum Deced: cause one Indian man Slave Named Jack Mingo of the said Decedts. Estate to be Inventoryed in the Inventory thereof and be duly appraised.

Nicholas Jarrard in Open Court acknowledged his Deed for Land (Indented and Sealed) bearing Date the thirteenth day of this Instant to Nathaniell Harrison Esqr. on whose motion the Same is admitted to record, and then also appeared in Court Elizabeth the Wife of the said Nicholas and being first privately Examined according to Law, freely relinquisht. her right of Dower of in and to the Lands &c in the said Deed mentioned. Ordered it be recorded.

In the Suit in Chancery Depending between Joshua Irby and John Melone it's Ordered that a Sums. Issue to the said Respondt. according to a former Order of this Court, and that a Due return thereof be made to the next Court.

In the Suit Depending between Randall Platt and John Hardyman, the plts. Demurrer being waved the Deft. Joins in the Issue Tendered by the said plt. which is referred to the next Court for Tyrall.

In the suit of Partition brot. by Stith Bolling against Robert Bolling and Thomas Bolling who is an Infant, for the Divideing one Tract or parcell of Land Containing One thousand Acres, more or Less, with the appurtenances, Lying and being in the Parrish of Bristoll in this County, the said Robert Bolling and Thomas Bolling by John Bolling who is Admitted as Guardian to the said Thomas Bolling by the Court to prosecute &c appear and file a plea to the plts. Declaration wherein the said Robert saith Nothing in barr of the action aforesaid of the said plt. by which the said Plaintiff remaineth against the said Robert thereof undefended and the aforesaid John Bolling Guardian of the aforesaid Thomas Bolling saith that he is not informed by the aforesaid Thomas Bolling of giveing any answer for the said Thomas Bolling to the said plt. and saith Nothing else thereof by which the said plt. remaineth against the aforesaid Thomas thereof undefended. Whereupon it's Considered by the Court that Partition between the plt. and Defendants of the Land and appurtenances be made and that a Writt of *De Partition facienda* Issue to the Sherriff of this County accordingly.

And then the Court adjourn'd till Court in Course. John Hamelin. Test: Wm. Hamelin, Cl. Cur.

[page 44]

Att a Court held in the County of Pr. George on the 13th Day of
December 1715; for Laying the County Leavy

Present	John Hamelin	Randall Platt	Robert Hall
	Robert Munford	James Thweatt	Robert Bolling
	Lewis Green	John Peterson	Gent. Justices

Pr. Geo: County Dr. 1715
Wolves Heads

					Tobo. £
Richard Smith	2	200	Brot. on		2600
Thos. Sambs	1	100	Abram Ally	1	100
Mathew Mayes	2	200	Wm. Butler	1	100
Henry Embry	1	100	Richard Scoggin	1	100
Robert Bolling	3	300	Wm. Coleman	1	100
Peter Wynn	1	100	Thos. Jones	1	100
Buller Herbert	2	200	John Phillips		2200
John Evans	5	500	Peter Mitchell	1	100
Stephen Evans	2	200	Joseph Stroud	1	100
Robert Munford	4	400	Richard Hudson junr.	1	100
Richard Derden	1	100	Edward Powell	1	100
Samuell Harwell	2	200			3700
	carried on 2600				

To Wm. Hamelin [C.C.] for the County Service One year	1000
To Sampson Merredeth Sherr: for Do.	500
To Thos. Simmons for Sweeping the Court house one year	250
To Capt. Goodrich for his attendance on the Last Session of Assembly as }	
a Burgess 40 Days, with ferryages included	5260
To 6 pct. allowed him on Do. for [Cask]	316

To Mr. Robt. Hall for 40 Days attendance as a Burgess, on the }	
Last Session of Assembly with ferryage included	5260
To 6 pct. allow'd him on Do. for [Cask]	316
To Do. on 650 l. Tob. to Capt. Goodrich not all owed him Last year	339
To Do. to Capt. Hamelin	339
To the Clerk of the House of Burgesses for a Copy of the Laws and }	
Leavy Anno 1714 and 1715, Vizt. 850 & 350	1200
To 4160 Tobacco for the Publick as Directed by an act for }	
Leavying the Same	4160
To Thos. Simmons for a Lock &c for the Prison	60
To the Sherriff for his attendance ten Days in [amounting] &c	2000
Pr. Geo: County Cr. 1715	24700
By Sampson Merredeth Sherr: over Leavied Last year	00138
By 1054 Tithables at 23¼ pr. pole is	24505
Due to the Sherriff to be Leavied next year	00042
	24700

[page 45]

Ordered that the Sherriff receive of every Tithable person within this County (by Distress in case of refusal or nonpayment) the Sum of twenty three pounds and a Quarter of Tobacco, the Same being their County Leavy for this present year and that the said Sherriff take care to pay the Same to the Severall persons to whom it's proportioned in the above Leavy.

Ordered that the Sherr: attend for accounting wth. the Severall Debtors to this County, in the Several precincts as Ordered at the Last Leavy Court.

On the motion of James Thweatt it's Entred. that he refused to allow the Burgesses the Tobacco above Leavied and allowed them.

And then the Court Adjourn'd. John Hamelin. Test. Wm. Hamelin, Cl. Cur.

Att the Court house in the County of Prince George on the Second Tuesday in
January Anno Domini 1715; being the tenth Day of the said month.

Pursuant to a Commission of the Peace from the Honble. the Lieut. Governour bearing Date at Williamsburgh the eighth Day of December 1715; and Dedimus for Swearing the Justices &c: which being read as usuall, Robert Bolling and John Hardyman Administred. the Oaths and Test therein mentioned to John Hamelin, Randall Platt, Robert Munford and Robert Hall, who Administred. the Like Oaths and Test to the said Robert Bolling, John Hardyman, John Peterson and Richard Hamelin. Test Wm. Hamelin, Cl. Cur.

Att a Court held for the County of Prince George on the Second Tuesday in
January Anno Dom: 1715, being the tenth Day of the said Month.

Present   John Hamelin   Randall Platt   Robert Munford
             Robert Hall   Robert Bolling   John Hardyman
             John Peterson   & Richard Hamelin Gent. Justices

William Stainback acknowledged his Deeds of Lease and Release of Land (Sealed) to John Hill and his heirs &c on whose motion they are Ordered to be recorded, and then also did Onah the Wife of the said William acknowledge the said Deeds to the said Hill and to him freely relinquish her right of Dower of in and to the lands &c in the said Deeds mentioned, she being first privately Examined according to Law. Ordered the Same also be recorded.

[page 46]

The Last Will and Testament of Mary Tatum Deced: was presented into Court by Nathaniel Tatum the Executor therein Named who made Oath thereto and it being proved by the Oaths of Richard Carlile and Xpher Tatum is Admitted to Record, and upon his giveing Security according to Law it's Ordered that a Certificate be granted him for Obtaining a Probate thereof whereupon Thomas Eldridge becomes his Security and with the sd. Executor enters into Bond &c.

Ordered that Nathaniel Tatum Executor of Mary Tatum Deced: return an Inventory of the said Decedts. Estate to the next Court.

Nathaniel Tatum Admr. of Saml. Tatum Deced: returns a further Inventory &c of the sd. Decedts. Estate. Ordered it be recorded.

A Power of Attorney from Sarah Evans (the Wife of John Evans) to Robert Munford, was proved in Court by the Oaths of the Witnesses thereto. Ordered it be recorded.

John Evans in Open Court acknowledged his Deeds of Lease and release of Land (Indented and Sealed) to Richard Jones and his heirs &c, also did Robert Munford Attorney of Sarah Evans the Wife of the said John Evans acknowledge the same to be her act and Deed and relinquisht. to the said Jones her right of Dower of in and to the Lands &c in the said Deeds mentioned, and on the motion of the said Jones the said Deeds &c are ordered to be recorded.

Peter Simmons an Orphan appears in Court and Chuses John Denton his Guardian.

John Denton appears in Court and together with Edward Goodrich his Security enters into Bond to Indemnifie this Court from any Claim or Demand that may at any time hereafter be made against any of the Members thereof by Peter Simmons an Orphan for his Estate formerly Committed to the Care of Thomas [Hunoby].

John Denton (& Elizabeth his Wife) made Complaint that Thomas Hunoby Stands Indebted to them the Sum of Seaven pounds ten Shillings Current money and one Cow and Set forth that the sd. Thomas hath unlawfully Departed this County that the Ordinary process at Law cou'd not be Served against him whereupon they by Virtue of an Attachment under the hands of one of his Majestys Justices for this County (returnable to this Court) have caused part of the Estate of the said Thomas to be attacht. for Sattisfaction thereof Vizt. 13 Sheep, 8 head of Cattle, 2 Chests, One beer Cask, two [hoggs], a parcell of which & Two Tobacco hds: and the said Thomas being called and failing to appear to replevye the said Goods &c attacht. as aforesaid on the plts. prayer Judgement is granted them against the said Defendt. for the aforesaid Sum of Seaven pound ten Shillings & Costs, and the said Cow to be Leavied [...]

[page 47]

paid out of the Goods &c attacht. Ordered that the Sherr: cause the said Goods &c to be duly appraised by John Bonner, William Hulm, William Cureton and John Cureton or any three of them, being first Sworn by Some Justice for that purpose (and Delivered the plts.) for and toward the payment and Sattisfaction of the above Sum &c and that he make report of his proceedings to the next Court and till then to Continue the said Attachment.

Randall Platt made Complaint that Thomas Hunoby Stands Indebted to him the Sum of Two thousand forty Seaven pounds of Tobacco &c as by the plts. Declaration is made appear, and Setts fforth yt. the said Thomas hath unlawfully Departed this Coty. that the Ordinary process at Law cou'd not be served against him, whereupon he by Virtue of an attachment under the hand of one of his Majestys Justices for this County returnable to this Court hath caused part of the Estate of the sd. Thomas to be Attacht. for Sattisfaction thereof, Vizt. A parcell of Indian Corn and a Loom -- -- -- and the said Thomas being called and failing to appear to repleve the same on the plts. prayer, Judgemente is granted him agst. the said Defendt. for the aforesaid Sum and Costs to be Leavied on and paid out of the said Goods &c attacht. Ordered that the Sherr: cause the said Goods &c to be Duly appraised by John Bonner, William Hulm, William Cureton & John Cureton or any three of them being first Sworn for that purpose, and Delivered the plt. for and toward the payment and Sattisfaction of the above sum &c and that he make report of his proceedings to the next Court and till then to Continue the sd. Attachmt.

ffrancis Mallory and ffrancis Poythres Exrs. of Jos: Patterson Deced: made complt: that Thomas Hunoby stands indebted to them the Sum of One thousand and Sixty pounds of Tobacco Due for Rent &c, and Set forth that the said Thomas hath unlawfully Departed this County that the Ordinary process at Law cannot be Served against him whereupon they by Virgue of an Attachmt. under the hands of one of his Majestys Justices of this County Returnable to this Court have caused part of the Estate of the sd. Thomas to be attacht. for payment therof, Vizt. A parcell of Tobacco -- -- -- and the said Thos. being called and failing to appear to replevye the Same, on the plts. motion Judgement is granted them agst. the said Deft. for the aforesaid Sum and Costs, to be Leavied on and paid out of the said Tobacco Attacht. Ordered that the same be Duly appraised by John Bonner, William Hulm, William Cureton & John Cureton or any three of them being first Sworn by Some Justice for that purpose, and Delivered the plts. for and toward the payment and Sattisfaction of the above Sum &c and that he make report of his proceedings to the next Court, and till then to Continue the said Attachment.

Ordered that the Sherr: Deliver one hundred and twenty pounds of Tobacco out of the [...] of Tobacco above mentioned, to John Hardyman, Churchwarden of Westopher Parrish in Discharge of two Leavys Due in the said Parrish from the said Hunobe an Inhabitant thereof.

23

[page 48]

The attachmt. granted John Hardyman agst. the Estate of Thos. Hunobe is Continued.

Jane Patterson made Complaing that Thomas Hunobe Stands Indebted to her in the Sum of three hundred Ninety four pounds of Tobacco by Bill &c and Setts forth that the said Thomas hath unlawfully Departed this County that the Ordinary process of aLaw cou'd not be Served afst. him whereupon she by Virtue of attachmt. under the hand of one of his Majestys Justices of this County hat caused part of the Estate of the said Thomas to be attacht., Vizt. A horse Colt and a poor Calfe -- -- -- and being called and failing to appear to replevye the Same and the sd. plt. proveing the said Sum be Justly due Judgement is thereupon granted her agst. the sd. Hunoby for the said Sum and Costs to be Leavied on the Goods &c attacht. Ordered that the Sherr: cause the same to be Duly appraised by John Bonner, William Hulm, William Cureton and John Cureton or any three of them being first Sworn and Delivered the plt. for and toward the payment and Sattisfaction of the above Judgement and that he make report of his proceedings therein to the next Court & till then to Continue the said Attachmt.

William Epes in Open Court acknowledged his Deeds of Lease and release of Land (Indented) to James [Pace] and his heirs &c and then also Sarah Wife of the said William acknowledged the Same to be her act and Deed and freely relinquished to the said [Pace] her right of Dower of in and to the Land &c in the said Deed mentioned she being first privately Examined according to Law and on the motion of the said James the said Deeds &c are Ordered to be recorded.

In the Suit in Chancery Depending Between Benjamin Braine of London and Peter Wynne Admr. of the Goods &c of Joshua Wynne Deced: the respondt. appears and files his answer upon Oath, whereupon it is Ordered that Messrs. Robert Hall and John Hatch View and Inspect the Books of accts. and proceedings of the said Deced. relateing to the Goods &c beloinging to this Complt: and use their endeavours to Settle the Same and make a report of their proceedings to the next court.

And then the Court Adjourn'd till Court in Course. Jn: Hamelin, Test. W. Hamelin, Cl. Cur.

[page 49]

Att a Court held for the County of Prince George on the second Turestay in ffebruary
Anno Dom: 1715; being the fourteenth Day of the said month.

Present   John Hamelin   Robert Munford
              Robert Hall   Robert Bolling   Gent. Justices

Nathaniel Urvin in Open Court acknowledged his Deed for Land (Indented and Sealed) bearing Date the 13 Day of ffebruary 1715, with Livery and Seizin endorst. therein to David Crawley and his heirs &c, on whose motion the same is Admitted to record, and then also appeared in Court Elizabeth the Wife of the sd. Urvin and being first privately Examined freely relinquished to the said Crawley her right of Dower in and to the said Lands &c. Ordered the Same also be recorded.

Elizabeth Dew came into Court and under Oath that John Dew (her Deced: Husband) Departed this Life Intestate as farr as she knew or believed, and upon her giveing Security for her just and faithful Administration of the said Decedts. Estate it was Ordered that a Certificate be granted her for Obtaining Letters of Administration in Due form thereupon Thomas Smith and William Hobbs became her Security and together wth. her entred. into Bond according to Law.

Adam Tapley, Alexander Tapley, John Lett and Edward Prince or any three of them are Ordered to appraise the Estate of John Dew Deced: they being first sworn by Some Justice for that purpose and that a report of their proceedings be made to the next Court when the Administratrix is to return the Inventory.

On the petition of ffrancis Kay It's Ordered that he be Exempted from paying County Leavy for the future.

In the Suit in Chancery Depending between John and Saml. Vaughn and James Sevecar who Intermarryed with Sarah Vaughn the relict of William Vaughn Deced: the Goods &c Confest by the Respondent being Duly appraised and a Discount allowed the said Sevecar of what Debts be paid against the sd. Decedts. Estate there appears to be due to the Same the Sum of four hundred Sixty Seaven pds: of Tobacco whereupon on the Complainants motion It is Ordered and Decreed that the said Respondent pay to the sd. Complaints. two Eights of the said Sum, being One hundred and Sixteen pounds of Tobo. with Costs.

In the suit Depending between Elizabeth Epes Exrx. &c of Wm. Epes Deced: and William Mayes, the plt. files a replication to the Defendts. plea, who has time to Consider the Same.

The Suit in Chancery Depending between William Smith and John Sherley is Dismist.

John Arnall in Open Court acknowledged his Deeds of Lease and release of Land (Indented and Sealed) to Robert Hall and his heirs &c on whose motion it's Ordered they be recorded.

[page 50]

In the Suit Depending between Joseph Pleasant and Abraham Odium for four pounds five Shillings Current money Due by Bill Dated the Ninth Day of November 1713, at the Last Court (the Deft. failing to appear) [words removed] Judgement was granted the plt. against ffrancis Mallory returned Security for the sd. Deft. upon Condition that if the said Defendt. Should appear at this Court and answer to this Suit that then the said Judgemt. to be Void and the sd. Defendt. being now called and failing to appear on the motion of the plts: Attorney Judgement is granted and Confirmed (to the sd. plt.) against the said ffrancis Mallory for the sd. Sum of four pounds five Shillings Current money with Costs. Als. Exec:

The Suit Depending between Charles and William Williams Admrs. &c and William Dickason is referred till the next Court.

In the Suit Depending between Richard Littlepage and Henry Duke from Seaven hundred Sixty five pounds of Tobacco Due by accot. Dated 1710: at the Last Court time was granted the Deft. till this Court to Consider the Same and being now called and failing to appear or Offer any thing in Barr or reclusion of the plts. action, therefore it is Considered by the Court and accordingly Ordered that the Deft. pay to the sd. plt. the aforesd. sum with Costs unless he ye sd. Deft. shall appear at the next Court and answer the said Action.

The suit Depending between Benjamin ffoster and John Tiller is referred.

And then the Court Adjourn'd till Court in Course. Jno. Hamelin. Test. William Hamelin, Cl. Cur.

Att a Court held for the County of Prince George on the second
Tuesday in March 1715: being the thirteenth day of the said month.

| Present | John Hamelin | Randall Platt | Robert Munford |
| | Robert Hall | & Robert Bolling | Gent. Justices |

George [Pace] in Open Court acknowledged his Deeds of Lease and release of Land (Indented and Sealed) bearing Date the twelfth and thirteenth days of March 1715: to John West and his heirs &c on whose motion it was Ordered they be recorded.

Adam Heath in Open Court acknowledged his Deeds of Lease and release of Land (Sealed) bearing Date the 12th and 11th Days of March 1715: to his son William Heath and his heirs &c on whose motion it was Ordered the said Deeds be recorded. {Memo. when the abovementioned (deeds) came to be recorded they apear to be only two Deeds of Lease for one and the same Tract of Land as may appear by the records. Test. W.H. Cl. Cur.}

[page 51]

William Heath and Elizabeth his Wife in Open Court acknowledged their Deed for Land (sealed) within Livery and Seizin endorsed thereon, bearing Date the tenth Day of March 1715: to John Smith and his heirs &c, the sd. Elizabeth being first privately Examined according to Law freely and voluntarily relinquisht. to the sd. Smith her right of Dower &c in and to the Lands &c the sd. Deed mentioned & on his motion the sd. Deed &c was Ordered to be recorded.

Present Mr. Peterson

On the motion of Adam Tapley it's Ordered that Peter an Indian Boy now under the care of the sd. Adam be bound to him the said Tapley by the Church Wardens of Westopher Parrish till he shall be Thirty one years of Age.

Present Mr. Hardyman

On the peto. of Sampson Merredeth Sherr: Setting forth that the two years now Last past he was Sheriff of this County and that it hath pleased the Almighty to afflict this part of the Country with such Dreadfull Droughts that the Inhabitants cou'd not possibly make Cropps to Discharge their Dues either of the said years and the same tending verry much to the Loss and prejudice of the sd. Sherr: it's Ordered that he be one of the three Gent. that are recommended the Honble. the Govr. as fitt &c to Execute the Office of Sherr: this ensueing Year.

Pursuant to the Act for appointing Sheriffs John Poythres, Sampson Merredeth, and Richard Hamelin Gent. Justices &c are recommended to the honbld. the Governour as fitt &c to Execute the Office of Sherriff this ensueing Year.

Thomas Potts came into Court and made Oath that his ffather Thomas Potts Deced: dyed without makeing any will as farr as he knew or believed, and upon his giveing Security for his just and ffaithfull adm: of the sd. Decedts. Estate, it is Ordered that a Certificate be granted him for Obtaining a Commission of Administration Due form, where upon Robert Hunnicutt and Thomas Chappell became his Securitys and enter into Bond according to Law.

Benjamin ffoster, William Reves, Thomas Chappell and Phillip Burrow or any three of them are ordered to appraise the Estate of Thomas Potts Deced: they being first Sworn by some Justice of this County for that purpose

25

and that a report of their proceeding's be made to the next Court when Thos. Potts the Admr. is to return the Inventory.

Pursuant to a Commission of the Peace &c Dated the Eighth Day of December 1715: John Poythres, James Thweatt and Lewis Green Junr. appear in Court take the usuall Oaths Sign the Test and are accordingly Sworn Justices of this County.

Ordered that the Sherriff Summon Charles Goodrich, Peter Jones, & Henry Duke to the next Court to take the Oaths of Justices &c.

The suit Depending between Dominick Skerrett and John Simmons (the plt. being not resident in this Collony and haveing failed giveing Security for the payment of Costs as the Law Directs) is Dismist.

[page 52]

The attachmt. awarded Samson Merredeth Sherr: agst. the Estate of John Simmons is Dismist.

On the peto. of James Westbrook a Servant boy belonging to Joshua Irby it's Ordered that the said Irby be Summoned to the next Court to answer the Same and that the said James be and remain with his brother John Westbrook till tryall.

In the suit in Chancery Depending between Benjamin Braine of London and Peter Wynne Administrator of the Goods and Chattells &c of Joshua Wynne the Gentlemen appointed at the Last [court] to View and Inspect the books of accot. &c of the said Decedt. relateing to the Goods &c belonging to this Complt. mentioned in his Bill of Complt. make the following report Vizt. Pursuant to the order of January Court Last in the suit Dependieng between Benjamin Braine of London, Merchant and Peter Wynne Administrator of the Goods and Chattels of Joshua Wynne Deced: we the subscribers have viewed and inspected the Books of accot. of the said Joshua Wynne relateing to the Goods and Debts of the said Braine and do find by the said Books that the Debts on the other side herewithin returned are seemingly Due unto the said Braine, Besides what is Confessed to be Due by the List of Debts annext. unto the said Peter Wynnes answer and we also find that the said Peter Wynne has a Certain Claime for Severall Services due for the said Braine since his Father Joshua Wynns Death which is humbly submitted to this Worshipfull Court by Robt. Hall & John Hatch, and the Deft. at a former Court haveing in his answer to the Complts. Bill, confest Sundry Bills and Goods to be in his possession, It is thereupon Ordered and Decreed that upon John Willcox (attorney for the said Benjamin Braine) his giveing the said Wynne a Discharge for the same the said Wynne Deliver and assign to the said Braine or his Order the said Goods Bills and Boos of accot. relateing to the sevll. Cargoes of Goods &c mentioned in the said Complaintants Bill saveing and reverring to him the said Wynne such and so many of the said Bills as will sattisfie and pay him what he hath actually Disburse for the use of the said Braine being one thousand and five hundred thirty and three pounds of Tobacco and Seaven pounds Seaven Shillings.

And then the Court adjourn'd till Court in Course. R: Hall. Test Wm. Hamelin, Cl. Cur.

[page 53]

Att a Court held for the County of Prince George on the second Tuesday in
Aprill Anno Dom: 1716, being the tenth Day of the said month

Present   John Hamelin   John Poythres   Randall Platt
       Robt. Hall   & Richard Hamelin   Gent. Justices

Ordered that the Sherriff Summon a Lawfull Grandjury to appear the next Court On the peto. of Thomas Adams it's Ordered that he be Exempted from paying County Leavy &c for the future.

Ordered that Capt. James Thweatt Administer the Oaths of Constable to Henry Thweatt and that Thomas Clay present Constable Summon the said Henry Thweatt to appear before the said James Thweatt for that purpose.

Elizabeth Dew Administratrix of John Dew Deced: returns upon Oath an Inventory &c of the said Decedts. Estate. Ordered it be recorded.

Present Mr. Peterson

The suit Depending between Thomas House and John Hines & uxor, neither party appearing is Dismist.

In the action of Debt Depending between ffrancis Wynne and Nathaniel Tatum Admr. &c of Samuell Tatum Deced: for Nine pounds two Shillings and five pence Sterl: Due by Bill Dated the Nineteenth Day of November 1713, the plt. appears by her son Buller Herbert and makes Oath that two pounds One Shilling and Eleaven pence Sterl: of the sd. Sum is now Justly Due, thereupon Judgement is granted the sd. plt. against the said Admr. for the aforesaid Sum of two pounds One Shilling and Eleaven pence Sterl: with Costs to be paid Out of the said Decedts. Estate. Als. Exec.

In the action on the Case Depending between Robert and Stith Bolling Consignees of Henry Offley and Nathaniel Tatum Administrator &c of Samuel Tatum Deced: for Six hundred Eighty One pounds of Tobacco Due by accot. Dated from the twenty Ninth Day of December 1714, to the twelfth of March following, the Deft. appears and prays the plts. may prove their accot. whereupon Robt. Bolling one of the sd. plts. makes Oath the said Sum is Justly Due & on his motion Judgement is granted them afsd. the said Administrator for the aforesaid Sum & Costs to be paid out of the said Decedts. Estate. Als. Exec.

The suit Depending between John Hatch and Samuell Burch neither party appearing is Dismist.

In the action on ye Case Depending between John Hatch and Nathaniel Tatum Administrator &c of Samuell Tatum Deced: for Six pounds Eleaven Shillings and four pence half penny Due by accot. dated the tenth Day of March 1714/15, the Deft. prays the plt. may prove his accot. whereupon the said plt. makes Oath the said Sum is Justly Due & on his Motion Judgement is granted him afst. the said Administrator for the said Sum to be paid out of the said Decedts. Estate with Costs. Als. Exec.

[page 54]

The action Depending between Ann Kemp Admx. of Jno. Kemp Deced: and Wm. Anderson (neigher party appearing) is Dismist.

The action Depending between Ann Kemp Admx. of Jno. Kemp Deced: and Henry Mayes (neither party appearing) is Dismist.

The action Depending between James Jones Junr. and John Anderson, neither party appearing is Dismist.

The Action Depending between Adam Heath and Richard Warthen (neither party appearing) is Dismist.

John Hamelin Complained against Peter Wynne Admr. of the Goods and Chattels &c of Joshua Wynne Deced: in plea by *scire facias* for that the said John Hamelin at a Court held for this County the twelfth Day of May 1713 did recover against the said Administrator the Sum of fifteen thousand three hundred and Nineteen pounds of Tobacco with Costs of the said Suit to be paid out of the said Decedts. Estate when the said Administrator should receive sufficient assetts of the said Decdts. Estate to Discharge the same, and the said John Hamelin saith that since the sd. twelfth Day of June 1713 the said Admr. hath reced: assetts of the sd. Decedts. Estate sufficient to pay the said Sum of fifteen thousand three hundred and Nineteen pounds of Tobacco and Costs and still hath the same in his possession, and the said Peter Wynne Admr. as aforesaid being Summoned to appear at this Court to shew cause if any have or know what to say why the said John Hamelin ought not to Have Judgement against him of the Debt and Damages aforesaid and he faileing to appear or make any plea in barr &c thereupon it is Considered by ye Court that the plt. have Judgement against the said Peter Wynne Administrator as aforesaid for the sd. Sum of fifteen thousand three hundred and nineteen pounds of Tobacco with the former and present costs to be paid out of the sd. Decedts. Estate. Als. Exec. the sd. plt. first allowing to the said Deft. all Just Discounts that may be made by the sd. Deft. since the granting the abovesaid Judgement.

Ordered that Elizabeth Nowlin Exrx. &c of Richard Nowlin Deced: be Summoned by the Sherr: to return an Inventory &c of the sd. Decedts. Estate to the next Court.

Ordered that the Sherr: Summon Thos. Collup Exr. &c of Susanna Jackson Deced: to return to the next Court an Inventory of the sd. Decedts. Estate.

Ordered that the Sherr: Summon Ann Blackman Exrx. of Thos. Blackman Deced: to return an Inventory &c of The sd. Decedts. Estate, to the next Court.

In the suit in Chancery Depending between Joshua Irby and John Melone at a former Court it was Ordered that the said Deft. shou'd be Summoned to rejoin in a replicatn. filed by the plt. or join in Commission &c: on return of the said Sum. the Sherr: makes oath he Left a Copy of the same at the late Dwelling house of the sd. Deft which is adjudged by the Court to be [in] Lawfull Service thereof, and the plt. failing further to prosecute his suit its thereupon Dismist.

[page 55]

Richard Smith Complains against Elizabeth Dew Admx. &c of John Dew Deced: for his part of his Deced: father Thomas Smith's Estate being twelve hundred twenty one and an half pounds of Tobacco, the said Elizabeth appears and Confesses the same to be due, whereupon Judgement is granted the said Richard Smith against the said Eliza: Dew Admx. as aforesaid for the said Sum of Tobacco wth. Costs. Als. Exec.

William Hobbs and Sarah his Wife complain against Elizabeth Dew Admx. &c of John Dew Deced: per pct. for the remainder of the sd. Sarah's part of her Deced: ffather Thomas Smith's Estate being Seaven hundred forth four pounds of Tobacco, the sd. Elizabeth appears and Confesses the same to be Justly Due whereupon Judgmt. is granted the said William Hobbs and Sarah his wife against the said Elizabeth Dew Admx. &c as aforesaid for the said Sum & Costs. Als. Exec.

William Smith Complains against Elizabeth Dew Admx. &c of John Dew Deced: for the remainder of his part of his Deced. ffather Thomas Smith's Estate being Nine hundred and five pounds of Tobacco, the said Elizabeth appears and Confesses the same to be Due whereupon Judgement is granted the sd. William against the said Eliza: Admx. &c as aforesaid for the said Sum wth. Costs. Als. Exec.

Mathew Anderson and William Anderson junr. in Open Court acknowledged their Deeds of Lea: and release of Land (Indented & Sealed) bearing Date the Ninth and tenth Instant, [to] James Anderson and to his heirs Exrs. &c, on whose motion they are ordered to be recorded.

The action Depending between Randall Platt and John Hardyman (neither party appearing) is Dismist.

The suit of partition between Stith Billing [sic] and Robt. and Thos. Bolling is Continued.

The suit Depending between ffrances Mallory and ffrancis Poythres Exrs. &c of Josh: Patterson Deced: and Thos. Hunoby (neither party appearing) is Dismist.

The suit Depending between Jane Patterson and Thos. Hunobe (neither party appearing) is Dismist.

The suit Depending between Edmond Irby and Thos. Hunobe (neither party appearing) is Dismist.

The suit Depending between Gilbert Hay and John Lett (neither party appearing) is Dismist.

The action Depending between Robert Bolling and John Stroud is Continued till next Court.

The action Depending between Edmond Irby plt. and Michall Rosser and Richard Tomkins Defts. [...] (neither party appearing[)] is Dismist.

In the action of Debt Depending between Abram Heath and Martin Sheffeild and Richard Harrison for Six hundred and thirty pounds of Tobacco Due by Bill &c the said Martin being returned arrested and as Bail returned for him and failing to appear on the motion of the plt. Judgemt. is granted him agst. Sampson Merredeth Sherr: of this County for the said Sum & Costs unless the Deft. appears at the next Court and answers the said Action.

[page 56]
Judgement being this Day pass to Abram Heath against Sampson Merredeth Sherr: for Six hundred thirty pounds of Tobacco by reason of the non appearance of Martin Sheffeild in an action of Debt at the suit of the said Heath, and then motion of the said Sherff: an attach: is granted him against the said Sheffeild's Estate for the said Sum & Costs returnable to the next Court for Judgement.

In the action on the case Depending between Peter Wynne and Michall Upchurch for [words removed] the Deft. being returned non est Inventus and not appearing on the motion of the plts. Attorney an attachment is awarded him against the said Defendants Estate for the said Sum and Costs returnable to the next Court for Judgement.

In the action on the case Depending between Peter Wynne Admr. &c of Joshua Wynne Deced: & William Mayes for Six hundred pds. of Tobo: Due by accot. Dated 1710 & 1711, the Defendt. appearing and makeing no Legall Defence, thereupon on the motion of the plts. Attorney Judgement is awarded the Deft. in his said Capacity agst. the said Defendt. for the aforesaid Sum and Costs. Als. Exec:

The action Depending between ffrancis Wynne and Henry King (neither party appearing) is Dismist.

Thomas Potts Admr. &c of Thomas Potts Deced: returns an Inventory &c of the Estate of The said Deced. upon Oath Ordered it be recorded.

The suit Depending between Thomas Hedger and George Ivey (neither party appearing) is Dismist.

The suit Depending between Edmond Irby and Nicholas Whitmore, (neither party appearing) is Dismist.

The suit Depending between Edmond Irby and John Collier (neither party appearing) is Dismist.

The action Depending between James Thweatt and George Hill, neither party appearing is Dismist.

The action Depending between George Tillman and Henry Baites, neither party appearing is Dismist.

The action Depending between Richard Pidgeon and Richard Wallpool, neither party appearing is Dismist.

The action Depending between Richard Pidgeon and William ffisher neither party appearing is Dismist.

The action Depending between Richard Pidgeon and John Poke, neither party appearing is Dismist.

Present Majr. Munford & Mr. Hardyman

In the action on the case Depending between Thomas Simmons and Robert Hix for Six hundred Sixty Seaven pds. of Tobacco Due by accot. Dated 1709, the Deft. being called and not appearing nor any Security returned for him on the motion of the plt.

[page 57]
Judgement is granted him against Sampson Merredeth Sherr: of this County for the said Sum & Costs unless the Defendt. appears at the next Court and answers the said action.

Judgement being [word removed] this Day past unto Thomas Simmons against Sampson Merredeth Sherr: of this County for Six hundred Sixty Seaven pds: of Tobacco by reason of non appearance of Robert Hix in an action on the case at the suit of the said Simmons, On the motion of the said Sherr: an attachmt. is granted him against the said Hix's Estate for the aforesaid Sum & Costs [&] Returnable to the next Court for Judgemt.

The order that Nathaniel Tatum Exr. &c of Mary Tatum Deced: return[s] an Inventory of the said Decedts. Estate is Continued till next Court.

John Denton vrs: Thomas Hunobe parla: is Continued till next Court.

Randall Platt vrs: Thomas Hunobe parla: is Continued till next Court.

ffrancis Mallory and ffrancis Poythres Exrs. &c of Joshua Patterson Deced: vrs. Thomas Hanoby parla: pursuant to an Order of the Last Court the plts. Exhibitt into Court an accot. relateing to the proceeding's on the sd. Atta: which being Examined and allowed is Ordered to be filed, and the said plts. Exrs. &c as aforesaid to have the Tobo. herein mentioned.

The attachmt. awarded John Hardyman agst. the Estate of Thomas Hunoby is by the plts. Order Dismist.

James Patterson vrs: Thomas Hunobe parla: is Continued till next Court.

The suit Depending between (James Bell plt. &) Edward Scott and William Smith (neither party appearing) is Dismist.

A Letter of Attorney from Prudence Hall to Mr. Richard Bland was proved in Open Court by the Oaths of Isham Randolph and Graves Parke the Witnesses thereto and on the motion of the said Isham the said is Admitted to record.

The suit Depending between James Bell plt. and John White and Bryan ffarrell Defts. neither party appearing is Dismist.

In the suit Depending between James Westbrook and Joshua Irby p. pct. for being unlawfully Detained by the sd. Irby as a Servant, the sd. partys appearing and the cause being well and Sufficiently argued by the Attorneys of the sd. party's the Court do adjudge that the said James was not Legally bound to the said Irby and that he's by Law a freeman.

On the peto. of Martha Tucker it is Ordered that a Crop and slitt and halfe moon under the Left ear and a slitt and halfe moon under the right ear be recorded her ear mark.

On the motion of Wm. Harrison it's Ordered that Rebecca Harrison Admx. &c of Hannah Harrison Deced: pay the charge of the Administration of the said Deceds. Este. formerly granted to the said William.

The action of Debt Depending between Joseph Pleasant and Thomas Hunobe is Continued till the next Court.

And then the Court adjourn'd till Court in Course. John Hamelin. Test Wm. Hamelin, Cl. Cur.

[page 58]

Att a Court held for the County of Prince George on the second
Tuesday in May Anno Dom: 1716: being the Eighth Day of the said Month.

Present   John Hamlin   Robert Hall
           Robt. Bolling   & John Hardyman   Gent. Justices

William Hamelin presented into Court a Commission from the honble. the Justices appointing him Clerk of this County Court, which being read is approved, and the said William Hamelin admitted and Continued Clerk as aforesaid, he haveing taken the Oaths enjoined by Law.

On the motion of Peter Bond, Thomas Eldridge is entred his Attorney in all Causes the said Bond now hath or may have Depending in this Court.

Elizabeth Avery als: Nowlin Exrx. &c of Richard Nowlin Deced: returns an Inventory &c of the said Decedents. Estate upon Oath, Ordered it be recorded.

Pursuant to the Direction of the act Concerning Tithables, James Thweatt Gent: is appointed to take the List of Tithables in Bristoll Parish.

Richard Hamelin in Martins brandon Parish

Randall Platt in Wyanoke Parrish

John Hamelin in Westopher Parish.

The Grandjury being called & Sufficient number of the Jurors failing to appear, those persons not appearing are acquitted the fine given by Law, for reason's Considered by the Court.

The peto. of William Tomlinson, on the motion of Goodrich Attorney of Adam Tapley is referred till the next Court to be Considered.

And then the Court adjourn'd till Court in Course. Jno. Hamelin. Test. Wm. Hamelin, Cl. Cur.

[page 59]

Att a Court held for the County of Prince George on the Second Tuesday in June
Anno Dom. 1716. being the twelfth Day of the said month.

Present   John Hamelin   John Poythres   Robert Munford

             Robert Hall   Robert Bolling   & Lewis Green junr., Gent. Justices

On the peto. of Henry Tally he's Exempted from paying the County Leavy for the future.

On the peto. of Majr. Charles Goodrich it's Ordered that John Hardyman Admr. of John Hardyman Deced: be Summoned to return to the next Court and accot. Dr. & Cr. of the Estate of the said John Hardyman Deced:

Mary Daniell came into Court and made Oath that her husband John Daniell Late of this County Deced: Dyed Intestate as farr as she knows or believes, and upon her giveing Security for her just and faithfull Administration of the said Decedts. Estate it is Ordered that a Certificate be granted her for Obtaining Letters of Administration in Due form whereupon Benjamin ffoster became her Security and with her enters into Bond according to Law.

Roger Reese, Richard Pace, Thomas Kirkland & Michal Rosser junr. or any three of them are Ordered to Appraise the Estate of John Daniell Deced: they being first Sworn for that purpose by Some Justice of this County, and make report of their proceedings therein to the next Court when Mary Daniell the Administratrix is to return the Inventory.

On the peto. of Edward Denton it's Ordered that Roger Taylor be Summoned to the next Court to answer the Same.

Pursuant to the Act Concerning Highways, Rivers & Creeks being Cleared &c It's Ordered that John Hill Junr. be Overseer of the Highways in the room of John Ledbetter.

Ordered that Duglas Irby be Overseer of the Highways instead of Mathew Smart.

Ordered that William Butler be Overseer of the road from Rowanty Bridge to Kings road.

Order'd that John Mayes be Overseer of the road from Mayes's Bridge to Lawts. run.

Ordered that Adam Tapley be Overseer of the Highway instead of John Lett.

Ordered that Thomas Simmons junr. be Overseer of Powells Creeke.

Ordered that Richard Cotten be Overseer of the Highways in Martin brandon instead of Nicho. Jarrard.

Ordered that Peter Jones Junr. be Overseer of the Highways instead of Majr. Robt. Bolling.

Ordered that the severall Surveyors of the Highways, Rivers and Creeks in this County appointed in the year Last past Continue in their Offices respectively and proceed therein according to Law.

Major Robert Bolling presented into Court a Commission from the Surveyor General of this Colony appointing him Surveyor of this County, which being read the said Bolling is admitted and Continued Surveyor as aforesaid, he haveing taken the Oath, enjoined by Law.

[page 60]

John Peterson & William Batte came into Court and made Oath that Joseph Holycross Late of this County Deced: Departed this Life Intestate as farr as they know and believe, and upon their giveing Security for their Just and faithfull Administration of the said Decedts. Estate, It's Ordered that a Certificate be granted them for Obtaining Letters of Administration in Due form, whereupon Edward Goodrich became their Security and with them enter into Bond according to Law.

Edward Mitchell, John Thweatt, Daniell Hardwick and Thomas Moor or any three of them are Ordered to appraise the Estate of Joseph Holycross Deced: being first Sworn (by Some Justice of this County) for that purpose, and make report of their proceedings to the next Court when John Peterson and William Batte the Administrators are to return the Inventory.

Elizabeth Dew Administratrix of John Dew Deced: returns upon Oath an accot. Dr. & Cr. of the said Decedts. Estate. Ordered it be recorded.

In the action of Debt Depending between Charles Goodrich and Daniell Higdon for Nineteen pounds Seaventeen Shillings and Nine pence halfe penny Due by Bills Dated the 24 Day of January 1710, the sd. Deft. haveing had time given him till this Court to plea, and being now called and failing to appear or offer any thing in Barr or preclusion of the plts. Action therefore it is Considered by the Court that the plt. recover against the said Defendt. the aforesaid Sum & Costs unless the Defendt. appears at the next Court and answers the said Action.

The action of Debt Depending between James Bell and John Arnall (neither party appearing) is Dismist.

The action of Debt Depending between James Bell Assignee of [Jil:] Stokes and Peter Talbutt (neither party appearing) is Dismist.

In the action of Debt Depending between James Bell plt. and Thomas Harrison and Edward Goodrich Defts. for Six hundred Ninety five pounds of Tobacco Due by Bill Dated the 12 of June 1714, the sd. Edward appears and pleads payment and the plt. Joining in the Issue the same is thereupon referred for Tryall till the next Court.

30

The action of Debt Depending between James Bell plt. and Henry Baites, John Hines and George Ivey (neither party appearing) is Dismist.

In the action of Debt Depending between James Bell plt. and John Lett & John Hamelin [Defts.] for five hundred and Eighty pounds of Tobacco Due by Bill and the Defts. motion Oyer of the plts. Bill is granted them and time to Consider the same till the next Court.

The action of Deft Depending Between James Bell plt. and ffrancis Willkins & Thomas Harrison Defts. (neither party appearing) is Dismist.

[page 61]

The action of Debt Depending between James Bell and James Loftin, neither party appearing is Dismist.

The action of Debt Depending between Mathew Marks and John Knight is Dismist by the plts. Order.

The action Depending between Peter Gaudey and Peter Mell, neither party appearing is Dismist.

The action of Debt Depending between Robert Hunnicutt and Wm. Heath, neither party appearing is Dismist.

The peto. of Mr. Richard Bland that a road be cleared in the out part of this County is Disapproved and Dismist.

The action Depending between Robert Rivers and John Bell neither party appearing is Dismist.

In the action of Debt Depending between John Allen and John Sherley for Eleaven hundred and thirty pounds of Tobacco Due by Bill Dated the 19 Day of November 1714, the Deft. being called and not appearing and Nathaniell Harrison Esqr. being returned Security for him on the motion of the plts. Attorney Judgement is granted him against the said Nathl. Harrison for the said Sum and Costs, unless the sd. Deft. appears at the Next Court and answers the sd. Action.

The action Depending between Robert Rivers and Richard Spencer neither party appearing is Dismist.

The action Depending between John Tomkins and James Bell, neither party appearing is Dismist.

In the action of Debt Depending between Peter Wynne plt. and Peter Talbutt and Michall Talbutt for four hundred Seaventy five pounds of Tobacco due by Bill Dated the 1st day of June 1715, the Defts. being called and not appearing and Edward Scott being returned Security for them on the motion of the plts. Attorney Judgement is granted him against the sd. Edward Scott for the said Sum & Costs unless the said Defts. appear'd at the next Court and answer the said action.

The action Depending between Mathew Marks and Benjamin Rix neither party appearing is Dismist.

In the action Depending between Peter Wynne Plt. and John Sherley and Thomas Loyd for Seaven hundred and Two pounds of Tobacco Due by Bill Dated the Nineteenth Day of May 1714, the said John Sherley came personally into Court and Confessed Judgmt. to the plt. for the said Sum of Seaven hundred and two pounds of Tobacco, whereupon it is Considered by the Court that the said Deft. pay unto the plt. the said Sum and Costs. Als. Exec:

[page 62]

The action Depending between Robert Hix and John Lee, neither party appearing, is Dismist.

The action Depending between Daniell Pellison and Wm. Matson, neither party appearing, is Dismist.

The action Depending between Math: Marks & Tho. Moor, neither party appearing, is Dismist.

The action Depending between Benja: Rix and John Berry, neither party appearing is Dismist.

The action Depending between Math: Marks and John Hill junr. neither party appearing is Dismist.

The action Depending between Geo: Hambleton & Edward Burchett, neither party appearing is Dismst.

The action Depending between Edwd. Goodrich and Joshua Woodleife, neither party appearing is Dismst.

The suit Depending between Peter Wynne Admr. &c of Jos: Wynne Deced: and John Rivers p. *Scire ffacias* neither party appearing is Dismist.

In the action on the case Depending between Peter Wynne Admr. &c of Jos: Wynne Deced: and Stephen Evans for twelve hundred pounds of tobacco Due by accot. Dated the 17 of July 1712, the Defendt. being returned *non est Inventus* and not appearing, on the motion of the plts. Attorney an attachment is granted him against the Estate of the said Defendt. for the said Sum & costs returnable to the next Court for Judgemt. for what shall appear to be Due.

In the suit Depending between Peter Wynne Admr. &c of Joshua Wynne Deced: and Martin Sheffeild pr. scire ffacias, the plt. setts forth that at a Court held for this County the Ninth day of June 1713, Judgement was granted him in the Capacity aforesaid against the said Defendt. for the Sum of two hundred Eighty Six pounds of Tobacco and Costs, which Costs amount to Seaventy four pounds of Tobacco, and that Execution of the Judgemt. aforesaid pt. remains to be done. And the said Martin being Summoned to Appear at this Court to Stand cause if any have or know what to Say why the said Plt. ought not to have Execution agst. him of the Debt and Damages aforesaid according to the form and Effect of the sd. Judgemt. accordingly appears and Confesses the said Sums of two hundred Eighty Six, and of Seaventy four pounds of Tobacco which amount to three hundred and Sixty pounds of

Tobacco to be [till] Justly Due. Therefore it is Considered by the Court and accordingly Ordered that the said plt. have Execution for his Debt and Damages aforesaid according to the form tenor and Effect of the said Judgemt. with present Costs.

The suit Depending between Henry Clay and David Collyshaw pr. *scire facias*, neither party appearing is Dismist.

The suit Depending between Ann Millner Admrx. &c of Isau Millner Deced: and Henry Duke is Dismist.

On the action of Debt Depending between Mansell Blagrave Assignee of John Lilly and Robert Davis for four pounds five Shillings Currt. money Due by Bill Dated the 30 Day of June 1715; the Defendant being called and not appearing, nor any Security

[page 63]

returned for him on the motion of the plts. Attorney Judgement is granted him against Sampson Merredeth Sherriff of this County for the said Sum and Costs, unless the Defendant appears at the next Court and answers the said Action.

Judgement being this day past unto Mansell Blagrave Assignee of John Lilley against Sampson Merredeth Sherriff of this County for four pounds five Shillings Currt. money by reason of the non appearance of Robert Davis in an Action of Debt at the suit of the said Mansell, On the motion of the said Sherriff an Attachmt. is granted him against the Estate of the said Davis for the said Sum & Costs returnable to the next Court for Judgement.

In the action of Debt Depending between David Owen and Robert West for two thousand four hundred pounds of Tobacco Due by Bond Dated the twenty Second Day of October 1712: the Defendt. Came personally into Court and Confessed the principle of the said bond (being twelve hundred pounds of Tobacco) to be justly Due. Therefore it is Considered by the Court and accordingly Ordered that the plt. recover agst. the said Deft. the sd. Sum of twelve hundred pounds of Tobacco, being his Debt aforesaid, together with Costs. Als: Exed.

In the action Depending between William Wheatley and Edward Goodrich, the plt. failing to prosecute on the Defts. motion it's Ordered that he be Nonsuited and pay the sd. Defendt. five Shillings with Costs. Als. Exec:

In the suit Depending between William Short and Randall Platt pr. *scire ffacias* the plt. Setts forth that at a Court held for this County on the 11 Day of May 1714, Judgement was granted him against the Deft. for Eleaven hundred twenty four pounds of Tobacco and Costs of the said Suit amounting to one hundred and Sixteen pds. of Tobacco, and that Execution of the Judgement aforesaid yet remains to be done, and the said Deft. being Summoned to appear at this Court to Shew cause if any have or know what to say why the said plt. ought not to have Execution agst. him of Debt &c aforesaid, accordingly appears and pleads payment and the plt. Joining in the Issue the same for Tryall is referred till the next Court.

The suit Depending between Edward Goodrich and Richard Hamelin pr. *scire ffacias* is Continued till the next Court.

The action of Debt Depending between Robert Rogers and Richard Pidgeon neither party appearing is Dismist.

The Suit Depending between James Jones & Thos. Millton neither party appearing is Dismist.

In the action on the Case Depending between Eliza: Epes Exrx. &c of Wm. Epes Deced: and Wm. Mayes, the plts. at the Last Court filed a replication to the Defts. plea, who non appears and Joins in the Issue Tendered by the plt. in her sd. replication, and the same is referred for Tryall to the next Court.

[page 64]

The action Depending between Charles Williams and William Williams Admrs. &c of Charles Williams Deced: and William Dickason is Continued till the next Court.

In the action on the Case Depending between Richard Littlepage and Henry Duke for Seaven hundred and Sixty five pounds of Tobacco Due by accot. Dated 1710, the Deft. by Edward Goodrich his Attorney appears and Confesses Judgement to the plt. for the said Sum, whereupon it is Considered by the Court and accordingly Ordered that the said Deft. pay unto the plt. the sd. Sum of Seaven hundred Sixty five pounds of Tobacco with Costs. Als. Exec:

On the motion of Robert Blaws Attorney of Richard Littlepage it's Entred that he the said Blaws refused accepting the Confession of the above Judgement in the suit Depending between the sd. Littlepage and Henry Duke and prayed the said suit might be Dismist.

Benja: ffoster returns an appraismt. of the Estate of John Tiller Attacht. by the said Benjamin, Ordered it be recorded, Vizt.

6 Head of Cattle at	1150}	
the rest of the Lumber at	230}	
rec. Test W.H. Cl. Clk.	1380	Appraised by Phillip Burrow & John Hines.

The action Depending between Robert Blaws and James Banks, neither party appearing is Dismist.

The action Depending between Rachel Watkins, Exrx. of Henry Watkins Deced: and James Banks, neither party appearing, is Dismist.

In the action on the Case Depending between John Baites and Henry Duke for two thousand and Eighty pounds of Sweet Scented Tobacco Due by accot. &c the Deft. by Edward Goodrich his Attorney appears and Confesses Judgement to the plt. for the said Sum, therefore it is Considered by the Court and accordingly Ordered that the said Defendt. pay to the said plt. the said Sum of two thousand and Eighty pounds of Sweet Scented Tobacco with Costs. Als. Exec:

The action of Trespass Depending between Richard Wallpole and Richard Pidgeon neither party appearing is Dismist.

The action of Debt Depending between Mary Stith Exrx. &c of John Stith Deced: and Edward Goodrich, neither party appearing, is Dismist.

The action Depending between Edward Burchett and Robert Poythres, neither party appearing, is Dismist.

The action Depending between Richard Pidgeon and Geo: Ivey, neither party appearing is Dismist.

The action Depending between John [H]ines and Adam Ivey, neither party appearing is Dismist.

[page 65]

The action Depending between William Cocke and John Sherley, neither party appearing, is Dismist.

The action Depending between Mathew Marks and Edward Scott, neither party appearing is Dismist.

The action Depending between Thos. Simmons Assignee &c and Adam Ivey is referred till next Court.

The action Depending between Robt. Short & James Bell, neither party appearing, is Dismist.

In the action Depending between Joshua Irby and John Wallbrook, the plt. faileing to appear to prosecute on the motion of the Defts. attorney it's Ordered that he be Nonsuited and pay the said Deft. five Shillings with Costs. Als. Exec:

In the action of Debt Depending between Thomas Eldridge and Richard Acock, the Deft. appearing on the plts: motion it's Continued till the next Court.

In the action Depending between Christopher Hinton and Randall Platt for two hundred pounds of Tobacco Due by accot. Dated 1713, the sd. Defendt. personally appears in Court and Confesses Judgemt. to the plt. for the said Sum, therefore it is Considered by the Court and accordingly Ordered that the sd. Defendant pay to the plt. the sd. Sum of two hundred pounds of Tobacco and Costs. Als. Exec:

The action Depending between Henry Harrison and George Ivey, neither party appearing is Dismist.

In the action of Debt Depending between Robert Rogers and John Sherley for Six hundred and thiry pounds of Tobacco Due by Bill Dated the Eleaventh Day of October 1713. On the motion of Richard Hamelin he is Entred Speciall Baile for the Deft. who thereupon came personally into Court and Convessed Judgemt. to the plt. for the said Sum therefore it is Considered by the Court and accordingly Ordered that the plt. recover agst. the sd. Defendt. and Baile the said Sum of Six hundred and thirty pounds of Tobacco with Costs. Als. Exec:

In the action on the Case Depending between Robert Bolling and Richard Pidgeon for two hundred Sixty five pounds of Tobacco due by accot. &c the Deft. Came personally into Court and Confessed Judgmt. to the plt. for the said Sum, thereupon it's Considered by the Court and accordingly Ordered that the said Deft. pay to the plt. the said Sum of two hundred Sixty five pounds of Tobacco with Costs. Als. Exec:

The action Depending between Robert Bolling and Thomas Booth neither party appearing, is Dismist.

In the action of Debt Depending between Robert Bolling and William Stainback junr. for five hundred pounds of Tobacco Due by Bill Dated the 18 day of May 1715, the Deft. being returned *non est Inventus* and not appearing on the plts. motion an attachmt. is granted him against the said Defendants Estate for the said Sum and Costs returnable to the next Court for Judgemt. for what shall appear to be Due.

The action Depending between Robert Bolling and John Lee, neither party appearing is Dismist.

[page 66]

In the action on the Case Depending between ffrancis Mallory and Samuell Harwell for two hundred pounds of Tobacco Due by a Note under the Defts. hand Dated 1715 the Defendt. being returned *non est Inventus* and not appearing on the plts. motion an Attachmt. is granted him against the said Defts. Estate for the said Sum & Costs returnable to the next court for Judgemt. for what shall appear to be Due.

In the action on the Case Depending between Instance Hall and ffrancis Hudson, an Imparlance is granted the Defendt. till the next Court.

In the action of Debt Depending between Peter Bond and Peter Wynne for two thousand pounds of Tobacco Due by Bill Dated the 27 Day of Aprill 1713, the Defendt. being returned *non est Inventus* and not appearing on the motion of the plts: Attorney an Attachmt. is granted him against the Defendts. Estate for the said Sum & Costs returnable to the next Court for Judgemt.

Thomas Collup Executor of the Last Will &c of Susanna Jackson Deced: returned upon Oath an Inventory of the said Decedts. Estate. Ordered it be recorded.

The Order that Ann Blackman Exrx. &c of Thomas Blackman Deced: returned an Inventory &c of the said Decedts. Estate is Continued till the next Court.

In the suit of Partition brought by Stith Bolling against Robert Bolling and Thomas Bolling, for the Divideing one Tract or parcel of Land Containing One thousand Acres more or Less, with the appurtenances, Lying and being in the Parrish of Bristoll in this County, Pursuant to an Order of this Court the Sherriff makes return of the said Partition which is Ordered to be recorded and it is therefore Considered that the former Judgemt. for partition be and remain firm and Stable forever.

Nathaniel Tatum Admr. of Saml. Tatum Deced: returns upon Oath an accot. Current of the said Decedts. Estate. Ordered it be recorded.

Nathaniel Tatum Exor. &c of Mary Tatum Deced: returns upon Oath an Inventory &c of the said Decedents Estate. Ordered it be recorded.

The action Depending between Robert Bolling and John Stroud, neither party appearing, is Dismist.

The action Depending between Peter Wynne and Michal Upchurch, neither party appearing is Dismist.

In the action Depending between Thomas Simons and Robert Hix for Six hundred Sixty Seaven pounds of Tobacco Due by accot. Dated 1709, at the Last Court (the Deft. not appearing) Conditionall Judgemt. was granted the plt. agst. Sampson Merredeth Sherriff of this County, that is the sd. Deft. shou'd appear at this Court and answer this action the said Judgemt. shou'd be Void and

[page 67]

the said Defendt. being now called and failing to appear, On the plts. motion Judgement is granted and Confirmed against the said Sampson Merredeth Sherr: for the said Sum of Six hundred Sixty Seaven pounds of Tobacco with Costs. Als. Exec:

The attachment granted Sampson Merredeth Sherr: against the Estate of Robert Hix is Continued till the next Court.

In the suit lately Depending between John Denton et Uxor and Thomas Hunobe pr. Atta. the Sherr: makes return of the appraismt. of the Goods &c of the sd. Defendts. attacht. by the plts. Ordered it be recorded, Vizt.

13	Sheep at	£3.5.0	
8	head of Cattle	7.15.0	
2	Chests	0.15.0	
1	beer Cask	0.3.0	
2	hoggs	0.9.0	
a	parcell of wheat	0.15.0	Appraised by John Boner [sic], Wm. Hulme
2	Tobo. hds:	0.4.6	& Wm. Cuerton

Ver. rec. Test W.H., Cl. Cur. £13.6.6

The Sherr: makes return of the appraisement of the Estate of Thomas Hunobe Attacht. by Randall Platt. Ordered it be recorded, Vizt.

A parcell of Indian Corn at	390 Tobo.	
A Loom at	80	

Ver. rec. W.H., Cl. Cur. 470 Appraised by John Bonner, Wm. Hulme & Wm. Cuerton

The Sherr: makes returns of the appraisement of the Estate of Thomas Hunobe attacht. by Jane Patterson. Ordered it be recorded, Vizt.

A horse Colt	300 Tobo.	
a poor Calf	25	

Ver. rec. W.H., Cl. Cur. 325 Appraised by John Bonner, Wm. Hulme & Wm. Cureton

In the action of Debt Depending between Abraham Heath and Martin Sheffeild for Six hundred and thirty pounds of Tobacco Due by Bill Dated the twenty Seaventh day of March 1714, at the Last Court the Deft. not appearing, Conditionall Judgemt. was granted the plt. against Sampson Merredeth Sherr: of this County that if the said Defendant did ~~not~~ appear at this Court and answer to this Suit then the sd. Judgement Shou'd be Void, and the said Defendt. being now called and failing to appear On the plts. motion Judgement is granted and Confirmed against the said Sampson Merredeth Sherr: for the said Sum of Six hundred and thirty pounds of Tobacco and Costs. Als. Exec:

Whereupon the sd. Sherr: was in arrest of Judgement and for cause [word removed] Sheweth, that the Plt. hath Entred an action of Debt against the said Martin Sheffeild and Richard Harrison for the above said Sum due by a Bill which sd. Bill is jointly made to the plt. and not Severally, and the plt. hath only prosecuted one of them which reason being argued by the Attorneys is Overruled and the Judgemt. Confirmed.

[page 68]

The attachment granted Sampson Merredeth Sherr: against the Estate of Martin Sheffeild is Continued till next Court.

In the action Depending between Joseph Pleasant (Consignee &c) and Thos. Hunobe for four hundred Seaventy one pounds of Tobacco Due by Bill Dated the 8d day of May 1712, the Defendant being called and not appearing on the motion of the plts: attorney Judgement is granted him against Edward Denton returned Security for the sd. Defendt. for the said Sum and Costs unless the said Defendt. appears at the next court and answers the said Action.

In the action Depending between ffrancis Mallory and Benjamin ffoster and Uxor an Imparlance is granted the Defts. till the next Court.

The action Depending between Henry Irby by Wm. Irby &c and George Woodleif and ffrancis Coleman, neither party appearing, is Dismist.

In the action on the Case Depending between John Hatch and John Scott for Eight hundred Sixty five pounds and an halfe of Tobacco due by accot. &c the Defendt. being called and not appearing nor any Security returned for him on the motion of the plt. Judgement is granted him against Sampson Merredeth Sherr: of this County for the said Sum & Costs, unless the Defendant appears at the next Court and answers the said Action.

Judgement being this Day past unto John Hatch against Sampson Merredeth Sherriff of this County for Eight hundred Sixty five pounds of Tobacco by reason of the Nonappearance of John Scott in an action on the Case at the suit of the said John Hatch, on the motion of the said Sampson Merredeth an Attachment is granted him against the State of the said John Scott for the aforesaid Sum & Costs returnable to the next Court for Judgemt.

In the action of Debt Depending between William Hamelin and Richard Pidgeon for three hundred and five pounds of Tobacco due by Bill Dated this twenty Seaventh Day of April 1716, the Defendt. by Edward Goodrich his Attorney Confessed Judgement to the plt. for the said Sum, therefore it is Considered by the Court and accordingly Ordered that the sd. Richard Pigeon pay to the said plt. the said Sum of three hundred and five pounds of Toacco with Costs. Als. Exec.

In the action Depending between William Hamelin and William Wheatley for two hundred and fifteen pounds of Tobacco due by accot. &c the Defendant being called and not appearing nor any Security returned for him on the motion of the plt. Judgement is granted him against Sampson Merredeth Sherr: of this County for the said Sum & Costs unless the Deft. appears at the next court and answers the said action.

[page 69]

The peto. of Nathaniel Tatum is Dismist.

On the peto. of William Tomlinson it's Ordered that Jack an Indian Boy be bound by the Churchwardens of Westopher Parrish, to the said Tomlinson till the said Boy shall attain to the age of one and twenty years.

Gilbert Hay, John Willkins, Peter Poythres & James Jones junr. or any three of them are ordered to appraise Jack an Indian boy now under the Care of William Tomlinson they being first Sworn by Some Justice for that purpose, and that they make report of the same to the next Court.

Richard Hamelin haveing produced a Commission from the honble. the Lieut. Govr. to be Sherr: of this County he accordingly takes the usuall Oaths &c he haveing first given Bond and Security as the Law Directs. Ordered the said Bond be recorded, Vizt.

> Know all men by these presents that we Richard Hamelin, John Hamelin and Sampson Merredeth of Prince George County are held and firmly bound to our Soveraign Lord the King his heirs and Successors in the Sum of One thousand pounds Sterl: for the honest and true payment whereof as aforesaid we bind Our Selves our heirs Executors and Admrs. Jointly and Severally firmly by these presents. Witness our hands and Seals this 12 Day of June 1716.
>
> The Condition of the above Obligation is such that whereas the above bounden Richard Hamelin by Virtue of a Commission from the Honble. the Lieut. Governour is this Day admitted and Sworn Sherriff of Prince George County. Now if the said Richard Hamelin shall well and truly Execute the said Office of Sherriff and faithfully do and perform all and Every act and acts thing and things relateing to and Enjoined him in the said Office of Sherriff Dureing his Sherrivalty by Virtue of the

Commission aforesaid, that then this Obligation to be Void and of None Effect otherwise to be and remain in full power force and Virtue.

Richard Hamlin. Sealed wth. a wafer
John Hamlin. Sealed wth. Do.

Ver: rec. Test W. Hamelin, Cl. Cur.   Samson Merredeth. Sealed wth. Do.

Thomas Simmons appears in Court and haveing taken the usuall Oaths is Sworn under Sheriff of this County. And then the Court Adjourn'd till Court in Course. John Hamlin. Test Wm. Hamelin, Cl. Cur.

[page 70]

Att a Court held for the County of Prince George on the Second
Tuesday in July Anno Dom 1716: being the tenth Day of the said month.

Present	Robert Munford	Robert Hall	Robert Bolling
	John Peterson	& John Hardyman	Gent. Justices

Jack, a Negro Boy belonging to John Peterson is judged Seaven years Old.

Jone, a Negro Girl belonging to John Peterson is judged Eight years old.

Dena, a Negro Girl belonging to William Batte is Judged Eight years Old.

The Last Will and Testament of William Gary Deced: was presented into Court by Sarah his relict and Executrix therein Named, who made Oath thereto and it being proved by the Oaths of the Severall Wittnesses thereto, is Admitted to record, and [word removed] the said Executrix's [giveing] Security according to Law it's Ordered that a Certificate be granted her for Obtaining a Probate in Due form, whereupon Francis Mallory and Joseph Carter became her Security and wth. her enter into Bond according to Law.

Ordered that Sarah Gary, Executrix of the Last Will and Testament of William Gary Deced: return to the next Court an Inventory of the said Decedts. Estate.

Present Capt. John Hamelin

John Peterson and William Batte Admrs. &c of Jos: Hollycross Deced: return upon Oath an Inventory &c of the said Decedts. Estate. Ordered, it be recorded.

Elizabeth Avery als. Osborn, Executrix &c of Elias Osborn Deced: returns upon Oath an accot. Dr. & Cr. of the said Decedts. Estate, Ordered it be recorded.

The Last Will and Testament of John Bishop Deced: was presented into Court by Sarah his relict and Executrix therein Named, who made Oath thereto, and the said Will togather with a Memorandum endorse on the back thereof, being proved by the Oath of Mr. Robert Hall is Admitted to record, and upon the said Executrix's giveing Security according to Law, it's Ordered that a Certificate be granted her for Obtaining a Probate in Due form, whereupon James Bishop becomes her Security and with her enters into Bond &c.

Thomas Adam's, Wm. Short, John Avery and Israel Marks or any three of them are Ordered to appraise the Estate of John Bishop Deced: they being first Sworn by some Justice of this County for that purpose, and that they make report of their proceedings to the next Court when Sarah Bishop the Executrix is to return the Inventory.

Mary Daniell Admx. &c of the Estate of John Daniel Deced: return's upon Oath an Inventory &c of the sd. Decedts. Estate. Ordered it be recorded.

[page 71]

Pursuant to a Comission of the Peace &c Mr. Sampson Merredeth takes the usuall Oaths [&] Signs the Test and is Sworn a Justice &c and takes his place.

John Hardyman Admr. &c of John Hardyman Deced: returns upon Oath a further accot. Dr. & Cr. of the sd. Decedts. Estate. Ordered it be recorded.

On the peto. of Benjamin Foster Overseer of the Lower Blackwater Bridge It's Ordered that he employ workmen to build plank Bridges over the severall watercourses of the said Swamp, and that he bring his accot. of the Charge thereof to the next Leavy Court for this County for allowance, and that the Overseers of the Rowanty and Abernathy's Bridges take the same Method for keeping the said Bridges in repair that is the workmen abovementioned are only to Saw the plank and put the said Bridges togather when the said plank and Timber are brought in place by the said Overseers &c.

On the Complt. of Edward Denton in behalfe of his son Peter Denton who was formerly bound an Apprentice to Roger Taylor, It's Ordered that the said Boy return to his sd. ffather and be acquitted from any further Service to the said Taylor.

Pursuant to an Order of the Last Court, Wm. Tomlinson returns the apprismt. of Indian Jack. Ordered it be recorded. Vizt. We the Subscribers in Obedience to an Order of Court (being first Sworn) have appraised an Indian Boy called Jack, belonging to William Tomlinson, at five Shillings Current money. [signed] Gil. Hay, John Wilkinson. Ver. rec. Test W. Hamelin, Cl. Cur.

In the action of Debt Depending between Charles Goodrich and Daniell Higdon, the Defendt. being permitted to plead Doubly, files his plea to the plts: Declaration who has time till the next Court to Consider the same.

The action Depending between James Bell plt: and Thomas Harrison and Edward Goodrich is referred to Mr. Robt. Hall to Settle. Ordered he be make report of his proceedings therein to the next Court.

In the action of Debt Depending between James Bell plt. and John Lett and John Hamelin Defts. for five hundred and Eighty pounds of Tobacco Due by Bill &c at the Last Court Oyer of the sd. Bill was granted the Defendts. and time to Consider the same till this Court, and they being now called and failing to appear or Offer any thing in Barr or preclusion of the plts. Action, therefore it's Considered by the Court that the plt. recover against the said Defts. the said Sum and Costs unless they shall appear at the next Court and answer the said action.

In the action of Debt Depending between John Allen and John Sherley for Eleaven hundred and thirty pounds of Tobacco Due by Bill Dated 19 Day of November 1714, at the Last Court the Defendt. failing to appear Judgemt. was granted the plt. agst. Nathaniell Harrison Esqr. returned Security for the sd. Deft upon Condition that if he shou'd appear at this Court and answer the said action then the said Judgemt. shou'd be Void, And the sd. Deft. being now called and failing to appear on the motion of the plts: Attorney Judgemt. is granted and Confirmed against the sd. Nathaniel Harrison Eqr. the said Sum of Eleaven hundred and thirty pounds of Tobacco. It's therefore Ordered that the sd. Nathaniel pay the sd. sum to the said Allen with Costs. Als. Exec.

[page 72]

In the action of Debt Depending between Peter Wynne plt: and Peter Talbu[tt] and Michael Talbutt for four hundred Seaventy five pounds of Tobacco Due by Bill Dated the first Day of June 1715, at the Last Court the Defendts. faililng to appear, Judgmt. was granted the plt. against Edward Scott returned Security for the Defendts. upon Condition that if they Shou'd appear at this Court and answer the said Action then the said Judgemt. to be Void, and the sd. Defts. being now called and failing to appear on the motion of the plts. Attorney Judgemt. is granted and Confirmed against the said Edward Scott for the said Sum of four hundred Seaventy five pounds of Tobacco and Costs. Als. Exec.

The attachmt. granted Pr. [Peter] Wynn Admr. &c against the Estate of Stephen Evans is Continued till the next Court.

In the action of Debt Depending between Mansell Blagrave Assignee of John Lilly and Robert Davis for four pounds five Shillings Current Money Due by Bill Dated the thirtyeth Day of June 1715, at the Last Court the Defendt. failing to appear Judgemt. was granted the plt: against Sampson Merredeth Sherr: for the sd. Sum upon Condition that if the said Deft. shou'd appear at this Court and answer the said Action then the said [word removed] Judgemt. to be Void, and the said Deft. being now called and failing to appear on the motion of the plts: Attorney Judgemt. is granted and Confirmed against the said Sampson Merredeth Sherr: for the said Sum of four pounds five Shillings Current Money with Costs. Als. Exec.

The attachmt: awarded Sampson Merredeth Sherr: against the Estate of Robert Davis is Continued till the next Court.

The suit Depending between William Short and Randall Platt by *Scire ffacias* is Continued till the next Court.

The suit Depending between Edward Goodrich and Richard Hamelin by *scire facias* is Continued till next Court.

The action on the Case Depending between Elizabeth Epes Exrx. &c and Wm. Mayes is Continued till the next Court.

The action on the Case Depending between Charles and William Williams Admrs. &c of Charles Williams Deced: and William Dickason, neither party appearing is Dismist.

The action of Debt Depending between Thomas Simmons Assignee &c and Adam Ivie, neither party appearing is Dismist.

The action of Debt Depending between Thomas Eldridge and Richard Acock neither party appearing is Dismist.

The attachment awarded Robert Bolling against the Estate of Wm. Stainback junr. is Continued till next Court.

[page 73]

Elizabeth Spell Widow and relict of George Spell Deced: appears in Court and relinquishes her right of Administration of the said Decedts. Estate to John Hardyman.

John Hardyman Came into Court and made Oath that George Spell of this County Lately Deced: Dyed Intestate as farr as he knew or believed, and upon his giveing Security for his Just and faithful Administration of the said Decedts. Estate it's Ordered that a Certificate be granted him for Obtaining Letters of Administration in Due form whereupon Thomas Eldridge became his Security and with him entred into Bond according to Law.

John Ledbetter, Richard Rains, John Hill and James Williams or any three of them are Ordered to appraise the Estate of George Spell Deced: they being first Sworn by some Justice for that purpose, and that they make report of their proceedings to the next court, when John Hardyman the Admr. is to return the Inventory.

The attachment granted ffrancis Mallory against the Estate of Samuell Harwell is Continued till the next Court.

Ordered that Charles Gillam be Overseer of the Highways from Moor's ffeild to Appomattox Chappell.

In the Action on the Case Depending between Instance Hall and ffrancis W[ood]son for One pound ten Shillings three pence Due by accot. &c the Deft. haveing had time given her to plead and being called failed to appear or offer any thing in barr or preclusion of the plts: Action, Therefore it's Considered by the Court that the plt. recover against the said Deft. the said Sum and Costs unless she shall appear at the next Court and answer the said Action.

In the action of Debt Depending between Peter Bond and Peter Wynne for two thousand pound of Tobacco Due by Bill Dated the (twenty) Seaventh Day of Aprill 17[0]3, the Deft. by Edward Goodrich his Attorney appears and Confesses Judgement to the plt. for the said Sum, whereupon it's Ordered by the Court that the said Defendt. pay to the said plt. the said Sum of two thousand pounds of Tobacco and Costs. Als. Exec.

The Order that Ann Blackman Exrx. &c of Thomas Blackman Deced: return an Inventory of the said Decedts. Estate is Continued till next Court.

The Attachmt. awarded Sampson Merredeth Sherr: against the Estate of Robert Hix is Continued till the next Court.

The attachment awarded Sampson Merredeth Sherr: against the Estate of Martin Sheffeild is Continued till the next Court.

The action of Debt Depending between Joseph Pleasant Consignee of Isau Millner and Thomas Hunobe (neither party appearing) is Dismist.

In the action on the Case Depending between ffrancis Mallory plt. and Benjamin ffoster and Elizabeth his wife, the Defts. being permitted to plead Doubly appear and file their plea to the plts: Declaration who has time till the next Court to Consider the Same.

[page 74]

In the action on the Case Depending between John Hatch and John Scott, the Defendt. appears and pleads in writeing to the plts. Declaration who Joins in the Issue Tendered by the said Defendt. and the same is referred till the next Court for Tryall.

The attachmt. awarded Sampson Merredeth Sherr: against the Estate of John Scott is Dismist.

In the action on the Case Depending between William Hamelin and William Wheatly for two hundred and fifteen pounds of Tobacco Due by accot. &c at the Last Court the Deft. failing to appear Judgement was granted the plt. against Sampson Merredeth Sherr: upon Condition that if the sd. Defendt. shou'd appear at this Court and answer the said action that then the said Judgemt. shou'd be Void and the sd. Deft. being now called and failing to appear on the motion of the plt. Judgemt. is granted and Confirmed against Said Sampson Merredeth for the said Sum of Two Hundred and fifteen pounds of Tobacco & Costs. Als. Exec:

Francis Wynne Executrix of the Last will and Testament of John Herbert Deced: assignee of William Mayes plt. against John Peterson and William Batte Admrs. of the Goods and Chattels &c of Joseph Holycross Deced: for three thousand four hundred and Eighty pounds of Tobacco Due by Bill Dated the 29 Day of August 1713, the Defts. appear and [...] their motion the plt. by her son Buller Herbert makes Oath the said Sum is Justly Due, thereupon it's Ordered that the plt. recover against the Defts. the said sum of three thousand four hundred and Eighty pounds of Tobacco to be paid out of the said Decedts. Estate with Costs. Als. Exec:

In the action of Debt Depending between William Byrd Esqr. and John Peterson and William Batte Admrs. &c of Joseph Holycross Deced: on the Defts. Motion Oyer of the plts. Bill is granted them and time till the next Court to Consider the same.

In the action of Debt Depending between ffrancis Epes Assignee of Charles Hudson and John Peterson and William Batte Admrs. &c of Jos. Hollycross Deced: on the Defts. motion Oyers of the plts. Bill is granted them and time to Consider the same till the next court.

In the action of Debt Depending between Thomas Jefferson Assignee of Mary Mattock and John Peterson and William Batte Admrs. &c of Jos. Hollycross Deced: on the Defts. motion Oyer of the plts. Bill is granted them and time till the next Court to Consider the same.

In the action of Debt Depending between Thomas Jefferson Assignee of Mary Mattock and John Peterson and William Batte Admrs. &c of Jos. Hollycross Deced: neither party appearing it's Ordered the same be Dismist.

[page 75]
In the action of Debt Depending between Edward Holloway and Mary Daniell Admx. &c of [John] Daniell Deced: on the motion of the Defts. attorney Oyer of the plts. Bill is granted her and time to Consider the same till the next Court.

Wm. Temple vrs. Thomas Addison, assault & Battery &c retraxit.

The action Depending between ffrancis Norten and Mathew Anderson, neither party appearing is Dismist.

In the action on the Case Depending between Lucy Boys Admx. &c of Saml. Boys Deced: And Henry Duke for fourteen hundred pounds of Tobacco Due by accot. &c the Deft. being called and not appearing (nor any Security returned for him) on the motion of the plts. Attorney Judgement is granted against Richard Hamelin Sherr: of this County for the said sum & Costs, unless the Deft. shall appear at the next Court and answer the said Action.

Judgement being this Day past to Lucy Boys against Richard Hamelin Sherr: of this County for fourteen hundred pounds of Tobacco by reason of the non appearance of Henry Duke in an action on the Case at the suit of the said Lucy Boys, On the motion of the said Sherr: an attachmt. is granted him against the Estate of the said Duke for the said Sum and Costs returnable to the next Court for Judgemt.

In the action on the Case Depending between Ann Millner Admx. &c of Isau Millner Deced: and Henry Duke, the plt. failing to prosecute, on the motion of the Defendts. Attorney it's Ordered that the said plt. be Nonsuit and pay the Deft. five Shillings with Costs. Als. Exec:

The action of Debt Depending between James Bell plt. and Phillip and John Burrow, neither party appearing is Dismist.

The action of Debt Depending between James Bell plt. and Cornelius Cargill and Richard Whittmore, neither party appearing, is Dismist.

In the action on the Case Depending between John Lett and John Soane Damage Six hundred pounds of Tobacco &c the Deft. being called and not appearing nor any Security returned for him on the motion of the plts. Attorney Judgement is granted him against Richd. Hamelin Sherr: of this County for the said Sum and Costs, unless the Deft. appears at the next Court and answers the said Action.

The action Depending between John Lett and Thomas Crafford, neither party appearing is Dismist.

In the action of Trespass &c Depending between Thomas Crafford and John Lett the plt. in his Declaration setts forth that whereas in the fifth Day of this Instant July in the Parrish of Westopher in this County he being possessed of the sum of forty one Shillings and Seaven pence halfe penny of good current money as of his own, the aforesaid John Lett on the Day and year aforesaid and in the Parrish & County aforesaid with force and arms, the aforesaid Sum of money out of the Hands & Possession of the

[page 76]
of the said Thomas Crafford did take and Carry away and him the said Thomas of the said Sum of such takeing and carrying away did wholely Deprive and Dispossess and other Enormitys to him did against the peace &c wherefore the said Thomas saith that he is Damnified and Damage hath sustained to the Value of ten pounds Current month. The Defendt. being returned *non est Inventus* and not appearing on the motion of the plts. Attorney an Attachmt. is granted him against the Estate of the said Defendt. for the said sum & Costs returnable to the next court for Judgemt.

The action Depending between John Willkinson Assignee &c and Adam Ivie neither party appearing is Dismist.

And then the Court Adjourn'd till Court in Course. Jno. Hamelin. Test. Wm. Hamelin, Cl. Cur.

Att a Court held for the County of Prince George on the Second Tuesday in August Anno Dom 1716: being the fourteenth Day of the said Month.

Present	John Hamelin	Randle. Platt	Robert Munford
	Sampson Merredeth	& John Hardyman	Gent. Justices

Sarah Gary Executrix &c of Wm. Gary Deced: returns upon Oath an Inventory of the said Decedts. Estate. Ordered it be recorded.

Sarah Bishope Executrix &c of John Bishope Deced: returns upon Oath an Inventory and appraismt. of the Estate of the said Decedt. Ordered it be recorded.

Thomas Cocke haveing produced a Commission from the Honble. the Lieut. Governour to be Agent of the publick Storehouses at Martins Brandon, he thereupon gives Bond and Security according to Law and is Sworn Agent as aforesaid.

The Last Will and Testament of James Cureton Deced: was presented into Court by Joseph Renn Executor therein Named upon Oath, and the same being proved by the Oaths of Roger Taylor, John Cureton and Phillip Claud witnesses thereto is admitted to record and upon the sd. Executors giveing Security for his Just & Faithfull Executorship &c it's Ordered that a Certificate be granted for Obtaining a probate in Due form whereupon Edward Goodrich became his security and with him enters into Bond accordingly.

[page 77]

John Hines Security for George Maine Admr. &c of Edward Maine Deced: returns upon Oath an accot. Dr. and Dr. of the said Decedts. Estate Ordered it be recorded, the same being Exd. & allowed by ye Clk.

Mary Daniell Admx. &c of John Daniell Deced: returns upon Oath an accot. Dr. & Cr. of the said Decedts. Estate and the same being Examined and allowed by the Court is Order'd to be recorded.

The Last Will and Testament of John Bishope Deced: was further proved in Court by the Oaths of Richard Warthen and Ailce his wife.

In the action of Debt Depending between William Byrd Esqr. and John Peterson and Wm. Batte Administrators of the Estate of Jos: Hollycross Deced: for tenn pounds fifteen Shillings Due by Bill Dated the 23d: Day of ffebruary 1715. On the Defendts. motion the plt. by Major Robert Munford his Attorney makes Oath the said Sum is Justly due, it's thereupon Ordered that the said Defendts. Admrs. as aforesaid pay to the sd. plt. the sd. Sum & Costs out of the said Decedts. Estate. Als. Exec:

John Peterson and William Batte Admrs. &c of Jos: Hollycross Deced: return upon Oath an accot. Dr. & Cr. of the said Decedts. Estate, Wch. being Examined and allowed by the Court is Ordered to be recorded.

The action of Debt Depending between James Bell plt. and Thomas Harrison & Edward Goodrich Defendts. is Continued.

George Crooke in Open Court acknowledged his Deed for Land with Livery of Seizin endorst. thereon (Indented and Sealed) bearing Date the fourteenthof this Instant to David Crawley and his heirs &c and on the motion of Major Munford Attorney of the sd. Crawley the said Deed with the Livery of Seizin &c is admitted to record. And then also appeared in Court Elizabeth the wife of the said George and being first privately Examined freely relinquisht. to the sd. Crawley her right of Dower of in and to the Lands &c in the said Deed mentioned. Ordered the same also be recorded.

George Crooke in Open Court acknowledged his Bond for performance of Covenants &c Dated the fourteenth Instant, to David Crawley. Ordered it be recorded.

In the action of Debt Depending between James Bell plt. and John Lett and John Hamelin Defendts. for five hundred and Eighty pounds of Tobacco Due by Bill &c the said John Lett appeared in Court and Confess Judgemt. to the plt. for the said Sum and at the Last Court Conditionall Judgemt. was granted the plt. against the Defendts. that if they did not appear at this Court and answer the said action then the sd. Judgemt. shou'd be Confirmed &c and the said John Hamelin being called and failing to appear &c the sd. Last Courts Judgemt. is Confirmed the plt. &c It's thereupon Ordered that the said Defendts. Jointly and Severally pay to the said plt. the said Sum of five hundred & Eighty pounds of Tobacco & Costs. Als: Exed.

The attachmt. granted Peter Wynne Admr. &c against the Estate of Step: Evans is Continued till next Court.

[page 78]

The attachmt. granted Sampson Merredeth Late Sherr: &c against the Estate of Robert Davis is Dismist.

The suit Depending between William Short and Randle Platt pr. *scire facias* is Continued.

In the suit Depending between Edward Goodrich and Richard Hamelin pr. *scire facias*, the Deft. files a Demurrer to the plts. Declaration who has time till the next Court to Consider the Same.

In the action on the case Depending between Elizabeth Epes Executrix &c of William Epes Deced: and William Mayes for two hundred Eighty three & an halfe pds: of Tobacco Due by Accot. Dated 1708 & 1810, the said partys Submitting themselves to the Court for Tryall and the plt. proving the sd. accot. to be Just by the Oath of her son ffra: Epes. Therefore it's Ordered by the Court that the sd. Defendt. pay to the said plt: the said Sum of two hundred Eighty three & an halfe pds: of Tobacco & Costs. Als. Exec:

The attachmt. granted Robert Bolling against the Estate of William Stainback junr. is Continued till the next Court.

In the action of Debt Depending between William Randolph and John Bishope for One thousand pounds of Tobacco Due by Bill &c the Deft. came personally into Court and Confest Judgemt. to the plt. for five hundred & thirty pounds of Tobacco, being the Ballance of the said Bill, thereupon [it is] Ordered that the said Deft. pay to the said plt. the said Sum & Costs. Als. Exec:

John Hardyman Admr. &cof Geo: Spell Deced: returns upon Oath an Inventory &c of the said Decedts. Estate, ordered it be recorded.

The attachment granted ffrancis Mallory against the Estate of Samuell Harwell is Continued till the next Court.

In the action on the case Depending between Instance Hall and ffrancis Hudson for thirty Shillings and three pence Due by accot. &c the Deft. appears and pleads *nil debit* and the plt. Joining in the Issue the same is referred for Tryall to the next Court.

The Order that Ann Blackman return an Inventory &c of the Estate of Thomas Blackman Deced: is Continued till the next Court.

On the Attachment granted Sampson Merredeth Late Sherriff of this County against the Estate of Robert Hix for Seaven hundred forty One pounds of

[page 79]

Tobacco, by reason of the Nonappearance of the said Robert at the suit of Thomas Simmons in an action on the Case, the Sherriff makes the following return, Vizt: Attachmt. a publick Debt Due from the Country to the said Robert Hix, being in the hands of the said Sampson Merredeth and the said Robert being called and failing to appear or Offer any thing in barr &c It's Ordered that the said Sampson Merredeth retain and keep in his hands so much of the said Publick Debt as will pay him the sd. Sum of Seaven hundred forty One pounds of Tobacco & Costs.

The attachmt. granted Sampson Merredeth agst. the Estate of Martin Sheffield is Continued.

The action Depending between ffrancis Mallory and Benja. ffoster & Uxor, neither party appearing is Dismist.

The action Depending between Charles Goodrich and Daniel Higdon, is Continued.

The action Depending between John Hatch & John Scott, is Continued.

The action Depending between ffrancis Epes Assignee of Charles Hudson and John Peterson and William Batte Admrs. &c of Jos. Hollycross Deced: neither party appearing is Dismist.

The action Depending between Thomas Jefferson Assignee of Mary Mattox and John Peterson and William Batte Administrators of Jos. Hollycross Deced: neither party appearing is Dismist.

In the action of Debt Depending between Edward Holloway and Mary Daniell Admx. of the Estate of John Daniell Deced: for One thousand and fifteen pounds of Tobacco Due to the plt. by reason of his being surety for and bound wth. the sd. Decedt: to one Willm: Cooke by Bill Dated the Eighty Day of August 1711, as by the plts. Declaration is sett forth, the Defendt. appearing on her motion the sd. Edward makes Oath that he hath paid the said Bill &c therefore it's Ordered by the Court that the said Mary Daniell Admx. as aforesaid pay to the said Edward the sum of five pounds One Shilling and Six pence (value of the sd. Tobo.) out of the sd. Decedts. Estate with Costs. Als. Exec.

In the action on the case Depending between Lucy Boys Admx. &c of Saml. Boys Deced: & Henry Duke the Deft. files a Demurrer to the plts. Declaration who has time till the next Court to Consider the same.

The Attachmt. granted Richd. Hamelin Sherr: agst. the Estate of Henry Duke is Dismist.

In the action Depending between Thomas Crafford and John Lett the Deft. files a plea to the plts. Declaration who has time to Consider the same till the next Court.

In the action Depending between John Lett & John Soane, the Deft. appears and pleads that he did not assume in Manner and fform as in the plts. Declaration is set forth and the plt. Joining in the Issue the same is referred for Tryall to the next Court.

And then the Court Adjourn'd till Court in Course. Rand: Platt. Test Wm. Hamelin, Cl. Cur.

[page 80]

Att a Court held for the County of Prince George on the second Tuesday
in September Anno Dom: 1716, being the Eleaventh Day of the said month.

Present			
	John Hamelin	Randll. Platt	Robert Hall
	Robert Bolling	& John Hardyman	Gent. Justices

John Patteson in Open Court acknowledged his Deeds of Lease and Release of Land (Indented and Sealed) bearing Date the tenth and Eleaventh Instant, to Richard Bland and his heirs &c on whose motion the sd. Deeds are Ordered to be recorded, also Ordered that a receipt written on the back of the above Deed of release for the Consideration therin Exprest be recorded, the sd. Patteson haveing acknowledged the same to be his act &c.

John Patteson and Richard Smith in Open Court acknowledge their Bond for performance of Covenants &c to Richard Bland and his heirs &c Ordered the Same be recorded.

Edmond Irby, Arthur Biggins, Nicholas Whitmo[re] & David Goodgame or any three of them are Ordered to appraise the Estate of James Curaton Deced: (they being first Sworn by some Justice for that purpose) and make report of their proceedings therein to the next Court, when Joseph Renn the Executor is to return the Inventory.

In the action of Debt Depending between John Allen and Richard Hamelin on the Defts. motion Oyer of the plts: Bill is granted him and time ill the next Court to Consider the same.

The action on the Case Depending between Randall Platt and John Lett (neither party appearing) is Dismist.

The action on the case Depending between John Hatch and John Lett, neither party appearing is Dismist.

In the action of Debt Depending between Edward Hawkins and Richard Harrison, William Short became Speciall Baile for the Deft. thereupon on his motion Oyer of the plts. Bills is granted him and time to Consider the same till the next Court.

In the action of Debt Depending between John Simmons Assignee of Edward Hawkins plt. and Richard Harrison Deft., William Short became Speciall Baile for the Deft. on whose motion Oyer of the plts. Bill is granted him and time till the next Court to Consider the same.

In the motion on the case Depending between Ann Millner, Admx. &c of Issau Millner of London Deced: and Henry Duke, the plt. failing to present &c its Ordered she be Nonsuited and pay the Deft. five Shillings with Costs. Als. Exec.

Absent Mr. Hardyman

On the peto. of Thomas Plains, It's Ordered that John Hardyman Admr. &c of George Spell Deced: pay to the sd. Thos: the Sum of Tenn Shillings for makeing a Coffin for the said Decedt. togather with Costs. Als. Exec.

[page 81]

In the action of Debt Depending between John Hardyman and Mary Daniell Admx. of the Goods and Chattels of John Daniell Deced: for four hundred and three pounds of Tobacco Due by Bill Dated the thirtyeth Day of Aprill 1761, on the Defts. motion the plt. makes Oaths the said Sum is Justly Due, thereupon it's Ordered that the said Adminx. pay to the said plt. the sum of forth Shillings and four pence out of the said Decedts. Estate, being the Value of the said Tobacco togather with Costs. Als. Exec.

Present Mr. Hardyman

In the action Depending between Nathaniel Harrison and Mary Daniell Admx. of the Goods and Chattels of John Daniell Deced: for Seaven hundred Seaventy Eight pounds of Tobacco Due by accot. &c on the Defts. motion the plt. by his booke keeper makes Oath the said sum is Justly Due thereupon it's Ordered that the said Admx. pay to the said plt. out of the said Decedts. Estate the sum of three pounds Seaventeen Shillings and ten pence, Value of the sd. Tobacco, with Costs. Als. Exec.

Absent Mr. Platt

In the action of Debt Depending between Randall Platt and John Lett for four pounds, four Shillings and Tenn pence to be paid in Tobacco at One penny per pound &c Due by Bill Dated the Eleaventh Day of January 1714, the Defendt. being called and not appearing nor any security returned for him, On the motion of the plt. Judgemt. is granted him against Richard Hamelin Sherriff of this County for the said Sum & Costs, unless the Defendt. appears at the next Court and answers the said action.

On the Suit Depending between John and Robert Bolling Executors of the Last Will and Testament of Robert Bolling Deced: and Daniell Higdon pr. *scire ffacias* the plts. Set forth that at a Court held for this County the Eleaventh Day of March 1711/12, Judgement was granted them in the Capacity aforesaid against the said Daniell Higdon for the sum of Eighteen pounds Eight Shillings and three pence Current money and four hundred Seaventy Eight pounds of Tobacco and Costs of suit amounting to One hundred thirty Eight pounds of Tobacco, and that Execution of the Judgement aforesaid yet remains to be Done, And the said Daniell being summoned to appear at this Court to Shew cause if any have or know what to say why the sd. plts. ought not to have Execution agst. him of the Debt and Damages aforesaid according to the force and Effect of the said Judgement accordingly appears and Confesses the said sums abovementioned to be still Justly Due. Therefore it's Considered by the Court and accordingly Ordered that the said plts. in their said Capacity have Execution against the said Daniell for their Debt and Damages aforesaid according to the forme and Effect of the said Judgemt. with present Costs.

Henry Thweatt vrs: William Anderson, Retraxit.

In the action of Debt Depending between Littlebury Epes and John Peterson on the motion of the Defts. Attorney an Imparlance is granted him till the next Court.

The action Depending between James Bell and Thos. Harrison & Ed. Goodrich is Continued till next Court.

[page 82]

The action Depending between Peter Wynne Admr. &c and Stephen Evans on the Defts. motion is Continued till the next Court.

Present Mr. Merredeth

In the suit Depending between William Short and Randall Platt pr. *Scire facias*, the plt. Setts forth that at a Court held for this County the eleaventh day of May 1714, Judgement was granted him against the said Defendt. for the sum of Eleaven hundred twenty four pounds of Tobacco and Costs amounting to One hundred and Sixteen pounds of Tobacco, and that Execution of the Judgement aforesaid yet remains to be done, and the said Randall being summoned to shew cause why the said plt. Ought not to have Execution against him of Debt and Damages aforesaid according to the force and Effect of the said Judgement accordingly appears and Exhibits a Discount of Nine hundred Ninety four pounds of Tobacco which being allowed by the Court, it's therefore Ordered that the said plt. have Execution against the said Deft. for two hundred forty Six pounds of Tobacco (being Ballance Due on the sd. Judgement) according to the forme and Effect thereof, with present Costs.

Present Mr. Platt

The action of Debt Depending between Sampson Merredeth and James Bell the plt. failing to prosecute, is Dismist.

In the action of Debt Depending between Robert Bolling and William Stainback junr. for five hundred pounds of Tobacco Due by Bill Dated the Eighteenth Day of May 1716, the Defendt. came personally into Court and Confessed Judgement to the plt. for the said sum, thereupon it's Ordered by the Court that the said Defendt. pay to the said plt. the said Sum of five hundred pounds of Tobacco & Costs. Als. Exec:

In the suit Depending between Edward Goodrich and Richard Hamelin pr. *scire facias*, the plt. setts forth that at a Court held for this County the Ninth Day of December 1713, Judgemt. was granted him against the said Deft. for Seaven hundred forty five pounds of Tobacco & five Shillings Current money it being the Damage and Costs awarded on a Nonsuit &c and that Execution of the Judgemt. aforesaid yett remains to be Done, and the said Richard being summoned to Shew cause why the said plt. Ought not to have Execution against him of the Debt and Damages aforesaid according to the force and Effect of the said Judgement accordingly appealed at the Last Court and filed a Demurrer to the plts. Declaration who had time till this Court to Consider the same, and the said partys now appearing and the Demurrer aforesaid being waved and the Deft. Exhibitting a Discount of five Shillings and Sixty Six and an halfe pounds of Tobo. It's therefore Ordered that the said plt. have Execution against the Deft. for Six hundred Eighty Eight and an halfe pounds of Tobacco the Ballance Due on the said Judgement, according to the forme and Effect thereof with present Costs.

[page 83]

The attachment granted ffrancis Mallory against the Estate of Samuell Hardwell is Continued till the next Court.

The action Depending between Instance Hall and ffrancis Hudson is Continued till next Court.

The Order that Ann Blackman return an Inventory &c of the Estate of Thomas Blackman Deced: is Continued till the next Court.

The attachment granted Sampson Merredeth against the Estate of Martin Sheffeild is by the sd. Merredeth's Order Dismist.

In the action on the case Depending between Lucy Boys Admx. &c of Samuell Boys Deced: and Henry Duke, the plt. failing to prosecute &c it's thereupon (on the motion of the Defendts. Attorney) Ordered that the said plt. be Nonsuit and pay the Defendts. five Shillings with Costs. Als. Exec:

On the Complaint of Richard Hamelin It's Ordered that John Lett be Summoned to the next Court to answer the same, also Ordered that the said Hamelin Cause his Evidence to be Summoned to the next Court to prove the said Complt. to be just &c.

And then the Court Adjourn'd till Court in Course. Rand: Platt, Test. Wm. Hamelin, Cl. Cur.

Att a Court held for Pr. George County on Tuesday the Ninth Day of
October Anno Dom: 1716.

Present	John Poythres	Randall Platt	Robert Munford	
	Robert Hall	John Hardyman	& Lewis Green Junr.,	Gent. Justices

On the Complt. of John Cross It's Ordered that Sarah Nants & John Nants [Nance] be Sumoned to the next Court to answer the said Complt.

On the Motion of Robert Mitchell It's Ordered that David Colyshaw be Sumoned to the next Court to give new Security for the Estate of Thomas Mitchell (an Orphan) Now under the Care of the said David.

Ordered that the Sherr: Summon a Lawful Grandjury to appear at next Court.

The action of Debt Depending between Charles Goodrich and Daniel Higdon is Continued till next Court.

The Last Will and Testament of Bryan ffarrell Late of this County Deced: was presented into Court by Elizabeth his relict and Executrix therein Named, who made Oath thereto and it being proved by the Oaths of the Severall Witnesses thereto is Admitted to record & upon

[page 84]

her giveing Security for her ffaithful performance &c of the sd. Will It was Ordered that a Certificate be granted her for Obtaining a probate in Due form whereupon Travis Morris became her Security and with her entred into Bond according to Law.

Thomas Adams, William Short, ffrances Willkins & John Bishope or any three of them are Ordered to appraise the Estate of Bryan ffarrell Deced: (they being first Sworn by Some Justice of this County for that purpose) & make report of their proceedings to the next Court when Elizabeth ffarrell the Executrix is to return the Inventory.

ffrancis Coleman and ffrancis Coleman junr. in Open Court acknowledged their Deed for Land (Indented and Seald) to Robert Bolling & his heirs &c on whose motion the same was Ordered to be recorded.

ffrances Coleman & ffrancis Coleman junr. in Open Court acknowledged their Deed for Land (Indented and Sealed) to John Coleman and his heirs &c on whose motion the same was Ordered to be recorded.

James Rivers in Open Court acknowledged his Deed for Land (Indented) to Robert Rivers and his heirs &c on whose motion the same was Ordered to be recorded.

Present Robert Bolling & John Peterson, Gent:

Ann Blackman returns by Robert Bolling an Inventory &c of the Estate of Thos. Blackman Deced: She haveing made Oath to the same before the said Bolling. Ordered it be recorded.

The action Depending between John Hatch and John Scott (neither party appearing to prosecute) is Dismist.

In the action of Trespass Depending between Thomas Crafford and John Lett, the Deft. haveing proved that the plt. hath reced: full sattisfaction for the Trespass mentioned in the plts. Declaration, thereupon the said suit is Dismist.

The peto. of John Nants for the Administration of his father's Estate is Dismist.

The action Depending between John Lett and John Soane (the plt. failing to presecute) is Dismist.

The action Depending between John Hardyman and John Lett (the plt. failing to prosecute) is Dismist.

In the action on the case Depending between Adam Tapley & Randall Platt, Oyer of the plts. is granted the Deft. and time to Consider the same till next Court.

In the action of Debt Depending between Randall Platt and Richard Pidgeon for Eight hundred twenty four pounds of Tobacco Due on Ballance of a Bill Dated the tenth day of November 1714, the Deft. being called and makeing no Legall Discounts, thereupon it's Ordered that the said Deft. pay to the said plt. the said sum of Eight hundred twenty four pounds of Tobacco & Costs. Als. Exec:

[page 85]

The action Depending between Randall Platt and William Ledbetter (the plt. failing to prosecute) is Dismist.

In the action of Debt Depending between Randall Platt and Thomas Harwell for two hundred and forty pounds of Tobacco Due by Bill &c the Deft. being called and not appearing and Robert Melone being returned Security for him, on the plts. motion Judgement is granted him agst. the sd. Deft. and Baile, unless the said Deft. shall appear at the next Court and answer the said action.

In the action of Debt Depending between Randall Platt and Chichester Sturdivant for three hundred Seaventy two pounds of Tobacco Due by Bill Dated the fifteenth Day of May 1714, the Deft. appears and Exhibits a Discount of Sixty pounds of Tobacco, Thereupon It's Ordered that the Deft. pay to the sd. plt. the Ball. of the sd. Bill being three hundred and twelve pounds of Tobacco & Costs. Als. Exec.

In the action on the case Depending between Randall Platt and Thomas Winingham for three hundred Sixty two pounds of Tobacco Due by Bill &c the Deft. being returned *non est Inventus* and not appearing, on the plts. motion an attachment is granted him against the sd. Defts. Estate for the sd. Sum and Costs, returnable to the next Court for Judgement for what shall appear to be Due.

In the suit Depending between Randall Platt and Henry Bates for Nine hundred forty Seaven pounds of Tobacco Due by Bill &c the Deft. being called and not appearing nor any Security returned for him, on the plts. motion

Judgement is granted him agst. the said Deft. and Sherr: &c for the said Sum and Costs, unless the sd. Deft. shall appear at the next Court and answer to the said action.

Judgement being this day past unto Randall Platt against Richard Hamelin Sherr: &c for Nine hundred forty Seaven pounds of Tobacco & costs &c by reason of the non appearance of Henry Baites in an action of Debt at the suit of the said Randall. On the motion of the said Sherr: an attachmt. is granted him against the Defts. Estate for the said sum & costs returnable to the next Court for Judgemt.

The action Depending between Randall Platt and Michael Hill, the plt. failing to prosecute, is Dismist.

In the action of Debt Depending between Randall Platt assignee of Charles Goodrich and Thomas House, an Imparlance is granted the Deft. till next Court.

In the motion on the case Depending between John Hatch and William Spiller for twenty Shillings and ten pence Due by accot. Dated 1716, the Deft. by Edward Goodrich his Attorney appears and Confesses Judgemt. to the plt. for the said Sum, therefore it's Ordered that the said Deft. pay to the said plt. the said Sum of twenty Shillings and ten pence with Costs. Als. Exec:

The action Depending between ffrancis Mallory & William Spiller, the plt. failing to prosecute is Dismist.

[page 86]

The action Depending between Thomas Sample & Henry Duke, the plt. failing to prosecute, is Dismist.

In the action of Debt Depending between Robert Rogers and John Lett for five hundred pounds of Tobacco Due by Bill Dated the thirteenth Day of December 1715, the Deft. came personally into Court and Confest. Judgemt. to the plt. for the said Sum, therefore it's Ordered that the said Deft. pay to the said plt. the said Sum of five hundred pounds of Tobacco & Costs. Als. Exec:

The suit in Chancery Depending between John Coleman & ffrancis Coleman, the plt. failing to prosecute is Dismist.

The suit Depending between William Randolph Admr. &c of Eusebius King Deced: & Richard Turbyfeild, pr. *Scire facias*, neither party appearing is Dismist.

In the motion of Detinue Depending between William Caratan and Joseph Renn, the Deft. pleads Non Detinue, the plt. Joins in the Issue which is referred till the next Court for Tryall.

In the suit Depending between William Randolph Admr. &c of the Goods and Chattels, rights & Credits of Eusebius King Deced: & Henry King pr. *Scire facias*, the plt. setts forth that at a Court held for this County the Ninth Day of September 1712, Judgement was granted him in the Capacity aforesaid against the said Deft. for Eleaven pounds four Shillnigs current money with Costs of suit amounting to One hundred pounds of Tobacco, and that Execution of the Judgement aforesaid yet remains to be done, and the said Henry being Summoned to Shew cause [words removed] if any have or know what to say why the said plt. ought not to have Execution agst. him of the Debt & Damages aforesaid according to the force and Effect of the said Judgement, accordingly appears and Exhibitts a Discount of forty Seaven Shillings and Nine pence, thereupon it's Ordered that the plt. have Execution agst. the sd. Deft. for the residue of his Debt & Damages aforesaid being Eight pounds Sixteen Shillings and three pence Current money and One hundred pounds of Tobacco together with Costs.

The order that Joseph Renn Exr. of James Curatan Deced: return an Inventory &c of the sd. Decedts. Estate is Continued till next Court.

In the action of Debt Depending between John Allen and Richard Hamelin for Six hundred & thirty pounds of Tobacco Due by Bill &c at the Last Court Oyer of the plts. Bill was granted the Deft. and time ill this Court to plead, andbeing called failed to appear or Offer any thing in barr or preclusion of the plts. Action, therefore it's Considered by the Court that the plt. recover agst. the said Deft. the said Sum & Costs unless he appear at thenext Court and answer the said action.

In the action of Debt Depending between Edward Horskins and Richard Harrison for Eleaven hundred and twenty pounds of Tobacco Due by two Severall Notes &c at the Last Court Oyer of the said Notes was granted the Deft. and time till this

[page 87]

Court to plead, and being called failed to appear or offer any thing in barr or preclusion of the plts. action, Therefore it's Considered by this Court that the plt. recover against the said Deft. the said Sum & Costs, unless he appear at the next Court and answer the said action.

In the suit Depending between John Simmons assignee of Edward Horskins plt. & Richard Harrison Deft. for One thousand five hundred pounds of Tobacco Due by Bill &c at the Last Court Oyer of the sd. Bill was granted the plt. and time till this Court to plead, and being called failed to appear or offer any thing in barr or preclusion of the plts.

action, thereupon it's Considered by the Court that the plt. recover against the said Deft. the said Sum & Costs unless he appears at the next Court and answers the said action.

In the action of Debt Depending between Randall Platt and John Lett, for four pounds four Shillings and ten pence to be paid in Tobacco at One penny pr. [..] Due by Bill Dated the Eleaventh Day of January 1714, at the Last Court the Deft. not appearing nor any Security returned for him on theplts. motion Conditionall Judgement was granted the plt. that if the Deft. shou'd appear at this Court and answer this action the said Judgemt. shou'd be Void &c & being now called and failing to appear, on the sd. plts. motion the sd. Judgemt. is Confirmed agst. the sd. Deft. and Richard Hamelin Sherr: It is therefore Ordered that they or either of them pay to the plt. the aforesaid Sum & Costs. Als. Exec:

In the action of Debt Depending between Littlebury Epes and John Peterson, for One thousand and thirty pounds of Tobacco Due by Bill Dated the fourteenth day of June One thousand Seaven hundred and fifteen, the Deft. Exhibitted a Discount of three hundred Sixty Nine pounds of Tobacco, thereupon it's Ordered that the sd. Deft. pay to the said plt. the residue of the aforesaid Bill being Six hundred Sixty One pounds of Tobacco and Costs. Als. Exec:

And then the Court adjourn'd till Court in Course. Jno. Poythres. Test Wm. Hamelin, Cl. Cur.

Att a Court held for the County of Pr. George on the Second Tuesday in November
Anno Dom 1716, being the thirteenth Day of the said month.

Present	John Hamelin	Randall Platt	Robert Munford	
	Robert Hall	James Thweat	and John Hardyman	Gent. Justices

Elizabeth Arnall (the Wife of John Arnall) appeared in Court and being first privately Examined freely relinquisht. to Robert Hall, her right of Dower in and to Certain Lands &c Conveyed to the said Hall in ffebruary Court Last by her sd. Husband, John Arnall, which by Order of the Court is here recorded.

On the peto. of Buller Herbert he is permitted to build a Water Mill on his Own Land on Wall['s] runn.

[page 88]

Present Majr. Bolling

William Renn haveing proved by the Oath of Joseph Renn junr. that James Curaton some time before his Decease gave to the said William a Coat and Hatt then belonging to the said James, therefore Ordered the same be Delivered him by the Exr. of the sd. James and not Inventoried in the Inventory of his Exr.

Nicholas Overby in Open Court acknowledged his Deeds of Lease and release of Land (Indented and Sealed) bearing Date the Eleaventh and twelfth Days Instant, to Bartholomew Crowder and his heirs &c on whose motion the same by Order of the Court are recorded.

Joseph Renn, Executor of James Curaton Deced: returns upon Oath an Inventory of the Estate of the said Decedt. Ordered it be recorded.

Elizabeth ffarrell Executrix of Bryan ffarrell Deced: returns upon Oath an Inventory &c of the sd. Decedts. Estate. Ordered it be recorded.

William Curaton in Open Court acknowledged his Deeds of Lease and release of Land (Sealed) Dated the twelfth and thirteenth Instant, to John Bonner, and his heirs &c on whose Motion they are Admitted to record.

Richard Smith appears in Court and (on the motion of Elizabeth Dew) makes Oath that at the time he Obtained Judgement agst. the sd. Eliza. the sum mentioned in the said Judgemt. was Justly Due to him.

William Smith appears in Court and (on the motion of Elizabeth Dew) makes Oath that at the time he Obtained Judgement agst. the said Elizabeth, the sum mentioned in the said Judgement was Justly Due to him.

The Last Will and Testament of John Tucker Deced: was presented into Court by Ann Jackson the Executrix therein Named who made Oath thereto, and it being proved by the Oath's of Thomas Daniel and Elizabeth Jackson, Witnesses thereto is Admitted to record, and upon the sd. Executrix's giveing Security according to Law it's Ordered that a Certificate be granted her for obtaining a probate in Due form, whereupon William Jackson became her Security and with her entred into Bond accordingly.

Edward Wyatt, Benjamin Rix, James Bell, and Michael Talbutt or any three of them (being first Sworn for that purpose) are Ordered to appraise the Estate of John Tucker Deced: and make report of their proceedings to the next Court when Ann Jackson the Executrix thereof is to return the Inventory.

A Power of Attorney from Robert Tucker (Attorney of John Tucker, Attorney to Mrs. Ann Millner Admx. &c of Issau Millner of Londo. Deced: and Mr. Peter [...]) to Capt. John Worsham was proved in Court by the Oath of Mr. John Hardyman a Witness thereto, who also makes oath that he saw Edward Jaquelin Subsribe the same as an Evidence. Ord. the said power be recorded.

The Question being put to this Court whither the Clerk thereof might Issue Executions on Indigents Obtained by any person or persons before one or more Justices of the

[page 89]

peace out of Court. It's the Opinion of the Court thereupon that the Clerke may and ought to receive and record the said Judgements and to Issue Execution thereon as in other cases he might Lawfully do.

William Scarbrough Admr. of the Estate of John Miles Deced: Exhibitts into Court an accot. Dr. & Cr. of the said Decedts. Estate upon Oath, and the same being Examined and allowed by the Court is Admitted to record.

James Thweatt Assignee of David Duke made Complt. that Hubbord Gibson stands Indebted to him as Assignee as aforesaid the sum of Sixteen good well Drest Doe Skins by bill Dated the 11th Day of July 1711, and sets forth that the said Hubbord Gibson hath unlawfully Departed this County that he Ordinary process of Law cannot be Served on him, whereupon he by Virtue of an Attachmt. under the hand of one of his Majestys Justices for this County returnable to this Court hath caused part of the Estate of the sd. Hubbord to be attacht. for payment thereof vizt. One Iron Pott and a pr. of Andirons, And the said Hubbord being called and failing to appear to replevy the same and the plt. proving (by his oath) the said Sum to be Due, and that the Defendt. owned the same since the assignment &c thereupon Judgement is granted him against the said Defendt. for the sd. Seum and Costs to be Leavied on and paid out of the said Goods attacht. &c Ordered that the Sherr: cause the said Goods to be Duly appraised by Robert Poythres, William Batte, George Rives & Edward Mitchell or any three of them (being first sworn for that purpose) and Delivered the plt. for and toward the payment and Sattisfaction of the abovesaid Sum & Costs, and that he make report of his proceedings therein to the next Court.

Pursuant to the Direction of the Act concerning Jurys, a Grandjury was Impannelled and Sworn by Name William Stainback, Chichester Sturdivant, Hugh Golightly, John Smith, William Short, Edward Woodleife, Thomas Booth, Benjamin ffoster, Phillip Burrow, William Wallice, Nathl. Overby, Henry Chamlis, ffrancis Willkinson, Edward Holloway & William Reves, and haveing had their charge withdraw and after some time spent return their presentmts. as follows, Vizt. Elizabeth Whittimore for haveing a Bastard Child & Ann Rosser for haveing a Bastard Child. William Stainback foreman.

Ordered that the Sherr: give Notice of the said presentmts. to the Church Wardens of Westopher Parrish.

John Hatch made complaint that Robert Burchet Stands Justly Indebted to him the sum of three pounds tenn Shillings and three halfe pence currt. money by accot. Dated from 1713 to 1715, inclusive and setts forth that the said Robert hath unlawfully Departed this County that the Ordinary process at Law cannot be Served on him whereupon he by Virtue of an Attachmt. under the hand of One of his Majestys Justices for this County returnable to this Court hath caused part of the Estate of the said Robert to be attacht. for Sattisfaction thereof, Vizt. One Indian Girl Named Sary, And the said Robert being called and failing to appear to replevye the same the plt. proveing (by his Oaths) the said sum to be Justly Due, thereupon Judgmt. is granted him agst. the said Deft: for the sd. Sum & Costs to be Leavied on and paid out of the sd. Girle Attach. &c: Ordered that the Sherr: cause the said Girle to be Duly appraised by James Gretion, George Woodleife, Duglas Irby and William Stainback or any three of them (being first Sworn for that purpose) and Delivered the plt. for payment and Sattisfaction of the said Sum and Costs and that he make report of his proceedings therein to this next Court.

[page 90]

The Attachmt. granted William Mattox agst. the Estate of Robert Burchett is Dismist.

William Mattox by his peto. set forth that Whereas he the said William at the Instance & request of Robert Burchett Late of this County did become bound with the said Robert as his Surety for the payment of the Estate belonging to the Orphans of John Duglas Deced: in the sum of Sixty pounds Sterl: as by his Bond in Court produced Dated the 21st Day of March 1712/13 appeared, and that there remains in the hands of the said Robert unpaid to the said Orphans the sum of thirty five pounds Sterl: and the sd. Burchet haveing unlawfully Departed this County so as the Ordinary process at Law cannot be served of him for recovery of the said Sum Due to the sd. Orphans nor for relief of the said William in his Suretyship as aforesaid. Whereupon he by Virtue of an Attachmt. under the hand of One of his Majestys Justices for this County returnable to this Court hath caused part of the Estate of the said Robert to be attacht. to sattisfie and pay the said Orphans, and to Indemnifie himselfe from the said Suretyship &c, Vizt. One Indian Man Named Skipper, two feather beds and some furniture, a Brass Kettle, One Iron pott, a parcell of Pewter & a Table, and the said Robert being called and failing to appear to replevye the same, thereupon Judgement is granted the said William against the said Robert for the said Sum of thirty five pounds Sterling & Costs, for the use aforesaid to be Leaved on the said Goods &c Attacht. as aforesaid. Ordered that the Sherr: cause the same to be Duly appraised by James Gretion, George Woodleife, Duglas Irby and William Stainback or any three of them (being first Sworn for that purpose) and Delivered the plt. for the use and Intent aforesaid, and make report of his proceedings therein to the next Court.

George Woodleife and William Wallice appeared in Court wth. William Mattox and Entred themselves Security for the sd. William Mattox's Due payment of the Estate of the Orphan's of John Duglas Deced: to the sd. Orphans &c.

William Wallice made complt. that Robert Burchet Stands Justly Indebted to him the sum of four pounds Eight Shillings and five pence by accot. Dated 1716, and set forth that the said Robert hath unlawfully Departed this County that the Ordinary process at Law cannot be served on him, whereupon he by Virtue of an Attachmt. under thehand of One of his Majestys Justices for this County returnable to this Court hath caused part of the Estate of the said Robert to be Attacht. for payment and Sattisfaction thereof, Vizt. a parcell of Coopers Tools, One Iron pott, one Horse Coller, one Mortarr and pestle, two pr. of Stillgards, One pr. of Bellows, One Sugar Box and one Gunn, One crosscutt saw, and warming pann, One candlestick, a fflesh forke and Skimmer, And the said Robert being called and failing to appear to replevye the same and the plt. makeing Oath the said Sum is Justly Due, thereupon Judgement is granted him agst. the sd. Defendt. for the said sum & Costs, to be Leavied on the goods attacht. Ordered that the Sherr: cause the said Goods to be Duly appraised by James Gretion, George Woodleife, Duglas Irby & William Stainback or any three of them (being first Sworn for that purpose) and Delivered the plt. for payment of the said sum & costs, and that he make report of his proceedings therein to the next Court.

[page 91]

John Golightly made complt. that Robert Burchet stands Indebted to him the sum of fifteen hundred pounds of Tobacco and five yards of Blew Linnen by Bill Dated the tenth Day of October 1716, and set fforth that the said Robert hath unlawfully Departed this County that the Ordinary process at Law cannot be served on him whereupon he by Virtue of an Attachmt. under the hand of One of his Majestys Justices for this County returnable to this Court hath caused part of the Estate of the said Robert to be attacht. for payment thereof, Vizt. One Large Chest and in four pewter plates, one small pewter Bason, one wyre riddler, one pewter porringer, one Gunn, one well Bucket and Chain, two wooden pales, One gallo. rimdlett, one La. Cyder Caske, four rush Bottom Chairs, one ffrying pann, one hatchet & two pr. of fire Tongs, one old chst, one old plaine, two Irons, four Augers, One Drawing knife, two Spoke staves, two Crossing Irons, seaven Chissells, One coopers ax and howell, two gauges, one handsaw and rest, one hilling hoe and a Coopers Adz, an auger, a par[...] and Wimblebitt, a small Table, a wooden peck, an Old bed & two Blanketts, One Gridiron, one pewter pott, a pameta bedcord, one chest and six old rush chairs, the surplusage of what is in the hands of William Mattox belonging to the said Burchett's Estate, as also his Debt Due to the said Burchet, and the said Robert being called and faililng to appear to replevye the same, and the plt. makeing Oath the said Sum is Justly Due, thereupon Judgemt. is granted him agst. the said Deft. for the said sum & Costs to be Leavied on the goods attacht. Ordered that the Sherr: cause the siad Goods to be Duly appraised by James Gretion, George Woodleife, Duglas Irby & Wm. Stainback or any three of them (being first sworn for that purpose) and Delivered the plt. for payment of the said sum and Costs, and that he make report of his proceedings therein to the next Court.

Peter Wynne Admr. &c of Joshua Wynne Deced: made Complt. that Robert Burchet Stands Indebted to him in the Capacity aforesaid by accot. the sum of One hundred thirty Nine pounds of Tobacco, and setts fforth that he the said Robert hath unlawfully Departed this Country that the Ordinary process at Law cannot be served on him, whereupon he Obtained an Attachmt. under the hand of One of his Majestys Justices for this County agst. the said Defendts. Estate for the said sum & Costs returnable to this Court, wch. being accordingly now returned Executed in the hands of John Woodleife who being sumoned to Deliver what he hath belonging to the said Burchet, appears and being sworn confesses to have in his possession the sum of fifteen shillings and tenn pence and the Deft. failing to appear to replevye the same and the plt. makeing Oath that the said Sum (of Tobo.) is Justly Due to him, thereupon Judgement is granted him agst. the said John Woodleife for the said sum of fifteen Shillings and tenn pence. Als. Exec: Ordered that the aforesaid Attachmt. continue in force till the next Court for recovery of the residue of the aforesaid sum & Costs.

Robert Bolling made complt. that Robert Burchet Stands Indebted to him the sum of Seaven pounds ten Shillings currt. money by Bond Dated the 11th Day of October 1712, and sets fforth that the said Robert Burchet hath unlawfully Departed this County that the Ordinary process at Law cannot be Served on him, whereupon he by Virtue of an Attachmt. under the hand of One of his Majestys Justices for this County returnable to this

[page 92]

to this Court hath caused part of the Estate of the said Robert to be Attacht. for payment thereof, Vizt. the service of a Sarvant Boy Named John Maynard, One Mair and Colt, and the said Robert being called and failing to appear to replevye the same, the the plt. makeing Oath that four pounds fifteen Shillings of the said Sum is now Justly Due to him thereupon Judgment is granted him agst. the said Defendt. for the said sum & Costs to be Leavied on the Goods &c Attach. Ordered that the Sherr: cause the said things Attacht. as aforesaid to be Duly appraised by James Gretion, George Woodleife, Duglas Irby and Wm. Stainback or any three of them (being first Sworn for that purpose) and Delivered the plt. for and toward the payment of the said Sum & Costs, and that he make rept. of his proceedings therein to the next Court.

George Rives made complt. that Robert Burchet stands Indebted to him by accot. Dated 1713 the Sum of thirty five Shillings, and set forth that the sd. Robert hath unlawfully Departed this County that the Ordinary process at Law cannot be served on him whereupon he by Virtue of an Attachmt. under the hand of one of his Majestys Justices for this County returnable to this Court hath caused part of the Estate of the said Robert to be attacht. for payment thereof, Vizt. three Hoggs, a Debt in the hands of Thomas Simmons, One Jointing Iron & a parcell of plank, and the sd. Robert being called and failing to appear to replevye the same, and the plt. makeing Oath the said sum is justly Due to him, thereupon Judgement is granted the plt. against the sd. Defendt. for the said sum & Costs, to be Leavied on the Goods attach. Ordered that the Sherr: cause the same to be Duly appraised by James Gretion, George Woodleife, Duglas Irby & Wm. Stainback or any three of them (being first sworn for that purpose) and Delivered the plt. for payment of the said sum & Costs, and that he make report of his proceedings therein to the next Court.

Mathew Smart junr. made Complt. that Robert Burchet Stands Indebted to him by accot. Dated 1716, the sum of five pound three Shillings, and set fforth that the said Robert hath unlawfully Departed this County that the Ordinary process at Law cannot be Served on him whereupon he by Virtue of an Attachmt. under the hand of one of his Majestys Justices for this County returnable to this Court hath caused part of the Estate of the sd: Robert to be Attacht. for payment thereof, Vizt. Six Cows and a Bull, three calves and a Bell, and the said Robert being called and failing to appear to replevy the same, and the plt. makeing Oath the said Sum if Justly Due, thereupon Judgmt. is granted him agst. the said Robert for the said Sum & Costs, to be Leavied on the sd. Cattle &c. Ordered that the Sherr: cause the said Cattle &c to be Duly appraised by James Gretion, George Woodleife, Duglas Irby & William Stainback or any three of them (being Sworn for that purpose) and Delivered the plt. for payment of the sd. Sums & Costs and make report of his proceedings to the next Court.

[page 93]

Sarah Nance and Richard Nance Executors appointed in the Last Will and Testament of John Nance Deced: personally appear in Court and refuse to accept the Executorship of the said Will, and relinquish their right to John Nance junr.

The Last Will and Testament of John Nance Deced: was Exhibited into Court by John Nance junr. and the Executors Named in the said Will haveing personally appeared in Court and refused to accept the Executorship &c, the said John Nance made Oath thereto, and it being proved by the Oath of William Stainback, William Epes & ffrancis Epes Witnesses thereto is admitted to record, and upon the said John Nance giveing Security according to Law it's Ordered that a Certificate be granted him for Obtaining a Commission of Administration within the said Wills annext. &c

Ralph Bradford appeared in Open Court and acknowledged his Deed for Land (Indented and Sealed) Dated the fourteenth Day of July 1716 to Edward Goodrich, David Goodgame and Joshua Goodgame and their heirs &c, on whose motion the said Deed is admitted to Record.

And then the Court Adjourn'd till Court in Course. Randll. Platt. Test Wm. Hamelin, Cl. Cur.

Att a Court held in the County of Pr. Geo: on Tuesday the 13th Day of November Anno Dom. 1716, for Laying the County Leavy.

Present	John Hamlin,	Randll. Platt,	Robert Munford }
	Robert Hall,	Robert Bolling,	James Thweatt }
	John Hardyman	& John Peterson	Gent. Justices

Pr. Geo. County Dr. 1716

For wolves killed, Vizt.

		Tobo.			Tobo.
William Coleman	1	100	Brot. on	16	1600
Richard Burch	1	100	John Golightly	1	100
Richard Vaughn	1	100	William Anderson	2	200
Joshua Irby	1	100	Wm. Epes junr.	1	100

Abram Ally	1	100	John Simmons 2d Swamp	1	100
Peter Mitchell	1	100	Buller Herbert	1	100
ffrancis Coleman	1	100	John Anderson	1	100
Thos. Clay pr. St. Evans	1	100	Charles Gee	1	100
James Thweatt, pr. W. Westbrook	2	200	John Tally	1	100
Wm. Hamelin, pr. Jos. ffowler	1	100	Saml. Harwell	1	100
George Rives	4	400	Wm. Temple junr.	1	100
Henry Maise	1	100	Xpher Hinton	1	100
	16	1600	==	28	2800

To Benja. ffoster overseeer of Blackwater Bridge for Disbursmts. abt. ye same   5500

carried over 8300

[page 94]   Tobo.

Brot. Over	8300
To James Thweatt Corroner for ye inquest of John Nisbett	133
To Colo. Harrison for a press to preserve the Records &c	400
To Wm. Hamelin for bringing the same from the sd. Harrisons to ye Coty. Office	070
To Do. Cl. for the County Service one year . . .	1000
To Richard Hamelin Sherr: for Do. 500	
To Thos. Simmons for Sweeping the Court house and work Done to the Prison 1715	300
To Samson Merredeth Late Sherr: for sundry insolvents &c	965
To Do. Due to him Last year not fully Leavied	042
To Thos. Simmons junr. for rope used in clearing Powells Creek	100
To 3889: Tobo. to the Publick as by an Act for Leavying the same is Directed	3889
To the Sherr: for his Attendance 10 Days in [accounting] &c	2000
Pr. Geo. County Cr. 1716	17699
By 1037 Tithables at 17 l. Tobo. pr. pole is	17629
Due to the Sherr: to be Leavied next year	70
	17699

Ordered that the Sherriff receive of every Tithathable [sic] person within this County (by Distress in case of refusall or Non payment) the Sum of Seaventeen pounds of Tobacco, the same being their County Leavy this present year. And that the sd. Sherr: take care to pay the same to the Severall persons to whom it's proportioned in the above Leavy.

Ordered that the Sherr: attend for accounting wth. the sevll. Debtors to the Coty. the severall precincts as Ordered at the Leavy Court Anno 1714.

Robert Hobbs and John Hines builders of the Blackwater Bridge, personally appeared in Court and acknowledged themselves to be jointly and Severally Indebted to the Justices of the peace for this County, and to theier Successors, in the Sum of Six thousand Eight Hundred pds. of Tobacco, with Condition that if they or either of them the said Robert Hobbs & John Hines shall maintain & keep the wooden worke of the said Bridge in Order and good repair the Space of Seaven years next comeing, then this recognizance to be Void and of None Effect, Otherwise to be & remain in full power force and Vertue.

And then the Court Adjourn'd. Jno. Hamlin. Test Wm. Hamelin, Cl. Cur.

[page 95]

On Tuesday the thirteenth Day of November Anno 1716, William Worsham, Desired that the following Judgemt. Awarded him agst. John Spain might be recorded that Ex[...] might Issue thereon, Vizt.

Whereas this Day William Worsham has caused John Spain to be brought before me to answer his Complaint for Seaventeen Shillings and three pence Current Mony Due to him pr. accot. the said Spain appearing and Confessing the same to be Due, I doe thereupon Odrder that the said Spain pay the sd. Worsham the said sum with Costs. Als. Exec. [signed Robert Bolling] ver: rec. Test: Wm. Hamelin, Cl. Cur.

Att a Court held for Prince George County the 8th Day of January 1716, being the
Second Tuesday in the said Month.

Present	John Hamelin	Randll. Platt,	Robert Munford }	
	Robert Hall,	Lewis Green,	& John Peterson }	Gent. Justices

Ordered that John Bell be Overseer of the Highways from Warthens Mill to Bleihleys Mill, and also from the said Warthins Mill to William Heeth's, and that with the Adjacent Inhabitants he take care to clear the first said Road as the Laws Direct and the other to be made [...] a good Bridle road.

On the peto. of William Mayes he is permitted to clear and Turn the main road by his plantation on the other side thereof.

Ann Jackson Executrix of John Tucker Deced: returns an Inventory of the said Decedts. Estate upon Oath. Ordered it be recorded.

Ordered that Thomas Simmons, Surveyor of the Highways in Merchts. hope with the people under his care, make a Bridge over Wards runn, where the main road crosses the same.

On the motion of Mr. Richard Bland and Majr. Robert Munford Admrs. of Wm. Byrd Esqr. It's Ordered that Thomas Eldridge be Entred Attorney for the said persons Attorneys as aforesaid in all causes for or concerning the said Byrd.

John Nance Admr. within the will Annext. of John Nance Deced: appears in Court & with ffrancis Epes and Wm. Gibbs enters into Bond for his ffaithfull Administration of the said Decedts. Estate according to Law.

On the peto. of William Pettypool junr. it's Ordered that a Crop and two slitts in the right Ear and a Small Square peice taken out of the Lower part of the crop or corner of the said Ear, and a Swallow for the [e]nd underlye and Over[high] in the Left be recorded his Ear Marke. Verte.

[page 96]

On the petition of John Curaton Its Ordered that a Crop and two Slitts in Each Ear and a halfe moon under the Left be recorded his Ear Marke.

Present James Thweatt, Gent.

Edward Epes, Nathaniel Tatum, John Lewis, and Thomas More, or any three of them are Ordered to appraise the Estate of John Nance Deced: by being first Sworn by some Majistrate for that purpose, and make report of their proceedings to the next Court when John Nance the Admr. &c is to return the Inventory.

In the action of Debt Depending between James Bell plt. and Thomas Harrison and Edward Goodrich Defendts. for Six hundred Ninety five pds. of Tobacco Due by Bill Dated the 13th Day of June 1714, at a former Court the Deft. pleaded payment and the plt. Joining in the Issue the same was referred to the [next] Court for Tryall, the the sd. partys not appearing and Edward Goodrich one of the Defendts. Exhibitting a Discount of four hundred and [forty] pds. of Tobacco which [he is] allowed thereupon Judgmt. is granted the plt. agst. the said Defendt. the residue of the aforesaid sum being two hundred forty five pds. of Tobacco, It's therefore Ordered that the said Defendts. or either of them pay to the said plt. the said Sum of two hundred forty five pds. of Tobo. & Costs. Als. Exec.

The Suit brot. by Peter Wynne Admr. &c against [word removed] Stephen Evans is Continued till next Court.

The Attachment granted ffrances Mallory against the Estate of Samuell Harwell is Continued till next Court.

The action Depending bweteen Instance Hall and ffrances Hudson (neither party appearing) is Dismist.

The Complt. made by Richard Hamelin Sherr: agst. John Lett (neither party appearing) is Dismist.

In the action of Debt Depending between William Randolph Administrator of the Goods and Chattells of Eusebius King Deced: not administred by William Randolph Deced: who was Executor of the Last Will and Testament of the said Eusebius King who Died intestate, and Stephen Evan's for tenn pds. three Shillings Sterling in good Buck and Doe skins Due by Bill Dated the 24th Day of August 1710, the Defendt. being called and not appearing and Robert Bolling being returned Security for him on the motion of the plts: Attorney Judgement is granted him against the said Defendt. and Robt. Bolling for the said Sum & Costs unless the sd. Defendt. shall appear at the next Court & answer to the said Action.

[page 97]

Judgement being this Day past unto William Randolph against Robert Bolling for ten pds. three Shillings Sterling in Buck and Doe Skins, by reason of the non appearance of Stephen Evans in an action of Debt at the suit of the said Randolph, on the motion of the said Bolling an Attachment is granted him against the Estate of the said Evans for the aforesaid sum & Costs returnable to the next Court for Judgemt.

The action Depending between Nathaniel Harrison Esqr. Attorney for Sr. Charles [Ingles] and Doctor Joshua Richardson of London plts. and Wm. Bleighton Deft. neither party appearing is Dismist.

The action Depending between Robert Bolling and Thos. Parram [Parham] the plt. failing to prosecute is Dismist.

In the action Depending between Roger Taylor and George Brewer for four pds. Due by Bill Dated the 21st Day of November 171[3], the Defendt. being returned *non est Inventus* and not appearing on the plts. motion an Attachment is awarded him against the said Defendts. Estate for the said Sum & Costs, returnable to the next Court for Judgement for what shall appear to be Due.

The Complt. made by John Cross against Sarah Nance and John Nance, neither party appearing is Dismist.

The Order that David Colyshaw give new Security for the Estate of Thos. Mitchell is Continued till next Court.

The action Depending between Charles Goodrich and Daniel Higdon is Continued till next Court.

The action Depending between Adam Tapley and Randall Platt, the plt. failing to prosecute is Dismist.

In the action Depending between Randall Platt & Thomas Harwell for two hundred and fivety pounds of Tobacco Due by Bill Dated the first Day of Aprill 1715, at the Last Court Conditionall Judgement was granted the plt. against the sd. Defendt. and Robert Melone his Security &c that is the sd. Defendt. did not appear at this Court and answer the sd. Action the sd. Judgement shou'd be Confirmed, And the sd. Defendt. being now called and failing to appear on the plts. motion the aforesaid Judgement is Confirmed against the sd. Deft. and Baile. It's therefore Ordered that the said Thomas Harwell and Robert Melone or either of them pay to the said plt. the aforesaid Sum of two hundred and fivety pds. of Tobacco and Costs. Als. Exec.

The Attachment granted Randll. Platt against the Estate of Thomas Winingham is Continued till next Court.

In the action of Debt Depending between Randll. Platt and Henry Bates for Nine hundred forty Seaven pds. of Tobacco Due by Bill &c the Defendt. appears and pleads paymt. and the plt. Joining in the Issue the same is thereupon referred to the next Court for Tryall.

The Attachmt. granted Richard Hamelin Sherr: agst. the Estate of Henry Bates is Dismist.

[page 98]

In the action Depending between Randll. Platt Assignee of Charles Goodrich and Thos. House for four hundred and Seaventy pds. of Tobacco and Cask Due for rent &c the said Defendt. haveing had time given him till this Court to plead, and being now called to do the same did not appear nor offer any thing in Barr or preclusion of the plts. action therefore it is Considered by the Court that the plt. recover agst. the said Deft. the aforesaid sum with Costs, unless the sd. Defendt. shall appear at the next Court and answer the said action.

The action Depending between Wm. Curaton and Jos. Renn the plt. failing to prosecute is Dismist.

In the action of Debt Depending between John Allen and Richard Hamelin the Defendt. files a plea to the plts. Declaration who has time till the next Court to Consider the same.

In the action Depending between Edward Horskins and Richard Harrison for Eleaven hundred and twenty pds. of Tobacco Due &c the Defendt. pleads paymt. and the plt. Joining in the Issue the same was thereupon referred to the next Court for Tryall.

In the action Depending between John Simons Assignee of Edward Horskins and Richard Harrison for One thousand five hundred pds. of Tobacco Due by Note &c the Defendt. pleads payment and the plaintiff Joining in the Issue the same is thereuon referred till the next Court for Tryall.

On the motion of Richard Pigeon Ordered that a Lycense Issue for his keeping an Ordinary at the usuall place he haveing Given Bond and Security as the Law Directs.

In the action Depending between Edward Holloway and Peter Wynne for Six hundred and thirty pds. of Tobacco Due by Bill Dated the 2d Day of June 1712, the Defendt. by Edward Goodrich his Attorney appears and Confesses Judgemt. to the plt. for the sd. Sum, It's therefore Ordered that the said Peter Wynne pay to the said plt. the said Sum of Six hundred and thirty pds. of Tobacco & Costs. Als. Exec.

In the action of Debt Depending between Joshua Irby and William Burge for One thousand and Sixty pds. of Tobacco Due by Bill &c the Defendt. being called and not appearing and John Hardyman being returned Security for him on the plts. motion Judgement is granted him agst. the sd. Defendt. and Baile for the said Sum & Costs, unless the Defendt. appears at the next Court and answers the said Action.

In the action Depending between Cornelius Cargill and John Robertson neither party appears, the same is thereupon Dismist.

The Action Depending between Robert Rogers and Michal Talbutt, neither party appearing, is Dismist.

[page 99]

The action brot. by James Jones against Martin Sheffeild, neither party appearing is Dismist.

The action brot. by Burrell Green agst. Cornelius Cargill, neither party appearing is Dismist.

In the action Depending between Thomas Simmons and Thomas Chamberlain for two hundred thirty pds. of Tobacco Due by accot. &c the Defendt. being called and not appearing nor any Security returned for him on the motion of the plt. Judgement is granted him against the said Deft. and Richard Hamelin Sherr: of this County for the said Sum & Costs unless sd. Defendt. shall appear at the next Court and answer to the said Action.

In the action of Debt Depending between Thomas Jackson and Henry Bates for Six hundred and fivety pds. of Tobacco Due by Bill &c the Defendts. being return'd *non est Inventus* and not appearing on the plts. motion an attachment is granted him agst. the said Defendts. Estate for the said Sum & Costs returnable to the next Court for Judgement for what shall appear to be due.

In the action Depending between John Stevens and Richard Griffith for Eleaven hundred pds. of Tobacco Due by accot. &c the Deft. on his motion has Oyer of the said accot. and time till the next Court to Consider the same.

The action of Dt. brot. by John Stevens assignee of John Tucker agst. Richard Griffith (neither party appearing) is Dismist.

On the motion of Edward Goodrich in behalfe of John Womack senr. Ordered that he be hereafter Exempt from paying Leavy.

Henry Mayes and Elizabeth his Wife Appear in Court and (the said Elizabeth being first privately Examined) Acknowledge their deeds of Lease and release of Land (Indented & Sealed) Dated the Seaventh and Eighth Days Instant, to Daniel Nance and his heirs &c. on whose motion the same are Ordered to be rec: and then also did the said Elizabeth freely relinquish to the sd. Daniell her right of Dower & to the said Lands &c. Ordered the same be Likewise recorded.

On the action brot. by Robert Rogers agst. Samuel Sentall for twenty Shillings Due by Bill &c the Defendt. being called and not appearing and Instance Hall being [word removed] returned Security for him on the plts. motion Judgement is granted him agst. the said Deft. and Baile for the sd. Sum & Costs, unless the said Deft. shall appear at the next Court and answer the said action.

In the action of Dt. brot. by James Bell and Martha his Wife agst. Daniel Marchand and John Scoggin the sd. Scoggin by Edwd. Goodrich his Attorney files a plea to the plts. Declaration who has time till next Court to Consider the same.

In the action of Dt. brot. by Richard Hamelin agst. John Lett, the Deft. appearing and assumeing to pay to the said Hamelin the Costs of this Suit he thereupon Directs the same to be Dismist.

[page 100]

The action brot. by [Geo.] Pasmore agst. Richard Hudson neither party appearing is Dismist.

The action brot. by Geo. Pasmore agst. John Womack junr. neither party appearing is Dismist.

The action brot. by Henry Peoples agst. Geo. Abby, neither party appearing is Dismist.

The action brot. by Robert Bolling agst. Stephen Evans, neither party appearing is Dismist.

The action brot. by John West agst. Geo. Pace, neither party appearing is Dismist.

The action brot. by Wm. Byrd Esqr. agst. ffra: Coleman junr., neither party appearing is Dismist.

In the action brot. by David Crawley agst. John Spain for two pds. fourteen Shillings and four pence halfe penny Due by Accot. Dated 1716, the Defendt. appears in Custody and Confesses Judgement to the plt. for the said Sum & Costs, And thereupon he is remanded to Prison in Custody of the Sherr: thereto remain untill he has fully paid the sd. plt. the sd. Sum & Costs.

In the action Depending between Thomas Simmons and John Spain for five hundred pds. of Tobacco Due by Bill Dated the 8th Day of June 1714, the Defendt. appears in Custody of the Sherr: and Confesses Judgement to the plt. for the said sum & Costs, And thereupon he is remanded to Prison in Custody of the Sherr: thereto remain untill he has paid to the sd. plt. the said sum & Costs.

In the action Depending between Wm. Byrd Esqr. and John Spain for Eight hundred Seaventy Eight pds. of Tobacco Due by Bill Dated the 24 Day of May 1716, the Deft. appears in Court in Custody of the Sherr: and Confesses Judgemt. to the plt. for the said Sum & Costs, And thereupon he is remanded to Prison in Custody of the Sherr: there to remain untill he has paid to the plt. the said sum & Costs.

In the action brot. by Richard Bland agst. John Spain for Eighteen hundred and Ninety pds. of Tobacco Due by bill Dated the 12th Day of December 1715, the Deft. appears in Court in Custody of the Sherr: and Confesses Judgement to the plt. for the said Sum & Costs, And thereupon he is remanded to Prison in Custody of the Sherr: there to remain till he has paid to the said plt. the said sum & Costs.

And then the Court Adjourn'd till Court in Course. Jno: Hamelin. Test Wm. Hamelin, Cl. Cur.

[page 101]

Att a Court held at Merchantshope for the County of Prince George on the Second
Tuesday in February Anno Dom: 1716, being the 12th Day of the said month.

Present   John Hemelin,   Randall Platt,   Robert Munford }
                Robert Hall,   Lewis Green,   John Hardyman &}
                      John Peterson   Gent. Justices

Upon the return of the accot. Dr. & Cr. of the Estate of James Boreman Deced: by James Bell the Exxecutor thereof, in Order to have the Value set on the Tobacco due from the aforesaid Estate, It's Ordered that the said Executor charge two pence pr. pd. on the said Tobacco Due and pd. Last year, and three halfe pence pr. pound on that hath been paid this year, and that he make up and return the said accot. at the next Court accordingly.

The Sherriff makes return of the appraisement of the Estate of Robert Burchet, Attacht. &c for John Hatch. Ordered it be recorded, Vizt.

One Indian Girle Named Sary at	£5:0:0.

Nov: the 13th 1716. In Obedience to an Order of Court Dated the 13 of Nov: 1716 the above Appraised by us. [signed] Wm. Stainback, Duglas Irby, George Woodleife, James Grestion.

Ver. rec. Test Wm. Hamelin, Cl. Cur.

The Sheriff makes return of the Appraisement of the Estate of Robert Burchet, Attacht. for William Mattox &c. Ordered the same be recorded, Vizt.

One Indian Man Named Skipper	£20.0.0
two feather beds and some furniture, One at £3.2.0}	
the other at 4	7.4.0
A Brass Kettle at 28/4, One Iron pot at 19/	2.7.4
A parcell of pewter 30/10, and a Table 8/	1.18.10
Nov. the 15th 1716.	£31.8.2

In Obedience to an Order of Court Dated the 13 Instant the above Appraised by us. [signed] Wm. Stainback, Duglas Irby, George Woodleife, James Grestion.

Ver. rec. Test Wm. Hamelin, Cl. Cur.

It appearing by the above Appraisement that the said Estate attacht. as aforesaid is insufficient to sattisfie and pay the Judgement granted the said William Mattox against the Estate of the said Robert Burchett by the sum of three pounds, Eleaven Shillings and ten pence Sterl: and Costs. Therefore it's Ordered that the said William have Execution against the Estate of the said Robert Burchett for the said sum of three pounds, Eleaven Shillings & ten pence Sterl: and Costs.

[page 102]

The Sherriff makes return of the Appraisement of the Estate of Robert Burchet, Attacht. by William Wallice. Ordered it be recorded, Vizt.

A parcell of Coopers Tools valued at	£1.5.0	
One Iron pott wt. 33 at 4 w 11/, One horse Collar 4/		0.15.0
One Mortar and pestle		0.6.0
two pr. of Sillyards		0.16.0
One pr. of Bellows 1/, 1 Sugar Box ¼	0.2.4	
One Gunn 20/, One Crosscutt saw 10/	1.10.0	
One warming pann 2/6, 1 Candlestick 6		[0].3.0
a fflesh forke and Skimmer		0.2.6
Nov. the 15th 1716		£4.19.10

In Obedience to an Order of Court Dated the 13 Instant the above appraised by us. [signed] Wm. Stainback, [name removed] Geo. Woodleife, James Grestion.

Ver. rec. Test Wm. Hamelin, Cl. Cur.

It appearing by the above appraisement that the said Estate attacht. as aforesaid is Insufficient to Sattisfie and pay the Judgemt. granted the said William Wallice against the Estate of the said Robert Burchet for the sum of four pounds Eight Shillings and five pence and Costs. Therefore it's Ordered that the said William have Execution against the Estate of the said Robert for the residue of the said Costs.

The Sheriff makes return of the appraisement of the Estate of Robert Burchet, attacht. for John Golightly. Ordered the same be recorded, Vizt.   Tobo.

One large chest 80 [Tobo.] four pewter plates & one small bason &c 48 128

One wyre ridle 30, One Gunn 120	130
One well Buckett and Chain 30, two wood corn pales 30, 1 gall. rundlet 30	130
One Large Cyder Caske 60, 4 rush Bottom chair 30, one frying pan 25 135	
One hatchett and two pr. fire Tongs 70, One old chest 50	120
One old plaine and two Irons 20, four Augers &c 30, one Drawing knife 085	
two Spoke S[t]aves 10, two crossing Irons 20, Seaven Chissells 30	085
One Coopers ax and howell 20, two Gouges, One handsaw and rest 25 045	
One hilling hoe and a Coopers Adze and an Auger p[...] Windlebitt	50
One Small Table 30, a wooden peck 15, and an old bed & two blanketts &c 300	365
One Gridiron, One [...] and Six old rush chairs 180	195
	1488

Nov. the 13th 1716. In Obedience to an order of Court Dated the 13th Instant the above appraised by us. [signed] Wm. Stainback, Duglas Irby, Geo. Woodleife, James Grestion. Sworn by me James Thweatt. Ver. rec. Test Wm. Hamelin, Cl. Cur.

It appearing by the above appraisement that the said Estate Attacht. as aforesaid is insufficient to Sattisfie and pay the Judgement granted the said John Golightly against the Estate

[page 103]

of the said Robert Burchett for the sum of fifteen hundred pounds of Tobacco and five yds. of Blew Linnen (Valued by the Court a thirty pds. of Tobacco) and Costs. It's therefore Ordered by the Court that the said John have Execution against the Estate of the said Burchett for the residue of the said Judgmt. being forty two pounds of Tobacco and Costs.

The attachment continued to Peter Wynne &c against the Estate of Robert Burchett is further Continued till the next court.

The Sheriff makes return of the appraisement of the Estate of Robert Burchett Attacht. for Robert Bolling. Ordered it be recorded, Vizt.

A Sarvant Boy Named John Mainard at	£6.0.0
a Mair and Colt	4.10.0
	£10.10.10

Nov. the 10th 1716. The above appraised in Obedience to an Order of Court Dated the 13 Instant by us. [signed] Wm. Stainback, Duglas Irby, Geo. Woodleife, James Grestion.

Ver. rec. Test Wm. Hamelin, Cl. Cur.

The Sheriff makes return of the Appraisement of the Estate of Robert Burchett, Attacht. for George Rives. Ordered it be recorded, Vizt.

three Hoggs at 8/. each	£1.4.0
A parcell of plank and Jointure Iron	10.6.0

Nov. the 15th 1716.   £1.10.1

In Obedience to an Order of Court Dated the 13 Instant the above appraised by us. [signed] Wm. Stainback, Duglas Irby, Geo. Woodleife, James Grestion.

Ver. rec. Test Wm. Hamelin, Cl. Cur.

It appearing by the above appraisement that the said Estate attacht. as aforesaid is Insufficient to sattisfie and pay the Judgement granted the said George against the Estate of the said Robert Burchett by the sum of five Shillings and Costs. It's therefore Ordered that the said George have Execution against the Estate of the said Robert for the said sum of five Shillings and Costs.

The Sherriff makes return of the appraisement of the Estate of Robert Burchett, Attacht. for Mathew Smart Junr. Ordered it be recorded, Vizt.

Six Cows at 26/. each, One Bull at 10/.	£8.0.0
three calves at 6/. each, One cow Bell 2/6	1.0.6
	£9.0.6

Nov. the 15th 1716. Appraised in Obedience to an Order of Court Dated the 13th Instant by us. [signed] Wm. Stainback, Duglas Irby, Geo. Woodleife, James Grestion. Sworn by me James Thweatt.

Ver. rec. Test Wm. Hamelin, Cl. Cur.

[page 104]

The order of the Last Court for ye return of the appraisement of the Estate of Hubbard Gibson attacht. for James Thweatt &c is Continued till the next Court.

Ordered that the Sherriff pay the Severall appraisers of the Estate of Robert Burchett attacht. &c the sum of thirty pds. of Tobacco each, out of the said Burchetts Estate.

On the motion of Nathaniell Harrison Esqr., Robert Rogers is entred his Genrall Attorney in all causes Depending in this Court for or against the said Harrison.

On the motion of Samuell Harwood, Robert Rogers is entred his Genrall Attorney in all causes Depending in this Court for or against the said Harwood.

Mathew Anderson in Open Court acknowledgd his Deeds of Lease and release of Land (Indented and Sealed) to Daniel Nance and his heirs &c. On whose motion the same are Ordered to be recorded.

Mathew Anderson in Open Court acknowledged his Bond for performance of Covenants to Daniell Nance. Ordered the same be recorded.

Henry Tally in Open Court acknowledged his Deeds of Lease and release of Land (Indented and Sealed) to [words removed] Christopher Hinton and his heirs &c on whose motion the same are Ordered to be recorded, and then also appeared in Court Mary the wife of the said Tally and being first privately Examined acknowledged the said Deeds and Voluntarily relinquisht. to the said Hinton her right of Dower in & to the sd. Lands, which is Likewise Ordered to be recorded.

John Nance Admr. &c of John Nance Deced: returns upon Oath an Inventory and Appraismt. of the said Decedts. Estate. Ordered it be recorded.

Ordered that Edward Goodrich be Overseer of the Highways in Merchantshope instead of Thomas Simmons.

And then the Court Adjourn'd till Court in Course. Jno. Hamelin. Test Wm. Hamelin, Cl. Cur.

[page 105]

Hugh Lee Exhibited the following Judgement the 12th of February 1716, and Desired the same might be recorded that Execution might Issue thereon, Vizt.

Pr. Geo. County St.

Upon complaint made before me James Thweatt one of his Majestys Justices of the peace of this County by Hugh Lee Senr. against Henry Ledbetter and John his son and haveing considered the cause doe hereby Order that the said Henry Ledbetter pay unto the said Hugh Lee five Shillings being the Costs. Als. Execution given under my hand this 5th Day of February 1716/17. James Thweatt. Truly recorded Test. Wm. Hamelin, Cl. Cur.

Att a Court held for Prince George County on Tuesday the twelfth Day of March
Anno Dom: 1716.

Present   John Hamelin,   Robert Hall }
               Lewis Green junr.   & John Peterson }   Gent. Justices

In the action on the case Depending Elizabeth Epes Executrix &c of William Epes Deced: and John Nance Administrator with the will annext. of John Nance Deced: for two hundred and Eighty and halfe pounds of Tobacco Due by accot. on the motion of the sd. Defendt., the plt. by ffrancis Epes her son makes Oath the said Sum is justly Due, thereupon it's Ordered by the Court that the said Defendant pay to the said plt. the said Sum and Costs, out of the said Decedts. Estate. Als. Exec.

In the action on the case Depending between David Crawley and John Sturdivant for two pounds five Shillings and a halfe penny current money Due by accot. &c the Deft. being called and not appearing and Edward Burchett being returned Security for him on the motion of the plts. Attorney Judgement is granted him against the said Deft. and Security for the said Sum & Costs, unless the said Defendt. shall appear at the next Court and answer the said action.

John Bolling vrs. John Gibson, for four pounds Sixteen Shillings & five pence Due by accot. &c the Defendt. geing called and not appearing and ffrances Mallory and John Hamelin being returned Securitys for him on the motion of the plts. Attorney Judgement is granted him against the said Defendt. and his Sd. Security for the said Sum & Costs, unless the said Defendt. shall appear at the next Court & answer to the said Action.

The action Depending between David Crawley and Mathew Anderson (the plt. failing to prosecute) is Dismist.

Richard Hamelin vrs. Kathrine Williams, no appearance Dismist.

Richard Hamelin vrs. Kathrine Williams, no appearance Dismist.   Verte.

[page 106]

In the action on the case Depending between Thomas Simmons and John Ellis junr. for Eight hundred and Eighteen pounds of Tobacco Due by accot. &c the Defendt. being returned *non est Inventus* and not appearing on the plts. motion an Attachment is granted him against the said Defendts. Estate for the said sum and Costs returnable to the next Court for Judgement for that shall appear to be Due.

The action Depending between Jane Dewell and Richard Jones (neither party Appearing) is Dismist.

The action of Debt Depending between William Cogill and John Sherley neither party appearing) is Dismist.

The action Depending Between John Smith and Edward Scott, neither party appearing) is Dismist.

The action Depending between James Niblett and Richard Jones, neither party appearing) is Dismist.

The action Depending between James Niblett and Edward Johnson (neither party appearing) is Dismist.

John Stevens vrs. Peter Anderson retraxit.

Thos. Billbro vrs. William Smith no appearance Dismist.

John Smith vrs. Saml. Lucy and Nicho. Brewer no appearance Dismist.

In the action of Debt Depending between John Hatch and John Nance Administrator with the Will annext. of John Nance Deced: for two thousand One hundred pounds of Tobacco Due by Bill Dated the fifth Day of April 1715, the plt. makes Oath the said Sum is Justly Due to him & the Defendt. makeing Oath that there is not Sufficient Tobacco of the said Decedts. Estate to pay the said Sum, thereupon the Court Values the said Tobacco at twelve Shillings and Six pence pr. hundred, and Orders the said Deft. to pay the said plt. out of the said Decedts. Estate the sum of thirteen pounds two Shillings and Sixpence, being the Value of the said Tobacco together with Costs. Als. Exec.

In the action on the case Depending between John Hatch and John Nance Admr. with the Will annext. of John Nance Deced: an Imparlance is granted the Defendt. till next Court.

In the action Depending between John Bolling and John Nance Admr. &c of John Nance Deced: an Imparlance is granted the Defendt. till the next Court.

John Spain came personally into Court and Confest. Judgement to John Hatch for Nineteen hundred and five pounds and an halfe of Tobacco Due to the plt. by accot. Dated from the 18th of October 1714 to the 23d of December 1715, Inclusive, thereupon It's Ordered that the said John Spain pay to the said John Hatch the said Sum & Costs. Als. Exec.

[page 107]

The action Depending between John Hatch and William Spain (neither party appearing) is Dismist.

The action Depending between Christopher Hinton and John Tally (the plt. failing to prosecute) is Dismist.

The action Depending between David Crawley and William Worsham (the plt. failing to prosecute) is Dismist.

In the action Depending between Joshua Irby and Peter Wynne, Imparlance is granted the Defendt. till the next Court.

In the action Depending between ffrancis Wynne and Will Mott Indian the plt. failing to Prosecute) is Dismist.

The action Depending between George Carter and Simon Naylor (the plt. failing to prosecute) is Dismist.

The action Depending between Robert Jones and Richard Womack (the plt. failing to prosecute) is Dismist.

The action Depending between Randall Platt and Xpher Robinson (neither party appearing) is Dismist.

In the action Depending between Randall Platt and Abraham Odium for three hundred Sixty four pounds of Tobacco Due by Bill &c the Defendant being returned *non est Inventus* and not appearing on the plts. motion an Attachment is granted him against the said Defendts. Estate for the said Sum & Costs returnable to the next Court for Judgemt.

The action Depending between Peter Wynne Admr. &c and Stephen Evans, is Continued till next Court.

The Attachmt. granted [word removed] Francis Mallory against the Estate of Samuell Harwell, is Continued till the next Court.

The action Depending between William Randolph Admr. &c and Stephen Evans (the plt. faililng to prosecute) is Dismist.

The action Depending between Robert Bolling and Stephen Evans (neither party appearing) is Dismist.

The Attachmt. granted Roger Taylor against the Estate of Geo: Brewer (the plt. failing to prosecute) is Dismist.

The Order that David Colyshaw give new Security for the Estate of Thomas Mitchell is Dismist.

[page 108]

The action Depending between Charles Goodrich and Daniel Higdon is Continued till the next Court.

The Attachment granted Randall Platt against the Estate of Thomas Winingham is Continued till the next Court.

57

Present Robt. Munford & Sampson Merredeth, Gent. Justices

In the action of Debt Depending between Randall Platt and Henry Bates for Nine hundred forty Seaven pounds of Tobacco Due by Bill &c at the Last Court the Deft. pleaded payment and the plt. Joining in the Issue the same for Tryall was referred to this Court and the said Defendt. being now called and failing to appear thereupon on the plts. motion it's Ordered that the said defendt. pay to the said plaintiff the said Sum and Costs. Als. Exec:

Ordered that John Hobbs, William Short and John Bell (Surveyors of the Highways) Jointly with the people under their Charge, meet and build a Bridge over the Head of Wards Creek at the usuall place of Crossing the same, near Warthins Mill.

In the action Depending between Randall Platt Assignee &c and Thomas House, the Defendt. being permitted to plead Doubly files his plea &c to the plts. Declaration who has time till the next Court to Consider the same.

In the Action Depending between John Allen and Richard Hamelin the plt. files a Demurrer to the Defendts. plea who has time till the next Court to Consider the same.

In the action Depending between Edward Horskins and Richard Harrison for Eleeven hundred and twenty pounds of Tobacco Due by two Severall Bills, whereon William Short is Special Bail for the sd. Defendt. he the sd. Defendant at the Last Court haveing pleaded payment and for Tryall put himself upon the Court and the plaintiff Likewise and both partys now appearing, the said Defendt. Offers his Oath that the Last of the said two Bills being for five hundred and Seaventy pounds of Tobacco includes the former for [five] hundred and fivety and the Ball. of the other Bills and amots. of the said plts. against him the said Defendt. which is Overruled by the Court and the plt. makeing Oath that the said Sum of Eleeven hundred and twenty pounds of Tobacco is Justly Due to him from the said Defendt. thereupon it's Ordered that the said Defendt. pay to the said plt. the said Sum & Costs. Als. Exec.

[page 109]

The Last Will and Testament of Susanna Tillman Deced: was presented into Court by Robert Abbernathy junr. the Executor therein Named who made Oath thereto and it being proved by the Oaths of Benjamin Bleike and William Gent is Admitted to record. And upon the said Executors giveing Security according to Law it's Ordered that a Certificate be granted the said Executor for Obtaining a probate in Due form whereupon John Tillman became his Security and Entred into Bond Accordingly.

Ordered that Robert Abbernathy Junr. return to the next Court an Inventory of the Estate of Susanna Tillman Deced:

Phillip Burrow in Open Court acknowledged his Deeds of Lease & release of Land (Indented and Sealed) to John Burrow. Ordered they be recorded.

Ordered that the Sheriff of this County take into his Custody & possession the Estate of Thomas Sadler Deced: and Sell the Same by way of Outcry and take Bills with Security payable to himselfe for the money that the same shall be sold for, and return an accot. of his proceedings thererin to the next Court.

In the action of Debt [word removed] Depending between John Simons assignee of Edward Horskins plt. and Richard Harrison Defendt. for One thousand five hundred pounds of Tobacco Due by Bill &c wherein William Short is Speciall Bail for the said Defendt., he the said Defendt. at the Last Court haveing pleaded payment and for Tryall put himselfe upon the Court and the plt. Likewise, and both partys now appearing the Defendt. Offers his Oath that the Bill for five hundred and Seaventy pounds of Tobacco mentioned in the Judgement granted Edward Horskins agst. the said Deft. was given for full payment of the abovesaid Bill for fifteen hundred pds. of Tobacco and all other Bills, which is Overruled by the Court and it appearing the said Sum is Justly Due thereupon it's Ordered that the said Defendt. pay to the said plaintiff the said Sum of fifteen hundred pounds of Tobacco & Costs. Als. Exec.

The action Depending between Joshua Irby and William Burge (neither party appearing) is Dismist.

In the action Depending between Thomas Simmons and Thomas Chamberlain, Edward Goodrich became Speciall Bail for the Defendt. who being permitted to plead Doubly files his plea to the plts. Declaration who has time till the next Court to Consider the same.

The Attachment granted Thomas Jackson against the Estate of Henry Bates (the plt. failing to prosecute) is Dismist.

John Stevens vrs: Richard Griffith Dismist.

[page 110]

Harman Read in Open Court acknowledged his Deeds of Lease and release of Land (Indented and Sealed) to Michael Wallice and his heirs &c Ordered they be recorded and then also appeared in Court Ann the Wife of the said Harman and being first privately Examined according to Law Voluntarily relinquisht. to the said Wallice her right of Dower in and too the said Lands, Ordered the same be Likewise recorded.

The action of Debt Depending between Robert Rogers and Saml. Sentall (the plt. failing to prosecute) is Dismist.

In the action Depending between James Bell and Martha his wife plts. and Daniell Marchand and John Scoggin Defts. the plts. Demurr. Genrally to the Defendts. plea and they Joining therein the said is referred to the next Court to be Argued &c

The action of Debt Depending between Robert Jones and Richard Harrison (the plt. failing to prosecute) is Dismist.

The action Depending between Robert Jones and Richard Harrison (the plt. failing to appear) is Dismist.

In the action brot. by Eliza. Jones agst. Robert Jones Exr. &c an Imparlance is granted the Defendt. till the next Court.

In the suit in Chancery brought by Samuel Harwood agst. ffrancis Mallory and Henry Offley, the Defendt. Mallory appears by Ed. Goodrich his Attorney and has time granted till the next Court to Consider the plts. Bill and Ordered that a resummons Issue against the said Offley &c

In the Suit in Chancery brot. by Nathaniell Harrison Esqr. against Robert Bolling and Henry Offley the said Harrison & Bolling Consent the same shall Stand referred to the next Court, which is Ordered accordingly also Ordered that a resumons Issue against the said Offley &c.

The action brot. by John Bolling agst. Nicho. Giles (neither party appearing) is Dismist.

Randll. Platt agst. Henry Duke, no appearance Dismist.

Randll. Platt agst. Nicho. Wyatt, no appearance, Dismist.

Robert Bland agst. John Lett, no appearance, Dismist.

James Jones junr. agst. John Lett, no appearance, Dismist.

Randll. Platt agst. Adam Tapley, no prosecution, Dismist.

Adam Taply agst. Randll. Platt, no appearance, Dismist.

Richard Hamelin agst. Kath. Williams, no prosecution, Dismist.

In the action Depending between John Peterson and John Nance Admrs. with the will annext. of John Nance Deced: an Imparlance is granted the Defendt. and time till the next Court.

[page 111]

William Byrd Esqr. agst. John Spain, no prosecution, Dismist.

Richard Bland against John Spain, no appearance, Dismist.

John Coleman agst. Xpher Robinson, he Retraxit.

John Hatch vrs. Adam Ivey, no appearance, Dismist.

In the action of Debt Depending between Thomas Goodwyn Assignee of Jos. Smith Marriner plt. and John Mayes Marriner, Oyer of the plts. Bill is granted the Defendt. and time till the next Court &c.

In the action of Debt Depending between Thomas Goodwyn Assignee of Jos. Smith and John Mayes, Oyer of the plts. Bill is granted the Defendt. and time till the next Court to Consider the Same &c.

John Willkinson agst. Adam Ivey, no appearance, Dismist.

Mathw: Marks agst. Thos. Hollinsworth, no appearance, Dismist.

In the action Depending between Cornelius Cargill and George Brewer a Speciall Imparlance is granted the Defendt. till the next Court.

The order that James Bell return the accot. Dr. & Cr. of James Boremans Estate is Continued till next Court.

The Attachment Continued to Peter Wynne Admr. &c agst. the Estate of Robert Burchett the plt. faililng to prosecute is Dismist.

The Order of the Last Court for the return of the appraisement of the estate of Hubbord Gibson Attacht. for James Thweatt &c is Continued till the next Court.

Robert Munford vrs: Robert Bolling and Henry Offley, Chancery, no appearance, Dismist.

Wm. ffloriday vrs. William Bobbitt, no appearance, Dismist.

Benja. ffoster agst. John Womack, no prosecution, Dismist.

In the action of Debt Depending between James Bell plt. and Henry Bates, John Hines and George Ivey Defendts. for Nineteen hundred and forty five pounds of Tobacco Due by Bill &c the Defendts. being called and not appearing nor any Security returned for them on the motion of the plt. Judgement is granted him against the said Defendts. and Richard Hamelin Sherriff for the said Sum & Costs unless the sd. Defendts. shall appear at the next Court and answer the sd. Action.

James Bell against Cornelius Cargill and Richard Whittmore, no prosecution, Dismist.

In the action Depending between John Hines and Henry Peoples, an Imparlance is granted the Defendt. till the next Court.

James Bell agst. Phillip and John Burrow, no prosecution, Dismist.

[page 112]

James Bell vrs: Edward Scott and William Smith, no prosecution, Dismist.

Robert Bolling against Henry Soane, no appearance, Dismist.

In the Action on the case Depending between Thomas Goodwyn and John Poake for two thousand Six hundred and fifteen pounds of Tobacco Due by accot. Dated from the Sixth of February 171[2], to the Sixth of February 1716, Inclusive, the Defendt. being returned *non est Inventus* and not appearing on the motion of the plts. Attorney an Attachment is granted him agst. the said Defendts. Estate for the said Sum & Costs returnable to the next Court for Judgement for what Shall appear to be Due.

Thomas Goodwyn vrs: Robert Burchett no prosecution Dismist.

Thomas Goodwyn vrs: Xpher Robinson, retraxit.

John Lett agst. James Loftin, Dt. no appearance, Dismist.

John Lett agst. James Loftin, case, no appearance, Dismist.

In the action of Debt Depending between Olive Poxson and [Edmond] Browder the plaintiff not appearing to prosecute, (on the motion of the Defendts. Attorney) It's Ordered that he be Nonsuited and that he pay the sd. Defendt. five Shillings with Costs. Als. Exec.

James Jones junr. agst. Martin Sheffeild, no prosecution, Dismist.

Sampson Merredeth agst. Robert Davis and Martin Sheffeild, Dismist.

In the action on the case Depending between Henry Harrison and John Sherley for twenty Eight pounds Current money by accot. &c the Defendant being returned *non est Inventus* and not appearing on the motion of the plts. Attorney an Attachment is granted him against the said Defendts. Estate for the said Sum & Costs, returnable to the next Court for Judgemt. for what shall appear to be Due.

Robert Bolling Assignee of Wm. Hamelin plt. agst. John Middleton, Dismist.

In the action of Debt Depending between John Hatch and Michael Hill for two thousand One hundred Eighty Nine pounds of Tobacco Due by Bill &c the Defendt. being returned *non est Inventus* and not appearing on the motion of the plts. Attorney an Attachmt. is granted him against the said Defendts. Estate for the said Sum & Costs returnable to the next Court for Judgemt.

Pursuant to the Direction of the Act for regulating Ordinarys & restraint of Tipling houses &c Ordered that the rate on Ordinary Liquors, Dyet Lodging, fodder and provander &c be as were formerly sett and rated by this Court.

Thomas Loyd vrs. Jane Dewell, retraxit.

And then the Court Adjourn'd till Court in Course. John Hamlin. Test Wm. Hamelin, Cl. Cur.

[page 113]

Att a Court held at Merchantshope for the County of Prince George on the Second Tuesday in Aprill 1717, being the Ninth Day of the said month.

Present   Robert Hall,   James Thweatt,   John Hardyman }
Lewis Green junr.   & John Peterson   } Gent. Justices

Upon the return of ye Execution on the Judgement awarded John Hatch at the Last Court agst. the Estate of John Spain which being that there is not Estate to be found of the said Spains whereon to Serve the said Execution, On the motion of the Attorney of the sd. Hatch it's Ordered that another Execution Issue agst. the Body of the said Spain for the sum mentioned in the abovesaid Judgemt. togather with Costs.

Peter Mitchell in Open Court acknowledged his Deeds of Lease and release of Land (Indented and Sealed) to William Russell and Elizabeth his wife, on whose motion the same are Ordered to be recorded.

On the petition of John Hobbs a Surveyor of the Highways It's Ordered that Capt. John Poythres Tythables, James Bishop, William Hobbs, Peter Poythres and William Poythres assist the said Hobbs in clearing the Highways &c of which he is Surveyor.

Richard Pigeon in Open Court acknowledged his Deeds of Lease and release of Land (Indented and Sealed) to Peter Gramer on whose motion the same are ordered to be recorded, and then also Elizabeth the Wife of the said Pigeon (being first privately Examined) freely and Voluntarily relinquisht. to the said Peter her right of Dower in and to the said Lands &c Ordered the same be Likewise recorded.

John Womack in Open Court ackowledged his Deed for Land (Indented and Sealed) with Livery and Seizin endorst. thereon, to his son Richard Womack on whose motion the said by order of the Court is truly recorded, and then did Mary the wife of the sd. John frely [sic] relinquish her right of Dower in and to the said Lands &c She being first privately Examined as the Law Directs. Ordered the same also be recorded.

In the action on the case Depending between David Crawley and John Sturdivant for two pounds five Shillings and a half penny Due by accot. Daged 1716 (the Defendt. failing to appear) Judgement is granted and Confirmed the plt. against the said Defendt. and Edward Burchett his Security pursuant to the Conditionall Judgement and Order therein of the Last Court, therefore it's Ordered that the said John Sturdivant and Edward Burchett or either of them pay to the said plaintiff the said Sum and Costs. Als. Exec:

In the action on the case Depending between John Bolling and John Gibson for four pounds Sixteen Shillings and five pence Due by accot. &c the Defendt. failing to appear pursuant to the Conditional Judgement and Order therein of the Last Court thereupon Judgement is granted and Confirmed the plt. agst. the sd. Defendt. and John Hatch, & ffrances Mallory his Securitys, and Ordered that the said John Gibson, John Hamelin & ffrancis Mallory or either of them pay to the said plt. the said Sum & Costs. Als. Exec.

[page 114]

The attachment awarded Thomas Simmons agst. the Estate of John Ellis junr. is Continued till the next Court.

In the action Depending between John Hatch and John Nance Admrs. &c of John Nance Deced: for three pounds three Shillings and Eleaven pence Due by accot. at the Last Court the Defendt. haveing had time given him till this Court to plead and being now called to do the same did not appear nor offer any thing in barr or preclusion of the plts. action. Therefore it's Considered by the Court that the plt. recover against the said Defendt. the sd. Sum & Costs unless he shall appear at the next Court and answer the said action.

George Bleighton one of the Orphans of George Bleighton Deced: came personally into Court and Chose Nathaniel Harrison Esqr. his Guardian who gave Bond with Security for his faithfull performance of his Guardianship according to Law.

Present John Hamelin & Robt. Munford, Gent. Justices

In the action on the case Depending between John Bolling and John Nance Administrator with the will annext. of John Nance Deced: for One thousand forty Six and a halfe pounds of Tobacco Due by acct. &c the sd. partys appearing and the plt. haveing made Oath the said Sum is Justly Due to him, and there being not Sufficient Tobacco of the said Deceds. Estate to pay the same, therefore the Court Values the Same at twelve Shillings and Six pence per hundred, and the Defendt. alledgeing that he hath in his hands of the sd. Decedts. Estate only the Sum of five pounds, thereupon it's Ordered that the sd. Administrator pay the said Sum of five pounds to the said plt. Als. Exec: and Judgement is granted the plt. agst. the sd. Admrs. for the residue of his Debt aforesaid being One pound ten Shillings and Nine pence three farthings, to be paid out of the said Decedts. Estate with Costs, when assetts thereof shall come to hand &c.

In the action Depending between Joshua Irby and Peter Wynne for Seaven hundred forty five pounds of Tobacco &c at the Last Court the Defendt. haveing had time given him till this Court to plead and being now called to do the same did not appear nor offer any thing in barr or preclusion of the plts. action. Therefore it's Considered by the Court that the plt. recover agst. the said Defendt. the sd. Sum & Costs unless he shall appear at the next Court and answer the said action.

The Attachment granted Randll. Platt agst. the Estate of Abra: O[dgan] the plt. failing to prosecute) is Dismist.

The action Depending between Peter Wynne and Stephen Evans on ye plts. motion is Continued till next Court.

[page 115]

The action Depending between Charles Goodrich and Daniell Higdon is Continued till next Court.

The attachment granted Randall Platt against the Estate of Thomas Winingham the plt. failing to appear to prosecute is Dismist.

Randall Platt assignee of Cha. Goodrich plt. vrs. Thos. House Deft. the sd. plt. appears and Joins in the plea and Demurrer of the Defendt. and the same is thereupon referred to the next Court to be argues and tryed.

In the action Depending between John Allen and Richard Hamelin the Deft. Joins in the Demurrer of the plt. filed at the Last Court and the same is thereupon referred to the next Court to be argued.

The order that Robert Abbernathy return [words removed] an Inventory of the Estate of Su. Tillman Deced: is Continued till next Court.

The order that the Sherr: make return of his proceedings in the Sale of Thomas Sadlers Estate is Continued till the next Court.

In the action Depending between Thomas Simmons and Thomas Chamberlaine the plt. files a Demurrer to the first plea of the Defendt. and Joins Issue in the second which is referred to the next Court for Tryall.

In the Action Depending between James Bell and Martha his Wife plt. and Daniell Marchand and John Scoggin Defts. at the Last Court the plts. Demurred Genrally to the Defendts. plea who Joined therein and the said partys now appearing & the sd. Demurrer being Sufficiently argued is overruled and the plea of the Deft. held [good] whereupon it's Ordered the suit be Dismist.

The Attachmt. granted ffrancis Mallory against the Estate of Samuel (Harwells) (the sd. Defendt. appearing and assumineing to pay the Costs) is Dismist.

In the action on the case Depending between Elizabeth Jones and Robert Jones Executor &c of William Jones Deced: for two Steers Due &c at the Last Court the Defendt. haveing had time given him till this Court to plead and being now called to do the same did not appear nor offer any thing in barr or preclusion of the plts. action, therefore it's Considered by the Court that the plt. recover agst. the said Defendt. the said Steers togather with the Costs unless he shall appear at the next Court and answer the said Action.

The suit in Chancery Depending between Samuell Harwood and ffra: Mallory and Henry Offley respondts. is Continued till next Court.

In the suit in Chancery brot. by Nathaniel Harrison Esqr. agst. Henry Offley Late of London Merchant and Robert Bolling Respondts. the sd. Complt. and ye respondt. Bolling appearing, the sd. Bolling files his answer upon Oath to the

[page 116]
the Complainants Bill where he Confesses to have in his hands and possession of the Estate of the sd. Henry Offley, in Goods and outstanding Debts Sufficient to Sattisfie and pay the Complaints. Debt & Demand being One hundred and thirteen pounds Seaventeen Shillings and Nine pence halfe penny Sterling, and five hogsheads of Sweet Scented Tobacco weighing neet four thousand Seaven hundred and three pounds in the hands of the sd. Offley unaccounted for to the said Complaint. which the Court Values at Seaventy five pounds Sterling. And the said Complainant fileing upon Oath an account Dr. & Cr. between the said Respondt. Offley and himselfe wherein he allows of a Discount to the sd. respondt. of twenty pounds Sterling by him paid and allowed to Richard B[l]and, and the Court haveing heard the Evidence produced by the Complt. and no further Objection [word removed] being made by the said respondants thereupon it is Decreed and Ordered that upon the said Complainants giveing the said Bolling Security to Indemnifie him agst. the said Offley for so much he the said Bolling do Sattisfie and pay the Complainant his Debt being One hundred Sixty Eight pounds Seaventeen Shilling and Nine pence halfe penny Sterl: togather with costs of this suite, out of the said Offleys goods in his hands and possession as aforesaid Advancing ten pr. Cent. upon the first [...] of the said Goods as they are rated and Valued in the Shopkeepers Notes. Whereupon the sd. Nathaniel Harrison Esqr. and Richard Bland appear in Court and acknowledge their Bond to Robert Bolling on whose motion the same is by the Court Ordered to be recorded.

In the action Depending between John Peterson and John Nance Admr. &c of John Nance Deced: for three pounds Due by accot. &c at the Last Court the Deft. haveing had time till this Court to plead and being now called to do the same did not appear nor offer any thing in barr or preclution of the plts. action, therefore it is Considered by this Court that the plt. recover agst. the said Defendt. the said Sum & Costs unless he shall appear at the next Court and answer the said action.

In the action of Debt Depending between Thomas Goodwyn assignee of Jos. Smith Marriner and John Mayes Marriner for three pounds Current money Due by Bill &c at the Last Court the Defendt. haveing had time given him to plead and being now called did not appear nor offer any thing in barr or preclusion of the plts. action, therefore it's considered by the Court that the plt. recover against the said Defendt. the said Sum & Costs unless he shall appear at the next Court and answer the said action.

[page 117 (Copy from Reel 7; filmed as page 117 and duplicated as page 147 on Reel 31)]
In the action of Debt brot. by Thomas Goodwyn assignee of Joseph Smith agst. John Mayes for One New Snaffle Bridle, one hackney [word removed], one pair of brass Spurrs and one hunting horswhip, Due by bill &c at the Last Court time was granted the Defefndt. till this Court to plead and being now called to do the same did not appear nor offer any thing in barr or preclusion of the plaintiffs action therefore tis Considered by the Court that the plt. recover against the said Defendt. the sd. Goods and Costs, unless the said Defendt. appears at the next Court and answers the said action.

In the action brot. by Cornelius Cargill agst. George Brewer the Defendt. being permitted to plead Doubly files his plea &c to the plts. Declaration who has time till next Court to Consider the said plea &c.

Daniel Nance and Elizabeth his Wife (being first privately Examined) in open Court acknowledge their Deeds of Lease and release of Land (Indented and Sealed) to Thomas Gregory on whose motion the same are ordered to be recorded, and the said Elizabeth also relinquisht. to the said Thomas her right of Dower in and to the said Lands &c. Ordered the same be Likewise recorded.

The Sherriff makes return of the appraisement of the Estate of Hubbard Gibson, Attacht. for James Thweatt. Ordered it be recorded, Vizt.

One Iron pott qt. 99 at 3½	£1.19.2
One pair Andirons qt. 81 at 4	1.10.4

The above Goods appraised by us [signed] Wm. Batte, Robt. Poythres, Edwd. [his M mark] Mitchell. The appraisers first Sworn by me John Peterson.

Ver. rec. Test Wm. Hamelin, Cl. Cur.

In the action brot. by James Bell agst. Henry Bates, John Hines and George Ivey for One thousand Nine hundred and forty five pounds of Tobacco Due by Bill Dated the 12 Day of June 1714, the Defends. failing to appear pursuant to the Conditionall Judgement and Order of therein of the Last Court thereupon Judgement is granted and Confirmed the plt. against the said Defendts. and Ordered that they the said John Hines, Henry Bates and George Ivey or either of them pay to the said plt. the said Sum & Costs. Als. Exec.

Elizabeth Cooper relict of John Cooper Deced: came into Court and made Oath that her said Husband Dyed Intestate as farr as She knew or believed and upon her giveing Security for her faithfull Administration of the said Decedts. Est: it's Ordered that a Certificate for Obtainining a Certificate of Administration be granted her, whereupon James Bell and Peter Anderson became her Security with her entred into Bond according to Law.

[page 118]

Edward Wyatt, Benja. Reeks, Paul Jones and Peter Talbutt or any three of them are Ordered to appraise the Estate of John Cooper Deced: they being first Sworn by Some Magistrate for that purpose and make report of their proceedings to the next Court when the Administratrix is to return the Inventory.

The order that James Bell return an accot. Dr. & Cr. of the Estate of James Boreman Deced: is continued till next Court.

The Suit Depending between John Hines and Henry Peoples (neither party appearing) is Dismist.

The attachment granted Henry Harrison agst. the Estate of John Sherley (the plt. failing to prosecute) is Dismist.

The attachment granted John Hatch agst. the Estate of Michael Hill is Continued till next Court.

In the action on the case Depending between John Womack and John Anderson for thirty Shillings Due by a Note &c the Defendt. being called and not appearing nor any Security returned for him on the plts. motion Judgement is granted him agst. the said Defendt. and Richard Hamelin Sherr: &c for the said Sum and Costs unless the said Defendt. appears at the next Court and answers the said Action.

The action brot. by John Roberts agst. Daniel Higdon (neither party appearing) is Dismist.

The action brot. by Thomas Goodwyn agst. John Spain (neither party appearing) is Dismist.

The action brot. by Cornelius Cargill agst. Nathl. Brewer junr. (neither party appearing) is Dismist.

The action brot. by John Hardyman Admr. agst. Thomas Simmons is by Consent Continued till the next Court.

In the action Depending between John Hatch and Saml. [Burch] for four hundred and fivety pounds of Tobacco Due by Bill &c the Defendt. being returned non est Inventus and not appearing on the plts. motion an Attachment is granted him against the sd. Defts. Estate for the said Sum & Costs returnable to the next Court for Judgement.

[page 119]

Ordered that a Grandjury of twenty four freeholders of this County be Summoned by the Sherr: to appear at the next Court.

The action brot. by John Hatch against Jeffrey Hawks (neither party appearing) is Dismist.

The action brot. by Fra. Wynne agst. John Ellington (neither party appearing) is Dismist.

The action brot. by Francis Wynne agst. John Stroud (neither party appearing) is Dismist.

The action brot. by Robert Rogers agst. Richd. Walpole (the plt. failing to prosecute and the Defendt. assumeing to pay the Costs) is Dismist.

The action brot. by Richard Hamelin agst. Samuel Harwood (neither party appearing) is Dismist.

In the action brot. by Richard Hamelin agst Samuel Harwood the plt. failing to prosecute on the Deffendts. motion it's Ordered that he be Nonsuited and pay the said Deft. five Shillings with Costs. Als. Exec.

The action brot. by John Allen agst. Mathew Smart (the plt. failing to prosecute) is Dismist.

The action brot. by John Allen agst. Adam Tapley (the plt. Failing to prosecute) is Dismist.

The action brought by John Allen agst. Henry Ivey (the plt. failing to prosecute) is Dismist.

The action brot. by John Allen agst. George Ivey (the plt. failing to prosecute) is Dismist.

The action brot. by John Allen agst. Abra. Odgan (the plt. failing to prosecute) is Dismist.

The action brot. by John Allen agst. Charles Gillam (the plt. failing to prosecute) is Dismist.

The action brot. by William Mayes agst. Thos. Sands (neither party appearing) is Dismist.

The action brot. by James Thweatt agst. Mathew Sturdivant (neither party appearing) is Dismist.

In the action brot. by Thomas Goodwyn Assignee of Elizabeth Epes agst. Henry Robertson for Six hundred and fourteen pounds of Tobacco Due by Bills &c the

[page 120]

Defendt. being returned *non est Inventus* and not appearing on the plts. motion an attachment is granted him agst. the said Defendts. Estate for the said Sum & Costs returnable to the next Court for Judgement.

In the action Depending between Thomas Goodwyn and John Poake for two thousand Six hundred and fifteen pds: of Tobacco Due by accot. &c at the Last Court the Defendt. being returned *non est Inventus* and not appearing an Attachment was granted the plt. agst. the said Defts. Estate for the said Sum & Costs returnable to this Court for Judgemt. which being now returned accordingly Executed on the sd. Defendts. Estate and the sd. partys being called William Mattox became Speciall Bail for the said Defendt. who thereupon appears and replevys his Estate Attacht. as aforesaid and Exhibitts a Discount, thereupon the accots. of the sd. partys were Examined in Court and there appearing to be Due to the plt. the Sum of One thousand Six hundred Sixty Six pounds of Tobacco. It's therefore Ordered that the said Deft. pay to the said plt. the said Sum and Costs. Als. Exec.

Robert Bolling in Open Court acknowledged his Deeds of Lease and release of Land (Indented and Sealed) to Stith Bolling on whose motion the Same are Ordered to be recorded.

On the petition of Edward Goodrich for the Administration of the Estate of Fra. Norten Deced: who Dyed (as is alledged) Intestate It's Ordered that Mary the relict of the said Deced. be Summoned to the next Court to accept or refuse the said Administration.

And then the Court Adjourn'd till Court in Course. Jno. Hamelin. Test Wm. Hamelin, Cl. Cur.

[page 121]

Att a Court held at Merchantshope for the County of Prince George on the
Second Tuesday in May being the fourteenth Day of the month Anno Dom: 1717.

Present — John Hamelin, John Poythres, Randll. Platt }
Robt. Hall, John Hardyman & Lewis Green junr. } Gent. Justices

Pursuant to the Direction of the Act concerning Tythables, Mr. Sampson Merredeth is appointed to take the List of Tithables in Martins Brandon Parrish. Mr. Randal Platt for Wyanoake, Capt. John Hamlin for Westopher and Major Robert Munford for Bristoll Parrish.

Elizabeth Cooper Administratrix of the Estate of John Cooper Deced: returns upon Oath an Inventory &c of the said Decedts. Estate. Ordered it be recorded.

The peto. of Robert Fellows that he be Leavy free is rejected and Dismist.

The peto. of Samuell Burch that he be Leavy free is rejected and Dismist.

On the peto. of John Bell he is Exempted from paying the County Leavy for ye future.

James Bell, Executor &c of James Boreman Deced: returns an accot. Dr. & Dr. of the Estate of the said James Boreman Deced: upon Oath. Ordered it be recorded.

ffrancis Wynne in Open Court acknowleged her Deeds of Lease and release of Land (Indented and Sealed) to William Stainback and his heirs &c on whose motion the same are ordered to be recorded.

Robert Tucker in Open Court acknowledged his Deed with Livery and Seizin endorsed thereon (Indented and Sealed) to David Crawley and his heirs &c on whose motion the Same is Ordered to be recorded.

On the peto. of George Pace its Ordered that a Crop and two Slitts in the right Ear and a Crop and Slitt and half moon under the Left be recd. his Ear marke.

In the action brot. by Thomas Simmons against John Ellis junr. for Eight hundred and Eighteen pounds of Tobacco Due by accot. &c the Defendt. being returned *non est inventus* and not appearing at a former Court an Attachment was granted the plt. agst. the Estate of the sd. Defendt. &c which being now returned Executed on part thereof, Vizt. about fifteen Bushells of Indian Corn, and the said Defendt. being called and failing to appear to replevye the same and the said plt. makeing Oath the said Sum is justly Due, thereupon Judgement is granted him agst. the said Defendt. for the said Sum and Costs. Ordered that the Sherr: cause the said Corn to be Duly appraised by John Coleman, Daniell Sturdivant and Justain Hall (they being first Sworn by Some Majestrate for that purpose) and Delivered the plt. for towards the payment and Discharge of the sd. Sum & Costs, and make report of his proceedings therein to the next Court.

[page 122]

Present Mr. Peterson

In the action brot. by Joshua Irby agst. Peter Wynne, the sd. Defendt. pleads non assumpsit, the plt. Joins in the Issue and the Cause for Tryall is referred till next Court.

Present Majr. Bolling

The action brot. by Peter Wynne Admr. &c agst. Stephen Evans, the plt. failing to prosecute is Dismist.

The action brot. by Charles Goodrich agst. Daniel Higdon, the plt. failing to prosecute is Dismist.

In the action brot. by Randll. Platt Assignee of Charles Goodrich plt. against Thomas House ye Defendt. haveing filed a plea and Demurrer to the plts. Declaration and he Joining therein, the same was referred to this Court for Tryall and the sd. partys now appearing and the Demurrer aforesaid being argued by he attys. is adjudged good, whereupon the suit is Dismist.

Richard Bland made Complaint that John Perry Stands Justly Indebted to him by accot. &c the Sum of four pound twelve Shillings and Six pence halfe penny and twelve hundred and eighteen pounds of Tobacco, and set forth that the sd. John Hath unlawfully Departed this County that the Ordinary process at Law canot be Served on him whereupon he by Virtue of an Attachmt. under thehand of one of his Majestys Justices for this County returnable to this Court hath cased part of the Estate of the sd. John to be attacht. for payment thereof, Vizt. One feather bed, one pair of Sheets, one rugg, one Small Chest, three Charis, one Table, one poll and poll hooks, one frying pann, one pair of fire Tongs, One Skillet, four puter Dishes, five puter plates, two puter porringers, four Spoons, Six glass bottles, one Spining wheel, one Spitt & Six Stools, and the said John being called and failing to appear to replevye the Same, and the sd. plt. makeing Oath the sd. Sums are Justly Due, thereupon Judgement is granted him agst. the sd. John for the sd. Sums & Costs, to be Leavi[e]d on the sd. Goods Attacht. Ordered that the Sherr: cause the same to be Duly appraised by William Rains, William Stainback junr., John Bonner and John Woodleife or any three of them (being first Sworn by some Majistrate for that purpose) and Delivered the plt. for and toward the payment of the said Sums and Costs, and make report of his proceedings therein to the next Court.

Pursuant to the Direction of the act Concerning Jurys, a Grandjury was Imipannelled and Sworn by Names John Scott, John Ledbetter, George Reves, Israel Marks, Chic[hester] Sturdivant, Richard Smith, Richard Raines, John Avery, James Bell, Thos. Booth, Robert Tucker, Thomas Clay,

[page 123]

John Bell, William Short, & John Hobbs, and haveing their charge were sent out and after Some time Spent return their presentments as follows, Vizt.

We present Richard Warthan for Spoiling the County road by placing his Mill in the road and the Gates Just above the road and that the said Worthan hath not made his Mill Dam according [to] Law

We present Robert Burchet for Turning away his wife and by Common fame Lives in Adultry with Hanah Hedsted. John Scott, foreman.

Ordered that prosecution be made by the Churchwardens of the Parrishes wherein the offences are Committed, according to Law.

The Last Will and Testament of William Santan [Santom] Deced: was presented into Court by James Bell one of the Executors therein Named who made Oath thereto and it being proved by the Oaths of William Cogill and Thomas Clifton two of the Witnesses thereto, is Admitted to record, and upon the sd. Executors giveing Security according to Law, It's Ordered that a Certificate be granted him for Obtaining a probate in Due form, whereupon John Bell and Israel Markes became his Security and with him entred into Bond accordingly.

William Smith appeared in Court and acknowledged his Deeds of Lease and release of Land (Sealed) to John Holloway on whose motion the same are Ordered to be recorded, and then also appeared in Court Susan the wife of the sd. William and being first privately Examined according to Law relinquisht. her right of Dower of in and to the Lands in the said Deed mentioned, to the sd. John Holloway on whose motion the same is Likewise Ordered to be recorded.

George Haynes an Indented Sarvant to Mr. Richard Bland being Suspected of ffelony and Burlary was brot. into Court by his sd. Master and sd. Bland and Richard Ruth being Sworn Evidences against him, the sd. Bland Declared that on or abt. the 1st Day of March last at night the sd. Blands Store was broken [up] in and that there was Stolen from thence upwards of Twenty pounds Current money and Suspecting the sd. Haynes to be Guilty of the robery, upon Search found Some such Like money as he had Lost, in the possession of the sd. George in a Letter Directed to a person in great Brittain, and that the sd. Haynes thereafter confest to him that he was in Company with a person who broke upon the sd. Store and that he the sd. George Stole the sd. money, which he the sd. George also upon

Examinationin Open Court Confest. And the sd. Richard Ruth being upon his Oath Declared that he reced. of the sd. George the Letter above mentioned to be Dleivered for him to the person to whom it was Directed

[page 124]
from all which the Court are of Opinion that the sd. George Haynes ought to be Tryed for the facts aforesaid before the Genrall Court or Court of Oyer & Terminer and thereupon Committ the sd. George Haynes to the County Gaol from thence to be Conveyed to the publick Gaol at Williamsburgh there to remain untill he be Delivered thence by Due course of Law.

Richard Bland in Open Court Acknowledged himself Indebted to our Soveraign Lord the King his heirs and Successors in the Sum of Tenn pds. Sterl: with Condition that if he the sd. Richard Bland shall appear before the Honble. the Genrall Court next on the fourth Day therefor before the next Court of Oyer and Terminer which shall first happen, and then and there give Evidence for our sd. Lord the King agst. George Haynes who stands Committed to the Common Gaol of this County on Suspition of ffelony and Burlary, then this recognizance to be Void, or Else to be and remain in full power and force.

Stith Bolling in Open Court acknowledged his Deed (Indented & Sealed) with Livery of Seizin endorsed thereon to Robert Poythres and his heirs on whose motion the same by the Court are Ordered to be recorded.

Stith Bolling in Open Court acknowledged his Bond for performance of Covenants to Robert Poythres on whose motion the (same) is Ordered to be recorded.

Edward Goodrich in Open Court acknowledged his Deed with Livery of Seizin endorsed thereon (Indented and Sealed) to Timothy Grammer and his heirs for ever, on whose motion the same is Ordered to be recorded, and then also appeared in Court Margaret the wife of the said Goodrich and being privately Examined according to Law relinquisht. to the said Grammer her right of Dower of in and to the Lands in the said Deed mentioned which by the Court is Likewise Ordered to be recorded.

Samuell Chappell appeared in Open Court and acknowledged his Discharge to James Jones junr. on whose motion the same is Ordered to be recorded.

On the motion of the Attorney of Nathaniel Harrison Esqr. Guardian to George Bleighton the son of George Bleighton Deced: It's Ordered that the sd. Nathaniel Harrison Esqr. take into his Custody & possession the Estate of the sd. Orphan.

[page 125]
In the action brot. by John Allen agst. Richard Hamlin for Six hundred & thirty pounds of Tobacco Due by Bill Dated the 26th Day of March 1714, the plt. haveing Demurred to the Defendts. plea and upon hearing the Arguments it appears to the Court that the plea of the Defendt. is not Sufficient to preclude the plt. from maintaining his action, whereupon on the plts. motion Judgement is granted him agst. the sd. Defendt. for the sd. Sum & Costs, the [sic] And it's Ordered that the sd: Defendt. pay unto the sd. plt. the sd. Sum of Six hundred and thirty pounds of Tobacco and Costs. Als. Exec.

The Last Will and Testament of Thomas Parram Deced: was presented into Court by Elizabeth his relict and Executrix therein Named who made Oath thereto and it being proved by the Oaths of George Tillman and Robert Abernathy junr. is Ordered to be recorded, and upon the sd. Executrix's giveing Security according to Law It's Ordered that a Certificate be granted her for Obtaining a probate thereof in Due form whereupon David Crawley and Edward Goodrich became her Securitys and wth. her entred into Bond accordingly.

In the action brot. by John Hatch agst. John Nance Administrator with the will annext. of John Nance Deced: for three pounds three Shillings and Eleaven pence Due by accot. &c the Defendt. pleads *plene administravit*, and the plt. Joining in the Issue the same for Tryall is referred till the next Court.

The order that Robert Abernathy return an Inventory of Su. Tillman's Est: is Continued till next Court.

In the action on the case Depending between Thomas Simmons and Thos. Chamberlain the Defendt. haveing pleaded to the plts. Declaration and he Demurring thereto the same was referred to this Court to be argued and then sd. partys now appearing and the Demurrer aforesaid being argued is Overruled and the plea of the Defendt. adjudged good whereupon the suit is Dismist.

In the action brot. by Elizabeth Jones agst. Robert Jones Exr. &c the Defendt. being permitted to plead Doubly, files his plea &c to the plts. Declaration, she has time till next Court to Considert he same.

The suit brot. by John Peterson agst. John Nance Admr. &c the plt. failing to prosecute is Dismist.

In the action brot. by Thomas Goodwyn assignee of Jos. Smith Marriner against John Mayes Marriner for three pounds Currt. money Due by Bills, the Defendt. pleads payment and the plt. Joining in the Issue the same is referred till next Court for Tryall.

[page 126]
In the action of Debt brot. by Thomas Goodwyn assignee of Jos. Smith agst. John Mayes the Defendt. pleads *nil Debit* the plt. Joins in the Issue and the cause for Tryall is referred till next Court.

In the suit in Chancery brot. by Samuel Harwood agst. Henry Offley Late of London Mercht. and ffrancis Mallory respondts. the sd. Complainant and the respondt. Mallory appearing the sd. Mallory files his answer upon Oath to the Complts. Bill wherein he confesses to have in his hands (of the sd. Offleys Estate) in Outstanding Debts sufficient to Sattisfie and pay the Complts. Debt Due from the sd. Offley being Nine pounds thirteen Shillings and a halfe penny Sterl: which the plt. makes oath is Justly Due to him and which also appears by accot. under the sd. Offleys hand, Thereupon it's Decreed by the Court that upon the Complainants giveing the said Mallory Security to Indemnifie him against the sd. Offley for so much the sd. Complainant do recover his aforesaid Debt to be paid out of the said Debts Contracted by the said Mallory with the said Offleys Goods, a full List of which Debts the said Mallory is to Deliver upon Oath to Mr. Randll. Platt and Mr. John Hardyman of which Debts the sd. Complainant is to have his Choice for payment of the sd. Sum and Costs, together with ten pr. Cent to make the same Equivalent wth. Sterling. Whereupon the sd. Samuel Harwood and Samuel Harwood junr. [entred] into Bond Accordingly and acknowledge the same to the sd. ffrancis Mallory which is Ordered to be recorded.

And then the Court adjourn'd till Court in Course. Randl. Platt. Test Wm. Hamlin, Cl. Cur.

Pr. Geo: County   November the 9th 1716
This Day ffrancis Coleman junr. was brought before us by the Complt. of Cornelius Cargill for that he stood Justly Indebted to him the sum of two Bushells and one halfe of Indian Corn, and refused payment, and the same being proved by the Oath of [one] Evidence to be Justly due, Judgement is granted to the said Cargill for the said Sum with Costs. Als. Execution. Pr. John Hamlin.

On the 11th day of June 1717, Cornelius Cargill Exhibited the above written Judgement and Defered the same might be recorded that Execution might Issue thereon, which accordingly is truly recorded and Execution is Issued against the Estate of the sd. Defendt. &c. Test. W. Hamelin, Cl. Cur.

[page 127]
Att a Court held for the County of Prince George on the second Tuesday in June being the Eleaventh Day of the month, Anno Dom: 1717.
Present   Randle Platt,   Robert Hall,   Robert Bolling }
                 John Hardyman   & Lewis Green Junr.   Gent. Justices
In the action Depending between Cornelius Cargill and George Brewer, on the plts: motion and paying Costs, he is permitted to amend his Declaration, whereupon the plt. has time till the next Court to Consider the same.

The action brot. by John Hatch agst. Michael Hill (the plt. failing to prosecute) is Dismist.

In the action brot. by John Womack agst. John Anderson for thirty Shillings due by a Note under his hand Dated the 18th of October 1706, the Defendt. being called and failing to appear pursuant to the Conditionall Judgement and Order therein of the Last Court, on the plts: motion Judgement is granted and Confirmed the plt. against the said Defendt. and Richard Hamlin Sherr: &c for the sd. Sum, It's therefore ordered that the sd. Defendt. and Richard Hamlin or either of them pay to the said plt. the sd. Sum of thirty Shillings and Costs. Als. Executed.

Judgement being this Day past unto John Womack agst. Richard Hamlin Sherr: of Pr. Geo. County for thirty Shillings & Costs by reason of the non appearance of John Anderson at the suit of the Sd. Womacke in an action on the Case, On the motion of the said Sherr: an Attachment is granted him agst. the said Defendts. Estate for so much thereof as will be of Value Sufficient to Sattisfie and pay the sd. Sum & Costs returnable to the next Court for Judgement.

Absent Mr. Hardyman. Present Capt. Jno. Hamlin
In the action Depending between John Hardyman Administrator of the Estate of John Hardyman Deced: and Thomas Simmons for One thousand and twenty three [pounds] of Tobacco due by accot. &c the Deft. appears and pleads *nil Debit* and the plt. Joining in the Issue the same for Tryall was Submitted to the Court and the accots. of the said Partys being Examined and Settle in Court and it appearing that the Ballance is Due to the Defendt. thereupon on his motion the suit is Dismist. with Costs.

Pompey a Negro Boy belonging to Major Robert Munford is Adjudged Eleaven years of Age.

Daniell Mallone in Open Court acknowledged his Deeds of Lease & release of Land (Indented and Sealed) to John Fitzgerrald and his heirs for ever on whose motion the same are Ordered to be recorded, And then also appeared in Court Mary the Wife of the said Daniell and being first privately Examined according to Law freely relinquisht. to the said John her right of Dower of in and to the Lands in the said Deeds mentioned. Ordered the same be Lilkewise recorded.

[page 128]
Robert Burchett in Open Court acknowledged his Deed with Livery of Seizin Endorst. thereon (Indented and Sealed) to Duglas Irby and his heirs for Ever on whose motion the Same is Ordered to be recorded.
Present Mr. Hardyman
In the action brot. by John Hatch agst. Samuell Burch for four hundred and fivety pounds of Tobacco Due by Bill Dated the 13 Day of December 1715, At a former Court the Defdt. being returned *non est Inventus* and not appearing an Attachment was granted the plt. agst. the sd. Defendts. Estate for the sd. Sum & Costs, returnable to this Court for Judgement, which being now returned Executed on part thereof, Vizt. One feather bed, One blankett & one Sheet, and the sd. Defendt. being called and not appearing to replevye the same, and the sd. plt. makeing Oath the said Sum is Justly Due thereupon Judgement is granted him agst. the said Defendt. for the sd. Sum & Costs. Ordered that the Sherr: cause the said Goods to be Duly appraised by Richard Jones, Daniell Jones, Peter Jones and William Davis or any three of them, being first Sworn by Some Justice for that purpose, and Delivered the plt. for and towards the paymt. of the said Sum & Costs, and make report of his proceedings therein to the next Court.
Present Majr. Robt. Munford
On the peto. of John Hobbs, John Bell and William Short, Surveyors of the Highways, who at a former Court were Ordered to build a Bridge over the Head of Wards Creek near Warthins Mill, the sd. Order is Dispensed with and made Null & Void.
The attachment granted Thomas Goodwyn assignee &c agst. the Estate of Henry Robertson is Continued till next Court.
Mary Norten, Relict of ffrancis Norten Deced: came into Court and made Oath that the sd. ffrancis Norten Dyed without any Will as farr as she knows or believes, and upon her giveing Security according to Law, it's Ordered that a Certificate be granted her for obtaining Letters of Administration in Due form, whereupon Robert Munford & Henry Batte became her Security and with her entred into bond accordingly.
Thomas Clay, Henry Thweatt, John Thweatt and Richard M[uns] or any three of them are Ordered to appraise the Estate of ffrancis Norten Deced: they being first Sworn by Some Justice for that purpose and make report of their proceedings to the next Court, when Mary Norten the Adminx. is Ordered to return the Inventory.
Thomas Addison is appointed Overseer of the Highways from We[stbr]ook to the Extent of the County, Instead of John Scott.

[page 129]
The peto. of John Westbrook concerning two Orphan Children now under the Care of Joshua Irby is refered till the next Court to prove the Allegations therein when the sd. Irby is Ordered to bring the said Orphans to Court.
The action brot. by Edward Goodrich agst. John Lett on the plts. motion is referred or Continued till the next Court.
The action brot. by Thomas Simmons Assignee of Samson Merredeth agst. Henry Duke the plt. failing to prosecute, is Dismist.
Robert Abbernathy junr. returns upon Oath an Inventory of the Estate of Susanna Tillman Deced:. Ordered it be recorded.
In the action of Debt brot. by James Jones Junr. agst. Martin Sheffeild for four hundred and ten pounds of Tobacco Due by Bill &c the Deft. being returned *non est Inventus* and not appearing an Attachment is granted the plt. against the sd. Defendts. Estate for the sd. Sum and Costs returnable to the next Court for Judgement for which shall appear to be Due.
The action brought by Peter Wynne agst. Edward Wyatt & Benjamin Rix is referred till the next Court by Consent.
The action brot. by William Hamlin agst. ffrancis Mallory the plt. failing to prosecute, is Dismist.
The action brot. by Henry Harrison agst. ffrancis Mallory, is Dismist, the sd. Deft. by Edward Goodrich, Assumeing to pay the Costs.
The action brot. by Randle Platt agst. John Perry, the plt. failing to prosecute is Dismist.
The action brot. by John Simmons Assignee &c agst. Robert Hobbs (neither party appearing) is Dismist.
The suit in Chancery brot. by Edward Goodrich, David Goodgame & Joshua Goodgame agst. James Sevakar, the plts. failing to prosecute, is Dismist.

In the action brot. by Benja. Ray et uxor. agst. John Doby, An Imparlance is granted the Defendt. till the next Court.

In the action brot. by David Crawley agst. Christopher Davis junr. for three pds. Eighteen Shillings and Eight pence halfe penny Due by accot. &c the deft. being called and not appearing and Christopher Davis Senr. being returned Security for him on the motion of the plts. Attorney Judgement is granted him agst. the sd. Defendt. and his Security for the said Sum & Costs, unless the said Defendt. shall appear at the next court and answer the said Action.

The action brot. by David Crawley against William Gent, the plt. failing to prosecute is Dismist.

[page 130]

In the action of Debt brot. by Elizabeth Hamlin against Simon Naylor for four Barrells of Indian Corn Due by Bill &c the Defendt. being returned *non est Inventus* and not appearing on the motion of the plts. Attorney an Attachment is granted her agst. the sd. Defendts. Estate for the said Sum and Costs returnable to th enext Court for Judgemt.

In the action on the Case brot. by Joshua Irby agst. John Evans, Oyer of the plts. accot. is granted the Defendt. and time till the next Court to Consider the same.

The action brot. by William Irby agst. William Davis, the plt. failing to prosecute is Dismist.

In the action brot. by Peter Wynne agst. Samuell Sentall for forty three Shillings Due by Bill &c the Defendt. being returned *non est Inventus* and not appearing on the motion of the plts. Attorney an Attachmt. is granted him agst. the sd. Defendts. Estate for the sd. Sum & Costs, returnable to the next Court for Judgemt.

The action brot. by Peter Wynne Admr. &c agst. Edwd: Denton, the plt. failing to prosecute is Dismist.

On the peto. of Charles Roberts he is Exempted from paying Leavy for the future.

In the action brot. by Henry Harrison agst. George Ivie for Six hundred Sixty five pounds of Tobacco Due by accot. &c the Defendt. being returned *non est Inventus* and not appearing on the motion of the plts. Attorney an Attachment is granted him agst. the said Defendts. Estate for the said Sum and Costs returnable to the next Court for Judgemt.

The action brot. by Henry Embry agst. Robert Glidewell, neither party appearing is Dismist.

The action brot. by Richard Hamlin agst. Instance Hall, neither party appearing, Dismist.

The Sherr: makes return of the appraisement of the Estate of John Ellis junr. Attacht. for Thomas Simons, which is Ordered to be recorded, Vizt. June the 4, 1717. In Obedience to an Order of Pr. Geo. Court, we the Subscribers being first Sworn have appraised the Corn Attacht. being fourteen Bushells to two Hundred [& twenty] pounds of Tobacco, witness our hands the Day and year above. [signed] Danl. [his DS mark] Sturdivant, Jas. Hall, John Coleman. Sworn before me Robert Munford. Ver. rec. Test W. Hamlin, Cl.

It appearing by the above appraisement that the same is insufficient to Sattisfie and pay the Judgement granted the said Thomas Simons against the Estate of the said

[page 131]

John Ellis junr. by the sum of five hundred Ninety Eight pounds of Tobacco & Costs, It's therefore Ordered by the Court that the said Thomas Simmons have Execution agst. the sd. Defendt. for the said Sum and Costs.

The action brot. by Joshua Irby against Peter Wynne is referred till next Court.

The order for the return of the appraisement of the Estate of John Perry Attacht. for Richard Bland is Continued till next Court.

The order that the Sherr: return his proceedings in the sale of Sadler's Estate is Continued till next Court.

In the action brot. by Eliza. Jones agst. Robert Jones Exr. &c the Deft. Joins in the Demurrer and Issue Tendered by the Defendt. which is referred till next court for Tryall.

Oder that John Nance Admr. &c of John Nance Deced: return to the next Court an accot. Dr. & Cr. of the sd. Decedts. Estate.

The action Depending between John Hatch and John Nance Admr. &c is referrd. till next Court.

The action Depending between Thomas Goodwyn Assignee of Jos. Smith & John Mayes for three pounds Due by Bill &c the Defendt. haveing pleaded payment and the plt. Joining in the Issue the same was Submitted to the Court for Tryall, and Severall Difficultys appearing the same is referred to the next Court for Tryall.

The action brot. by Tho: Goodwyn Assignee of Jos: Smith &c agst. John Mayes is referred till next Court.

In the action of Tresspass on the case Depending between Thomas Webb Surviveing Executor of the Last Will and Testament of Giles Webb Deced: for the Detaining of Nine geldings of the price of ten pounds Sterl: each & also of one Cart of the Value of five pounds Sterl: and One pair of Cart Wheels, of the Value of five pounds Sterl: and to the plts. Damage two thousand pounds Sterl: the Defendt. being called and appearing, and failing to make any plea or offer any thing in barr or preclusion of the plts. Action. Therefore it's Considered by the Court that the said plt. ought to recover against the said Defendt. his Damages by means of the Detainer aforesaid but because it is unknown to the Court what Damages the said plt. in that part hath sustained, therefore it is Commanded that the Sherr: cause to come before his Majestys Justices at the next Court twelve good and Lawfull men of his Bailywick by whose Oaths Dilligent Enquiry may be made of the said Damage.

Robert Rogers Entred himselfe Security to pay all costs and Damages that may be awarded Henry Randolph in an action of Tresspass on the Case Depending between Thomas Webb and the said Randolph.

[page 132]

In the case Depending between William ffarrar and Henry Randolph for One thousand four hundred and Six pounds of Tobacco Due by accot. &c the Defendt. appears and pleads payment, and the plt. Joining in the Issue the same for Tryall is referred till next Court.

The Suit in Chancery brot. by Richard Bradford agst. ffrancis Mallory and Henry Offley is referred till next Court.

In the action Depending between Jerre: Turner &c and ffrancis Mallory, Robert Rogers enters himselfe Security to pay all costs and Damages that may be awarded the Deft. agst. the sd. plt. whereupon an Imparlance is granted the sd. Defendt. till the next Court.

In the action of Debt brot. by Seth Ward against Edward Goodrich the plt. failing to prosecute on the Defendts. motion it's Ordered that he be Nonsuit and pay the sd. Deft. five Shillings with Costs. Als. Exec:

In the suit in Chancery Depending between Thomas Goodwyn and Joseph Smith and Cornelius Cargill respondts. on the motion of the said Cargill time is granted him till the next Court to answer the Complts. Bill.

The action brot. by Thomas Goodwyn agst. John Poke, neither party appearing is Dismist.

In the suit in Chancery brot. by Thomas Goodwyn agst. Jos. Smith and ffrancis Mallory, Ordered the same be referred till next Court.

The suit in Chancery brot. by Charles Anderson agst. John Poythres and Henry Offley, neither party appearing is Dismist.

Charles Anderson haveing filed a Bill in Chancery agst. John Poythres Surviveing Executor of John Poythres Deced: and Henry Offley Late of London Merchant It's Ordered that a Supa. Issue agst. the said John Pythres and Henry Offley to appear at the next Court and answer the said Bill.

In the action brot. by John Cargill Assignee of Peter Wynne Admr. &c agst. Elizabeth Parham Executrix of the Last Will of Thos. Parham Deced: for Six hundred pounds of Tobacco Due by Bill &c the Defendt. being called and not appearing nor any Security returned for her on the plts. motion Judgemt. is granted him agst. the sd. Deft. & Richard Hamlin Sherr: &c for the sd. Sum unless the sd. Deft. shall appear at the next Court and answer the sd. Action.

The action brot. by Richard Walpole agst. Charles Bowen, neither party appearing, is Dismist.

[page 133]

In the action brot. by Randle Platt agst. Nicholas Overby Junr. for five hundred and five pounds of Tobacco Due by Bill &c the Defendt. being returned *non est Inventus* and not appearing on the plts. motion an Attachment is granted him agst. the sd. Defendts. Estate for the said Sum & Costs returnable to the next Court for Judgement.

The attachment granted Powell Cock against the Estate of Joseph Smith neither party appearing is Dismist.

The peto. and Complt. of Mary Batte agst. James Parham is Dismist.

And then the Court Adjourn'd till Court in Course. John Hamlin. Test W. Hamlin, Cl. Cur.

At a Court held at Merchantshope for the County of Prince George on the Second Tuesday in July being the Ninth Day of the month Anno Dom. 1717.

Present   John Poythres,   Robert Bolling,   John Hardyman }
         Lewis Green junr.   & John Peterson   Gent. Justices }

Adam Tapley in Open Court acknowledged his Deeds of Lease and Release of Land (Indented and Sealed) to Randle Platt and his heirs &c On whose motion the Same are Ordered to be recorded, And then also appeared in Court Elizabeth the Wife of the said Adam Tapley and being first privately Examined as the Law Directs, Voluntarily relinquisht. to the sd. Platt her right of Dower in and too the Lands &c in the sd. Deeds mentioned which is Likewise Ordered to be recorded.

Adam Tapley in Open Court acknowledged his Bond (Sealed) for performance of Covenants to Randle Platt. Ordered the same be recorded.

Present Randle Platt Gent.

Martha Cocke returns upon Oath a List of Sundry Debts that she has paid and Stands Obliged to pay out of the Estate of her Deced: husband Stephen Cocke. Ordered it be recorded.

On the petition of John Peterson for One Acre of Land belonging to the heirs of Joseph Holycross Deced: for the said Peterson's Convenience to build a water Mill on, It's Ordered that Martha Holycross Mother to the said Heirs be summoned to the next Court to answer the same.

In the action on the case Depending between Cornelius Cargill and George Brewer Damage One thousand pds: of Tobacco, the Defendt. haveing had tie given him till this Court to plead and being now called did not appear &c thereupon Judgemt. is granted the plt. by *Nihil Dicit* &c.

[page 134]

The attachment granted Richard Hamlin Sherr: &c against the Estate of John Anderson is Dismist.

Francis Coleman and Francis Coleman junr. in Open Court acknowledged their Deed for Land (Indented and Sealed) to David Crawley and his heirs whose motion the same is Ordered to be recorded.

The attachmt. granted Thomas Goodwyn Assignee of Eliza. Epes agst. the Estate of Henry Robertson the plt. failing to prosecute is Dismist.

William Cuerton in Open Court acknowledged his Deeds of Lease & release of Land (Indented & Sealed) to John Risby and his heirs &c with a receit. on the back thereof for the Consideration money, and on the motion of the said Risby the same are Ordered to be recorded.

In the suit in Chancery brought by Richard Bradford agst. Henry Offley late of London Merchant and ffrancis Mallory respondents, the said Complainant and the respondt. Mallory appearing the said Mallory files his answer upon Oath to the Complainants Bill wherein he Confesses to have in his hands of the said Offleys Estate in outstanding Debts Sufficient to Sattisfie and pay the Complainants Debt Due from the said Offley being Eight pounds five Shillings and Nine pence Sterling which the plt. makes Oath is Justly Due to him and which also appears by accot. under the said Offleys hand, togather with thirty two Shillings Sterl: being the Charge and protest of a Bill of Exchange Drawn by this Complainant on the said Offley for the said Sum of Eight pounds five Shillings and Nine pence Sterl: which said Bill was returned protested for non payment &c Whereupon the Decree by the Court that upon the Complainants giveing the siad Mallory Security to Indemnifie him against the said Offley for so much the sd. Complainant do recover the aforesaid Sum amounting to Nine pounds Seaventeen Shillings and Nine pence Sterling, to be paid out of the said Debts contracted by the said Mallory with the said Offleys Goods, a full list of which Debts the said Mallory is to Deliver upon Oath to Mr. Platt and Mr. John Hardyman, of which Debts the sd. Complainant is to have his choice for payment of the said Sum of Nine pounds Seaventeen Shillings and Nine pence Sterling and Costs, togather with ten pr. Cent to make the same Equivalent with Sterling.

William Tomlinson Exhibited into Court the Last Will of his Deced: Wife Jane Tomlinson and Desired that he might be permitted to prove the same and Adam Tapley eldest son to the Deced: objecting agst. the same It's Ordered that the Same be referred till the next Court.

Mary Norten Admx. of ffra. Norten Deced: returns upon Oath an Inventory of her Deced: husbands Estate. Ordered it be recorded.

[page 135]

Ordered that the Order of the Last Court concerning two Orphans under the care of Joshua Irby be continued till the next Court.

In the action of Debt Depending between Edward Goodrich and John Lett for Six hundred and Eighty pounds of Tobacco Due by Bill &c the Defendt. failing to appear, on the plts. motion Judgement is granted him agst. the said Deft. for the said Sum & Costs, unless the sd. Defendt. shall appear at the next Court and answer the said Action.

In the action of Debt brot. by James Jones junr. agst. Martin Sheffeild for four hundred and ten pounds of Tobacco Due by Bill Dated the 5th Day of May 1713, at a former court the Defendt. being returned *non est Inventus* and not appearing an Attachmt. was granted the plt. against the Defendts. Estate for the said Sum & Costs returnable to this Court for Judgement which being now returned Executed on part thereof, Vizt. On two Cows and one Calfe, and the said Deft. being called and not appearing to replevye the same, and the said plt. makeing Oath the said Sum is justly Due, thereupon Judgement is granted him agst. the said Defendt. for the said Sum & Costs to be Leavied on the sd. Cattle attacht. as aforesaid. Ordered that the Sherr: cause the same to be Duly appraised by Gilbert Hay, James Harrison, John and ffrancis Wilkins, or any three of them being first Sworn by some Majistrate for that purpose

71

and Delivered the plt. for and towards the payment of the sd. Sum & Costs, and make report of his proceedings therein to the next Court.

Martha Tucker an Orphan appears in Court and Chuses Majr. Robert Munford her Guardian who is Ordered to give Security at the next Court &c.

In Order of the Last Court for the appraisement of Sundry goods of the Estate of Saml. Burch, Attacht. for Mr. John Hatch is made Null and Void by consent of the sd. Hatch.

In the action of Debt brot. by Peter Wynne agst. Edward Wyatt and Benja. Ricks for Seaven hundred thirty five pounds of Tobacco Due by Bill Dated the 5th Day of Jany. 1716, the Defendts. appear and offer a Discount of Six hundred and One pds. Tobo. which being Examined is allowed by the Court & Judgement is granted the plt. for the residue, thereupon it's Ordered that the said Defendts. Jointly and Severally pay to the said plt. the said Sum of One hundred thirty four pounds of Tobacco and Costs. Als. Exec:

In the action brot. by Benja. Ray et Uxor agst. John Doby for Slander &c the Defendt. by his Attorney pleads not Guilty and the plts. Joining in the Issue the same is thereupon referred till next Court for Tryall.

In the action brot. by David Crawley agst. Christopher Davis junr. for three pounds Eighteen Shillings and Eight pence one halfe penny Due by accot. the Defendt. failing to appear pursuant to the conditionall Judgemt. and Order therein of the Last Court on the motion of the plts. Attorney Judgemt. is granted and Confirmed agst. the sd. Defendt. and Christopher Davis Senr. for the said Sum & Costs. It is thereupon Ordered that the said Defendt. & Christopher Davis Senr. his Security or either of them pay to the sd. plt. the said Sum & Costs. Als. Exec.

[page 136]

The Attachment granted Elizabeth Hamlin agst. the Estate of Simon Naylor is Continued till the next Court.

The action brot. by Joshua Irby agst. John Evans, the plt. failing to prosecute is Dismist.

The Attachment granted Peter Wynne agst. the Estate of Saml. Sentall is Continued till the next Court.

The attachment granted Henry Harrison agst. the Estate of George Ivie the plt. failing to prosecute is Dismist.

In the action brot. by Joshua Irby agst. Peter Wynne for Seaven hundred forty five pounds of Tobacco Due by Assumpsit &c the Deft. haveing pleaded non Assumpsit and the plt. Joining in the Issue and the sd. partys Submitting themselves to the Court for Tryall, who after haveing heard the several proofs & allegations and the plt. proveing only a triviall and inconsiderable Sum to be Due and that the Defendt. assumed as further, are of Opinion the same is not Actionable and thereupon Dismist the suit.

The Sherr: makes return of the appraisement of the Estate of John Perry Attacht. for Mr. Richard Bland. Ordered it be recorded, Vizt.

The Estate of John Perry Attached pr. Mr. Richard Bland Appraised by us the
Subscribers being first Sworn by Mr. John Hardyman, this 6: Day of June 1717, Vizt.

1 feather bed and furniture with bedstead & Cord	£3.12.0
1 Chest and Table 12/.	0.12.0
4 Dishes and 5 plates & two porringers & 3 Spoons	1.3.0
1 Skillet 6/, 1 Iron pot & frying pan, 1 Spit & 1 pr. fire Tongs 19/	1.0.10
1 Spining Wheel 4/, 3 chairs 4/6, and 3 Stools at 18. & 6 glass bottles 2/	0.12.0
	£6.19.10

[signed] William [his WR mark] Raines, John Woodleife, John [his B mark] Bonner.
Truly recorded. Test W. Hamlin, Cl. Cur.

The Order that the Sherr: return his proceedings in the sale of Sadler's Estate is Continued till the next Court.

In the action brot. by Elizabeth Jones agst. Robert Jones Executor of the Last Will and Testament of William Jones Deced: for two Steers given to the sd. plt. by the Last Will and Testament of the sd. Deced: The Defendt. haveing filed a Demurrer & plea to the plts. Declaration and she Joining therein and the Demurrer aforesaid being argued by the Attornys of the said partys is Overruled, whereupon A Jury to try the Issue on the Defendts. plea was Impanneled and Sworn by Name John Poythres, [John] [Pook]

[page 137]

Thomas Lewis, William Harrison, William Batte, William Reves, Joshua Irby, Arthur Biggins, John Bonner, Edward Wyatt, Adam Tapley & John Gerrald, who haveing heard the Evidence and reced: their charge were sent out and soon after return into Court & brot. in their Verdict, We find for the plt. Damage four pounds three Shillings and four pence Sterl: John Poythres foreman, which Verdict on the motion of the plts. Attorney is recorded, and thereupon it is Ordered that the said Defendt. Executor as aforesaid pay to the sd. plaintiff the said Sum of four pounds three Shillings and four pence Sterl: out of the said Decendts. Estate togather with Costs. als. Executed.

The order that John Nance return an accot. Dr. & Cr. of the Estate of John Nance Deced: is Continued till the next Court.

In the action brot. by John Hatch against John Nance Administrator with the Will annext. of John Nance Deced: for three pounds three Shillings and Eleaven pence Due by accot. the Defendt. haveing pleaded *plene Administravit* and the plt. Joining in the Issue the same was Submitted to the Court for Tryall and the Deft. failing to prove and make good his said plea and the plt. makeing Oath the said Sum is Justly Due to him thereupon it's Ordered that the sd. Defendt. Admr. as aforesaid pay to the said plt. the said Sum & Costs out of the said Decedts. Estate. Als. Exec:

Ordered that Martha Holycross be acquitted from paying Leavy for her Negro Woman for the future.

Ordered that Robert Brawn be Exempt from paying Leavy for the future.

In the action of Debt Depending between Thomas Goodwyn Assignee of Joseph Smith plt. and John Mayes Defendt. for three pounds Due by Bill Dated the 20th day of October 1714, the Defendt. haveing pleaded payment and the plt. Joining in the Issue the same was Submitted to the Court for Tryall and the Deft. proveing a Discount of thirty One Shillings and Eight pence thereupon Judgemt. is granted the plt. agst. the Deft. for the Residue being twenty Eight Shillings and four pence, and it's Ordered that the sd. Defendt. pay to the sd. plt. the said Sum of twenty Eight Shillings and four pence with Costs. Als. Exec:

The action brot. by Thomas Webb Exr. &c of Giles Webb Deced: agst. Henry Randolph the plt. failing to prosecute, is Dismist.

The action brot. by William ffarrar agst. Henry Randolph the plt. failing to prosecute is Dismist.

In the action of Debt brot. by John Cargill Assignee of Peter Wynne Admr. of the Estate of Joshua Wynne Deced: agst Elizabeth Parham Executrix of the Last Will and Testament of Thomas Parham Deced: for Six hundred pounds of Tobacco Due by Bill Dated the 17 day of March 1713/4, the Defendt. failing to appear pursuant to the Conditionall Judgemt. and Order therein of the Last Court, and the plt. makeing Oath the said Sum is Justly Due, thereupon Judgemt. is granted and Confirmed agst. the Deft. Exor. as aforesaid and Richard Hamlin Sherr: for the said Sum, and it is Ordered that the said Defendt. Exr. as aforesaid and Richard Hamlin Sherr: or either pay to the sd. plt. the said Sum and Costs. Als. Exec:

[page 138]

Judgemt. being this Day past unto John Cargill against Richard Hamlin Sherr: of Prince Geo. County for Six hundred pounds of Tobacco & Costs of Suit by reason of the non appearance of Elizabeth Parham at the suit of the said Cargill, On the motion of the sd. Richard Hamlin an Attachmt. is granted him agst. the Estate of the said Parham for the said Sum & Costs returnable to this next Court for Judgemt.

Richard Womack haveing attended one day as an Evidence for Robert Jones in the action brot. agst. him by Elizabeth Jones, therefore it's Ordered that the said Robert Jones pay to the sd. Womack for the Same forty pounds of Tobacco and Costs. Als. Exec:

And then the Court Adjourn'd till Court in Course. Jno. Poythres. Test Wm. Hamlin, Cl. Cur.

At a Court holden at Merchantshope for the County of Prince
George on the second Tuesday in August being the thirteenth Day of
the said month Anno Dom: 1717.

William Gower appeared in Open Court and acknowledged his Deeds of Lease & Release of Land (Indented and Sealed) to Lewis Green and his heirs on whose motion the same are ordered to be recorded.

The action Depending between Thomas Goodwyn Assignee of Jos. Smith & John Mayes, (the plt. failing to prosecute) is Dismist.

In the action Depending between Jerremiah Turner &c and Francis Mallory for four pounds and Six pence Current money Due by accot. the Deft. haveing had time given him (at the Last Court), till this Court to plead and being now called to do the same did not appear nor offer any thing in barr or preclusion of the plts. action therefore it's considered by the Court that the plt. recover against the sd. Defendt. the aforesaid Sum & Costs unless he shall appear at the next court and answer the sd. Action.

In the suit in Chancery brot. by Thomas Goodwyn agst. Jos. Smith and Cornelius Cargill at the Last Court time was given the sd. Cargill till this Court to answer the Complainants Bill and being now called and failing to answer to the sd. Bill on the motion of the Complainants Attorney an Attachment is granted him

[page 139]

against the Body of the sd. respondt. returnable to the next Court.

The suit in Chancery brot. by Thomas Goodwyn agst. Jos. Smith & ffra. Mallory is referred till the next Court.

In the suit in Chancery brot. by Charles Anderson agst. Henry Offley Late of London Merchant and John Poythres Surviveing Exr. of the Last Will &c of John Poythres Deced:, Thomas Simmons sub Sherr: makes Oath to the service of the writt on the said Poythres and he failing to appear an Attachmt. is granted the Complainant against the Body of the sd. Poythres returnable to the next Court and it's Ordered that a resummons Issue agst. the sd. Offley returnable to the next Court.

The attachment granted Randle Platt agst. the Estate of Nicho. Overby junr. is continued till next Court.

The action brot. by Phillip Claud agst. Thomas Goodwyn the plt. failing to prosecute is Dismist.

In the action of Tresspass on the case brot. by John Pook agst. Thomas Goodwyn, ffrancis Mallory and George Hambleton are chose by the sd. partys and appointed by the Court to meet and setle the Difference between the sd. partys and make report of their proceedings therein to the next Court.

In the action on the case Depending between John Pook and John Poythres, ffrancis Mallory and George Hambleton are chose by the sd. partys and appointed by the Court to meet and setle the Difference between the sd. plts. and Deft. and make report of their proceedings therein to the next Court.

In the action of & Depending between Edward Goodrich and Mary Norten Admx. &c of ffrances Norten Deced: for forty Shillings Due by Bill &c the Deft. being called and not appearing nor any Security returned for her on the motion of the plt. Judgemt. is granted him agst. the said Defendt. and Richard Hamlin Sherr: &c for the sd. Sum & Costs unless the sd. Deft appears at the next Court and answers the sd. action.

In the action Depending between David Crawley and Mary Norten Admx. &c of ffrancis Norten Deced: for four pounds and Eleaven pence Due by accot. &c the Deft. being called and not appearing nor any Security for her, on the motion of the plts. Attorney Judgemt. is granted him agst. the sd. Deft. and Richd. Hamlin Sherr: for the sd. Sum & Costs unless the sd. Deft. shall appear at the next Court and answer the sd. action.

In the suit in Chancery brot. by Robert Munford agst. Henry Offley Late of London Mercht. and Robert Bolling, the sd. Bolling on his motion has time till the next Court to answer the Complainants Bill, and it's Ordered that a resummons Issue agst. the sd. Offley returnable to the next Court.

The action brot. by Phillip Burrow agst. John Smith, neither party appearing is Dismist.

The action brot. by Adam Tapley agst. Randle Platt, the plt. failing to prosecute is Dismist.

[page 140]

An[n] Williams's relinquishmt. of her right to the Administration of the Estate of her deced: Husband Wm. Williams, to her son Cha. Williams was proved in Court by the Oath of Edward Goodrich And Ordered to be recorded, Vizt. Worthy Gents. I doe hereby relinquish my right of Admo. of my Deced: husband William Williams Estate, and Desire the same may be granted to my son Charles. Witness my hand this 13 Augst. 1717. [signed] Ann [A] Williams marke. [Wits.] E. Goodrich. To the Wr'full Justices of Pr. Geo. Court.

Charles Williams came into Court and made Oath that William Williams deced: dyed without any Will as farr as he knows or believes and upon his giveing Security as the Law Directs it's Ordered that a Certificate be granted him for Obtaining Letters of Administration in Due form, whereupon John Pook became his security and with him entred into bond accordingly.

Gilbert Hay, James Harrison, William Harrison and Robert Hobbs or any three of them being first Sworn by some Justice for that purpose, are Ordered to appraise the Estate of Wm. Williams Deced: and make report of their proceedings therein to the next Court when Charles Wms. the Administsrator is Ordered to return the Inventory.

William Grigg appeared in Open Court and acknowledged his Deed for Land (Indented and Sealed) with Livery of Seizin Endorst thereon, to John Peterson and his heirs on whose motion the same are Ordered to be recorded, and then also appeared in Court Susan the wife of the sd. Grigg and being first privately Examined acknowledged the sd. Deed and relinquisht to the sd. Peterson her right of Dower in and to the said Land &c in the sd. Deed mentioned, which by Order of the Court is Likewise recorded.

The action brot. by Kath: Williams agst. Richard Hamlin (the Deft. failing pleavin abatement &c and the plt. thereupon failing to prosecute) is Dismist.

On the petition of John Peterson setting forth that he has Land one One side of Balys runn convenient to Erect a water Mill on, and praying an Order of this Court for One Acre of Land on the other side the said runn beloniging to the Heirs of Joseph Holycross Deced: convenient for the sd. use, Martha Holycross Mother of the sd. Heirs was by Order of the Last Court Summoned to appear at this Court and answer the said Petition, and she signifying to the Court by an attested Note under her hand that she is willing thereto, It's Ordered thereupon that Robert Poythres and Edward Mitchell Lay out one Acre of the sd. Land for the purpose aforesaid and Value the same, and upon the said Petersons paying the Value thereof, to put him into possession of the sd. Acre of Land.

[page 141]
In the action Depending between Cornelius Cargill and George Brewer, the Deft. being permitted to plead Doubly, pleads in writing to the plts. Declaration who has time till the next Court to consider the same.

Robert Davis in Open Court acknowledged his Deed for Land (Indented and Sealed) wth. Livery of Seizen endorst thereon, to John Hardyman and his heirs on whose motion the same is Ordered to be recorded, And then also appeared in Court Elizabeth the wife of the said Robert and being first privately Examined freely relinquisht. to the said Hardyman her right of Dower in & to the Lands &c in the sd. Deed mentioned, which is Likewise Ordered to be recorded.

The order of the Last Court concerning the proveing of the Last Will &c of Jane Tomlinson Deced: late wife of Wm. Tomlinson, which was then objected agst. by Adam Taply Eldest Son of the sd. Deced: for reasons to be Shewn at this Court (neither of the partys therein concernine, appearing) is made Null & Void.

On the petition of John Westbrook for and in behalfe of Henry and Margarett Westbrook Orphans & Children of James Westbrook Deced: now under the care of Joshua Irby, setting forth that the sd. Irby unlawfully Detains the sd. Orphans as Sarvants and them doth abuse in a most Violent and gross manner, and praying the sd. Orphans (as they are not Lawfully bound) may be released from their Servitude and barbarous useage. And the said Irby being summoned to answer to the sd. Complt. and he being called and failing to appear, thereupon it's Ordered that the sd. Orphans be acquitted and released from any further service to the sd. Irby and for & Dureing their Minority to remain wth. the sd. John Westbrook.

In the action of Debt brot. by Edward Goodrich agst. John Lett for Six hundred and Eighty pounds of Tobacco Due by Bill &c the Defendt. being called and not appearing pursuant to the Conditionall Judgement and Order therin of the Last Court the plt. makeing Oath the said sum is Justly Due thereupon it's Ordered that the sd. John Lett pay to the sd. Edwd. Goodrich the aforesaid Sum of Six hundred and Eighty pounds of Tobacco and Costs. Als. Exec:

The Order of the Last Court concerning the Appraismt. &c of the Estate of Martin Sheffeild Attacht. &c for James Jones junr. is made Null & Void the Deft. haveing paid his Dr. to the plt.

Major Robert Munford, Guardian to Martha Tucker an Orphan Girle appears in Court and gives Bond and Security for the performance of his trust &c.

The action Depending between Benjamin Ray et Uxor plts. and John Doby Deft. is referred till the next Court, the Deft. paing ths cost of this reference.

The Attachment granted Peter Wynne agst. the Estate of Saml. Sentall is Continued till next Court.

[page 142]
In the action of Debt brot. by Elizabeth Hamlin agst. Simon Naylor for four Barrels of Indian Corn Due by Bill &c the Defendt. being returned *non est Inventus* and not appearing at a former Court an Attachmt. was granted the plt. agst. the sd. Defts. Estate for the sd. Sum returnable to this Court for Judgemt. and the sd. Attachmt. being now returned Executed on part thereof, Vizt. One pewter Dish, and the sd. Deft. appearing replevye the same, and he haveing paid ten bushells and an halfe of the said corn since the Entry of the sd. action and Confessing Judgemt. to the plt. for the residue thereupon it's Ordered that the sd. Deft. pay to the plt. Nine bushells and an halfe of Indian corn being the residue as aforesaid and Ball: Due on the sd. Bill togather with Costs. Als. Exec:

The order that John Nance Admr. &c of John Nance Deced: return an Accot. Dr. & Cr. of the sd. Deceds. Estate is Continued till next Court.

The Attachmt. granted Richard Hamlin Sherr: agst. the Estate of Elizabeth Parram [Parham] is Continued till next Court.

In the action of Debt brot. by George Robertson against [James?] Thweatt, Thomas Simmons became Speciall Bail for the sd. Deft. whereupon Oyer of the plts. Bond is granted him and time till the next Court to Consider the Same.

The action on the case Depending between David Crawley and James Thweatt, the plt. failing to prosecute, is Dismist.

In the action of Trespass on the case brot. by Kathrine Bristow and Robert Bristow Executors of the Last Will and Testament of Robert Bristow junr. Esqr. Deced: and ffrancis Willis agst. Randle Platt and Henrietta his wife Executrix of the Last Will and Testament of John Taylor Deced: for fifty Seaven pounds four pence Sterling, Due from the Estate of the sd. Deced: John Taylor to the sd. plts. in their said Capacity by accot. Dated from the sixth Day of November One thousand Seaven hundred and One, to the twenty first Day of March One thousand Seaven hundred and four, the sd. plts. and Defendts. being called the sd. Randle Platt appeared and Confest Judgemt. to the plts. for the said Sum thereupon it's Ordered that the sd. Defendants pay to the said plts: out of the Estate of the sd. John Taylor Deced: the aforesaid Sum of fifty Seaven pounds and four pence Sterl: together with Costs. Als. Exec:

    The action brot. by Mathew Marks agst. Edwd. Wyatt, neither party appearing is Dismist.

[page 143]

    In the action brot. by John Peterson agst. John Nance Admr. &c of John Nance deced: an Imparlance is granted the sd. Deft. till the next Court.

    In the action of Deninue brot. by Mary Batte agst. James Parram, an Imparl: is granted the Defendt. till the next Court.

    Mr. John Hardyman is appointed Overseer of the Highways and Bridges over Carltons Swamp, Instead of John Woodleife.

    And then the Court Adjourn'd till Court in Course. John Hamlin. Test W. Hamlin, Cl. Cur.

At a Court held at Merchantshope for the County of Prince George on
the second Teusday in September being the tenth Day of the month 1717:

Present	Robert Munford,	Robert Hall,	Robert Bolling }	
	James Thweatt	Lewis Green junr.	& John Peterson	Gent. Justices

Robert Coleman on his motion is acquitted from paying County Leavy for the future.

Henry King on his motion is acquitted from paying County Leavy for the future.

Thomas Lewis on his motion is acquitted from paying County Leavy for the future.

    In the action on the case brot. by Jerremiah Turner Master and Comander of the Ship *Spotswood* against Francis Mallory for four pounds and Six pence Due by accot. dated 1715, at the Last Court the Defendt. failing to appear or offer any thing in barr or preclusion of the plts. action thereupon Judgement was granted him by *Nihil Dicit* and the sd. Deft. being now called appears and Vacates the sd. Judgemt. and makes Oath that there is Due to the plt. only thirty Shillings on ball. of his accot., whereupon it's Ordered by the Court that the sd. Francis Mallory pay to the sd. Jeremiah Turner the sd. Sum of thirty Shillings with Costs. Als. Exec:

    Thomas Goodwyn's Letter of Attorney to Capt. Henry Harrison was proved in Court by the Oath of Edward Goodrich, and is Ordered to be recorded.

    In the suit in Chancery brot. by Thomas Goodwyn agst. Jos. Smith and Cornelius Cargill, at the Last Court the Defendt. failing to answer to the Complainants bill on the motion of his Attorney an Attachment was granted him agst. the body of the said respondt. returnable to this Court and he still failing to appear &c on the motion of [the] said Attorney it's Ordered that another Attachment issue agst. the sd. respondt. returnable to next Court.

[page 144]

    The suit in Chancery brot. by Thomas Goodwyn agst. Jos. Smith & ffrancis Mallory, is Continued till next Court.

    In the suit in Chancery brot. by Charles Anderson agst. Henry Offley Late of London Merchant and John Poythres Surviveing Executor of the Last Will and Testaement of John Poythres Deced: the said Complainant and the respondt. Poythres appearing, the sd. Poythres Executor of the aforesaid Confesses to have in his hands of the said Offley's Estate sufficient to pay the Complainants Debt being Nineteen pounds one Shilling and three pence Sterl: Due from the said Offley, which the sd. Complainant makes Oath is Justly Due to him and which also appears by an accot. under the sd. Offley's hand, wherefore it's Ordered by the Court that upon the Complainants giveing the said Poythres Security to Indemnifie him agst. the said Offley for so much, the said Complainant do recover against the sd. Respondts. Executor as aforesaid his said Debt and Costs to be paid out of the said Offleys Estate in his hands and possession, and thereupon the said Anderson enters into bond with Security accordingly.

    Ordered that a road be cleared from the upper Inhabitants of Nottoway River in unto Appomattox river, with respect to the conveniency of the Inhabitants of Stony Creek, Gravelly runn and Hatchers runn, and that William Davis be Overseer thereof.

    Major Munford is Appointed Overseer of Rowanty Road.

    Robert Abbernathy Senr. is appointed Overseer of the road from Stony Creek to Monksneck.

    The Attachment granted Randle Platt agst. the Estate of Nicholas Overby Neither party appearing is Dismist.

    In the action on the case brot. by John Pook agst. Thomas Goodwyn for Scandalous words Spoke of the plt. by the sd. Deft. at the Last Court ffrancis Mallory and George Hambleton were chose and appointed to Settle this

Difference between the said partys and Ordered he make report of their proceedings to this Court, who accordingly make the following report, Vizt.

Pr. Geo. County Sct.

In Obedience to an Order of this County Court Dated the 13 this Instant, We the Subscribers have this Day met Setled and adjusted the Difference Depending between John Pook and Thomas Goodwyn and are of Opinion (haveing heard the proofs and Allegations of both partys) that John Pook is not any ways Damnified by the words Spoke by Capt. Thomas Goodwyn agst. him nor Does his witnesses prove the said Goodwyn ever Spoke any Such words are are mentioned in his said Declaration. Given under our hands this 19 of Augst. 1717. [signed] Francis Mallory, George Hambleton. Thereupon on the motion of the Defts. atto: the Suit is Dismist.

[page 145]

In the action on the case brot. by John Pook against John Poythres for two hundred pounds of Tobacco Due for the striping two weighty hds. of Tobacco &c at the Last Court ffrancis Mallory and George Hambleton were chose and appointed to Settle the Difference between the said partys and Ordered to make report of their proceedings to this Court, who accordingly make the following report, Vizt.

Pr. Geo. County Sct.

In Obedience to an Order of this County Court Dated the 13 Instant, We the Subscribers have this Day met Setled and Adjusted the Difference Depending between John Pook plt. and John Poythres Defendt. and are of opinion that the said Poythres Oought [sic] to pay the said Pook one hundred and forty pounds of Tobacco. Given under our hands this 19 August. 1717. [signed] Fran. Mallory, Geo. Hambleton. Whereupon Judgement is granted the plt., the said Defendt. for the said Sum and it's Ordered that the said John Poythres pay to the said John Pook the said Sum of one hundred and forty pounds of Tobacco and Costs. Als. Exec:

In the action of Debt brot. by Edward Goodrich against Mary Norten Admx. of the Goods and Chattels of Francis Norten Deced: for forty Shillings Due by bill Dated the 20 Day of June 1716, the sd. Defendt. appearing vacates the Conditionall Judgemt. and Order of the Last Court, and she failing to make any Legall plea or Discount to the sd. Bill thereupon it's Ordered that the said Mary pay to the said plt. out of the said Decedts. Estate the sd. Sum of forty Shillings and Costs. Als. Exec:

The action of ye case brot. by David Crawley agst. Mary Norten Admx. &c of ffrancis Norten Deced: (the plt. failing to prosecute) is Dismist.

The Order that Charles Williams Admr. of Wm. Williams's Estate return an Inventory thereof, is Continued till next Court.

In the action brot. by Cornelius Cargill agst. Geo. Brewer, the sd. plt. Joins in the Demurrer and first plea of the Defendt. and files a Demurrer to the second plea of the sd. Defendt. who also Joins therein, and the whole are referred till the next Cort. to be Tryed.

In the action brot. by Benjamin Ray and Sarah his wife agst. John Doby for that the said John on or abt. the 1[2] day of March Last past in the Parrish of Westover and County of Prince George those false & Scandalous English words & Lyes following in the presence of hearing of many Leige people of Our Lord the King did Openly and publicly Speak and Declare, Vizt. that she (the said Sarah Ray meaning) is a thief and hath Lately S[t]olen out of his house a New Cotton Shift, a Coat, a Pillowbarr, an Apron and a handkerchiefe, and he (meaning the said John) would prove the same, when as she the said Sarah never was Guilty of the said Theft or robbery or any other whatsoever and by reason of which false feigned and Scandalous words aforesaid by him the sd. John Spoken the sd. Benja. Ray and Sarah his wife is much hurt and Damge hath sustained to the Value of fifty pounds

[page 146]

as is set forth in the plts. Declaration, the Defendt. by his Attorney appeared and pleaded not Guilty and for Tryall put himself upon the County and the plt. Likewise whereupon a Jury was Impannelled and Sworn to try the matter [at] Issue by Name Lewis Green, Wm. Batte, John Lewis, Barthow: Crowder, Thomas Booth, Nicho. Overby, Wm. Short, Wm. Davis, Richard Reece, John Cuerton, Benjamin ffoster, & Wm. Cuerton, who haveing heard the Evidence and reced. their charge were sent [out] and some after return into Court & brought in their Verdict, We find for the Plaintiff five pounds Sterl: Lewis Green, fforeman, which Verdict on the motion of the plts. Attorney is recorded. And thereupon it's Considered by the Court that the plts. recover against the said Defendant the aforesaid Sum of five pounds Sterl: being their Damage aforesaid by the Jurors in manner aforesaid assessed, with Costs. Als. Exec:

Whereupon the Defendt. moves in arrest of Judgement and for cause Shews the following reasons, Which are referred till the next Court to be Argued.

Pr. Geo. County Sct.   Sept. Court 1717

In the suit Depending between Benjamin Ray and Sarah his Wife plts. and John Doby Defendt. wherein the Jury have assessed for the plts. five pounds Sterl: Damages, and on which the Court have given Judgement with Costs, the Deffendt. therefore humbly moves to arrest the said Judgment for the reasons following, Vizt.

First.   For that it is not alledged in the Declaration that the words said to be therein Spoken by the Defendt. were Spoken of the plts. or either of them but only in the following words that (she the sd. Sarah Ray meaning) is a thief &c which is not a sufficient Declaration in Law to maintain their action.

2ndly.   For that the Jury who tryed the Issue Assessed their Damages for the plt. Generally, whereas part of the words in the Declaration mentioned were not proved to be Spoken by the Defendt. and therefore they ought to have given Damages only for the words that were Spoken by him.

[signed] Thos. Eldridge, for the Deft.

The Attachment granted Peter Wynne agst. the Estate of Samuell Sentall, the plt. failing to prosecute is Dismist.

Robert Munford and John Butler prove their accot. agst. the Estate of Thomas Sadler Deced: for three pounds thirteen Shillings and Eleaven pence, therefore Ordered that the sd. Munford's bill of four pounds two Shillings pa[ss] to the Sherr: for goods bt. of the said Estate be Delivered him (for payment of the sd. Suit and Costs) and that he pay the Ballance Due to the said Estate being Six shillings & one penny (after ye Charges Deducted) to Hen: Batte.

John Hatch haveing proved his accot. agst. the Estate of Thomas Sadler Deced: for three pounds Nine Shillings, therefore Ordered that Thomas Simmon's Bill past to the Sherr: for four pounds ten Shillings, for goods bot. of the said Estate be Delivered him for payment of all sd. Sum and that he pay the Ballance Due to the Estate being Nineteen Shillings after the Charge Deducted, vizt. Six Shillings & Nine pence to John Peterson, two & four pence to Henry Batte and Nine and Eleaven pence to the Sherriff.

[page 147 (Copy from Reel 7)]

Henry and William Batte haveing proved their accots. against the Estate of Thomas Sadler deced: for thirty Six Shillings and Seaven pence, therefore Ordered that their Bill of thirty one Shillings and two pence past to the Sherr: for goods bought of the said Estate be delivered them for payment of the said Sum & Costs, and Six Shillings and one penny in the hands of Robert Munford, and two Shillings and four pence in the hands of John Hatch.

John Peterson proves his accot. agst. the Estate of Thomas Sadler Deced: for forty Shillings and five pence, therefore Ordered that his bill of thirty five Shillings and Eight pence past to the Sherr: for goods bought of the said Estate be Delivered him for payment of the said Sum and Costs, and Six Shillings and Nine pence in the hands of Mr. Hatch.

Elizabeth Anderson being Summoned an Evidence for Benjamin Ray and Sarah his wife plts. against John Doby Deft. and haveing attended one Day, Ordered that the said Benjamin pay her for the same the sum of forty pounds of Tobacco wth. Costs. Als. Exec:

In the suit in chancery brot. by Robert Munford agst. Henry Offley and Robert Bolling, the sd. Bolling files a plea to the plts. Bill &c who has time till the next Court to Consider the same.

The order that John Nance Admr. of the Estate of John Nance Deced: return an accot. Dr. & Cr. of the sd. Decedts. Estate is Continued till next Court.

The attachment granted Richard Hamlin Sherr: &c agst. the Estate of Elizabeth Parram is Continued till next Court.

In the action of Debt brot. by George Robertson agst. James Thweatt for Sixteen thousand three hundred and fifty two pounds of Tobacco Due by Bond &c at the Last Court time was given the Defendt. till this Court to plead and being now called to do the same did not appear or offer any thing in Barr of the plts. action, therefore it's Considered by the Court that the plts. recover agst. the sd. Deft. the said Sum & Costs, unless he shall appear at the next Court and answer the said action.

In the action on the case brot. by John Peterson agst. John Nance Admr. &c of John Nance Deced: for three pounds Due by accot. &c at the Last Court time was given the Deft. till this Court to plead and being now called to do the same did not appear or offer any thing in barr of the plts. action. Therefore it's Considered by the Court that the plt. recover agst the sd. Deft. the sd. Sum & Costs, unless he shall appear at the next Court and answer the said Action.

In the action of Detinue brot. by Mary Batte agst. James Parram, the Deft. pleads *non Detinet*, and the plt. Joining in the Issue the same is referred till the next Court for Tryall.

And then the Court Adjourn'd till Court in Course. John Poythres. Test Wm. Hamlin, Cl. Cur.

[page 148]

Att a Court held at Merchantshope for the County of Prince George on
the second Tuesday in October being the Eighth Day of the month, 1717.

Present   John Poythres,   Randle Platt,   Robert Munford }
                 Robert Bolling,   James Thweatt,   John Peterson & }
                  Lewis Green Junr.   Gent. Justices.

Dick, a Negro Boy, Belonging to ffrancis Epes is adjudged twelve years old.

In the action of Trover &c brot. by Joseph Fowler agst. Barth. Crowder the Defendt. being permitted to plead Severall pleas, files his pleas to the plts. Declaration who has time till the next Court to Consider the same.

In the action on ye Case brought by Richard Hyde and Mary his wife against David Jones Surviveing Executor of the Last Will and Testament of Benjamin Evans Deced: for fourteen pounds Eleaven Shillings and Seven pence Curt. money Due by accot. Dated from the Second Day of June 1714 to the twentyeth of Aprill 1717, Inclusive, the sd. David Executor as aforesaid appears in Court and Confesses Judgement to the plts. for the sum of thirteen pounds Sixteen Shillings and Seaven pence Curt. money being the Ballance of their account. Thereupon it is Ordered that the said Executor pay to the plts. out of the said Decedts. Estate the said Sum of thirteen pounds Sixteen Shillings & Seaven pence Current money with Costs. Als. Exec:

In the actoin of Trespass brot. by John Berry et Uxor agst. Stephen Evans, an Imparlance is granted the said Deft. till the next Court.

In the action of Trespass brot. by John Berry against George Crook, an Imparlance is granted the sd. Deft. till the next Court.

James Lundy appeared in Open Court and acknowledged his Deed (Indented and Sealed) with Livery of Seizin endorst. thereon, to David Meadows and his heirs on whose motion the same is Admitted to record. And then also appeared in Court Elizabeth the Wife of the said James and being first privately Examined freely relinquisht. to the said David her right of Dower in and to the Lands &c in the sd. Deed mentioned, which is Ordered to be recorded.

In the suit in Chancery brot. by John Lewis Junr. agst. Henry Offley and Robert Bolling, the said Bolling has time till the next Court to answer the Complainants Bill.

[page 149]

In the action of Trespass brought by Cornelius Cargill against William Cuerton, the said Defendt. appears and pleads not Guilty, and the plt. Joining in the Issue, the same is thereupon referred till the next Court for Tryall.

In the action on the case brot. by Robert Bolling agst. Stephen Evans, for five hundred pounds of Tobacco Due by Accot. the Defendt. appeard. and Confest. Judgement to the plt. for the said Sum, therefore it is Ordered that the said Stephen Evans pay to the said Robert Bolling the said Sum & Costs. Als. Exec.

The action brot. by Da[niel] Vaughn agst. Cornelius Fox, neither party appearing, is Dismist.

The action on the case brot. by Richard Bland agst. Nicholas Brewer junr., neither party appearing, is Dismist.

James Thweatt vrs. William Grigg, retraxit.

The action on the case brot. by Richard Hyde et Uxor agst. David Jones, Surviveing Executor &x of Ben: Evans Deced: neither party appearing is Dismist.

In the action of Debt brot. by John Hatch agst. Charles Williams Admr. &c of William Williams Deced: Oyer of the plts: Bill is granted the Defendt. and time till the next Court to Consider the same.

In the action of Debt brot. by Richard Pigeon agst. Charles Williams Admr. &c of William Williams Deced: Oyer of the plts: Bill is granted the Defendt. and time till the next Court to Consider the same.

In the action of Debt brot. by George Pasmore against Charles Williams Administrator of the Goods and Chattels of William Williams Deced: for One pound ten Shillings and Nine pence Due by Bill Dated the Ninth Day of February 1711/12, the Deft. appearing and failing to make any Legall plea and the plt. makeing Oath the said Sum is Justly Due, thereupon it is Ordered that the said Defendt. Admr. as aforesaid pay to the said plt. out of the said Decedts. Estate the said Sum & Costs. Als. Exec.

In the action of Debt brot. by John Allen agst. Charles Williams Admr. of Wm. Williams' Deced: Oyer of the plts. Bill is granted the Defendt. and time till the next Court to Consider the same.

[page 150]

In the suit in Chancery brot. by Thomas Goodwyn agst. Jos. Smith and Cornelius Cargill, the said Cargill appears and files his answer upon Oath and on the motion of the Complainants Attorney time is granted him till the next Court to Consider the same.

The suit in Chancery brot. by Thomas Goodwyn agst. Jos. Smith & ffrancis Mallory is Continued till the next Court.

Present John Hamlin, Gent. Just.

In the action on the case Depending between Cornelius Cargill and George Brewer, the Deft. haveing Demurred to the plts. Declaration and he Joining therein the same was referred till this Court to be argued, and the sd. partys now appearing & and the Demurrer aforesaid being argued by their Attorneys, is adjudged good, whereupon the suit is Dismist. with Costs.

Randle Platt made complaint that John Middleton stands Justly Indebted to him by Bill Dated 20th Day of May 1714, the sum of Six hundred & twenty nine pounds of Tobacco, And set forth that the said John hath unlawfully Departed this County so that the Ordinary process at Law cannot be served on him, whereupon he by Virtue of an Attachment and on hand of one of his Majestys Justices of the peace for this County returnable to thie Court hath caused part of the Estate of the said John to be attacht. for payment thereof, Vizt. two Cows and one yearlling heifer, and the said John being called and failing to appear to replevye the same, and ye said plt. makeing Oath the said sum is Justly Due to him, Thereupon Judgement is granted him agst the said John Middleton for the said Sum & Costs. Ordered that the sherr: cause the said Cattle to be Duly appraised by John Smith, William Jackson, James Niblet and James Bell or any three of them (being first Sworn for that purpose) and Delivered the plt. for and towards the payment of the said Sum & Costs, and make report of his proceedings herein to the next Court.

James Parram in Open Court acknowledged his receit. to Lewis Green which is Ordered to be recorded.

Lewis Green and Ephraim Parram in Open Court acknowledged their Deed (Indented and Sealed) with Livery of Seizin endorst. thereon, to Lewis Green Junr. on whose motion the same is Ordered to be recorded.

[page 151]

The Last Will and Testament of John Wall Deced: was presented into Court by Sarah his Relict and Executrix named in the sd. Will, who made Oath thereto, and it being proved by the Oaths of John Livesay, John Cleton and Phillip Claud is Ordered to be recorded and upon the said Executrix's giveing security and according to Law it's Ordered that a Certificate be granted her for Obtaining a probate in Due form, whereupon Thomas Wicks and Phillip Claud became her securety and with her entred into Bond &c.

Edmond Irby, Arthur Biggins, Daniel Higdon and David Goodgame or any three of them are Ordered to appraise the Estate of John Wall Deced: (they being first sworn for that purpose) and make report of their proceedings therein to the next court when Sarah Wall the Executrix is Ordered to return the Inventory.

Charles Williams Admr. of William Williams Deced: returns upon Oath an Inventory &c of the said Decedts. Estate, which is Ordered to be recorded.

Edward Burchet proves his accot. agst. the Estate of Thomas Sadler Deced: for twenty Shillings and Six pence therefore Ordered that the Sherr: pay the said Burchet the said Sum & Costs out of the said Decedts. Estate.

Ordered that the Sheriff Summon a Grandjury of twenty four freeholders of this County to appear at the next Court.

In the action brought by Benjamin Ray and Sarah his Wife agst. John Doby, at the Last Court Judgemt. past for the plts. agst. the said Defendt. for five pounds Sterling Damages, and the Defendt. moveing in arrest of Judgement and fileing his Errors the same were referred till this Court to be argued, and the said partys now appearing and the Errors aforesaid being argued by the Attorneys of the partys aforesaid are adjudged good & Sufficient to arrest the Judgemt. aforesaid, whereon the suit is Dismist with Costs.

The action on the case brot. by John Hatch agst. Charles Williams Admr. of William Williams Deced: the plt. failing to prosecute, is Dismist.

And then the Court Adjourn'd till Court in Course. John Hamlin. Test William Hamlin, Cl. Cur.

[page 152]

At a Court held at Merchantshope for the County of Prince
Geo: on Tuesday the twelfth Day of November 1717, being the second
Tuesday of the month.

Present	John Hamlin,	Randle Platt,	Robert Munford }	
	James Thweatt,	Lewis Green Junr.	& John Peterson }	Gent. Justices

The Last Will and Testament of Thomas Wheatley Deced: was presented into Court by James Baker One of the Executors therein Named who made Oath thereto and it being proved by the Oath of Adam Kirkwood one of the Witnesses thereto is admitted to record, and upon the said Executors giveing Security according to Law it is Ordered that Certificate be granted the said James Baker and Nathaniell Harrison Esqr. the Executors named in the said Will for Obtaining a Probate in Due form, whereupon Edward Goodrich became his security and with him entred into Bond accordingly.

James Bell, Edward Wyatt, Benja. Rix and Paul Jones or any three of them are ordered to appraise the Estate of Thomas Wheatley Deced: (they being first sworn for that purpose by some Justice of this County) and make report of their proceedings to the next Court, where[on] James Baker & Nathl. Harrison Esqr. the Exrs. are Ordered to return the Inventory.

Janey a Negro Girl belonging to Thomas Epes is adjudged Seaven years old.

James Parram in open Court acknowledged his Deed for Lease (Indented and Sealed) bearing Date the tenth of October Last past, with Livery of Seizin endorst thereon to Lewis Green Junr. and his heirs &c on whose motion the same is Ordered to be recorded.

William Temple in Open Court acknowledged his Deeds of Lease and Release to Land (Indented & Sealed) bearing Date the Eleaventh and twelfth Instant, to Samuel Temple and his heirs &c on whose motion the same are ordered to be recorded.

Elizabeth Parram Executrix of the Last Will and Testament of Thomas Parram Deced: returns upon Oath an Inventory [words removed] of the Estate of sd. Deceds. which is Ordered to be recorded.

[page 153]

James Thweatt in Open Court acknowledged his Deeds of Lease and Release of Land (Indented and Sealed [)] bearing Date the Eleaventh and twelfth Instant, to William Eaton and his heirs &c on whose motion the same are ordered to be recorded. And then also appeared in Court Judith the Wife of the said James Thweatt and being first privately Examined freely relinquisht. to the sd. Eaton her right of Dower in & to the Lands &c in the sd. Deed mentioned which is Likewise Ordered to be recorded.

Arthur Biggins in Open Court acknowledged his Deed for Land (Indented and Sealed[)], Date the thirteenth Day of August Last past, to Thomas W[eiks] and his heirs &c on whose motion the same is Ordered to be recorded. And then also appeared in Court Hester the wife of the sd. Biggins and being first privately Examined freely relinquisht. to the said Thomas her right of Dower in and to the Lands &c in the said Deed mentioned which is Likewise Ordered to be recorded.

Upon Examining the accot. Dr. & Cr. of the Estate of William Williams deced: It is the Opinion of the Court that if Charles Williams the Admr. prove that he received no sattisfaction of Robert and Saml. Clerke for the sum therein mentioned to be paid them and that it was the proper Debt of the Deced: then the said Article to be allowed him in the said accot.

Pursuant to the Direction of the Act concerning Jurys, a Grandjury was Impannelled and Sworn by Name John Scott, Thomas Simmons, Thomas Burge, Jas. Hall, John Tillman, John Lewis, John Wall, Barth. Crowder, Jos. Woodleife, George Crook, John Patteson, John Lett, Peter Gramer, Thomas Harrison & William Temple, who haveing reced: their charge withdrew and after some time spent therein return there presentments as follows, Vizt.

We present Hannah Headstead for haveing a Bastard Child.

We Likewise present Eliza. Daniel for haveing a Bastard Child.

We Likewise present Mary Aldridge for haveing a Bastard Child.

[signed] John Scott, foreman.

Ordered that the Sheriff give Notice of the said presentments to the Churchwardens of the Severall Parrishes where the said Women reside.

On the peto. of Peter Talbut for the Administration of the Estate of Michael Talbut Deced: it's Ordered that Michael Talbut eldest son of the said Deced: be Summoned to appear at the next Court to accept or refuse the sd. Administrat[ion].

[page 154]

John Tillman files a Bill in Chancery agst. George Tillman Administrator &c of Roger Tillman Deced: Ordered that he be sumoned to answer the sd. Bill at the next Court.

In the suit in Chancery Depending between Robert Munford Complt. and Henry Offley and Robt. Bolling Respondts. the sd. Complt. files a Demurrer to the plea of the respondt. on whose motion time is granted till the next Court to Consider the same.

John Nance Admr. &c of John Nance Deced: files the accot. Dr. & Cr. of the sd. Decedts. Estate which is referred till the next Court to be Considered and Examined.

In the action of Debt Depending between Geo. Robertson and James Thweat, at a former Court Oyer of the plts. Bond was granted the Deft. and the sd. plt. haveing failed fileing the same, thereupon its Ordered that he now file the sd. Bond, which he accordingly does, and time is granted the Deft. till the next Court to plead.

The action on ye case brot. by John Peterson agst. John Nance Admr. &c of John Nance Deced: is Continued till next Court.

Resolved that the Court will Lay the County Leavy at the next Court in Course.

John Wall is appointed Overseer of the Highways instead of Wm. Davis.

The Attachment granted Richard Hamlin Sherr: &c agst. the Estate of Elizabeth Parram is Continued till the next Court.

Ordered that Henry Peoples be Summoned to appear at the next Court to take the Oath of a Constable instead of Cornelius Cargill.

And then the Court Adjourn'd till Court in Course. Jno. Hamlin. Test Wm. Hamlin, Cl. Cur.

[page 155]

At a Court held at Merchantshope in the County of Prince George for Laying the Leavy of the sd. County, on Tuesdy the tenth Day of December 1717.

Present

John Hamlin, John Poythres, Randle Platt, James Thweatt Robert Munford, Robert Bolling, John Hardyman & John Peterson. Gent. Justices.

Pr. Geo: County Dr. Decembr. 10, 1717.

For Wolves killed, Vizt:

		Tobo.						
			Brot. over	17	1700	Brot. over	32	3200
To Richard Herbert for	1	100	Thomas Jones	1	100	Majr. Robert Munford	27	
To Edmond Browder for	1	100	Thos. Mathews	1	100	by Severall parties, Vizt.		
Geo. Rives	4	400	Fra. Epes by St. Evans	1	100	Fra. Coleman	4	400
Hugh Lee	1	100	Peter Mitchell	2	200	Wm. Lawes	1	100
Richd. Smith Senr.	1	100	William Russell	2	200	Jos. Stroud	1	100
Saml. Lee	1	100	Capt. Pr. Jones	1	100	Stephen Evans	4	400
Math. Anderson Senr.	1	100	William D[ittee]	1	100	Wm. Matta	3	300
James Anderson	1	100	John Ellington	1	100	Saml. Harwell	1	100
John Womacke Junr.	1	100	Wm. Gillam	1	100	Wm. Westbrook	1	100
Richard Burch	2	200	Abram Alley	1	100	Wm. Tucker	9	900
Nicho. Overby	1	100	Fra. Coleman	1	100	Richard Burch	2	200
Thos. Hobby	1	100	Saml. Harwell	1	100	John Wall	3	300
Thos. Whood	1	100	Richard Hudson Junr.	1	100		59	5900
	17	1700		32	3200			

To Capt. James Thweatt Corroner for two Inquests &c	266
To John Scott for Timber used about Warrick Bridge	135
To Majr. Robert Munford for Disbursmts. about Rowanty Bridge as by accot.	7196
To Richard Hamlin Sherr: for Services and Disbursements abt. Geo. Haynes a Criminal	1540
To Do. for 11 Insolvents of the Coty. Leavy Last year at 17 p. poll	187
To Do. for the County Service one year	500
To William Hamlin Clerk for Do. one year	1000
To Do. for Services abt. George Haynes	092
To Thomas Simmons for Sweeping the Courthouse one year	250
To Mr. Richard Hamlin Sherr: not Leavied Last year	070
	17136
To Sallary for 17136 at 10 p. Ct.	1713
To Caske of Do. at 8 pr. Ct.	1370
Pr. Geo: County Cr. Decembr. ye 10, 1717.	20219
By 1061 Tithes at 19l Tobacco pr. poll is	20159
Due to the Sherr: to be Leavied & paid next year	60
	20219

Ordered that the Sheriff Collect and receive of every Tithable person within this County (by Distress in case of refusall or Non payment) the sum of Nineteen pounds of Tobacco the same being their County Leavy this present year, and that the said Sheriff pay the Same to the severall persons to whom it is proportioned in the above amount.

And then the Court Adjourn'd. John Hamlin. Test W: Hamlin, Cl. Cur.

[page 156]

At a Court held at Merchantshope for the County of Prince George
on the second Tuesday in December being the tenth Day of the Month
Anno Dom. 1717

Present   John Hamlin,   Randle Platt,   Robert Munford
                 John Poythres,   John Peterson   Gent. Justices.

A Proclamation was read, Concerning Prohibitting the Entertaining or harbouring of Seamen Deserting His Majestys Ships of Warr.

Also a Proclamation Prohibitting Trade with the ffrench Settlements is America.

Also a Proclamation for publishing the repeal of the act of Assembly for preventing frauds in Tobacco payments &c the act for Continuing the said Act, and also for the Act for the Better regulation of the Indian Trade.

On the petition of John Woodleife, he is permitted to build & keep a Rowling house near his Landing at Jordans on James River.

Phillip Jean in Open Court acknowledged his Deeds of Lease and release of Land (Indented and Sealed, bearing Date the Ninth & Tenth Instant) to John Cheese and his heirs &c on whose motion the same are Ordered to be recorded. And then also appeared in Court Elizabeth the Wife of the said Phillip Jean and being first privately Examined freely relinquisht. to the said John her right of Dower in and to the Lands &c in the sd. Deed mentioned, which is Likewise Ordered to be recorded.

And then the Court adjourn'd till Tenn of the Clock Tomorrow Morning. Jno. Hamlin. Test W: Hamlin, Cl. Cur.

[page 157]

Att a Court held at Merchantshope for the County of Prince George on Wednesday
the Eleventh Day of December Anno Dom: 1717.

Present   John Hamlin,   John Poythres,   Randle Platt }
                 James Thweatt,   & John Peterson,   Gent. Justices }

On the petition of Majr. Robert Bolling, he is permitted to build and keep a Rowling house at the Usuall place called Prawtons or the Point on Appomattox River.

In the action on the case brot. by Rowland Thomas agst. Richard Hamlin, the Deft. files a plea &c and time is granted the plt. till the next Court to Consider ye same.

In the action of Tresspass brot. by Kathrine Williams agst. Richard Hamlin, the Deft. files a plea &c and time is granted the plt. till the next Court to Consider the same.

The action of Debt brot. by Richard Hamlin agst. John Lett, the plt. failing to prosecute, is Dismist.

Present Robt. Munford, Gent. Justice.

In the action of Debt brot. by Richard Hamlin agst. John Anderson for Thirty Shillings Current money and One hundred and fifteen pounds of Tobacco Due by Bill &c the Deft. being returned *non est Inventus* and not appearing on the plts. motion an Attachment is granted him agst. the said Defendts. Estate for the said Sum and Costs returnable to the next Court for Judgemt.

In the suit in Chancery brot. by Walter Vernon agst. John Poythres Surviveing Executor of the Last Will &c of John Poythres Deced: the respondt. appears and on his Motion time is granted him till the next Court to answer the Complainants Bill.

The action brot. by Edward Scott agst. ffrancis Longmore, neither party appearing, is Dismist.

In the suit in Chancery brot. by James Anderson agst. John Ellis Junr. the Summons being returned Executed and the respondt. being called and not appearing, and Thos. Simmons Sub Sherr: makeing Oath to the Service of the Summons on the sd. Ellis thereupon on the motion of the plts: Attorney an Attachment is granted him agst. the Body of the said respondt. returnable to the next Court.

In the suit in Chancery brot. by William Anderson Junr. agst. John Ellis Junr. the Summons being returned Executed and the respondt. being called and not appearing and Thomas Simmons Sub: Sherr: Makeing Oath to the Service of the Sumons on the said Ellis, thereupon on the motion of the plts. Attorney an Attachment is granted him agst. the Body of the sd. respondt. returnable to the next Court.

[page 158]

In the action of Trespass brot. by John Berry agst. Stephen Evans, the Deft. appears by his Attorney and pleads not Guilty, and the plt. Joining in the Issue, the same is thereupon referred till the next Court for Tryall.

The action on the case brot. by ffrancis Mallory agst. William Spiller neither party appearing is Dismist.

Absent John Poythres and James Thweatt, Gent.

In the action of Detinue brot. by Mary Batte agst. James Parram, for the Detaining one Negro Girl Slave Named Isbell of the Price of thirty pounds Sterl: and to the plts. Damage forty pounds Sterl: the Deft. by his Attorneys appeared &c pleaded *non Detinet* and for Tryall put himselfe upon the Country and the plt. Likewise, whereupon a Jury was Impannelled and Sworn to Try this matter in Issue by Name Gilbert Hay, George Hambleton, Abram Hoeth, John Wilkins, Henry Ivie, John Nance, Phillip Jan[e], Edward Burchet, William Reves, Cornelius Cargill, John Lett & James Moody, who haveing heard the Evidence and reced: their charge were sent out and after sometime return into Court & brought in their Verdict We find for the Deft. Gil. Hay foreman, which Verdict on the motion of the Defts. Attorney is recorded, and the suit Dismist with Costs.

Present John Poythres and James Thweatt, Gent.

The Last Will and Testament of Thomas Parram Deced: (being formerly proved and recorded) was further proved by the Oath of John Patteson a third Witness thereto which is Ordered to be recorded.

Charles Williams admr. &c of William Williams Deced: returned upon Oath and accot. Dr. & Cr. of the said Decedts. Estate, which being Examined & allowed by the Court is Ordered to be recorded.

In the action of Trover &c brot. by Jos. Fowler agst. Barthol: Crowder, the plt. amending his Declaration, thereupon time is granted the Deft. till the next Court to Consider the same.

In the action of Trespass brot. by John Berry et Uxor agst. Stephen Evans, the plt. failing to prosecute thereupon on the motion of the Defts. Attorney it's Ordered that he be Nonsuit and pay the sd. Deft. five Shillings with Costs. Als. Exec.

Jonathan Carter makeing Oath that he attended at this Court three Days as an Evidence for James Parram agst. Mary Batte, thereupon Ordered that the said James Parram pay him for the same One hundred and twenty pounds of Tobacco with Costs. Als. Exec.

[page 159]

In the action of Trespass brot. by John Berry agst. George Crook, the Defendt. by his Attorney pleading not Guilty and the plt. Joining in the Issue the same is referred till the next Court for Tryall.

In the suit in Chancery brot. by John Lewis Junr. agst. Henry Offley and Robert Bolling, the Deft. Bolling files a plea &c and time is granted the plt. till the next Court to Consider the same.

The action of Trespass brot. by Cornelius Cargill agst. William Cuerton, neither party appearing, is Dismist.

In the action of Debt brot. by David Parker agst. Charles Williams administatr. &c of Wm. Williams Deced: for three thousand Nine hundred Seventy two pounds of Tobacco Due by Bond &c on the motion of the Defendts. attorney Oyer of the sd. Bond is granted him and time till the next Court to Consider the same.

In the action of Debt brot. by John Hatch agst. Charles Williams Admr. & of Wm. Wm's. Deced: the plt. failing to prosecute, is Dismist.

In the action of Debt brot. by Richard Pigeon agst. Charles Williams Admr. &c of Wm. Wm's. Deced: the Deft. by his attorney pleading fully Administred and the plt. Joining in the Issue the same is thereupon referred till the next Court for Tryalls.

In the action of Debt brot. by John Allen agst. Charles Williams Admr. of Wm. Wm's. Deced: the Deft. by his attorney pleading fully Administred and the plt. Joining in the Issue the same is thereupon referred till the next Court for Tryall.

In the suit in Chancery Depending between Thomas Goodwyn Complt. and Jos. Smith & Cornelius Cargill respondts. the Complainant files a replication to the answer of the respondt. Cargill who has time till the next Court to consider the same.

The Sherriff makes return of the appraisement of the Estate of John Midleton Attacht. for Randle Platt, which is Ordered to be recorded, Vizt.

In Obedience to an Ordr. of Court we the Subscribers (being first Sworn) have appraised two Cows and one Yearling heifer of Mr. John Middletons upon accot. of Randle Platt, haveing Obtained Judgemt. for the same, and do value the said two Cows and Calfe at three pounds five Shillings as witness our hands the 22d Day of Novber. 1717. [signed] James Bell, Wm. Jackson, John [his I mark] Smith.

The above £3.5.0 in Tobacco as Valued by the Court at 12/6 pr. Ct. is 520. Test Wm. Hamlin, Cl. Truly recorded Test. Wm. Hamlin, Cl. Cur.   Verte

[page 160]

In the Suit in Chancery brought by Thomas Goodwyn agst. Joseph Smith and ffrancis Mallory, the Complt. sets forth in his Bill that the said Joseph Smith Stands Indebted to him the sum of five pounds Current money and hath withdrawn and removed ouf ot this Colony, that he cannot have reliefe by the ordinary course of the common Law and being Informed that the sd. ffrancis Mallory hath in his hands &c Estate of the sd. Smith's, thereupon a Supa. Issued &c and the sd. Mallory appearing files his answer upon Oath to the Complts. Bill wherein he confesses that the said Joseph Smith in the Bill mentioned did Leave in his hands and possession One Small Shalloop, One Silver Spoon, One silver Snuff box, one old watch & seal as a pledge or Pawne untill he the sd. Josh. Smith shou'd Sattisfie & pay the sd. Mallory the sum of Ten pounds Six Shllings & Six pence which he the sd. Smith Stands Indebted unto him, and failing to make any further plea, and the Complainant haveing made Oath that the sd. Sum of five pounds is Justly Due to him from the said Smith (as Appears by a Certificate under the hand of Nathl. Harrison Esqr.) thereupon it is Decreed by the Court that upon the sd. Complainants giveing the sd. Mallory Security to Indemnifie him agst. the sd. Smith for so much, the said Goods be appraised by John Hamlin, Randle Platt, John Hardyman and William [T]roughton, Gent. or any three of them being first Sworn for that purpose, and the surplusage or remainder thereof (after the said Sum of ten pounds Six Shillings and Six pence Due to the sd. Mallory be fully paid) or so much of the sd. Surplusage as will sattisfie and pay the said Sum of five pounds & Costs be paid & Delivered by the said ffrancis Mallory to the said Thomas Goodwyn for & towards the Discharge of his said Debt.

And then the Court Adjourn'd till Court in Course. Jno. Poythres. Test: Wm. Hamlin, Cl. Cur.

[page 161]

At a Court held at Merchants=hope for the County of Prince George
on the second Tuesday in January being the fourteenth Day of the month
Anno Dom: 1717.

Present   Randle Platt,   Robt. Bolling }
         Lewis Green   & John Peterson }   Gent. Justices.

William Mayes in Open Court acknowledged his Deeds of Lease and Release of Land (Indented and Sealed) to Buller Herbert and his heirs &c On whose motion the same are ordered to be recorded. And then also appeared in Court Mary the Wife of the said William and being first privately Examined freely relinquisht. to the said Buller Herbert her right of Dower in and to the Lands &c in the said Deeds mentioned which is Likewise ordered to be recorded.

Present James Thweatt, Gent.

On the petition of Richard Cureton he is permitted to build and keep a Rowling House at his house and the usuall place near the Head of Powells Creek.

The Last Will and Testament of David Parker Deced: was presented into Court by John Holloway the Executor Named therein who made Oath thereto and it being proved by the Oaths of Severall Witnesses thereto is Admitted to record. And upon the said Executors giveing Security as the Law Directs it is Ordered that a Certificate be granted Him for Obtaining a Probate in Due form whereupon John Hines and Thomas Griffith became his Security and with him entred into Bond.

John Lovesay, John Bonner, Edmond Irby and Benja. ffoster or any three of them (being first Sworn for that purpose by Some Majistrate of this County) are Ordered to appraise the Estate of David Parker Deced: and make report of their proceedings therein to the next Court when the Executor is to return the Inventory.

Sarah Wall Executrix of John Wall Deced: returns upon Oath an Inventory &c of the said Decedents Estate. Ordered it be recorded.

Absent Randle Platt, Gent.

In the action on the case Depending between Randle Platt and James Lundy an Imparlance is granted the Deft. till the next Court.

The action brot. by Randle Platt agst. Jeffrey Hawks, the plt. failing to prosecute, is Dismist.

[page 162]

Present John Hamlin, John Poythres and John Hardyman, Gent.

In the action Depending between Randle Platt and George Bolling for four hundred twenty four pounds of Tobacco Due by accot. &c the Deft. being called and not appearing nor any Security returned for him on the plts. motion Judgement is granted him agst. the said Deft. and Richard Hamlin Sherr: for the said Sum & Costs, unless the said Deft. shall appear at the next Court and answer the said action.

The action brot. by Randle Platt agst. John Stroud, the plt. faililng to prosecute, is Dismist.

In the action brot. by Randle Platt agst. William ffloriday for two Hundred forty one pounds of Tobacco Due by accot. the Deft. appearing and faililng to make any Just plea or Discount thereto, on the plts. motion Judgemt. is granted him agst. the said Deft. and it is Ordered that the said Deft. pay to the sd. plt. the said Sum & Costs. Als. Exec:

The action brot. by Randle Platt agst. Olive Poxson, the plt. failing to prosecute, is Dismist.

The action brot. by Randle Platt agst. Richard Ledbetter, the plt. failing to prosecute, is Dismist.

In the action brot. by Randle Platt agst. Henry King, an Imparlance is granted the Deft. till the next Court.

The action brot. by Randle Platt agst. Nicholas Vaughn, the plt. failing to prosecute, is Dismist.

The action brot. by Randle Platt agst. Richard Ledbetter, the plt. failing to prosecute, is Dismist.

In the action brot. by Elizabeth Parram Executrix of the Last Will &c of Thomas Parram Deced: agst. Joshua Wynne, the plt. failing to prosecute on the motion of Edward Goodrich Attorney for the Deft. it's Ordered that the sd. plt. be Nonsuit and pay the Deft. five Shillings with Costs. Als. Exec:

In the action brot. by David Crawley agst. William Anderson for one pound Seven Shillings and two pence halfe penny Due by accot. the Deft. being returned *Non est Inventus* and not appearing on the plts. motion an Attachment is granted him agst. the Estate of the said Deft. for the said Sum & Costs returnable to the next Court for Judgemt. for what shall appear to be Due.

[page 163]

In the action brot. by David Crawley agst. William Mitchell for two pounds Sixteen Shillings and four pence half penny Due by accot. the Defendt. being returend *Non est Inventus* and not appearing an Attachment is granted the plt. against the said Defendts. Estate for the said Sum and Costs, returnable to the next Court for Judgemt. for what shall appear to be due.

The action on the case brot. by David Crawly agst. Saml. Sentall, the plt. failing to prosecute is Dismist.

The action on the case brot. by David Crawley agst. Daniel Vaughn, the plt. failing to prosecute, is Dismist.

In the action on the case &c brot. by George Tillman agst. John Pattison, Damage twenty pounds Current money &c the Deft. being called and not appearing nor any Security returned for him on the plts. motion Judgement is granted him agst. the sd. Deft. and Richard Hamlin Sherr: for the said Sum & Costs unless the said Deft. shall appear at the next Court and answer the said action.

The action on the case brot. by George Tillman agst. Robert Abbernathy Junr. Exr. &c of Su. Tillman Deced:, the plt. failing to prosecute is Dismist.

In the action of Debt brot. by Joshua Irby agst. Mathew Smart Junr. the plt. failing to prosecute. On the motion of the Defts. Attorney it is Ordered that he be Nonsuit and pay the said Deft. five Shilling wth. Costs. Als. Exec:

In the action of Debt brot. by Joshua Irby agst. Cornelius Fox, the plt. failing to prosecute, on the motion of the Defts. Attorney it is Ordered that he be Nonsuit and pay the said Deft. five Shillings with Costs. Als. Exec:

The action of Debt brot. by Stephen Evans agst. Thomas Hackney neither party appearing, is Dismist.

The action of Debt brot. by William Baugh agst. William Anderson Junr. the plt. failing to prosecute, is Dismist.

The action on the case brot. by William Ranye agst. Thomas Burge the plt. failing to prosecute, is Dismist.

In the action on the case for Assault and Battery brot. by Richard Pigeon agst. Richard Whitmore, Damage fifty pounds Current money, the Deft. being returned *non est Inventus* and not appearing on ye motion of the plts. Attorney an Attachmt. is granted him agst. the said Defendts. Estate for the said Sum and Costs returnable to the next Court.

[page 164]

The action brot. by John Acre agst. Charles Bowen is withdrawn by ye plt.

In the action of Debt brot. by Benjamin Arnold agst. Stephen Hausman for three hundred Seventy five pounds of [fresh] Scented Tobacco and Cask Due by Bill, the Deft. being called and not appearing and Wm. Troughton being returned Security for him, on the motion of the plts: attorney Judgement is granted the said plt. agst. the sd. Deft. and his sd. Security for the said Sum & Costs, unless the said Deft. shall appear at the next Court and answer the said action.

A Deed for Land (Sealed) from John Nickells to Thomas Griffith was proved in Open Court by the Oaths of Thomas Posford, Thomas Posford Junr. and William Dunn Witnesses thereto to be the Act and Deed of the sd. Nickells to the said Griffith on whose motion the same is Ordered to be recorded.

The Order that James Baker &c return an Inventory of the Estate of Thomas Wheatley Deced: is Continued till next Court.

Michal Talbott and Peter Talbott came into Court and made Oath that their Father Michal Talbott Deced: dyed without any Will as farr as they know or believe and upon their giveing Security according to Law, It is Ordered that a Certificate be granted them for Obtaining a Commission of Administration in Due form, whereupon William Colgill and William Talbott became their Security & with them entred into Bond.

Edward Wyatt, Benjamin Reeks, Paul Jones and James Bell or any three of them being first Sworn for that purpose by some Majistrate are Ordered to appraise the Estate of Michal Talbott Deced: and make report of their proceedings to the next Court when the Admrs. are to return the Inventory.

The suit in Chancery brot. by John Tillman agst. George Tillman Admr. of Roger Tillman Deced: the Complt. failing to prosecute is Dismist.

In the suit in Chancery Depending between Robt. Munford Complt. and Henry Offley and Robert Bolling respondts. the Defendt. Bolling waves his plea &c and by consent the suit is referred till the next Court but the said Bolling has Liberty hereafter to file another plea.

In the Action of Debt Depending between Geo. Robertson and James Thweatt, [the] Deft. appearing and having Liberty to plead Doubly files his plea's to the plts. Declaration, who Joins therein and the same is referred till next Court for Tryall.

[page 165]

In the action on the case Depending between John Peterson and John Nance Admr. with the will annext. of John Nance Deced: for three pounds Due by accot. &c the Deft. pleading fully administred and the plt. Joining in the Issue the same was Submtited to the Court for Tryall, and the said Deft. makeing his said plea good thereupon the suit is Dismist.

John Nance Administrator with the Will annext. of John Nance Deced: returns upon Oath an accot. Dr. & Cr. of the said Decedts. Estate, and the same being Examined and allowed by the Court is Ordered to be recorded.

The Order that Henry Peoples be Summoned to Take the Oath of a Constable of Wyanoke Parrish is made Void.

The action on the case brot. by William Firth agst. John [B]uston neither party appearing is Dismist.

The action on the case brot. by Benjamin ffoster agst. Thomas Chappell neither party appearing is Dismist.

In the action on the case brot. by John Wilkins agst. Adam Ivie an Imparlance granted the said Deft. till the next Court.

In the action on the case for Slander brot. by John Wilkins agst. Adam Ivie, an Imparlance is granted the said Deft. till the next Court.

In the action brot. by John Hatch agst. Daniel Higdon for One thousand Eight hundred pounds of Tobacco Due for Rent &c the Defendt. appearing pleads *Nil Debit*, and the plt. Joining in the Issue the same is referred till the next Court for [word removed] Tryall.

The action brot. by John Hatch agst. Danl. Higdon for Two pounds Eleven Shillings and one penny halfe penny Due by accot. the plt. failing to prosecute is Dismist.

In the action on the case brot. by Charles White agst. John Lett, the sd. John came personally into Court and Confest. Judgemt. to the sd. plt. for two pounds fourteen Shillings and three pence halfe penny, it is therefore Ordered that the said Deft. pay to the sd. plt. the said Sum & Costs. Als. Exec:

In the action on the case brot. by Robert Gillmore agst. John Lett, the sd. John came personally into Court and Confest. Judgemt. to the plt. for twenty Shillings and three pence, it is thereupon Ordered that the sd. Defendt. pay to the said plt. the said Sum & Costs. Als. Exec:

[page 166]

Robert Gilmore made Complaint that Stephen Hausman Stands Indebted to him the sum of One pound Sixteen Shillings and three half pence Due by accot. Dated 1717, and set forth that the said Stephen hath unlawfully Departed this County that the Ordinary process at Law cannot be served on him whereupon he Obtained an Attachment under the hand of one of his Majestys Justices of this County agst. the Estate of the sd. Stephen for the sd. Sum returnable to this court for Judgemt. on which the Sherr: makes the following return, Vizt. Esecuted one the said Estate in the Hands of Randle Platt and the said Stephen being called and failing to appear to replevye the same and the sd. plt. makeing Oath the sd. Sum is Justly Due to him, It is thereupon Ordered that the sd. Randle Platt (who confesses to have Sufficient of the sd. Hausmans Estate in his possession) do pay to the said Robert Gilmore the sd. Sum and Costs, out of the sd. Estate. Als. Exec:

On the Attachment granted Richard Hamlin Sherr: of this County against the Estate of Elizabeth Parram for Six hundred Seventy Seven pounds of Tobacco, by reason of the Non appearance of the said Parram at the suit of John Cargill in an action of Debt, the Corroner makes the following return, Vizt. Executed on two ffeather bedds and bolsters, two pair of Blanketts and one rugg, And the said Parram being called and failing to appear to replevye the same, thereupon on the motion of the said Richard Hamlin Judgement is granted him agst. the said Elizabeth Parram for the said Sum of Six hundred Seventy Seven pounds of Tobacco and Costs, to be Leavied on the said Goods attacht. as aforesaid. Ordered that the Corroner cause the said Goods to be Duly Appraised by Richard Smith and William

Smith, James Williams and Thomas Gent or any three of them, being first Sworn by Some Justice of this County for that purpose, and Delivered the plt. for and toward the payment of the said Sum & Costs, and make report of his proceedings to the next Court.

On the motion of Richard Pigeon It's Ordered that a Lycence Issue for his keeping an Ordinary at the usuall place near the Court house of this County, he haveing given Bond and Security as the Law Directs.

An[d] then the Court adjourn'd till Court in Course. Jno. Hamlin. Test Wm. Hamlin, Cl. Cur.

[page 167]

At a Court held at Merchantshope for the County of Prince George
on the Second Tuesday in ffebruary being the Eleaventh Day of the
month, Anno Dom: 1717.

Present   Robert Munford,   Randle Platt
         Lewis Green   and John Patterson }   Gent. Justices

Michal Talbutt and Peter Talbutt, Admrs. &c of Michal Talbutt Deced: return into Court upon Oath, an Inventory &c of the said Decedts. Estate which is Ordered to be recorded.

William Blackley in Open Court acknowledged his Deeds of Lease and release of Land &c (Indented and Sealed) bearing Date the tenth and Eleventh Instant, to John Simmons of Surry County, on whose motion the same are ordered to be recorded.

James Parram in Open Court acknowledged his Deeds of Lease and release of Land (Indented and Sealed) bearing Date the tenth and Eleventh Instant, to Joshua Poythres, on whose motion the same are Ordered to be recorded.

Nathaniel Harrison Esqr. one of the Executors of Thomas Wheatley deced: returns into Court upon Oath an Inventory of the said Decedts. Estate which is Ordered to be recorded.

On the motion of Nathaniel Harrison Esqr. Guardian to George Bleighton the son of George Bleighton Deced: It"s Ordered that the said Nathaniel Harrison Esqr. take into his Custody and Possession the Estate of the said Orphan in the hands of ffrancis Clements and Lydia his Wife Administratrix of the Goods and Chattels of the sd. George Bleighton Deced: being three hundred and tenn pounds, twelve Shillings and One penny halfe penny, and Tenn Thousand Nine hundred Seventy One pounds and three Quarters of Toacco. Pursuant to the accot. Dr. & Cr. of the Estate of the said George Bleighton Deced: returned into Court by the said ffrancis Clements and Lydia his wife Administratrix as aforesaid, the Eleventh Day of February Anno Dom: 1712. Ordered that the said ffrancis Clements and Lydia his wife Administratrix as aforesaid, do Deliver the same accordingly unto the said Nathaniel Harrison, togather with Costs. Als. Exec:

And then the Court adjourn'd till Court in Course. Randl. Platt. Test Wm. Hamlin, Cl. Cur.

[page 168]

At a Court held at Merchants=hope for the County
of Prince George on the Second Tuesday in March being
the Eleventh Day of the month Anno Dom: 1717.

Present   John Hamlin,   John Poythres }
         Robert Munford,   & Robert Bolling }   Gent. Justices

John Holloway Executor of David Parker Deced: returns upon Oath an Inventory of the said Decedts. Estate. Ordered it be recorded.

Ordered that Thomas Moor be Summoned to the next Court to take the Oath of a Constable instead of Henry Thweatt.

Pursuant to the Direction of ye Act for appointing Sherriffs John Poythres, Robert Munford, and James Thweatt Gent. Justices are recommended to the Honble. the Governor as fit and able to Execute the Office of Sherriff of this County this Ensueing year.

James Bell came into Court and made Oath that Mortilla Boreman Late of this County Deced: Dyed without any Will as farr as He knows or believes, and upon his giveing Security according to Law it is Ordered that a Certificate be granted him for Obtaining Letters of Administration in Due form, whereupon Robert Rivers became his Security and with him entred into Bond.

In the action on the case Depending between Rowland Thomas and Richard Hamlin, the plt. Demurrs Genrally to the Defts. plea, who has time till next Court to Consider the same.

On the petition of Benjamin ffoster it is Ordered that Richard Hamlin Sherr: of this County be summoned to the next Court to answer the same.

In the action of Tresspass Depending between Kathrine Williams and Richard Hamlin, the plt. Demurrs Genrally to the Defendts. plea who has time till next Court to consider the same.

The Attachment granted Richard Hamlin agst. the Estate of John Anderson the plt. failing to prosecute, is Dismist.

[page 169]

In the suit in Chancery brot. by Walter Vernon agst. John Poythres Surviveing Executor &c of John Poythres Deced: the respondent files his answer uon Oath to the Complainants Bill who has time till next Court to Consider the same.

The suit in Chancery Depending between James Anderson, and John Ellis Junr. the plt. failing to prosecute, is Dismist.

The suit in Chancery Depending between William Anderson Junr. and John Ellis Junr., the plt. failing to prosecute, is Dismist.

In the action of Trespass brot. by John Berry agst. Stephen Evans for that the said Stephen on the Seventh Day of August now Last past in the Parrish of Bristoll in this County, upon him the said John Berry an Assault Did make, and him with force and Arms, that is to say with Swords Staves and knives did then and there beat bruse wound and Evilly Intreat so that of his Life he greatly Dispaired, whereupon the said John Berry Saith that he is Damnified and Damage hath Sustained to the Value of ffifty pounds Sterl: as in the plts. Declaration is set forth the Deft. by his Attorney pleads not Guilty and the plt. Joining in the Issue thereupon a Jury was Impannelled and Sworn to Try the matter, by Name William Stainback, John Bonner, Cuthbert Williams, John Cureton, Thomas Weeks, Roger Taylor, Nicholas Overby, Abraham Heeth, George Tillman, John Pattison, John Lewis and Richard Pace, who haveing heard the Evidence and reced. their charge, were sent out and soon after returned into Court and brot. in their Verdict. We find for the plt. twenty Shillings Sterling. Wm. Stainback, foreman, which Verdict on the motion of the plts. Attorney is recorded and thereupon it is Considered by the Court that the plt. recover of the sd. Deft. the aforesaid Sum of twenty Shillings Sterling being his Damages aforesaid by the Jurors aforesaid assessed, togather wth. costs. Als. Exec:, the Court being of Opinion that the Battery was proved.

The action of Trover &c Depending between Joseph ffowler and Barth. Crowder, the plt. failing to prosecute is Dismist.

The action of Trespass Depending between John Berry and George Crook, neither party appearing is Dismist.

The suit in Chancery Depending between John Lewis Junr. and Henry Offley &c Robert Bolling respondts. is continued till next Court.

The action of Debt Depending between David Parker and Charles Williams Admr. &c of Wm. Williams (the plt. being Dead) is Dismist.

[page 170]

The action of Debt Depending between Richard Pigeon and Charles Williams Admr. of Wm. Williams Deced: the plt. failing to prosecute is Dismist.

The action of Debt Depending between John Allen and Charles Williams Admr. of William Williams Deced: is continued till next Court.

The suit in chancery brot. by Thomas Goodwynn agst. Joseph Smith and Cornelius Cargill, the plt. failing to prosecute is Dismist.

In the action of Debt brot. by John Acre Junr. agst. Charles Bowen for Eight pounds fifteen Shillings and five pence Sterl: and One hundred pounds of Tobacco Due by Bill &c the Deft. being returned *non est Inventus* and not appearing on the motion of the plts. Attorney an Attachment is granted him agst. the sd. Defts. Estate for the said Sum and Costs returnable to the next Court for Judgemt. for what shall appear to be Due.

The suit in Chancery brot. by John Bolling agst. Henry Offley & Robert Bolling, the plt. failing to prosecute is Dismist.

In the action of the case Depending between Elizabeth Parram Exrx. of Thomas Parram Deced: and Joshua Wynne, the plt. failing to prosecute It's Ordered that she be Nonsuit and pay the sd. Deft. five Shillings with Costs. Als. Exec:

In the action of Debt brot. by John Smith and Thomas Potts agst. Benjamin ffoster, Oyer of the plts. Bill is granted the Deft. and time to Consider the same till the next Court.

The action of Debt brot. by Randle Platt agst. Jane Byrd, the plt. failing to prosecute is Dismist.

In the action of Debt Depending between Randle Platt and John Hardyman, Oyer of the plts. bill is granted the Deft. and time till the next Court to Consider the same.

In the action on the case brot. by George Har[vie] agst. David Colyshaw for two hundred and thirteen pounds of Tobacco Due by accot. &c the Deft. being returned *non est Inventus* and not appearing on the plts. motion an attachment is granted him agst. the said Defendts. Estate for the said Sum & Costs, returnable to the next Court for Judgemt. for what shall appear to be Due.

[page 171]

In the action brot. by George Harvie agst. John Spain for Nineteen Hundred Ninety Six pounds of Tobacco Due by accot. &c the Defendt. being returned *non est Inventus* & not appearing on the plts. motion an Attachment is granted him agst. the said Defendts. Estate for the said Sum and Costs returnable to the next Court for Judgement for what shall appear to be Due.

In the action brot. by George Harvie agst. John Berry for five hundred Ninety Eight pounds of Tobacco Due by accot. by the Defendt. being returnen *non est Inventus* and not appearing an Attachment is granted the plt. agst. the sd. Defts. Estate for the said Sum and Costs returnable to the next Court for judgemt. for what shall appear to be Due.

In the action brot. by Drury Bolling against John Spain for fifty four Shillings current money and One hundred pounds of Tobacco Due by accot. &c the Deft. being returned *non est Inventus* and not appearing on the motion of the plts: Attorney an Attachment is granted him agst. the said Defendts. Estate returnable to the next Court for Judgemt. for what shall appear to be due.

In the action Depending between George Carter and Simon Naylor, the Court being Informed that the said have agreed, thereupon the suit is Dismist.

In the action of Debt brot. by James Moody Assignee of Benja. Reeks against John Berry, the plt. failing to prosecute, thereupon the same is Dismist.

The suit in chancery brot. by John Tillman agst. Geo. Tillman Admr. &c of Roger Tillman Deced: the plt. failling to prosecute is Dismist.

On the petition of Severall of the Inhabitants of Nan[bcends] It's Ordered that a road be cleared from Powhiponock Bridge to Namounds Bridge and that the Inhabitants of Namocends and Powhiponock assist John Tally who is appointed Overseer thereof, in performing the same.

In the action on the case Depending between David Crawley and Cornelius ffox for [line blank] the Deft. being returned *non est Inventus* and not appearing on the plts. motion an attachment is granted him agst. the said Defendts. Estate for the said Sum & Costs returnable to the next Court for Judgement for what shall appear to be due.

In the action on the case Depending between Joshua Irby and John Bonner for Nine hundred and fifteen pds: of Tobacco Due by accot: the Deft. by his Attorney pleads *Nil Debit* and the plt. Joining in the Issue the same is referred till the next Court for Tryall.

[page 172]

The suit Depending between Abram Heeth and Sampson Merredeth Late Sherr: &c pr. *Scire ffacias* is Continued till next Court.

William Low's Deeds of Lease and release of Land (Sealed) were proved in Open Court by the Oaths of Majr. Robert Munford, Buller Herbert and George Tillman Witnesses thereto to be the act and Deed of the said William Low to George Pace therein Named, on whose motion the said Deeds are Ordered to be recorded.

The action on the case brot. by Thomas Harrison agst. William Hines, Neither party appearing is Dismist.

The Last Will and Testament of Thomas Loyd Deced: was presented into Court by Jane his relict and Executrix therein Named who made Oath thereto and it being proved by the Oaths of John Gill and Robert Rivers Witnesses thereto is Ordered to be recorded, and upon the said Executrix's giveing Security as the Law Directs It is Ordered that a Certificate be granted her for Obtaining a Probate in Due form, whereupon Benjamin ffoster and Robert Rivers became her Securitys and with her entred into Bond.

The Last Will and Testament of Hugh Mackmehan Deced: was presented into Court by Jane Loyd and Thomas Loyd the Executor Named in the said Will being Dead, the said Jane made Oath thereto and it being proved by the Oaths of Wm. Jackson and William Hutcheson witnesses thereto is Ordered to be recorded, and upon the said Janes giveing Security as the Law Directs it is Ordered that a Certificate be granted her for Obtaining Letters of Administration with the said will annex. in Due form, whereupon Benjamin ffoster became her Security and with her entred into Bond.

Richard Cotten, James Niblet, Thomas Bilbro and William Jackson or any three of them being first Sworn by Some Majistrate for that purpose, are Ordered to appraise the Estates of Thomas Loyd and Hugh Mackmehan Deced:

and make report of their proceedings to the next Court when Jane Loyd the Executrix of the Wills of the said Decedents is Ordered to return the Inventorys of the said Estates.

The action on the case brot. by Nath. Harrison Esqr. agst. John Buston the plt. failing to prosecute is Dismist.

George Crook haveing attended three Days as an Evidence for John Berry agst. Stephen Evans, Ordered that the said Berry pay him One hundred and twenty pounds of Tobacco for the same with Costs. Ats. Exec:

George Crook haveing attended three Days as an Evidence for Stephen Evans at the suit of John Berry. Ordered that the said Stephen pay him for the same One hundred and twenty pounds of Tobacco with Costs. Als. Exec.

[page 173]

Pursuant to the Direction of the Act for regulating Ordinarys and restraint of Typling Houses, Ordered that the rates on Ordinary Liquors, Dyet, Lodging, fodder and provender &c be as were set and rated the Last year.

Ordered that Duglas Irby Surveyor of the blackwater road, be summoned to the next Court to answer for his contempt in refusing to clear the said road.

And then the Court adjourn'd till court in Course. Jno: Poythres. Test. Wm. Hamlin, Cl. Cur:

On the first Day of Aprill 1718, William Short Exhibitted the following Judgement and Desired the same might be recorded that Execution might Issue thereon, Vizt.

Pr. Geo: County Sct.   9ber the 9th 1717

This Day William Short and John Hobbs caused Richard Worthin to appear before us on their complaint for that the said Worthin hath Stopt. the main road and caused it to be Spoilt., the same being made plainly appear Judgement is granted him agst. the sd. Warthin as the Law Directs in Such cases, the sum of tenn Shillings currt. money with cost, als. Execution. Given under my hand the day and year above mentioned. [signed] John Hamlin.

Truly recorded Test. Wm. Hamlin, Cl. Cur.

At a Court held for Merchantshope for the County of Prince
George on the second Tuesday in Aprill being the Eighth Day of
the month Anno Dom: 1718.

Present	Randle Platt,	Robert Munford,	Robert Hall
	Robert Bolling,	John Hardyman,	Lewis Green
	and	John Peterson	Gent. Justices

James Bell Admr. of the Goods and Chattels of Mortella Boreman Deced: returns into Court an Inventory of the said Decedts. Estate, which is Ordered to be recorded.

The petition of Timothy Bridges for the Administration of the Estate of Richard Cotten and Elizabeth his wife Lately Deced: is referred till next Court & till then the said Bridges is Ordered to take care of the said Estate.

[page 174]

Present Capt. John Hamlin

Elinor Walpole Relict of Richard Walpole Deced: came into Court and made Oath that the said Richard Walpole Deced: Dyed without any Will as farr as she knows or believes and upon her giveing Security for Her Just and ffaithfull Administration of the said Decedts. Estate it is Ordered that a Certificate be be [sic] granted her for Obtaining Letters of Administration in Due form, whereupon John Hatch and Edward Goodrich became her Securitys and with her entred into Bond &c.

Gilbert Hay, William Harrison, James Harrison and Joseph Carter or any three of them (being first Sworn for that purpose by some Majistrate of this County) are Ordered to Appraise the Estate of Richard Walpole Deced: and make report of their proceedings to the next Court when Elinor Walpole the Administratrix thereof is to return the Inventory

Henry Lee in Open Court acknowledged his Deed for Land Indented and Sealed, with Livery of Seizin endorst thereon to John Butler on whose motion the same is Ordered to be recorded, And then also appeared in Court Ann the wife of Henry and being first privately Examined, acknowledged the same to be her act and Deed and Voluntarily relinquisht. to the said Butler her right of Dower in & to the Lands &c in the said Deed mentioned which is Likewise Ordered to be recorded.

John Robberds and Thomas Winingham in Open Court acknowledged their Deed for Land with Livery of Seizin endorst thereon & Indented and Sealed, to Dorrell Young Junr. on whose motion the same is Ordered to be recorded.

Ordered that John Hatch be Summoned to the next Court to answer the petition of Randle Platt and others.

John Wyatt one of the Orphans of Anthony Wyatt Deced: appeared in Court and chose Edward Wyatt his Guardian. Ordered the said Edward give Security accordingly.

The action Depending between Randle Platt and George Bolling Neither party appearing is Dismist.

[page 175]

In the action on ye case Depending between Randle Platt and James Lundy for five hundred Sixty three pounds of Tobacco Due by accot. at the Last Court the Defendt. haveing had time given him till this Court to plead and being now called to do the same did not appear nor offer anything in barr or preclusion of the plts. action thereupon it is considered that the plt. recover against the said Deft. the said Sum & Costs, unless he shall appear at the next Court and answer the said action.

Pursuant to the Direction of the act concerning Jurys It's Ordered that a Grandjury of twenty four freeholders of thie County be summoned to the next Court to Inquire into the breaches of the penall Laws &c.

In the action on the case Depending between Randle Platt and Henry King for four hundred and Tenn pounds of Tobacco Due by accot. at the Last Court the Deft. haveing had time given him till this Court to plead and being now called to do the same did not appear nor offer any thing in Barr or preclusion of the plts. Action, thereupon it is Considered that the plt. recover agst. the said Defendt. the said Sum and Costs, unelss he shall appear at the next Court and answer the said action.

The action on the case brot. by David Crawley agst. William Anderson the plt. failing to prosecute, is Dismist.

The action on the case brot. by David Crawley agst. William Mitchell the plt. failing to prosecute, is Dismist.

In the action brot. by George Tillman against John Patteson, Major Robert Bolling became Speciall Bail for the Deft. who being permitted to plead Doubly files his plea's to the plts. Declaration who has time till next Court to consider the same.

Jane Loyd Executrix &c of Thomas Loyd Deced: returns upon Oath an Inventory of the said Decedts. Estate, which is Ordered to be recorded.

Jane Loyd Administratrix with the will annext. of Hugh Mackmehan Deced: returns upon Oath an Inventory of the said Decedts. Estate which is Ordered to be recorded.

In the action of Trespass for Assault and Battery brot. by Richard Pigeon against Richard Whitmore, the Deft. appears by his Attorney and pleads not Guilty and the plt. Joining in the Issue the same is referred till next Court for Tryall.

[page 176]

In the action of Debt brot. by Benjamin Arnold against Stephen Hausman for three hundred Seventy five pounds of Tobacco and Caske Due by Bill &c: the Deft. failing to appear Edward Goodrich Attorney for William Troughton who is Bail for the appearance of the sd. Deft. appears and pleads payment and the plt. Joining in the Issue the same is thereupon referred for Tryall till the next Court.

The action of Debt Depending between George Robertson and James Thweatt, the plt. failing to prosecute is Dismist.

In the action of Trespass for Assault and Battery brot. by John Wilkins agst. Adam Ivye, Damage fifty pounds Current money &c at the Last Court the Deft. haveing had time till this Court to plead and being now called to do so the same did not appear nor offer any thing in Barr or preclusion of the plts. action, thereupon Judgemt. is granted the plt. agst. the sd. Deft. by *Nihil Dicit*.

In the action [brot.] by John Wilkins agst. Adam Ivey for Slander Damage fifty pounds Current money &c at the Last Court the Deft. haveing had time till this Court to plead and being now called to do the same did not appear nor offer any thing in barr or preclusion of the plts. action thereupon Judgement is granted the plt. agst. the sd. Deft. pr. *Nihil Dicit*.

The action of Debt Depending between John Hatch and Daniel Higdon the plt. failing to prosecute is Dismist.

The order of the Last Court for the appraisment of the Estate of Elizabeth Parram Attacht. for Richard Hamlin Sherr: &c is made Null and Void the said Elizabeth haveing paid the Debt for which the said Goods were Attacht. as appears by the Corroners return on the said Order.

The suit in Chancery brot. by Robert Munford agst. Henry Offley and Robert Bolling is Continued till next Court.

The action of Detinue Depending between William Mitchell by Peter Mitchell his Guardian & Cuthbert Williamson, the plt. failing to prosecute is Dismist.

[page 177]

In the action on the case Depending between Cornelius ffox and William Wallice for fourteen pounds One shilling and four pence Due by accot. the Deft. appears and pleads [*Nihil*] *Dicit* and the Plaintiff Joining in the Issue the same is referred till next Court for Tryall.

The action on the case brot. by Michael Rosser Junr. agst. Sarah Wall Executrix &x of John Wall Deced: neither party appearing is Dismist.

The action of Debt brot. by Edward Goodrich against James Sevekar the plt. failing to prosecute is Dismist.

In the action of Debt Depending between Isham Randolph Assignee of Peter Wynne Admr. of Joshua Wynne Deced: Late factor of Benjamin Braine Merchant in London, and Richard Hudson for two pounds Seven Shillings Current money Due by Bill &c the Deft. Hudson being returned *non est Inventus* and not appearing on the motion of the plts. Attorney an Attachment is granted him agst. the said Defendts. Estate for the said Sum and Costs returnable to the next Court for Judgement.

The action on the case brot. by William Hamlin agst. Daniel Higdon the plt. failing to prosecute is Dismist.

In the action of Debt brot. by Richard Munns agst. William Anderson for four pounds two Shillings Current money Due by Bill &c the Deft. being returned *non est Inventus* and not appearing on the motion of the plts. Attorney an Attachment is granted him agst. the said Defendts. Estate for the said Sum and Costs, returnable to the next Court for Judgement.

The action on the case brot. by John Wilson against John Duffeild neither party appearing is Dismist.

The action of Debt brot. by John Acre Junr. agst. Charles Bowen is withdrawn by the plt.

The action of Debt brot. by ffrancis Mallory agst. George Ivie is Continued till the next Court on the motion of the plts. Attorney.

The action on the case brot. by Littlebury Epes agst. Thomas Simmons, the plt. failing to prosecute, is Dismist.

[page 178]

In the action of Debt brot. by William Randolph against ffrancis Mallory for fifteen pounds current money &c the Deft. being called and not appearing nor any Security returned for him on the motion of the plts. attorney Judgement is granted him agst. the said Defendt. and Richard Hamlin Sherr: &c for the said Sum and Costs, unless the said Deft. shall appear at the next Court and answer the said action.

In the action of Debt Depending between Thomas Simmons and Daniel Crawley and Elizabeth his Wife Executrix of the Last Will and Testament of Bryan ffarrell Deced: for five hundred and fivety pounds of Tobacco Due by Bill &c the Defendts. being returned Non Suit *Inventi* and not appearing on the plts. motion an Attachmt. is granted him against the Estate of the sd. Defendts. for the said Sum and Costs returnable to the next Court for Judgement.

The action on the case brot. by Littlebury Epes against Peter Wynne, is continued till next Court.

In the action on the case brot. by ffrancis Epes against John Poythres, the plaintiff failing to prosecute on the motion of Edward Goodrich Attorney for the Deft, it is Ordered that he be Nonsuit and pay the said Defendt. five Shillings with Costs. Als. Exec:

In the action on the case brot. by Nathaniel Harrison Esqr. agst. John Brewer for four hundred twenty Six and an halfe pounds of Tobacco Due by accot. &c the Defendt. being returned *non est Inventus* and not appearing on the motion of the plts. Attorney an Attachment is granted him against the said Defendts. Estate for the said Sum and Costs, returnable to the next Court for Judgement.

In the action on the case brot. by Joshua Woodleife against Thomas Burge for two hundred pounds of Tobacco Due by accot. &c the Defendt. appearing pleads *Nil Debit* and the plt. Joining in the Issue the same is thereupon referred till next Court for Tryall.

In the action on the case brot. by Joshua Woodleife against Edward Woodleife for two hundred pounds of Tobacco Due by accot. on the motion of the Defts. attorney Oyer of the plts. accot. is granted him and time till next Court to consider the same.

[page 179]

The action of Debt brot. by Robert Rogers against John Hamlin, the plt. failing to prosecute is Dismist. & the Deft. assumes to pay the costs.

The action of Debt brot. by Robert Rogers against John Pooke, the plt. failing to prosecute, is Dismist.

In the action on the case brot. by Joshua Irby against Mathew Smart junr. Damage fivety pounds Current money the Deft. being returned *non est Inventus* and not appearing on the motion of the plts. attorney an Attachment is granted him against the said Defendts. Estate for the said Sum and Costs, returnable to the next Court for Judgement.

In the action on the case brot. by Joshua Irby against Cornelius ffox Damage twenty pounds Current money, the Defendt. being returned *non est Inventus* and not appearing on the motion of the plts. attorney an Attachment is granted him against the said Defendts. Estate for the said Sum and Costs, returnable to the next Court for Judgement.

In the action of Debt brot. by Nathaniel Harrison Esqr. against Edward Crossland for Eight hundred fivety Eight pounds of Tobacco Due by Bill Dated the fifteenth Day of March 1714, the Defendt. came personally into Court and Confest Judgement to the plt. for the said Sum, it is thereupon Ordered that the said Defendt. pay to the said plt. the said Sum & Costs. Als. Exec.

The Last courts Order that Thomas Moor be Summoned to take the Oath of a Constable is made Void and it is Ordered that John Sturdivant be Summoned in his stead.

In the action on the case brot. by Rowland Thomas agst. Richard Hamlin, the Defendt. by his attorney appears and Joins in the Demurrer of the Plaintiff and the same is referred till next Court to be argued.

In the action of Trespass Depending between Kathrine Williams and Richard Hamlin, the Defendt. appears by her attorney and Joins in the plts. Demurrer & the same is referred till next Court to be argued.

The suit in Chancery brot. by Walter Vernon agst. Henry Offley &c and John Poythres Surviveing Executor &c of John Poythres Deced: the Complainant failing to prosecute, is Dismist.

[page 180]

The suit in Chancery brot. by John Lewis Junr. agst. Henry Offley and Robert Bolling is Continued till next Court.

In the action of Debt Depending between John Allen and Charles Williams Administrator of the Goods and Chattels of William Williams Deced: for Six hundred and thiry pounds of Tobacco in Caske Due by Bill Dated the twenty sixth of March 1714, the plt. haveing made Oath the said Sum is Justly Due to him, thereupon by consent of ye said Deft. it's Ordered that he the said Defendt. Administrator as aforesaid pay to the said Plaintiff the aforesaid Sum of Six hundred and thirty pounds of Tobacco in Caske out of the said Decedts. Estate with Costs. Als. Executio[n].

The attachment granted John Acre Junr. against Charles Bowen is Continued till the next Court.

The action of Debt Depending between John Smith and Thomas Potts plts. and Benjamin ffoster Deft. the plts. failing to prosecute is Dismist.

On the petition of Benjamin ffoster against Richard Hamlin Sherrif of this County Setting forth that the said Hamlin Sherr. as aforesaid Stands Indebted to him for Tobacco Leavied in the sd. County in the year 1716, the sum of two thousand Ninety Seven pounds of Tobacco, at the Last Court when the said Petition was first preferred the said Hamlin being absent it was Ordered (Pursuant to the Direction of the act concerning the Collection of the Publick and County Leavys and for the better payment of the same to the respective Creditors therein concerned) that the said Hamlin shoud be Summoned to appear at thie Court and answer the same and he being called and failling to appear or offer any thing in barr of the plts. said claime, and there appearing to [...] him the sum of One thousand Nine hundred and fifteen pounds of Tobacco, thereupon it is Ordered that the said Richard Hamlin pay to the said Benjamin ffoster the said Sum of Nineteen hundred and fifteen pounds of Tobacco & Costs. Als. Exec:

In the action of Debt Depending between Randle Platt and John Hardyman for fivety pounds &c by Bill at the Last Court the Deft. haveing had time till this Court to plead and being now called to do the same did not appear nor offer any thing in barr or preclusion of the plts. action, thereupon it is Considered by the Court that the plt. recover against the said Deft. the said Sum and Costs, unless he shall appear at the next Court and answer the said Action.

[page 181]

The action on the case brot. by Richard Hamlin against William Haynes, the plt. failing to prosecute is Dismist.

The action of Trespass on the case brot. by Richard Hamlin against William Haynes, the plt. failing to prosecute is Dismist.

And then the Court adjourn'd till Tomorrow Tenn of Clock. Jno: Hamlin. Test Wm. Hamlin, Cl. Cur.

At a Court held at Merchants=hope for the County of Pr.
George on Wednesday the Ninth Day of Aprill Anno Dom. 1718.

Present   John Hamlin   John Poythres }
             Randle Platt   & Robert Hall }   Gent. Justices

The Attachment granted George Harvy against the Estate of David Collishaw, is continued till next Court.

The attachment granted George Harvy against the Estate of John Spain is Continued till next Court.

The Attachment granted George Harvy against the Estate of John Berry is continued till the next Court.

The attachment granted Drury Bolling against the Estate of John Spain is Continued till the next Court.

The attachment granted David Crawley against the Estate of Cornelius ffox, is continued till the next Court.

The action Depending between Joshua Irby and John Bonner is continued till next Court.

The suit Depending between Abram Heeth and Sampson Merredeth pr. *Scire facias* is Continued till the next Court.

[page 182]

The Order of the Last Court against Duglas Irby is continued till the next Court.

The action brot. by Mathew Marks against Edward Wyatt the plt. failing to prosecute is Dismist.

In the action of Debt brot. by Mathew Marks agst. Thomas Simmons the Deft. Fileing a plea in abatement, the plt. thereupon fails to prosecute and the suit is Dismist.

In the action of Debt brot. by Henry Soane against Richard Hamlin Sherr: &c for three thousand Nine nundred pounds of Tobacco Due by a Note Drawn on the sd. Hamlin and by him accepted, the Deft. being returned *non est Inventus* and not appearing on the motion of the plts. Attorney an Attachment is granted him against the said Defendts. Estate for the said Sum & Costs, returnable to the next Court for Judgement for what shall appear to be Due.

The action of Debt brot. by Randle Platt against Richard Ledbetter the plt. failing to prosecute is Dismist.

In the action on the case brot. by John Mayes against Samuell Sentall for three pounds Seven Shillings and Six pence Due by account, the Defendt. being returned *non est Inventus* and not appearing on the plts. motion an Attachment is granted him against the said Defendts. Estate for the said Sum & Costs, returnable to the next Court for Judgement for what shall appear to be Due.

And then the Court Adjourn'd till court in course. Jno. Hamlin. Test Wm. Hamlin, Cl. Cur.

[page 183]

At a Court held at Merchantshope for the County of Prince George
the Ninth Day of Aprill 1718, for receiving and Certifying to the next
Session of Assembly the Propositions and Grievances and Publick Claims
of the said County.

Present   John Hamlin,   John Poythres }
                Randle Platt   & Robert Hall }   Gent. Justices

Sundry Propositions and Grievances of the Inhabitants of this County written on one Sheet of paper were presented into Court by the freeholders of the said County Subscribed thereto which are ordered to be certified to the next Session of the Genrall Assembly. And whereas upon reading the Proclamation for Enforceing the Laws for the better regulating the maner of Signing and Certifying Propositions and Grievances to the Genrall Assembly the freeholders at the Barr signing and presenting the said Propositions & Grievances are Surprized and Concerned to think the said Propositions and Grievances shoud come before the Assembly with so few Subscribers, they being Sensible the same contains the Genrall propositions and Grievances of the freeholders of this County and Expecting the same might have been signed at any other place or time as has been used heretofore, therefore on the motion of the said ffreeholders It is Ordered that the Clerk Certifie on the Back of the said Propositions and Grievances that the Sherr: Omitted Publishing the said Proclamation at the Election of Burgesses by which means the freeholders were Ignorant of their Duty therein.

And then the Court Adjournd. Jn. Hamlin. Test W: Hamlin, Cl. Cur.

[page 184]

At a Court held at Merchantshope for the County of Prince
Geo: on the second Tuesday in May being the thirteenth Day of the
month Anno Dom: 1718.

Present   John Hamlin,   John Poythres,   Randle Platt,
                Robert Munford,   & John Hardyman   Gent. Justices

Mr. Sampson Merredeth is appointed to take the List of Tythables in Martins brandon Parrish on the Tenth day of June Next.

Capt. John Poythres in Wyanoke.

Capt. John Hamlin in Westover.

& Majr. Robt. Bolling in Bristoll Parrish.

Present Mr. Sampson Merredeth, a Just.

The order that Elinor Walpole Admrx. &c of Richard Walpole Deced: return an Inventory of the said Decedts. Estate is Continued till next Court.

The petition of Randle Platt and others agst. John Hatch is referred till the next Court.

The order that John Sturdivant be summoned to take the Oath of a Constable is Continued till next Court.

Robert Wynne in Open Court acknowledged his Deeds of Lease and Release of Land (Indented and Sealed) to Richard Carlile, and then also appeared in Court Martha the wife of the said Wynne and being first privately Examined acknowledged the same to be her act and Deed to the said Carlile and to him freely and Voluntarily relinquisht. her right of Dower in and to the Lands &c in the said Deeds mentioned, which with the said Deeds are Ordered to be recorded.

Robert Wynne in Open Court acknowledged his Deeds of Lease & release of Land (Indented and Sealed) to William Cotten, and then also appeared in Court Martha the Wife of the said Wynne and being first privately Examined acknowledged the same to be her act and Deed to the said Cotten and to him freely and Voluntarily relinquisht. her right of Dower in and to the Lands &c in the said Deeds mentioned, which with the said Deeds are Odered to be recorded.

Duglas Irby a Surveyor of the Highways, being Summoned to appear at this Court to answer for his Contempt in refuseing to clear the Blackwater Road, and he failing to appear accordingly It is Ordered that he be taken into Custody of the Sherr: till he shall give Bond with Security for his appearance at the next Court.

[page 185]

The action on ye Case Depending between Randle Platt and James Lundy is continued till the next Court.

The action on ye Case brot. by Randle Platt agst. Henry King is continued till the next Court.

The action on ye Case Depending between Geo: Tillman and John Patteson is continued till next Court.

The action of Trespass Depending between Richard Pigeon and Richard Whitmore is continued till the next Court.

The action of Debt Depending between Benjamin Arnold and Stephen Hausman is continued till next Court.

The action on the case for Slander brot. by John Wilkins against Adam Ivie is Continued till the next Court.

The action of Trespass brot. by John Wilkins agst. Adam Ivie is Continued till the next Court.

The suit in Chancery Brot. by Robt. Munford agst. Henry Offley and Robt. Bolling is continued till next Court.

The action on the case Depending between Cornelius ffox and William Wallice is Continued till next Court.

The Attachment granted Isham Randolph Assignee &c against the Estate of Richard Hudson is continued till next Court.

The Attachment granted Richard M[unn] against the Estate of William Anderson Junr. is continued till the next Court.

The action of Debt Depending between ffrancis Mallory and Geo: Ivie is Continued till the next Court.

In the action of Debt brot. by Randle Platt agst. David Goodgame for two Hundred and Nineteen pounds of Tobacco Due by Bill &c the Defendt. being called and not appearing nor any Security returned for him on the motion of the plts. Attorney Judgement is Granted him against the said Defendt. and Richard Hamlin Sherr: &c for the said Sum and Costs, unless the said Defendt. shall appear at the next Court and answer the said action.

[page 186]

Pursuant to the Direction of the Act concerning Jurys, a Grandjury was Impannelled and Sworn by Name ffrancis Epes Junr., Benjamin ffoster, Edwd: Holloway, Jno. Pattison, Richard Cureton, Wm. Short, John Wilkins, John Lett, Thos. Burge, Robt. Tucker, Richard Carlile, Cornelius ffox, Geo: Hambleton, Geo: Tillman & Thos. Mitchell who haveing their charge were sent out and Soon after return into Court with the following presentments, Vizt.

We the Grandjury do present Mary Bishope and Allice Larrance for haveing Bastard Children.

[signed] ffra. Epes Junr., fforeman.

Mary Bishope being this Day presented by the Grandjury for haveing a Bastard Child It is Ordered that the sherr: Summons the said Mary Bishope to appear at the next Court and answer the said presentment.

Allice Larrance being this Day presented by the Grandjury for haveing a Bastard Child, It is Ordered the Sherr: Summons the said Allice Larrance to appear at the next Court and answer the said presentment.

Timothy Bridges came into Court and made Oath that Richard Cotten Late of this County Deced: Dyed without any will as farr as he knows or believes and upon his giveing Security for his Just and faithfull Administration of the said Decedts. Estate It is Ordered that a Certificate be granted him for Obtaining Letters of Administration in Due form, whereupon Sampson Merredeth became his Security and with him entred into Bond accordingly.

Thomas Bilbro, James Niblett, Edward Avery and William Jackson or any three of them, being first Sworn by Some Majistrate of this County for that purpose, are Ordered to appraise the Estate of Richard Cotten deced. and make report of their proceedings therein to the next Court when Timothy Bridges the Admr. is to return an Inventory thereof.

John Lett came into Court and made Oath that Sarah Drayton Late of this County Deced: Dyed without any Will as farr as he knows or believes and upon his giveing Security for his Just and ffaithfull Administration of the said Decedts. Estate It is Ordered that a Certificate be granted him for Obtaining Letters of Administration in Due form, whereupon James Moody became his Security and with him entred into Bond accordingly.

John Lett came into Court and made Oath that Roger Drayton Late of this County Deced: Dyed without any Will as farr as he knows or believes and upon his giveing Security for his Just and ffaithfull administration of the said Decedents Estate It is Ordered that a Certificate be granted him for Obtaining Letters of Administration in Due form, whereupon James Moody became his Security and with him entred into Bond accordingly.

[page 187]

William Harrison, Adam Tapley, Alexr. Taply and Richard Smith or any three of them being first Sworn by Some Majistrate of this County for that purpose, are Ordered to appraise the Estates of Sarah Drayton and Roger Drayton Deced: and make report of their proceedings to the next Court when John Lett the Admr. is to return Inventorys thereof.

In the action of Debt brot. by Randle Platt against Henry Duke for the breach of Covenants &c to the plts. Damage fivety pounds Sterling[...] the plts: Declaration is set forth, the Defendt. being returned *non est Inventus* and not appearing on the plts. motion an Attachment is granted him against the said Defendants Estate for the said Sum and Costs returnable to the next Court for Judgement.

And then the Court Adjourn'd till Court in Course. John Hamlin. Test W: Hamlin, Cl. Cur.

At a Court held at Merchantshope for the County of Prince
George on the Second Tuesday in June being the Tenth Day of
the month Anno Dom. 1718.

| Present | John Hamlin, | John Poythres, | Robert Munford } | |
| | Robert Hall, | Lewis Green Junr. | & John Peterson } | Gent. Justices |

James Thweatt haveing produced a Comission from the Honble. the Lieut. Governor to be Sherr: of this County, he accordingly Takes the Usuall Oaths Signes the Test and is Sworn Sherriff, he haveing given bond and Security as the Law Directs. Ordered the said Bond be recorded, Vizt.

Know all men by these presents that we James Thweatt, John Simmons and David Crawley of Prince George County are held and firmly bound to our Soveraign Lord the King his heirs and Successors in the Sum of One thousand pounds Sterling for the honest and true payment whereof to our sd. Soveraign his heirs and Successors we bind our Selves our heirs, Executors and Administrators Jointly and Severally firmly by these presents Witness our hands and Seals this 10: Day of June 1718.

The Condition of the above Obligation is Such that whereas the above bounden James Thweatt by Virtue of a Commission from [page 188] the Honble. the Lieut. Govr. is this Day Admitted and Sworn Sherriff for Prince George County. Now if the said James Thweatt shall well truly and ffaithfully Execute the said Office of Sherriff and faithfully do and perform all and every act and Acts thing and things relateing to and enjoined him in the said Office of Sherriff Dureing his Sherrivalty by Virtue of the Commission aforesaid, that then this Obligation to be Void and of None Effect otherwise to be and remain in full power force and Vertue.

[signed] James Thweatt, sealed wth. a wafer

Truly Recorded Test W: Hamlin, Cl. Cur.
[signed] Jno. Simmons, Seale of ye same
[signed] David Crawley, Seale of ye Same.

Thomas Simmons is Sworn under Sherriff to James Thweatt Sherr: he haveing first taken the Usuall Oaths and Signed the Test.

Richard Warthen in Open Court acknowledged his Deed (Indented and Sealed) Wth. Livery of Seizin endorst thereon, to Randle Platt on whose motion the same is admitted to record and then also appeared in Court Ailce the Wife of the said Richard Warthen and being first privately Examined freely relinquisht. to the sd. Platt her right of Dower in and to the Land and part of the mill mentioned in the said Deed, which is Likewise Ordered to be recorded.

Richard Warthen in Open Court Acknowledged his Bond for performance of Covenants to Randle Platt. Ordered it be recorded.

Randle Platt haveing produced a Comission from the Honble. the Lieut. Governor to be One of the Corroners of this County, he Accordingly takes the Usuall Oaths &c Signes the Test and is Sworn a Corroner.

Sarah Wall Executrix of John Wall Deced: returns a further Inventory of the said Decedts. Estate. Ordered it be recorded.

Nicholas Robyson in Open Court acknowleged his Deeds of Lease and release of Land (Indented and Sealed) to George Tillman on whose motion the same are Ordered to be recorded.

[page 189]

The Last Will and Testament of Richard Atkins Deced: was presented into Court by Sarah his Relict and Executrix therein Named who made Oath thereto and it being proved by the Oaths of William Cocke, William Short and Vol: Williamson the witnesses thereto Ordered to be Recorded, and upon the said Executrix's giveing Security according to Law it is Ordered that a Certificate be granted her for Obtaining a Probate in Due form, whereupon William Cocke and William Short became her Securety and with her entred into Bond.

John Beard, John Scoging, Vol: Williamson and William Heath or any three of them being first Sworn by some Majistrate of this County for that purpose are Ordered to appraise the Estate of Richard Atkins Deced: and make report of their proceedings thereinto the next Court [word removed] when Sarah Atkins the Executrix thereof is to return the Inventory.

On the petition of Thomas Harwell he is Exempt from paying Coty. Leavy for the future.

Francis Tucker in Open Court acknowledged his Deed (Indented and Seald) with Livery of Seizin endorst. thereon to David Crawley on whose motion the same is Ordered to be recorded, and then also appeared Mary the Wife of the said Tucker and being first privately Examined freely relinquisht. to the said Crawley her right of Dower in and to the Lands &c in the said Deed mentioned which is Likewise Ordered to be recorded.

Ellinor Walpole Administratrix &c of Richard Walpole Deced: returns upon Oath an Inventory &c of the sd. Decedts. Estate which is Ordered to be recorded.

The Last Will and Testament of Mathew Anderson Junr. was presented into Court by James Anderson the Executor therein Named who made Oath thereto and it being proved by the Oaths of James Thweatt and Buller Herbert the Witnesses thereto is Ordered to be Recorded, and upon the said Executors giveing Security according to Law it is Ordered that a Certificate be granted him for Obtaining a Probate in Due form, whereupon James Thweatt & Buller Herbert became his Security and with him entred into Bond.

William Batte, Henry Batte, John Thweatt and Henry Thweatt or any three of them are Ordered to appear to appraise the Estate of Mathew Anderson Junr. deced. they being first Sworn by Some [word removed] Magistrate of this County for that purpose and make report of their proceedings to the next Court, when James Anderson the Executor is to return the Inventory thereof.

[page 190]

West a Negro Boy belonging to ffrancis Epes is adjudged Seven Year Old.

Bernard Sykes the son of Bernard Sykes Deced: came into Court and made Oath that the said Bernard Sykes Deced: Dyed without any Will as farr [word removed] as he knows or believes, and upon his giveing Security for His Just and faitnfull Admin. of the sd. Decedts. Estate it is Ordered that a Certificate be granted him for Obtaining a Commission of Administration in Due form whereupon Richard Cureton became his Security and with him entred into Bond.

William Harrison, James Harrison, Gilbert Hays and James Jones or any three of them being first Sworn by some Majistrate of this County for that purpose, are Ordered to Appraise the Estate of Bernard Sykes Deced: and make report of their proceedings to the Next Court when Bernard Sykes the Administrator is Ordered to return the Intentory thereof.

John Robberds and Edward Winningham in Open Court acknowledged their Deed for Land (Indents and Sealed) with Livery of Seizin thereon to John Woodleife, on whose motion the same is Ordered to be recorded.

On the petition of Benjamin ffoster he is Exempt from being Surveyor of the Blackwater Road and Bridge, and Robert Honycutt is appointed Surveyor in his Stead and Ordered to proceed therein according to Law.

The peto. of Nicholas Robyson that he be Exempt from paying County Leavy is rejected.

The petition of Richard Munn that he be Levy free is rejected.

In the action of Debt brot. by Benjamin Arnold against Stephen Hausman for three hundred Seventy five pounds of Sweett Scented Tobacco & Caske Due by Bill Dated the twenty Second Day of July 1714, at the Last Court the

Defendt. failing to appear, William Troughton Security for the said Defendt. appeared by his Attorney and pleaded payment and the plt. Joining thereon the same was referred till this Court for Tryall, and the

[page 191]

said action being now called and the said Troughton failing to make good his sd. plea thereupon It's Ordered that the said William Troughton pay to the said Benjamin Arnall the said Sum and Costs. Als. Exec:

Elizabeth Whitmore Relict of Nicholas Whitmore Deced: came into Court and made Oath that the said Nicholas Departed this Life without any Will as farr as she knows or believes, and upon her giveing Security for her Just and faithfull Administration of the said Decedts. Estate, it is Ordered that a Certificate be granted her for Obtaining a Commission of Administration in Due form, whereupon Thomas Adams became her Security and with her entred into Bond.

Thomas Simmons Junr., David Goodgame, Arthur Biggins and Joseph Renn or any three of them being first Sworn for that purpose by some Majistrate of this County, are Ordered to appraise the Estate of Nicholas Whitmore Deced: and make report of their proceedings therein to the next Court when Elizabeth Whitmore the Admx. is to return the Inventory thereof.

The petition of William Mattox that his Negro Jack be Leavy free is rejected.

The Last Will and Testament of John Epes Deced: was presented into Court by Thomas Epes the Executor therein Named who made Oath thereto and it being proved by the Oaths of Francis Epes Junr. and William Epes Junr. two of the Witnesses thereto is Ordered to be recorded, and upon the said Executors giveing Security according to Law it is Ordered that a Certificate be granted him for Obtaining a Probate in Due form, whereupon ffrancis Epes Junr. became his Security and with him entred into Bond.

John Lewis, John Gerrald, John Nance and Thomas Moor or any three of them being first Sworn for that purpose are Ordered to appraise the Estate of John Epes Deced: and make report of their proceedings to the next Court when Thomas Epes the Executor is Ordered to return an Inventory thereof.

And then the Court adjourn'd till Court in Course. John Poythres. Test W: Hamlin, Cl. Cur.

[page 192]

At a Court held at Merchantshope for the County of Prince
Geo: on the second Tuesday in July being the Eighth Day of the
month Anno Dom: 1718.

Present   John Hamlin   John Poythres }
          Robt. Hall   & Sampson Merredeth }   Gent. Justices
Present John Hardyman Gent.

Timothy Bridges Admr. &c of Richard Cotten Deced: returns upon Oath an Inventory and appraisment of the sd. Decedts. Estate which is Ordered to be recorded.

Francis Ree's Deeds of Lease and Release of Land (Indented and Sealed) were proved in Open Court by the Oaths of John Baird, William Hall & Nathaniel Edwards Witnesses thereto, to be the act of the sd. ffrancis to Nathaniel Harrison Esqr. Named therein, and are Odered to be recorded.

Sarah Atkins Exrx. &c of Richard Atkins Deced: haveing [proved] by the Oath of William Short that it was the Desire of the sd. Deced: that his Estate shou'd not be Appraised, thereupon the Court reced. from their Order therein of the Last Court, and the sd. Sarah returns an Inventory only of the sd. Decedts. Estate which is Ordered to be recorded.

In the action of Debt Depending between William Randolph and ffrancis Mallory, for fifteen pds. Due by Notes &c on the Defts. motion oyer of the plts. Notes is granted him and time till the next Court to Consider the same.

The Attachment granted Thos. Simmons agst. the Estate of David Crawly &c is Continued till next Court.

The action on the case brot. by Littlebury Epes agst. Peter Wynne, is Continued till the next Court on the Defts. motion.

In the action on ye Case brot. by Joshua Woodleif against Thomas Burge for Two hundred pds. of Tobacco Due accot. Dated 1716, the Deft haveing pleaded *Nil Debit* and the plt. Joining in the Issue the same was Submitted to the Court for Tryall and the Deft. produceing a Discount of One hundred Eighty two pounds and a Quarter of Tobacco, which being allowed, Judgement is granted the plt. for Seventeen pounds and three Quarters of Tobacco being the Ballance, and it is Ordered that the sd. Deft. pay to the plt. the sd. Sum of Seventeen pounds and three Quarters of Tobacco and Costs. Als. Exec:

[page 193]

In the action on the case brot. by Joshua Woodleife agst. Edward Woodleife for Two hundred pounds of Tobacco Due by accot. Dated 1716, the Deft. appearing and pleading *Nil Debit* & the plt. Joining in the Issue the same was Submitted to the Court for Tryall, and the plt. failing to prove his accot. thereupon the suit is Dismist.

The action on the case brot. by Josh: Irby against Mathew Smart the plt. failing to prosecute, is Dismist.

The action on the case brot. by Joshua Irby agst. Cornelius ffox, the plt. failing to prosecute, is Dismist.

The action of Detinue brot. by Rowland Thomas against Richard Hamlin, the plt. failing to prosecute, is Dismist.

The action of Trespass brot. by Kathrine Williams agst. Richard Hamlin, the plt. failing to prosecute, is Dismist.

The suit in Chancery brot. by John Lewis Junr. agst. Henry Offley and Robert Bolling is Continued till the next Court.

Ned, Dina, Bridget and Tomazin, Negro's belonging to Mr. Richard Bland are adjudged Nine years old, each.

Robin and George, Negro's belonging to the sd. Bland are adjudged Seven years old each.

Jack a Negro belonging to the sd. Bland is adjudged four years old.

The action of Debt brot. by John Acre Junr. agst. Charles Bowen, the plt. faileing to prosecute is Dismist.

In The action of Debt brot. by Randle Platt agst. John Hardyman for fivety pds. Sterling &c the Deft. appears and pleads payment, and the plt. has time till the next Court to Consider the same.

The attachment granted George Harvie agst. the Estate of David Colleshaw is Continued.

The Attachment granted George Harvie agst. the Estate of John Spain is Continued.

The Attachment granted George Harvie agst. the Estate of John Berry is Continued.

The Attachment granted Drury Bolling agst. the Estate of John Spain is Continued.

The action on the case brot. by Joshua Irby agst. John Bonner the plt. faileing to prosecute on the Defts. motion it is Ordered that he be Nonsuit and pay the sd. Deft. five Shillings with Costs. Als. Exec:

[page 194]

Absent Mr. Merredeth

Abram Heeth agst. Sampson Merredeth Late Sherr: of this County pr. *Scire ffacias* &c the Deft. appears and pleads payment of the Judgement mentioned in the plts. Declaration and he Joining in the Issue the same was Submitted to the Court for Tryall and the sd. Deft. proveing the payment of the said Judgement thereupon the suit is Dismist.

Present Mr. Merredeth

The action of Debt brot. by Henry Soane agst. Richard Hamlin the plt. failing to prosecute is Dismist.

The action on the case brot. by John Mayes agst. Saml. Sentall, the plt. failing to prosecute is Dismist.

The attachment granted Nathl. Harrison Esqr. agst. the Estate of John Brewer is Continued till next Court.

The action on the case brot. by Thomas Mitchell agst. Randle Platt, the plt. failing to prosecute, is Dismist.

The action of Debt brot. by David Crawley agst. Samuel Sentall, the plt. failing to prosecute, is Dismist.

The action on the case brot. by Jonathan Carter agst. Jos[ep]h Greenhill, the plt. failing to prosecute, is Dismist.

The petiton of Randle Platt &c agst. John Hatch, the sd. Platt &c failing to appear, is Dismist.

The Order of the Last Court that John Sturdivant be Summoned to take the Oath of a Constable is made Null & Void, and it is Ordered that William Mitchell be Summoned in his Stead.

Duglas Irby being Summoned to answer for his Contempt in refuseing to clear the Blackwater Road, accordingly appears and upon reasons given to the Court he is acquitted & Discharged.

James Gretion is appointed Surveyor of the Blackwater Road & Bridge instead of Duglas Irby, Ordered that he proceed therein according to Law.

William Jackson is appointed Surveyor of the Roads from Warthens Mill & to Brandon Church, Ordered he proceed therein according to Law.

Ordered that all the Surveyors of the Highways be appointed in the year Last past Continue in their Offices.

[page 195]

In the action on ye Case brot. by Randle Platt against James Lundy for five hundred Sixty three pounds of Tobacco Due by accot. &c the Deft. by his attorney pleads *Nil Debit* and the plt. Joining in the Issue the same is referred till the next Court for Tryall.

In the action on the case brot. by Randle Platt agst. Henry King, the Deft. being permitted to plead Doubly, files his plea's to the plts: Declaration who has time till the next Court to Consider the same.

In the action brot. by George Tillman agst. John Patteson, the plt. Joins in the Demurrer and plea of ye Defendt: and the same is referred till the next Court for Tryall.

In the action of Trespass brot. by Richard Pigeon against Richard Whitmore for that the Deft. on the Eighth day of October Last past in the Parrish of Westover in this County, on him the sd. plt. an assault did make and him did then and there with force and Arms Vizt. Swords Staves and knives, beat wound & Evilly intreat so that of his Life he greatly Dispaired &c to the Damages of the sd. plt. fivety pds. Current money of Virginia as is set forth in the plts: Declaration, the Deft. by his Attorney appeared and pleaded not Guilty and for Tryall put himself upon the Country and the plt. Likewise, whereupon a Jury was Impannelled and sworn to try the matter in Issue by Name Duglas Irby, James Bell, John Bonner, John Sturdivant, Jos: Woodleife, John Womacke Junr., Richard Cureton, James Moody, John Robertson, John Scoggan, John Holloway & William Wallice, who haveing heard the Evidence and reced: their charge were sent out, and soon after return into Court & brought in their Verdict, We Jurrors find for the plt: Tenn Shillings Current money, Duglas Irby foreman, which Verdict on the motion of the plts: Attorney is recorded, and thereupon it is considered by the Court that the plt. recover agst. the aforesaid Deft. the aforesaid Sum of Tenn Shillings Current money being his Damages aforesaid by the Jurors in manner aforesaid assessed, togather with Costs. Als. Exec: the Court being of opinion that the Battery was proved.

In the action on the case of Slander brot. by John Wilkins against Adam Ivie the Deft. appears by his Attorney and pleads Not Guilty and the plt. Joining in the Issue the same is referred for Tryall till the next Court.

In the action of Trespass for Assault and Battery brot. by John Wilkins against Adam Ivie, the Deft. appears by his Attorney and pleads Not Guilty and the plt. Joining in the Issue, the same is referred for Tryall till the next Court.

Robert Gilmore being Summoned to appear at the next Court as a Witness for John Wilkins in his Actions against Adam Ivie, he makes Oath he cannot attend according to the sd. Summons, it is thereupon on his motion Ordered that a Commission Issue for the takeing his Evidence, and that the Deft. have Legall notice of the same from the plt.

[page 196]

In the suit in Chancery brot. by Robert Munford against Henry Offley and Robert Bolling is Continued till next Court.

In the action of Debt brot. by Isham Randolph Assignee &c against Richard Hudson, the Attachment granted the plt. agst. the Defts. Estate is Continued till next Court.

The Attachment granted Richard Munn agst. the Estate of William Anderson Junr. is Continued till next Court.

The action of Debt Depending between ffrancis Mallory and George Ivie is Continued.

The action of Debt Depending between Randle Platt and David Goodgame on the motion of the plts. Attorney is Continued till next Court.

The Order that Mary Bishope be Summoned to answer the presentment of the Grandjury is made Null and Void, the sd. Mary being removed out of this County.

The Order that Ailce Larrance be Summoned to answer the presentment of the Grandjury is made Null & Void.

John Melone the son of Robert Melone is Exempt from paying County Leavy for the future.

In the action on the case brot. by Cornelius ffox against William Wallice for fourteen pounds one Shilling and four pence Due by accot. Dated the 13th of January 1717, the Deft. haveing pleaded *nil Debit* and the plt. Joining in the Issue the same was Submitted to the Court for Tryall and the Deft. produceing a Discount of Six pounds One Shilling and Eleaven pence, which being allowed, Judgement is granted the plt. for the Ballance being Seven pounds Nineteen Shillings and five pence, and it is Ordered that the sd. Deft. pay to the sd. plt. the sd. sum of Seven pounds Nineteen Shillings & five pence with Costs. Als. Exec:

The Order that John Lett return Inventorys of the Estates of Sarah & Roger Drayton Deced: is Continued till next Court.

The Attachment granted Randle Platt agst. the Estate of Henry Duke, the plt. failing to prosecute, is Dismist.

Cornelius Cargill haveing attended one Day as an Evidence for Richard Pigeon agst. Richard Whitmore, Ordered the sd. Pigeon pay him for the same forty pounds of Tobacco & Costs. Als. Exec:

John Price haveing made Oath that he attended two Days as an Evidence for Cornelius ffox against William Wallice, Ordered that the sd. ffox pay him for the same Eighty pounds of Tobacco and Costs. Als. Exec:

[page 197]

John Womacke Junr. haveing made Oath that he attended two Days as an Evidence for Cornelius ffox, against William Wallice, Ordered that the sd. ffox pay him for the same Eighty pounds of Tobacco and Costs. Als. Exec:

And then the Court adjourn'd till Court in Course. John Hamlin. Test W: Hamlin, Cl. Cur.

At a Court held at Merchantshope for Prince George County on the
Second Tueday in August being the twelfth Day of the Month Anno Dom: 1718.

Present   John Hamlin,   John Poythres,   Randle Platt,   Robt. Hall
             Sampson Merredeth,   John Hardyman   & Lewis Green Junr.   Gent. Justices

On the petition of Hugh Lee It is Ordered that James Baugh the Overseer of the Nottoway River Road from John Colemans on Appomattox River to the south end of the Blackwater Bridge, and that Capt. James Thweatts, Henry Thweatts, John Thweatts, David Crawleys, Thomas Gregorys, Edward Burchetts, James Andersons, Edmd. Browders, Daniel Vaughn's & Thomas Spain's Male Labouring Tithable persons assist clearing the sd. Road.

Elizabeth Whittmore Administratix of the Estate of Nicholas Whittmore Deced: returns an Inventory and Appraisement of the Estate of the sd. Decedt. which is Ordered to be recorded.

The petition of John Wyatt agst. Timo: Bridges Admr. of Richard Cotten Deced: is referred till the next Court.

Timothy Bridges Admr. of Richard Cotten Deced: returns an accot. Dr. & Cr. of the Estate of the said Decedt. upon Oath and it being Examined by the Court is Admitted to record.

Elizabeth Marks Relict of Israel Marks deced: came into Court and made Oath that the sd. Israel Marks Deced: Dyed without any Will as farr as she knows or believes and upon her giveing Security as the Law Directs, It's Ordered that a Certificate be granted her for Obtaining Letters of Administration in Due form, whereupon James Harrison and John [Avery] became her Security and with her entred into Bond.

[page 198]

Thomas Adams, John Wilkins and ffrancis Wilkins and William Harrison or any three of them (being first sworn by some Majistrate of this County for that purpose) are Ordered to Appraise the Estate of Israel Marks Deced: and make report of their proceedings therein to the next Court, when Elizabeth Marks the Administratrix is to return the Inventory.

William Mitchell in Open Court acknowledged his Deeds of Lease and Release of Land (Indented and Sealed) to Stith Bolling on whose motion they are admitted to record. And then also appeared in Court Kathrain the Wife of the sd. Mitchell and being first Examined according to Law, acknowledged the same to be her act and Deed and freely and Voluntarily relinquisht. her right of Dower in and to the Lands &c in the sd. Deeds mentioned which is Likewise Ordered to be recorded.

William Mitchell in Open Court acknowledged his Deeds of Lease and Release of Land (Indented and Sealed) to Stith Bolling on whose motion they are admitted to Record. And then also appeared in Court Kathrain the Wife of the sd. Mitchell and being first Examined according to Law, acknowledged the same to be her act and Deed and freely and Voluntarily relinquisht. her right of Dower in and to the Lands &c in the sd. Deeds mentioned, which is Likewise Ordered to be recorded.

William Mitchell in Open Court acknowledged his Bond for performance of Covenants to Stith Bolling on whose motion it is Admitted to Record.

Drury Bolling in Open Court acknowledged his Deeds of Lease and Release of Land (Indented and Sealed) to Stith Bolling on whose motion they are admitted to record.

James Anderson Executor of Mathew Anderson Deced: returns an Inventory and appraisement of the sd. Decedts. Estate which is admitted to record.

The Last Will and Testament of Robert Hobbs Deced: was presented into Court by Sarah his Relict and Executrix therein Named who made Oath thereto and it being proved by the Oaths of Thomas Hobbs, James Hobbs and Nicholas Brewer Witnesses thereto is Admitted to Record, and upon the said Executrix's giveing Security according to Law it is Ordered that a Certificate be granted her for Obtaining a Probate in Due form, whereupon Wm. Harrison & James Moody became her Security and with her entred into Bond &c.

James Jones, Gilbt. Hay, William Short and William Adams or any three of them (being first Sworn for that purpose by some Majistrate of this County) are Ordered to appraise the Estate of Robert Hobbs Deced: and make report of their proceedings therein to the next Court when Sarah Hobbs the Executrix is to return the Inventory.

[page 199]

Bernard Sykes Admr. &c of Bernard Sykes Deced: returns an Inventory and appraisement of the Estate of the sd. Decedts. [Estate] which is Ordered to be recorded.

The Last Will and Testament of William Farrell Deced: was presented into Court by Sarah his Relict and Executrix therein Named who made Oath thereto, and it being proved by the Oath of Sampson Merredeth One of the Witnesses thereto is Admitted to record, and a Certificate is granted the sd. Executrix for Obtaining a Probate in Due form.

The action on the cast brot. by George Pasmore agst. Michal Hill, neither party appearing is Dismist.

In the action on the case brot. by John Hamlin agst. Timothy Bridges Admr. of the Estate of Richard Cotten Deced: for three hundred twenty Seven pounds of Tobacco Due by accot. the sd. Deft. appearing and haveing returned an accot. of the sd. Decedts. Estate and there being Due on the same only five Shillings and Eight pence, on the plts. motion Judgement is granted him for the same, and it is Ordered that the sd. Defendt. Admr. as aforesaid pay out of the sd. Decedts. Estate to the sd. plt. the said Sum of five Shillings and Eight pence. Als. Exec:

The action of Debt brot. by Thomas Mitchell agst. John Ward (neither party appearing) is Dismist.

The Depositions of Susan Naylor and Lewis Epes, Concerning a Negro belonging to Drury Bolling were taken in Open Court.

Drury Bolling appeared in Court and made Oath that his Negro man which was shott by John Nance, cost him thirty pounds Sterling.

In the action of Debt brot. by David Crawley agst. Mary Norten for four pounds Eleven Shillings and three pence, Due by Bill Dated 1716, the Defendt. came personally into Court and Confest Judgemt. to the plt. for the said Sum, it is therefore ordered that the said Defendt. pay to the said plt. the said Sum & Costs. Als. Exec.

In the action of Debt brot. by William Batte agst. Henry Robertson for three hundred forty Eight pounds of Tobacco Due by bill &c the Deft. being returned *non est Inventus* and not appearing on the plts: motion an Attachment is granted him agst. the sd. Defendts. Estate for the sd. Sum and Costs returnable to the next Court for Judgement for that shall appear to be Due.

The action on the case brot. by William Kennon agst. Joshua Wynne, neither party appearing is Dismist.

The action on the case brot. by William Cocke agst. Nathaniel Moss, neither party appearing is Dismist.

[page 200]

In the action on the case brot. by James Bell agst. Thomas Clifton for Eleven hundred and fivety pounds of Tobacco Due by accot. Dated 1715, the Deft. being returned *non est Inventus* and not appearing on the motion of the plts. Attorney an Attachment is granted him against the sd. Defts. Estate for the sd. Sum & Costs returnable to the next Court for Judgement for what shall appear to be Due.

In the action of Debt brot. by Robert Bolling against George Hambleton, on the motion of the Defts. Attorney Oyer of the plts: Bond is granted him and time till the next Court to Consider the same.

In the action of Debt brot. by John Hardyman and Compa. agst. Elizabeth Whittmore Administratrix of the Estate of Nicholas Whittmore Deced: for five hundred Sixty three pounds of Tobacco Due by Bill Dated the 13th of Aprill 1715, the Deft. appearing and makeing no Legall plea or Discount thereto, and the plt. makeing Oath that five hundred thirty three pounds thereof is Justly Due on Ballance of the sd. Bill, thereupon it is Ordered that the sd. Deft. pay to the said plt. out of the sd. Decedts. Estate the sum of four pounds Eight Shillings and Tenn pence, Value of the sd. Tobacco, togather with Costs. Als. Exec:

John Worsham Junr. appears in Court and Enters himselfe Security to pay all costs and Damages that shall be awarded Edward Wyatt at the suit of Joseph Goffe.

In the suit in Chancery brot. by Joseph Goffe agst. Edward Wyatt, the respondts. motion time is granted him till the next Court to answer the Complainants Bill.

The actoin on the case brot. by Joseph Greenhill agst. John Thompson neither party appearing is Dismist.

The action on the case brot. by Drury Bolling agst. Samuel Sentall the plt. failing to prosecute is Dismist.

The action on the case brot. by Robert Gilmore agst. Instance Hall neither party appearing is Dismist.

The action on the case brot. by David Crawley agst. Instance Hall the plt. failing to prosecute is Dismist.

In the action on the case brot. by Thomas Oliver agst. John Liles, Majr. Robert Munford became Speciall Bail for the Deft. who thereupon appears and plead *Nil Debit* and the plt. Joining in the Issue the same is referred till the next Court for Tryall.

[page 201]

In the action of Debt brot. by William Randolph agst. ffrancis Mallory for fifteen pounds Current money &c at the Last Court Oyer of the plts. Notes was granted the Deft. and time till this Court to consider the same, and he being now called to plead, did not appear nor offer any thing in barr or preclusion of the plts: action therefore it is considered by the Court that the plt. recover agst. the sd. Deft. the sd. Sum and Costs, unless he shall appear at the next Court and answer the sd. action.

In the action of Debt brot. by Thomas Simmons agst. Daniel Crawley and Elizabeth his Wife Executrix of the Last Will and Testament of Bryan Farrrell Deced: for five hundred and fivety pounds of Tobacco Due by Bill Dated the Ninth Day of March 1710/11, the sd. partys appearing the plt. allows of a Discount of One hundred twenty five pounds of Tobacco, thereupon Judgement is granted him for the residue of the sd. Bill being four hundred twenty five pounds of Tobacco and it s Ordered that the sd. Deft. pay to the said plt. the said Sum and Costs out of the sd. Decedts. Estate. Als. Exec:

In the suit in Chancery brot. [by] Robert Munford agst. Henry Offley Late of London Merchant and Robert Bolling Respondts. the sd. Complainant and the Respondent Bolling appearing, the said Bolling confesses to have in his hands of the said Offleys Estate in Goods and outstanding Debts Sufficient to pay the Complainants Debt Due from the sd. Offley being twenty Six pounds Eighteen Shillings and four pence halfe penny Sterling wch. the Complainant makes Oath is Justly Due to him, thereupon it is Decreed by the Court that upon the said Munfords giveing the said Bolling Security to Indemnifie him against the said Offley for so much, thhe sd. Bolling do Sattisfie and pay the sd. Munford his said Debt and Costs out of the sd. Offley's Goods and Debts in his hands & possession as aforesaid, advanceing Tenn per Cent upon the first cost of the sd. Goods as they are rated and Valued in the Shopkeepers Notes.

The suit in chancery brot. by John Lewis Junr. agst. Henry Offley and Robert Bolling is Continued till next Court.

In the action on the case brot. by Littlebury Epes agst. Peter Wynne, the Deft. appears and pleads *Nil Debit* and the plt. Joining in the Issue the same is referred till the next Court for Tryall.

Ann Hamlin relict of Richard Hamlin Deced: appears in Court and relinquishes her right to the Admininstration of her Deced: Husbands Estate to John Hamlin, who also appears in Court and Assumes to Indemnifie Sampson Merredeth one of the Securitys of the said Richard Hamlin Late Sherriff of this County as farr as the sd. Richards Estate will thereto Extend.

John Hamlin came into Court and made Oath that Richard Hamlin Deced: Dyed without any will as farr as he knows or believes, and upon his giveing Security as the Law Directs It is Ordered that a Certificate be granted him for Obtaining a Commission of Administration in Due form, whereupon Francis Poythres & Peter Wynne became his Securitys and with him entred into Bond &c.

[page 202]

George Hambleton, Gilbert Hay, James Jones and William Harrison or any three of them being first sworn for that purpose by some Majistrate of this County, are Ordered to Appraise the Estate of Richard Hamlin Deced: and make report of their proceedings thereunto the next Court when John Hamlin the Administrator thereof is to return the Inventory.

In the action of Debt brot. by Randle Platt against John Hardyman for fivety pounds &c the plt. Joins in the plea of the Defendt. and the Issue is referred till the next Court for Tryall.

On the motion of John Bolling Ordered that Robert Rogers be entred his Attorney in all causes Depending in this Court wherein the sd. Bolling is concerned.

John Bolling Exhibitted into Court a Bond from Thomas Wynne deced. to himselfe and made Oath thereto, Ordered it be Certified thereon.

John and Robert Bolling Exhibitted into Court a Bond from Thomas Wynne Deced: to them the sd. Bollings and made Oath thereto, Ordered it be certified thereon.

William Short haveing made Oath that he attended two days as an Evidence for Benjamin Arnold against Stephen Hausman, Ordered the said Arnold pay him for the same Eighty pounds of Tobacco and Costs. Als. Exec:

Mary Whittmore relict of Nicholas Whittmore senr. Deced: haveing relinquisht. her right to the Administration of her Deced. Husbands Estate, Richard Whitmore comes into Court and makes Oath that the sd. Nicholas Whittmore Deced: Dyed without any will as farr as he knows or believes & upon his giveing Security according to Law, it is Ordered that a Certificate be granted him for obtaining Letters of Administration in Due form where upon Edward Goodrich became his Security and with him entred into Bond.

Daniel Higdon, Jos. Carter, Wm. Reese and Richard Rees[e], or any three of them being first Sworn for that purpose by some Majistrate of this County, are Ordered to appraise the Estate of Nicholas Whittmore senr. Deced: and make report of their proceedings therein to the next Court when Richard Whittmore the Admr. is to return an Inventory thereof.

And then the Court Adjourn'd till Court in Course. Jno. Hamlin. Test W: Hamlin, Cl. Cur.

[page 203]

At a Court held at Merchantshope for the County of Prince George on the
Second Tuesday in September being the Ninth day of the month Anno 1718.

Present   John Hamlin,   Randle Platt,   Robert Munford
           Sampson Merredeth,   Robert Bolling,   John Hardyman
           & John Peterson   Gent. Justices

George Tillman and James Williams are appointed Surveyors of [Monksnak] Bridge and the Roads thereto belonging, Ordered they proceed therein according to Law.

Elizabeth Marks Admx. of Israel Marks Deced: returns into Court an Inventory and Appraisement of the said Decedts. Estate, which is Ordered to be recorded.

Anthony Wyatt One of the Orphans of Francis Wyatt Deced: appeared in Court and chose John Wyatt his Guardian, who gives Bond and Security according to Law.

Francis Wyatt and Susan Wyatt, Orphans of Francis Wyatt Deced: appeared in Court and chose Timothy Bridges their Guardian, who gives Bond and Security according to Law.

Sarah Vaughn relict of Samuell Vaughn Deced: came into Court and made Oath that the said Samuell Vaughn Deced. Dyed without any Will as farr as she knows or believes, and upon her giveing Security according to Law, it is Ordered that a Certificate be granted her for Obtaining a Commission of Administration in Due form whereupon William Wells became her Security and with her entred into Bond.

John Peterson, Henry Batte, William Batte and Arthur Kavanaugh, or any three of them being first Sworn by Some Majistrate of this County for that purpose are Ordered to Appraise the Estate of Samuel Vaughn Deced: and make report of their proceedings therein to the next Court when Sarah Vaughn the Admx. is to return an Inventory thereof.

Benjamin Evans one of the Orphans of Benjamin Evans Deced: appeared in Court and Chose Richard Hyde his Guardian, who gives Bond and Security accordingly.

The Last Will and Testament of Thomas Bilbro Deced: was presented into court by James Niblett, and the Executrix therein Named being Dead, the said James Niblett made Oath thereto, and it being proved by the Oaths of Edward Avery, James Niblett and William Bleighton the Severall Witnesses thereto is Admitted to record and upon the said James Niblett's giveing Security according to Law it is Ordered that a Certificate be granted him for Obtaining a Commission of Administration with the said Will annexed in Due form, whereupon Timothy Bridges became his Security and with him entred into Bond.

[page 204]

John Smith, Edward Avery, William Jackson and Robert Rivers or any three of them being first sworn for that purpose by some Majistrate of this County, are Ordered to appraise the Estate of Thomas Bilbro Deced: and make report of their proceedings therein to the Next Court when James Niblett the Admr. is to return the Inventory thereof.

In the action of Debt brot. by John and Robert Bolling Executors of the Last Will and Testament of Robert Bolling Deced: against James Vaughn for two thousand five hundred Seventy One pounds of Tobacco Due by Bill the Deft. came personally into Court and Convest. Judgement to the plts: for Nineteen hundred and Eighty pounds of Tobacco being the Ballance due on the said Bill, it is therefore Ordered that the said Defendt. pay to the said plts. the said Sum of Nineteen hundred and Eighty pounds of Tobacco and Costs. Als: Exec:

Richard Sykes one of the Orphans of Bernard Sykes Deced: appeared in Court and Chose Thomas Simmons Junr. his Guardian, who gives Bond &c.

John Sykes one of the Orphans of Bernard Sykes Deced: appeared in Court and Chose Richard Cureton his Guardian, who gives Bond &c.

Thomas Epes Executor &c of John Epes Deced: returns an Inventory and appraisement of the Estate of the said Decedt. which is Ordered to be recorded.

Richard Whittmore Admr. &c of Nicholas Whittmore senr. Deced: returns an Inventory and appraisement of the Estate of the said Decedt. which is Ordered to be recorded.

The Attachment granted George Harvie against the Estate of David Collyshaw is Continued till next Court.

The Attachment granted George Harvie against the Estate of John Spain is Continued till the next Court.

The Attachment granted George Harvie against the Estate of John Berry, the plt. failing to prosecute is Dismist.

The Attachment granted Drury Bolling against the Estate of John Spain is Continued till the next Court.

The Attachment granted Nathaniel Harrison Esqr. against the Estate of John Brewer is Continued till next Court.

[page 205]

John White appeared in Open Court and acknowledged his Deed for Land (Indented and Sealed) with Livery of Seizin thereon to John Hamersly on whose motion the same are ordered to be recorded, and then also appeared in Court Elizabeth the Wife of the said John White and being first privately Examined freely and Voluntarily acknowledged the same to be her act and Deed to the said John Hamersly and to him relinquisht. her right of Dower in and to the Lands &c in the said Deed mentioned which is Likewise Ordered to be recorded.

In the action on the case brot. by Robert Bolling agst. James Vaughn for five pounds Sixteen Shillings and five pence current mony Due by accot: Doctor Jos: Irby became Speciall Ball for the said Defendt. who thereupon appears and pleads *Nil Debit* and the plt. Joining in the Issue the same was Submitted to the Court for Tryall who haveing heard the proofs and allegations of the said partys give Judgement to the plt. for the said Sum, and Order that the said Defendt. pay to the said plt. the said Sum of five pounds Sixteen Shillings and five pence Currt. mony and Costs. Als: Exec:

And then the Court Adjourn'd till Court in Course. Jno. Hamlin. Test Wm. Hamlin, Cl. Cur.

At a Court held at Merchantshope for the County of Prince George on the second Tuesday in October being the fourteenth Day of the sd: month Anno Dom: 1718.

Present: Randle Platt, Robert Hall, Samson Merredeth, Robert Bolling, John Hardyman, Lewis Green Junr. & John Peterson Gent. Justices.

Wat a Negro Boy belonging to Roger Taylor is adjudged Seven years old.

Dick, a Negro Boy belonging to Drury Bolling is adjudged Tenn years old.

Harry, a Negro Boy belonging to Drury Bolling is adjudged Seven years old.

Jenny, a Negro Girl belonging to Samuel Lee is adjudged Six years old.

John Womacke Junr. in Open Court acknowledged his Deed for Land (Indented and Seald) with Livery of Seizin thereon, to Hannah Headworth, which with the said Endorsemt. of Livery and Seizin are Ordered to be recorded, And then also appeared in Court Mary the Wife of the said John Womack and being first privately Examined, Voluntarily

[page 206]

relinquisht to the said Hannah Hedworth her right of Dower in & to the Lands &c in the said Deed mentioned which is Likewise ordered to be recorded.

Present Robert Munford Gent. a Justice.

John Hatch made complaint that Joseph Greenhill stands Indebted to him by account Dated 1718, the Sum of Six hundred pounds of Tobacco and Seven Shillings and Nine pence, and Set forth that the sd. Joseph Greenhill hath unlawfully Departed this County that the Ordinary process at Law cannot be served on him, whereupon he by Virtue of an Attachment under the hand of one of his Majestys Justices for this County returnable to this Court hath caused part of the Estate of the said Greenhill to be attacht. for payment thereof, Vizt. One Desk, one Chest of Drawers, one small Ovall Table, One Small Looking glass, One Ditto, and one Doz: of Leather chairs, and the said Greenhill being called and failing to appear to replevye the Same, and the said plt. makeing Oath the said Sums are Justly Due, thereupon Judgement is granted him agst. the said Joseph Greenhill for the said Sums & Costs, to be Leavied on the said Goods Attacht., Ordered that the Sherriff cause the said Goods to be Duly appraised by Gilbert Hay, James Jones, William Harrison, and James Harrison, or any three of them (being first Sworn by some Majistrate of this County for that purpose) and Delivered the plt. for and toward the payment of the said Sum & Costs, and make Due report of their proceedings.

Thomas Goodwin made complaint that Joseph Greenhill Stands Indebted to him by Bond Dated the 14th Day of July 1718, the Sum of Forty pounds current money, and Set forth that the said Joseph Greenhill hath unlawfully Departed this County that the Ordinary process at Law cannot be Served on him, whereupon he by Virtue of an Attachment under the hand of one of his Majestys Justices for this County returnable to this Court hath caused part of the Estate of the said Greenhill to be Attacht. for payment thereof, Vizt. A certain Sum of Money in the hands of Mr. John Hardyman who is Sumoned to render account thereof upon Oath, and on the Surplussage one Negro man named Limbrick Attached by George Pasmore, And the said Greenhill being called and failling to appear to replevye the same, and the said plt. makeing Oath the said sum is Justly Due, thereupon Judgement is Granted him against the said Joseph Greenhill for the said Sum and Costs, to be Leavied on the said Estate attacht. as aforesaid

[page 207]

and the said John Hardyman who was Summoned as aforesaid accordingly appears and Confesses to have in his hands of the said Greenhills Estate the Sum of twenty five pounds Current money, there upon it is Ordered the said Hardyman pay the said Sum to the said Goodwyn Toward the payment of the plt. Goodwyns Judgement Obtained agst. the aforesaid Greenhill and it is further Ordered that the said Goodwyns Attachment against the Estate of the sd. Greenhill do continue in force till the next Court if Need be.

Robert Munford and William Kennon in Open Court acknowledged their Bond to Robert Bolling and whose motion the same is Admitted to Record.

Drury Bolling made a complaint that Joseph Greenhill stands Indebted to him by accot. Dated 1718: the sum of four pounds Current money, and set forth that the said Joseph Greenhill hath unlawfully Departed this County so that the Ordinary process at Law cannot be served on him, whereupon he by Virtue of an Attachment under the hand of one of his Majestys Justices for this County returnable to this Court hath caused part of the Estate of the said Greenhill to be Attacht. for payment thereof, Vizt. One Steel whipsaw with one rest and file, Six wood chairs, one Flock bed, and One pair of Sheets, One rugg, One plow, the Surplusage (if any) of Mr. Greenhills Estate in the hands of Mr. Hatch, One pr. Andirons, And the said Jos. Greenhill being called and failing to appear to replevye the same, and the said plt. makeing Oath the said Sum is Justly Due, thereupon Judgement is granted him agst. the said Joseph Greenhill for the said Sum & Costs, to be Leavied on the said Goods Attacht., Ordered that the Sherriff cause the said Goods to be Duly appraised by Gilbert Hay, James Jones, James Harrison, and William Harrison, or any three of them (being first Sworn by Some Majistrate of this County for that puspose) and Delivered the plt. for and toward the payment of the said Sum and Costs, and make due report of their proceedings.

John Williamson made complaint that Joseph Greenhill stands Indebted to him by Note under his hand Dated the twenty Sixth Day of February 1717, the Sum of Nine pounds Eight Shillings and Six pence currt. money, and set forth that the said Joseph Greenhill hath unlawfully Departed this County so that the Ordinary process at Law cannot be served on him, whereupon he by Virtue of an Attachment under the hand of one of his Majestys Justices for this County, returnable to this Court, hath caused part of the Estate of the said Greenhill to be attacht. for payment thereof, Vizt. twenty Gallons of rum and Sugar, One pair Stillyards, One Suit of Curtains and Vallains, One brass candlestick, one Grindstone, One [purear], One Cow and Calfe, One Iron Dragg, twelve Sawed plank in the woods, and Sevll. under the wheat in the store, and the unthrashed wheat in the store, and the said Jos. Greenhill being called and failing to appear to replevye the same, and the said plt. makeing Oath the said Sum is Justly Dew, thereupon Judgement is granted him against the said Joseph Greenhill for the sd. Sum and Costs, to be Leavied on the said Goods Attacht., Ordered that the Sherriff cause the said Goods to be Duly appraised by Gilbert Hay, James Jones, James Harrison, and William Harrison or any three of them (being first sworn by Some Magistrate of this County for that purpose) and Delivered the plt. for and toward the payment of the said Sum and Costs and make report of their proceedings.

[page 208]

George Pasmore made complaint that Joseph Greenhill stands Indebted to him by two Notes under his hand, one Dated the first Day of January 1717, and the other Dated the Seventh Day of March 1717, the sum of Nineteen pounds Current money, and Set forth that the said Greenhill hath unlawfully departed this County that the Ordinary process at Law cannot be served on him, whereupon he by Virtue of an Attachment under the hand of one of his Majestys Justices for this County returnable to this Court hath caused part of the Estate of the said Joseph to be attacht. for payment thereof, Vizt. One Negro named Limbrick, and the said Greenhill being called and failing to appear to replevye the same, and the said plt. makeing Oath the said Sum is Justly Due to him, thereupon Judgement is granted him agst. the said Greenhill for the said Sum and Costs, to be Leavied on the said Negro Attacht., Ordered that the Sherriff cause the said Negro to be Duly appraised by Gilbert Hay, James Jones, James Harrison, and William Harrison, or any three of them (being first Sworn by Some Magistrate of this County for that purpose) and Delivered the plt. for and toward the payment of the said Sum and Costs, and make Due report of their proceedings.

Ordered that the Sherriff do pay to Thomas Goodwyne (upon the appraisement of the Negro of Joseph Greenhills Attacht. by George Pasmore) the Surplusage of the money in the said Pasmores hands more than will pay his Judgement obtained against Jos. Greenhill for Nineteen pounds & costs, Provided the sd. Surplusage do not Exced fifteen pounds and the costs of the said Goodwyns Judgement agst. the said Jos. Greenhill.

Peter Wynne complained against Joseph Greenhill that he stands Indebted to him by account Dated 1718: the sum of Six pounds fourteen Shillings & Two pence currt. money, and set forth that the said Greenhill hath unlawfully Departed this County so that the Ordinary process at Law cannot be served on him, whereupon he by Virtue of an Attachment under the hand of one of his Majestys Justices for this County returnable to this Court, hath caused part of the Estate of the said Joseph to be attacht. for payment thereof, Vizt. fifteen pewter plates, two Iron potts, one pot rack and two pair pott hooks, Seven pewter Dishes and two Basons, One Iron Kettle, One Skillet, One feather bed and furniture, One Cart and wheels and Harness, One frying pann, three brass Candlesticks, Eight pewter plates more, & one bason, One bedstead and cord, One pair fire Tongs, two hair brushes & one Tin funnell, and the said Greenhill being called and failing to appear to replevye the same, and the plt. makeing Oath the said Sum is Justly Due, thereupon Judgement is granted him against the said Greenhill for the said Sum of Six pounds fourteen Shillings and two pence and Costs, to be Leavied on the said Goods Attacht. Ordered that the Sherriff cause the said Goods to be Duly appraised by Gilbert Hay, James Jones, James Harrison, and William Harrison, or any three of them (being first Sworn by Some Majistrate of this County for that purpose) and Delivered the plt. for and toward the payment of the said Sum and Costs, and make report of their proceedings.

[page 209]

John Dunbarr made complaint that Joseph Greenhill stands Indebted to him by account Dated 1718, the sum of One pound Nineteen Shillings and one penny half penny & set forth that the said Greenhill hath unlawfully Departed this County that the Ordinary process at Law cannot be served on him, whereupon he by Virtue of an Attachment under the hand of one of his Majestys Justices for this County returnable to this Court hath caused part of the Estate of the said Joseph to be attacht. for payment thereof, Vizt. Seventeen Bushells of wheat, Six empty caske, Eight porke barrells, One halfe bushell, one peck, One butter Tubb, and the said Greenhill being called and failling to appear to replevy the same, and the said plt. makeing Oath the said Sum is Justly Due to him, thereupon Judgement is granted him against the said Greenhill for the said Sum and Costs, to be Leavied on the said Goods Attacht. Ordered that the Sherriff cause the said Goods to be Duly appraised by Gilbert Hay, James Jones, James Harrison, and William Harrison, or any three of them (being first Sworn by some Magistrate of this County for that purpose) and Delivered the plt. for and toward the payment of the said Sum & Costs, and make due report of their proceedings.

John Wilkins made complaint that Joseph Greenhill stands Indebted to him by a Note under his hand Dated the fourteenth Day of June 1718: the sum of twenty Shillings Current money and set forth that the said Greenhill hath unlawfully Departed this County that the Ordinary process at Law cannot be served on him whereupon he by Virtue of an Attachment under the hand of One of his Majestys Justices for this County returnable to this Court hath caused part of the Estate of the said Greenhill to be Attacht. for payment thereof, Vizt. the Surplusage in the Hands of John Williamson of Mr. Greenhills Estate and the said Greenhill being called and failing to appear to replevye the same, and the said plt. makeing Oath the said Sum is Justly Due to him, thereupon Judgement is granted him against the said Greenhill for the said Sum and Costs, And it is Ordered that the Sherriff do pay to the said John Wilkins (upon the appraismt. of the Estate of Joseph Greenhill Attacht. by John Williamson) the Surplusage of the money in the said Williamsons hands more than will pay his Judgement Obtained against Jos. Greenhill for Nine pounds Eight Shillings and Six pence Curt. money & Costs, Provided the said Surplusage Exceed not the above mentioned Judgement of Twenty Shillings and Costs obtained against the said Greenhill.

William Troughton made complaint that Joseph Hawks Stands Indebted to him by accot. Dated 1717: the sum of Nine pounds one Shilling and Nine pence halfe penny currt. money, and set forth that the said Joseph hath unlawfully Departed this County that the Ordinary process at Law cannot be Served on him whereupon he by Virtue of an Attachment under the hand of one of his Majestys Justices for this County returnable to this Court hath caused

[page 210]

part of the Estate of the said Joseph to be attacht. for payment thereof, Vizt. One Anvill, One brake Iron, three Screw plates, one Vice, one Sledge, three pair of Tongs, One parcell of old Iron, fifteen files, three old pistolls and two barrs of new Iron, and the said Joseph Hawks being called and failing to appear to replevye the same, and the said plt. makeing Oath the said Sum is Justly Due to him, thereupon Judgement is granted him against the said Joseph Hawks for the said Sum & Costs to be Leavied on the said Goods Attacht. Ordered that the Sherriff cause the said goods to be Duly appraised by Gilbert Hay, James Jones, James Harrison, & William Harrison or any three of them (being first Sworn by some Majistrate of this County for that purpose) and Delivered the plt. for and toward the payment of the said Sum and Costs, and make report of their proceedings.

George Bleighton an Orphan of George Bleighton Deced: came into Court and Chose his mother Lydia Clements his Guardian, who gives Bond & Security accordingly.

The Last Will and Testament of Francis Rea Deced: was presented into court by Thomas Farmar, and the Executrix therein named being dead, the said Thomas Farmar made Oath thereto, and it being proved by the Oath of Mr. Robert Hall, one of the Witnesses thereto is Admitted to record, and upon the said Thomas Farmars giveing Security as the Law Directs, It's Ordered that a Certificate be granted him for Obtaining Letters of Administration with the said Will annext. in Due form, whereupon E. Goodrich and Robert Nicholson became his Securitys and with him entred into bond.

John Bell, Richard Winkles, William Savage and John Wyatt, or any three of them being first Sworn by Some Magistrate of this County for that purpose, are Ordered to Appraise the Estate of ffrancis Rea Deced: and make report of their proceedings to the next Court when Thomas Farmar the Administrator is to return the Inventory.

Sarah Hobbs Executrix of the Last Will and Testament of Robert Hobbs Deced: returns into Court an Inventory and appraisement of the said Decedts. Estate, which is Ordered to be recorded.

The Last Will and Testament of William Bishope Deced: was presented into Court by Sarah Bishope the Executrix therein Named who made Oath thereto and it being proved by the Oaths of William Harrison

[page 211]

and John Bishope Junr. is Admitted to record, and upon the said Executrix's giveing Security according to Law, it is Ordered that a Certificate be granted her for Obtaining a Probate in Due form, whereupon John Bishope and James Bishope became her Security and with her entred into Bond.

Ordered that Sarah Bishop Executrix of the Last Will and Testament of Wm. Bishope Deced: do return an Inventory of the said Decedts. Estate to the next Court.

Francis Rea the son of Francis Rea Deced: came into Court and chose Thomas Farmar his Guardian, Ordered that he give bond and Security at the next Court, Otherwise not to be admitted Guardian &c.

Sarah Vaughn Administratrix of Samuel Vaughn Deced: returns into Court an Inventory and Appraisement of the Estate of the said Decedt. which is Ordered to be recorded.

On the petition of John Acre for the Administration of the Estate of Charles Bowen Deced: It's Ordered that Margery Bowen relict of the said Decedt. be Sumond to the next Court to accept or refuse the said Administration.

Sarah Rea being Summoned to prove the Last Will of Francis Rea Deced: on her motion it is Ordered that Thomas Farmar Admr. &c of the said Deced: do pay to the said Sarah for the same One hundred thirty five pounds of Tobacco she haveing come out of another County twenty five miles and attended one Day togather with costs. Als. Exec:

In the suit in Chancery brot. by John Lewis Junr. against Henry Offley Late of London Merchant and Robert Bolling respondts. the said Complainant and the respondt. Bolling appearing, the said Bolling confesses to have in his hands of the sd. Offleys Estate in Goods and outstanding Debts sufficient to pay the Complainants Debt due from the said Offley being fifteen pounds thirteen Shillings and tenn pence Sterling, which the Complainant makes Oath is Justly Due to him, thereupon it is Decreed by the Court that upon the said Complainants giveing the said Bolling Security to Indemnifie him against the said Offley for so much, the said Bolling do sattisfie and pay the said John Lewis his said Debt and Costs out of the said Offleys Goods and Debts in his hands and possession as aforesaid, advanceing ten pr. Cent on the first cost of the said Goods as they are rated and Valued in the Shopkeepers Notes. Whereupon the said John Entred into Bond with Security, and the same being acknowledged in Court is Ordered to be recorded.

And then the Court Adjourn'd till court in Course. Rand. Platt. Test W: Hamlin, Cl. Cur.

[page 212]

At a Court held at Merchantshope for the County of
Prince George on the second Tuesday in November being
the Eleventh Day of the month A.Dom 1718.

Present   John Hamlin   Robert Munford }
     Samson Merredeth,   John Hardyman }
     Lewis Green Junr.   & John Peterson }   Gent. Justices

Dick a Negro Boy belonging to John Edwards is adjudged five years old.

James Niblet Admr. &c of Thomas Bilbro Deced: returns an Inventory and appraisement of the said Decedts. Estate which is Ordered to be recorded.

Present Robt. Bolling, Gent.

On the motion of James Niblet it's Ordered that William Jackson be Summoned to the Next Court to take the Oath of a Constable.

Pursuant to the Direction of the Act concerning Jurys, A Grandjury was Impannelled and Sworn by Name Gilbert Hay, John Ledbetter, Richard Smith Senr., John Wilkins, Saml. Temple, John Womacke Junr., Edmond Browder, William Wallice, George Woodleife, John Pooke, Thomas Simmons, Thomas Epes, William Harrison, James Jones, James Harrison, & William Reves, who haveing their charge were sent out and soon after make the following return into Court, Vizt. We the Grandjurors return *Ignoramus*. Gilbt. Hay, Foreman.

On the petition of Randle Platt, setting forth that his Sarvant John Thompson absented himselfe from his Service seven Days and praying Judgemt. agst. him according to Law, and the said John appearing and makeing no Defence, it is thereupon Ordered, that the said John do Serve the said Platt in Lieu thereof fourteen Days, and also Nine days over and above being for the Costs of this Judgement, after the time of the said John's Service by Indenture is Expired.

The Last Will and Testament of John Tidmarsh Deced: was presented into Court by Elizabeth his relict, and there being as Executor appointed therein, the said Elizabeth made Oath thereto, and it being proved by the Oaths of George Woodleife and Tillman Patteson, Witnesses thereto is Ordered to be recorded, and on the motion of the said Elizabeth and her giveing Security as the Law Directs, it's Ordered that a Certificate be granted her for Obtaining a Commission of Administration with the said Will annexed in Due form.

[page 212a]

Wm. Mattox, Wm. Wallice, Duglas Irby, and John Pooke, or any three of them being first Sworn by some Majistrate of this County for that purpose, are Ordered to appraise the Estate of John Tidmarsh Deced: and make report of their proceedings to the next court when the Administratrix &c is to return the Inventory.

Richard Bland made complaint that Joseph Greenhill stands Indebted to him by accot. &c three pounds Eight Shillings and Six pence, and set forth that the said Joseph hath unlawfully Departed this County that the Ordinary process at Law cannot be served on him, whereupon he by Virtue of an Attachment under the hand of one of his Majestys Justices for this County returnable to this Court hath caused part of the Estate of the said Joseph to be attacht. for payment thereof, Vizt. four Cows, and the said Joseph being called and failing to appear to replevye the same, and the said plt. makeing Oath the said Sum is Justly Due to him, thereupon Judgement is granted him agst. the said Joseph for the said Sum & Costs to be Leavied on the said Cattle attacht. Ordered that the Sherr: cause the said Cattle to be Duly appraised by Gilbert Hay, James Jones, James Harrison, and William Harrison or any three of them (being first Sworn by some Magistrate of this County for that purpose) and Delivered the plt. for and toward the payment of the said Sum & Costs, and make report of their proceedings.

The Attachment granted Charles Chiswell agst. the Estate of Joseph Greenhill is Continued till the next Court.

John Wilkins made Complaint that Joseph Greenhill stands Indebted to him by a Note under his hand Dated 1718, the sum of twenty Shillings, and set forth that the said Joseph hath unlawfully Departed this County so that the Ordinary process at Law cannot be served on him, whereupon he by Virtue of an Attachment under the hand of One of his Majestys Justices for this County returnable to this Court hath caused part of the Estate of the said Joseph to be attacht. for payment thereof, Vizt. About twelve Hoggs, One old horse, three Long two Inch plan, about twenty bushells of Salt, and the said Joseph being called and failing to appear to replevy the same, the said plt. makeing Oath the said Sum is Justly Due to him, thereupon Judgement is granted him agst. the said Joseph for the sd. Sum and Costs, to be Leavied on the said Estate Attachmt. Ordered that the Sherr: cause the said Estate ([words removed]) to be Duly appraised by Gilbert Hay, James Jones, James Harrison, and William Harrison, or any three of them (being first Sworn by some Magistrate of this County for that purpose) and Delivered the plt. for payment of the above Judgement, and make report of their proceedings.

[page 213]

Robert Honycutt made Complaint that Joseph Greenhill stands Indebted to him by accot. Dated 1718: the sum of twenty Shillings and Nine pence, and set forth that the said Joseph hath unlawfully Departed this County that the Ordinary process at Law cannot be served on him whereupon he by Virtue of an Attachment under the hand of one of his Majestys Justices for this County returnable to this Court, hath caused part of the Estate of the said Joseph to be Attacht. for payment thereof, Vizt. A Debt Due to the said Greenhill in the hands of Francis Mallory, and the said Joseph being called and failing to appear to replevye the same, and the said plt. (being a Quaker) made his Affirmation the said Sum is Justly Due to him, thereupon Judgement is granted him agst. the said Greenhill for the said sum and Costs, to be Leavied on the Estate attacht. as aforesaid, And the said Francis Mallory being Sumoned to render accot. of the said Debt upon Oath accordingly appears, and Confeses to have in his hands of the said Greenhills Estate Sufficient to pay the above Judgement and Costs, it is thereupon Ordered that the said Francis Mallory do pay to the said Robert out of the mony in his hands Due to the said Greenhill, the above mentioned sum and Costs. Als. Exec:

On the Attachment continued at the Last Court to Thomas Goodwynne against the Estate of Joseph Greenhill the Sherr: makes the following return, Vizt. ye 21st of October 1718, then Executed this Attachment farther on twenty one Shillings and one penny in the hands of Peter Wynne being the Surplus of his Attachment vrs. Greenhills Estate on one pound fifteen Shillings and Seven pcne in Mr. John Hatchs hands, on Sundry porke barrells at Warthins Mill, being abt. twenty four in Number, on a Large Copper, and the sd. Greenhill being called and failing to appear, it is thereupon Ordered that the said Peter Wynne above Named do pay to the said Thomas Goodwyn the said Sum of twenty one Shillings and one penny of the sd. Greenhills Estate in his hands. Als. Exec: also Ordered that the above Named John Hatch do pay to the said Thomas Goodwyn the said Sum of thirty five Shllings and Seven pence of the said Greenhills Estate in his hands attacht. as aforesaid. Als. Exec: and it is further Ordered that the Sherr: cause the Goods above mentioned to be Duly appraised by Gilbert Hay, James Jones, James Harrison, and William Harrison, or any three of them (being first Sworn by a Magistrate of this County for that purpose) and Delivered the plt. toward the payment of his Judgemt. agst. the said Joseph Greenhill, and make report of their proceedings

[page 214]

The petition of ffrancis and Jos. Rea that they be admitted to choose their Guardians &c is rejected.

The Last Will and Testament of John Hill Deced: was presented into Court by Ann his relict and Executrix who made Oath thereto and it being proved by the Oaths of William Mattox, George Woodleif and John Pook witnesses thereto is ordered to be recorded, and on her motion Certificate is granted her for Obtaining a Probate in Due forme.

Ordered that Ann Hill Exrx. of John Hill Deced: return an Inventory of the said Decedents Estate to the next Court.

John Hamlin Admr. &c of Richard Hamlin Deced: returns an Inventory and appraisement of the said Decedts. Estate which is Ordered to be recorded.

Nicholas Overby is appointed overseer of the Highway from Lieuts. runn to Wallices, and it is Ordered that he with his own male Tithables Join with the Inhabitants of that precinct in clearing the said Road.

Ordered that Francis Coleman be Overseer of the Highway from butterwood [runn] to John Tallys.

Mr. Randle Platt is appointed overseer of the Roads in Maycocks Neck Instead of Adam Tapley.

And then the Court Adjourn'd till Court in Course. Jno. Hamlin. Test W: Hamlin, Cl. Cur.

At a Court held at Merchantshope in Prince George County the
29th Day of October 1718: for Proof of Publick Claims, and for receiving
and Certyfying to the Genrall Assembly the propositions and Grievances of
the Inhabitants of this County.

Present	John Hamlin,	Randle Platt,	Robt. Hall }	
	Samson Merredeth	and Robert Bolling }		Gent. Justices

Drury Bolling presented into Court his claim for a certain Negro man, which was killed by John Nance of this County. Ordered the said Claim be Certified to the Next Session of the Genl. Assembly for Allowance.

And then the Court Adjourn'd. Jno. Hamlin. Test W: Hamlin, Cl. Cur.
this ought to preceed the Minutes of November Court 1718.

[page 215]

At a Court held at Merchantshope for the County of
Prince George, on the second Tuesday in December, being
the Ninth Day of the said month, Anno Dom: 1718.

Present	John Hamlin,	Robert Munford }	
	John Hardyman	& Lewis Green Junr. }	Gent. Justices

Rebecca Spencer relict of Richard Spencer Late of this County Deced: came into Court and made Oath that the said Richard Spencer Departed this Life without any Will as farr as she knows or believes, and on her motion and performing what is usuall in Such cases, certificate is granted her for Obtaining a Commission of Administration in Due form.

John Bishope, Travis Morris, William Warthen & William Short or any three of them being first Sworn by some Majistrate of this County for that purpose are Ordered to appraise the Estate of Richard Spencer Deced: and make report of their proceedings to the next Court then Rebecca Spencer the Admx. is to return the Inventory thereof.

The Last Will and Testament of Thomas Smith Late of this County Deced: was presented into Court by Judith Smith his relict and one of the Executrs. therein Named, and Richard Smith the other Executor haveing refused to take on him the burthen of the Execution of the said Testament, the said Judith made Oath thereto, and it being proved by the Oaths of Edward Prince and Francis Sheffeild Witnesses thereto is Admitted to record, and on her motion and performing what is usuall Certificate is granted her for Obtaining a Probate in Due form.

Ordered that Judith Smith Exrx. &c of Thomas Smith Deced: return an Inventory of the said Decedts. Estate to the next Court.

Valentine Minge, Edward Wyatt, Benjamin Reeks and James Bell or any three of them first sworn by some Majistrate of this County for that purpose, are Ordered to appraise that part of the Estate of Francis Clements Deced: that is within this County and make report of their proceedings.

Charles Chiswell made complaint that Joseph Greenhill stands Indebted to him by Bill Dated 1717, the sum of Six hundred pounds Currt. money, and set forth that the said Joseph hath unlawfully

[page 216]

absconded so that the Ordinary process at Law cannot be served on him, whereupon he by Virtue of an Attachment under the hand of one of his Majestys Justices for this County hath caused part of the Estate of the said Jos. to be attacht. for payment thereof, Vizt. One ps. of Damask, 2½ yds: broadcloth, two peices of Buckram, one ps. of Stuff, 5 yds. cullored Kersay, 2½ yds. Dto., 6¾ yds. of Sagathy, 8½ yds. of Drugget, 2½ yds. Ditto, 3½ yds. Stuff, 23¾ yds. Ditto, 2 yds. of Shalloon, 18 yds. of Drugget, One ps. of Buckram, 5¾ yds. of Stuff, 7¼ yds. of Dto., 1¾ yds. of Kersey, 8 yds. of Serge, 12¼ yds. white Ozenbriggs, 8 yds. Ditto, 27½ yds: of bro. Ozenbriggs, 4½ yds. blew Linnan, 1½ yds. Ditto, 2½ yds. white Ozenbriggs, 13 yds. white Sheeting Linnen, 11 papers of coat and waistcoat buttons, 5 bundles of Mohair, 8 cards of white thred buttons, 1 pr. womans Shoes, One papr. of coat buttons more two Doz. and 1 pr. of Snuffers, One Doz. and three case knives, three Tobacco boxes, and three inkhorns, One ps. of Stay Tape, 1 ps. Do., Seven Silk Laces, One pr. gloves, a bunch of Ribbon, Eleven pr. womens and Boyd Stockings, 1 pr. Snuffers, twelve felt hatts, three pair pumps, 4 pr. womans shoes, 17 Sine buttons, one Looking Glass, Six yds. of Stuff, 19 Large sifters, One horse collar and cart, Saddle, three barrls. of Shot, One Tinn pann of Shott, One Jugg of Ditto, half a Large barrell of Drapp shotts, a barrl. of powder about 100 wt., 86 Hs and 6 Doz. Dove tails, 3 pr. X garnetts, 12 pr. hooks and hinges, [6] Hs more, 6 pr. X garnetts more, one chest of pipes, 16 axes, 3 more, 4 pr. more of Hooks and hinges, One crosscut Steel plate saw, One whip saw, Six rests and Eight files, One adze, One barrl. of Nails and 6 more that have small parcells in them, Six Sickles, One handsaw, three weeding hoes, & two Narrow Dto. all the chests and barlls. in the room, Vizt. the store, one cask of Earthen ware, two Stele saws, one Fent. 1 x cutt, the Residue of his cattle which is not now attacht., all his book Debts, the Ball: Due from Mr. Platt to Mr. Greenhill, all Mr. Greenhills Estate in Mr. Hardyman's hands, One old boat, and the said Greenhill being called and failing to appear to replevye the same, the the sd. Chiswell makeing Oath the sum of four hundred and Nine pounds, thirteen Shillings and Seven pence half penny currt. mony is Justly Due to him thereupon Judgement is granted him for the said Sum and Costs, to be Leavied on the sd. Estate Attacht. &c. Ordered that the Sherr: cause the said Goods and Chattels to be Duly Appraised by John Hatch, James Jones, Gilbert Hay, and James Harrison, or any three of them, (being first Sworn by some Majistrate of this County for that purpose) and Delivered the plt. toward the payment of the said Sum and Costs, and make report of their proceedings.

John Hardyman above named being Summoned to render an account of what parts of the said Jos. Greenhills Estate he has in his hands, accordingly appears, and Confesses to have in his hands & possession of the said Greenhills Estate, the sum of Eighty Eight pounds thirteen Shillings currt. money, whereupon it is Ordered that the said John Hardyman do pay to the said Charles Chiswell the said Sum. Als. Exec:

[page 217]

Randle Platt being Summoned to render an accot. of what part of the estate of Joseph Greenhill he has in his hands or how much he stands Indebted to him, the same being Attacht. by Charles Chiswell, and the sd. Platt failing therein It's Ordered that he make up and return to the next Court an accot. Dr. & Cr. between the said Greenhill and himselfe.

Benjamin Foster in Open Court acknowledged his Deeds of Lease and release of Land, sealed, to John Hynes on whose motion they are Admitted to record, and then also appeared in Court Elizabeth the wife of the sd. Benjamin and being first privately Examined freely and Voluntarily relinquisht. to the sd. John her right of Dower in and to the Lands &c in the sd. Deeds mentioned which is Ordered to be recorded.

Elizabeth Duke relict of Henry Duke Late of this County Deced: came into Court and made Oath that the said Henry Duke Dyed without any Will as farr as she knows or believes and on her motion and giveing Security as the Law Directs Certificate is granted her for Obtaining a Commission of Administration in Due form.

Mr. John Hatch, Capt. John Hamlin, Capt. John Poythres and Gilbert Hay or any three of them, being first Sworn by some Majistrate of this County for that purpose, are Ordered to appraise the Estate of Henry Duke Deced: and make report of their proceedings therein to the next Court when Elizabeth Duke the Admx. is to return the Inventory thereof.

Elizabeth Titmarsh Administratrix with the Will Annext. of John Titmarsh Deced: returned an Inventory and Appraisment of the said Decedts. Estate, which is Ordered to be recorded.

William Mitchell is Sworn a Constable of Bristoll Parrish.

In the action on the case brot. by Randle Platt agst. James Lundy for five hundred Sixty three pds. of Tobacco Due by accot. Dated 1713, the Deft. haveing pleaded *Nil Debit* and the plt. Joining in the Issue the same was referred till this Court for Trayll and the sd. partys being called and the Deft. failing to appear and the plt. makeing Oath the said Sum is Justly Due to him, thereupon it is Ordered the said Deft. pay to the said plt. the said Sum & Costs. Als. Exec:

[page 218]

Bernard Sykes Admr. of Bernard Sykes Deced: returns a further Inventory & Appraisment of the said Decedts. Estate, which is Ordered to be recorded.

In the action on the case brot. by Randle Platt agst. Henry King, the plt. files a Demurrer to the plea's of the Deft. who has time till the next Court to consider the same.

The action brot. by George Tillman agst. John Pattison the plt. failing to prosecute is Dismist.

In the action on the case brot. by John Wilkins agst. Adam Ivie for certain false feigned Scandalous words and Lyes Spoke, publisht. Declared & Affirmed by the Deft. of the sd. plt: to his the sd. plts. Damage fivety pounds currt. money as in his Declaration is set forth, the Deft. haveing pleaded not Guilty and the plt. Joining in the Issue the same was referred till this Court for tryall, and the said partys by their Attorneys appearing a Jury was Impannelled and Sworn to trye the same, by Name Richard Smith, Arthur Biggins, Hugh Golightly, Richard Carlile, Thomas Simmons, William Reves, Phillip Burrow, Richd. Pace, Geo: Woodleife, William Wallice, John Hines and Geo. Tillman who haveing heard the Evidence and reced: their charge were sent out and soon after returned into Court with the following Verdict, Vizt. Wee the Jurors find for the plt: forty Shillings Currt. money, Richard Smith, Foreman, which Verdict on the motion of the plts. Attorney is recorded and it is considered by the Court that the plt. recover agst. the Deft. the aforesaid Sum being his Damage aforesaid in manner aforesaid by the Jurors Assessed togather with Costs. Als. Exec:

In the action of Debt brot. by Isham Randolph Assignee &c agst. Richard Hudson, the plt. failing to prosecute is Dismist.

The action brot. by Richard Munn agst. William Anderson junr. neither party appearing is Dismist.

In the action of Debt brot. by Francis Mallory agst. George Ivie for two thousand twenty Six pds: of Tobacco Due by Bill, at the Last Court time was given the Deft. till this Court to plead, and being now called to do the same did not appear or offer any thing in barr or preclusion of the plts. Action, thereupon it's Considered by the Court that the plt. recover agst. the Deft. the aforesaid Sum and Costs, unless he shall appear at the next Court and answer the said action.

In the action of Debt brot. by Randle Platt agst. David Goodgame the Deft. failing to appear &c Judgement is granted the plt. by *Nil Decit* &c.

[page 219]

The Order that John Lett Admr. of Sarah and Roger Drayton Deced: return Inventory of the said Decedts. Estate, is Continued till the next Court.

In the action of Debt. brot. by John Bolling against Richard Bland Admr. with the Will annext. of Thomas Wynne Deced: for Twenty Nine pounds One Shilling and Six pence Sterl: Due by Bond Dated the Last Day of January 1717/18, for the payment of fourteen pounds tenn Shillings and Nine pence, in buck and Doe Skins at two Shillings each buck Skin and One Shilling and Six pence each Doe Skins, which the Court Values at Twenty One pounds Current money, and the plt. haveing made Oath he has reced. no Sattisfaction for the said Bond, and the Deft. pleading that he has in his hands of the said Decedts. Estate only seven pounds two Shillings and four pence, thereupon it is Ordered that he pay the same to the said plt. Als. Exec:, and it is also Ordered that the sd. Deft. pay to the said plt. the sum of thirteen pounds Seventeen Shillings and Eight pence with costs out of the said Decedts. Estate when Assetts thereof Shall come to hand.

Francis Poythres the Elder his Deed for Land (Indented and Seald) to Richard Pace, was proved in Open Court by the Oaths of Peter Wynne, John Bonner and Thomas Poythres Witnesses thereto and Admitted to record.

Francis Poythres the Elder his Deed for Land (Seald) to Thomas Goodwyn, was proved in Open Court by the Oaths of Peter Wynne, John Bonner and Thomas Poythres Witnesses thereto and Admitted to record.

Francis Poythres the Elder and Richard Pace their Deed for Land (Indented and Seald) to Thomas Goodwyn, was proved in Open Court by the Oaths of Peter Wynne, John Bonner and Thomas Poythres Witnesses thereto and Admitted to record.

Ordered that the Livery of Seizin on the back of the said Deed be also recorded.

And then the Court Adjourn'd till Tomorrow Morning Tenn a Clock. John Poythres. Test W: Hamlin, Cl. Cur.

[page 220]

At a Court held at Merchantshope for the County of Prince George
the Tenth Day of December 1718: for Laying the County Levy.

Present   John Poythres,   Robert Hall, }
               Robert Bolling   & Lewis Green Junr. }   Gent. Justices.

Pr. George County Dr. December the 10th 1718.

	Q Tobo.
To Edward Goodrich for 72 Days Attendance on the Sevll. Assemblys } this year as Burgess &c and ferrages included	9705
To Mr. Robert Hall for 69 Days Do. and ferryages	9315
To Sampson Merredeth Corroner for an Inquest	0133
To James Thweatt Sherr: for the County Service one year	1080
To William Hamlin Clk. for Do.	1080
To Thomas Simmons for Sweeping the Court house	0250
To George Tillman and James Williams Overseers of Monksneck } Bridge for their Expence &c in building and repairing the same }	3000
To John Hamlin Admr. of Richard Hamlin Late Sherr: not fully } Levied Last Year	60

For Wolves Killed.

	Q Tobo.			Q Tobo.
To E. Goodrich pr. Richd. Womack	200		John Womack Junr.	100
To James Thweatt	100		Richard Smith senr.	200
To Majr. Robt. Bolling for			Thomas Gent	100
Danl. Jones	1		To Majr. Robert Munford for	
Indian Will	3		Joseph Tucker	4
Wm. Jones	1		Wm. Tucker	9
John Williamson	1		Francis Coleman	5
Richard Burch	3			18
Henry Embro	3		To Wm. Gamlin	100
Stephen Evans	1		To Wm. Tucker	100
Thos. Sisson	2		To John Tucker	100
Saml. Harwell	5		To Capt. Pr. Jones	300
Math. Mayes	3		Joseph Stroud	100
Nicholas Overby	2		Pr. Mitchell Junr.	100
Pr. Mitchell	1		Pr. Mitchell senr.	100
Richard Vaughn	1		John Ellington	100
Wm. Spain	1		William Butler	299
	28	2800	Phillip Burrow	100
carried ovr.		9100	Brought ovr.	3100

(18 × 100 = 1800)

	Q Tobo.
	91223
To Cask and Sallary on 31223 at 18 pr. Cent is	5619
Due to the County to be paid next year	14
Pr. Geo: County, December 10th 1717. Cr.	36856
By 1084 Tithables at 34 pr pole is [Verte]	36856

[page 221]

    Ordered that the Sherr: collect and receive of every Tithable person within this County (by Distress in case of refusall or Non payment) the Sum of thirty four pounds of Tobacco, the same being their County Levy this present year, and that the sd. Sherriff pay the same to the severall persons for whom it is raised and proportioned in the above account.

    And then the Court Adjourn'd. Randle Platt. Test W: Hamlin, Cl. Cur.

At a Court held at Merchantshope for the County
of Prince George on Wednesday the Tenth Day of
December Anno Dom: 1718.

Present   Randle Platt,   Robert Munford,   Robert Hall
               Robert Bolling,   John Hardyman   & Lewis Green junr.   Gent. Justices

John Gillam made Complaint that David Collyshaw stands Indebted to him by account Dated 1718, the sum of Eight pounds two Shilings and Six pence and set forth that the said David hath unlawfully absconded himself so that the Ordinary process at Law cannot be served on him whereupon he by Virtue of an Attachment under the hand of one of his Majestys Justices for this County hath Caused part of the Estate of the sd. David to be Attacht. for payment thereof, Vizt. One feather bed, One old rugg, One old Ozenbrigg Sheet, One bolster, One bedstead and Cord, One hyde, One Trunk, One Chest of Drawers, one brass kettle, one spice Mortar and pestle, one paster pottle pott, One flatt Iron, one brass Ladle, one Tin pale, three Tables, one Iron rack, one Spitt, three ;ewter Dishes, One Small Bason, one Iron pott, one Small Looking glass, one box, two Small pillows, and the said David being called and failing to appear to replevye the same and the plt. makeing oath the sum of Eight pounds five Shillings and Dix pence is Justly Due to him, thereupon Judgement is granted him for the said Sum and Costs to be Leavied on the Goods Attacht. Ordered that the Sherr: cause the said Goods to be Duly appraised by John Lewis, Henry Tatam, Thomas Moor and John Moor or any three of them being first Sworn by some Majistrate of this County for that purpose, and Delivered the plt. for and toward the payment of the said Sum and Costs and make report of their proceedings.

[page 222]

The action brot. by Sampson Merredeth agst. Timothy Bridges Admr. &c neither party appearing is Dismist.

In the action of Debt brot. by John and Robert Bolling against Richard Bland Administrator with the Will annext. of Thomas Wynne Deced: for fifty four pounds thirteen Shillings and Eight pence Sterl: Due by Bond Dated the Last Day of January 1717/18 for the payment of Twenty seven pounds Six Shillings and Tenn pence to be paid in buck and Doe skins as two Shillings Each buck Skinn and One Shilling and Six pence each Doe Skinns which the Court Values at forty one pounds and three pence current money, and the plts. haveing made oath they have reced. no sattisfaction for the said Bond and the Deft. pleading fully administred, thereupon Judgement is granted the plts. agst. the said Defendt. for the said sum of forty one pounds and three pence and Costs to be paid out of the said Decedents Estate when assetts thereof Shall come to hand &c.

John Hardyman and Company agst. Richard Poland Admr. with the will annext. of Thomas Wynne Deced: for Eleven pounds Seventeen Shillings and three pence Current mony Due by Bill Dated the thirtyeth of January 1715, the Defendt. appears and pleads fully administred, thereupon the plt. makes Oath the said Sum is Justly Due and Judgement is granted him agst. the said Defendt. for the same with Costs, to be paid out of the said Decedts. Estate when assetts thereof Shall come to hand &c.

In the action of Detinue brot. by Mary Wiggins agst. Richard Winkles for the Detaining Sundry Goods and Chattles of the plts. to her Damage fifteen pounds Current money, the Defendt. being called and not appearing and Richard Harrison being returned Security for him on the motion of the plts. Attorney Judgement is granted her against the said Defendt. and his Security for the said Sum and Costs unless the said Defendt. shall appear at the next Court and answer the said action.

The action of Debt brot. by John Williamson agst. Joseph Greenhill, neither party appearing is Dismist.

In the action of Debt brot. by Nathl. Harrison Esqr. agst. Lydia Clements Executrix &c of Francis Clements Deced: for thirty Nine pounds four Shillings and two pence Sterl: and four thousand four hundred Sixty Seven pounds of Tobacco, the Defendant being returned *non est Inventus* and not appearing on the motion of the plts. Attorney an Attachment is granted him agst. the Estate of the Decedt. in the hands of the said Executrix for the said Sum and Costs, returnable to the next Court.

[page 223]

The action of Debt brot. by David Crawley agst. Titus Creacher neither party appearing is Dismist.

The action on the case brot. by David Crawley agst. Titus Creacher neither party appearing is Dismist.

The petition of John Wyatt agst. Timothy Bridges &c the sd. John failing to prosecute is Dismist.

The attachment granted William Batte agst. the Estate of Henry Robertson, neither party appearing is Dismist.

The attachment granted James Bell agst. the Estate of Thomas Clifton is Continued till the next Court.

In the action of Debt brot. by Robert Bolling against George Hamelton, the Defendt. files his plea's to the plts: Declaration and he Joining in the same is referred till the next Court for Tryall.

The action of Trespass brot. by John Wilkins agst. Adam Ivie is Continued till the next Court.

In the suit in Chancery brot. by Joseph Goffe agst. Edward Wyatt, at the Last Court time was granted the respondt. till this Court to answer the Complainants Bill and being now called did not appear therefore on the motion of the plts. Attorney an Attachment is granted him agst. the body of the said Defendt. returnable to the next Court.

The action on the case brot. by Thomas Oliver agst. John Liles neither party appearing is Dismist.

In the action of Debt brot. by William Randolph agst. Francis Mallory for Fifteen pounds Current money Due by two Notes under his hand both Dated the 14th Day of May 1717, the Defendt. came personally into court and Confest Judgement to the plt. for Six pounds thirteen Shillings and five pence Current money being the Ballance Due on the sd. Notes, thereupon it is Ordered that the sd. Deft. pay to the sd. plt. the said Sum of Six pounds thirteen Shillings and five pence & Costs. Als. Exec:

[page 224]

In the action on the case brot. by Littlebury Epes agst. Peter Wynne for Twelve hundred and Nine pounds of Tobacco Due by accot. Dated 1715, the Defendt. haveing pleaded *Nil Debit* and the plt. Joining in the Issue the same was Referred till this Court for Tryall and the said partys being now called and the Defendt. failing to appear, and the plt. haveing made Oath the said Sum is Justly Due, thereupon it is Ordered that he pay the same to the said plt. togather with Costs. Als. Exec:

The action of Debt brot. by Randle Platt agst. John Hardyman is Continued till the next Court.

In the action of Debt brought by *John Hardyman and Company* agst. Sarah Hobbs Executrix of the Last Will and Testament of Robert Hobbs Deced: for five thousand and two hundred and fifteen pounds of Tobacco Due by Bill Dated the 24th Day of March 1716: which said sum of Tobacco the Court Values at two pence pr. pound, the Defendt. appearing pleads she has only Twenty Six pounds of the said Decedts. Estate in her hands, and the plt. makeing Oath the sum of four thousand Six hundred and fifteen pounds of the sd. Tobacco is Justly Due, thereupon Judgement is granted the plt. agst. the said Defendt. for the said Sum of Twenty Six pounds to be paid out of the said Decedents Estate. Als. Exec: and also Judgement is granted the plt. agst. the Defendt. for twelve pounds Nine Shillings and two pence and Costs to be paid out of the said Decedts. Estate when Assetts thereof Shall come to hand &c being with the aforesaid Sum of Twenty Six pounds the Value of the said Sum of four thousand Six hundred and fifteen pounds of Tobacco.

In the action of Debt brot. by John Hatch against Sarah Hobbs Executrix of the Last Will and Testament of Robert Hobbs Deced: for five pounds Seventeen Shillings and Eleven pence halfe pany Current money Due by Bill Dated the 13th of March 1717: the Defendt. appears and pleads She has fully Administred, thereupon the plt. makes Oath the said Sum is Justly Due, and Judgement is granted for the sd. Sum and Costs to be paid out of the said Decedts. Estate when Assetts thereof Shall come to hand &c.

In the action on the case brot. by Richard Smith agst. Sampson Merredeth for Seven hundred forty three pounds of Tobacco Due by accot. &c the Defendt. not appearing nor any Security returned for him on the plts. motion Judgement is granted him against the sd. Deft. and James Thweatt Sherr: for the said Sum and Costs unless the Defendt. shall appear at the next Court and answer the said action.

[page 225]

In the action on the case brot. by William Wallice against Cornelius Fox for three pounds one Shilling and Tenn pence, Due by accot. &c Geo. Hamelton, Gilbert Hay & Richard Pigeon or any two of them are appointed to Audit the accots. of the plt. and Defendt. and Ordered to make report of their proceedings to the next Court.

The action brot. by Robert Munford agst. Wm. Mitchell the plt. failing to prosecute is Dismist.

The action brot. by David Crawley agst. Robert Hix, the plt. failing to prosecute is Dismist.

The action brot. by David Crawley agst. James Mayo, the plt. failing to prosecute is Dismist.

The action brot. by Nathl. Lee agst. Richard Womack, the plt. failing to prosecute is Dismist.

In the action brot. by John Hatch agst. William Coleman for fourteen hundred and Forty pounds of Barrow Porke Due by Bill &c the writt being Executed and the Defendt. not appearing and Bartho: Crowder being returned Security for him on the motion of the plt. Judgement is granted him against the said Defendt. and his Security for the said Sum and Costs, unless the sd. Defendt. shall appear at the next Court and answer the said action.

The action brot. by John Ellis agst. Thomas Price, the plt. failing to prosecute is Dismist.

In the action on the case brot. by John Berry against Wm. Gent the plt. failing to prosecute on the motion of the Defendts. Attorney it's Ordered that he be Nonsuit and pay the said Defendt. five Shillings with Costs. Als. Exec:

In the action of Trespass brot. by John Berry agst. William Gent, the plt. faililng to prosecute, on the motion of the Defendts. Attorney, It's Orderd that he be Nonsuited and pay the said Deft. five Shillings with Costs. Als. Exec:

116

In the action on the case brot. by Elizabeth Millner agst. Wm. Gent, the plt. failing to prosecute on the motion of the Defendts. Attorney It's Ordered that she be Nonsuit and pay the said Defendt. five Shillings with Costs. Als. Exec:

[page 226]

In the action on the case brot. by Peter Bond against John Hamlin Admr. &c of Richard Hamlin Deced: for Nineteen hundred and forty pds. of Tobacco which the Defendt. Detains &c to the plts. Damage Twenty pounds Sterling the Deft. by his Attorney pleads *Non Detinet* and the plt. Joining in the Issue the same is referred till the next Court for Tryall.

In the action brot. by Robert Munford against John Hamlin Admr. of Richard Hamlin Deced: an Imparlance is granted the Defendt. till the next Court.

In the action brot. by Henry Soane agst. John Hamlin Admr. of Richard Hamlin Deced: for three thousand Nine hundred pounds of Tobo. Due by the Acceptance of a Note &c on the motion of the Defendts. Attorney Oyer of the sd. Note is granted him and time till the next Court to consider the same.

In the action brot. by John Hatch agst. John Hamlin Admr. of Richard Hamlin Deced: for Eight pou[n]ds Nineteen Shillings and four pence due By Bill and accot. &c on the motion of the Defendts. Attorney Oyer of the sd. Bill and Accot. is granted him and time to Consider the same till the Next Court.

In the action of Debt brot. by Robert Rogers agst. John Hamlin Admr. of Richard Hamlin Deced: for three pds. Eight Shillings Due by Bill &c on the motion of the Defendts. Attorney Oyer of the plts. Bill is granted him and time till the next Court to Consider the same.

In the action of Debt brot. by Randle Platt agst. Elizabeth Duke Executrix of the Last Will and Testament of Henry Duke Deced: for breach of covenants &c to the plts. Damage Fivety pounds Sterling the Defendt. being returned *non est Inventus* and not appearing on the motion of the plts: Attorney an Attachment is granted him agst. the Estate of the said Decedt: in the hands of his sd. Executrix for the said Sum and Costs returnable to the next Court.

In the action of Debt brot. by *John Hardyman and Company* against Richard Whittmore Admr. &c of Nicholas Whittmore senr. Deced: for two thousand Six hundred Ninety two pounds of Tobacco Due on Ballance of a Bill Dated the Ninth of February 1713: the Deft. by his Attorney moves that the plt. may prove his Debt, whereupon he makes Oath the said Sum is Justly Due and Judgement is granted him agst. the said Deft. for twenty two pounds Eight Shillings and Eight pence & Costs, to be paid out of the said Decedts. Estate. Als. Exec: the same being the Value of the said Tobacco as it is Valued by the Court.

[page 227]

In the action brot. by John Hatch against Elizabeth Whittmore Admx. of Nicholas Whittmore Junr. Deced: for three pounds Eleven Shillings and two pence Due by accot. Dated 1717, the Defendt. moves the plt. may prove his accot. whereupon he makes Oath the same is Justly Due and Judgement is granted him agst. the said Defendt. for the said Sum and Costs, to be paid out of the said Decedts. Estate. Als. Exec:

In the action brot. by John Hatch agst. Elinor Walpole Admx. of Richard Walpole Deced: for Six pounds Six Shillings and Six pence Due by Bill Dated 1717: the Defendt. by her Attorney moves the plt. may prove his Debt whereupon he makes Oath the same is Justly Due and Judgemt. is granted him for the said Sum and Costs to be paid by the said Defendt. out of the said Decedts. Estate. Als. Exec.

The action on the case brot. by Stith Bolling agst. Timothy Bridges, neither party appearing is Dismist.

Richard Cureton haveing made Oath that he attended five Days as an Evidence for John Wilkins in his action on the case agst. Adam Ivie. Ordered that the said John pay him for the same Two hundred pounds of Tobacco and Costs. Als. Exec:

And then the Court Adjourn'd till Court in Course. Rand. Platt. Test W: Hamlin, Cl. Cur.

[page 228]

At a Court held at Merchantshope for the County of Prince George on
the second Tuesday in January being the thirteenth day of the said month, Anno Dom: 1718[/9].

Present	John Hamlin,	John Poythres,	Robert Munford
	Robert Hall	& Robert Bolling	Gent. Justices.

Bernard Sykes Admr. &c of Bernard Sykes Deced: returns upon Oath an accot. Dr. & Cr. of the said Decedts. Estate, and it being Examined by the Court is Admitted to Record.

In the suit in Chancery Lately Depending in this Court between John Lewis Junr. Complaint. and Henry Offley and Robert Bolling respondts. the said John Lewis Obtained a Decree agst. the said Bolling for fifteen pounds, thirteen Shillings and tenn pence Sterl: and Costs, to be paid in Goods and Outstanding Tobacco Debts of the said Offleys Estate in the hands of the said Bolling. And he being apprehensive that there is not Sufficient Goods of the said Offleys in his hands to discharge and pay the said Decree and praying that a Certain Value may be set on the said Outstanding Tobacco Debts, Therefore it is Ordered that whatsoever Sum or part of the sd. Decree shall be paid in Tobacco the same shall be Valued and accounted for at twelve Shillings and Six pence Sterl: pr. Cent, and that the said Bolling Value and Charge the same at Sixteen Shillings & Eight pence Currt. money pr. Cent in his accot. with the said Offley.

Sarah Hobbs Executrix of the Last Will and Testament or Robert Hobbs Deced: returns upon Oath an Accot. Dr. & Cr. of the said Decedts. Estate, which being Examined by the Court is Admitted to record.

The peto. of Thomas Mitchell agst. Robert Mitchell is referred till the next Court.

And then the Court Adjourn'd till Court in Course. Jno. Hamlin. Test W: Hamlin, Cl. Cur.

[page 229]

At a Court held at Merchantshope for the County of Prince
George on the Second Tuesday in February being the Tenth
Day of the month Annoq Dom. 1718[/9].

Present   John Hamlin,   Robert Munford }
   Robert Hall,   John Hardyman }
   Lewis Green   & John Peterson }   Gent. Justices

On the peto. of William Cooper and Thomas Wilkins Guardians to William and Ralph Rachell two of the Orphans of William Rachell Deced: It's Ordered that Mr. Robert Hall who was Security for the Administration of the Estate of the said William Rachell Deced: and in whose hands the said Decedts. Estate is, do pay to the said William Cooper and Thos. Wilkins on their giveing Security &c Seven hundred Eighty two pounds of Tobacco being so much Due to the sd. Orphans. Whereupon the sd. William Cooper and Thomas Wilkins, togather with William Heath and Richard Winkles their Securitys acknowledged themselves Jointly and Severally indebted to the Justices of the peace for this County and to their Successors in the sum of fifteen hundred Sixty four pounds of Tobacco wth. Condition that if they the said Wm. Cooper and Thomas Wilkins Shall well and Truly pay to the sd. Orphans or their heirs the sd. Sum of Seven hundred Eighty two pounds of Tobacco when they or either of them Shall & may Lawfully Demand the same, then this recognizance to be Void, otherways to be of Force, whereupon the sd. Hall is Discharged therefrom.

John Duffin a Sarvant Boy belonging to John Golightly is Adjudged fourteen years old.

John Owen in Open Court acknowledged his Deed for Land (Indented and Seald) to William Troughton, on whose motion the same is Ordered to be recorded.

Benjamin Foster in Open Court acknowledged his Deed for Land (Indented and Seald) with Livery and Seizin thereon, to John Leonard on whose motion the same is Ordered to be recorded. And then also appeared in Court Elizabeth the Wife of the said Benjamin and being first privately Examined freely and Voluntarily relinquisht. to the said John Leonard her right of Dower of in and to the Lands &c in the said Deed mentioned which is Likewise Ordered to be recorded.

[page 230]

The Last Will and Testament of Michal Talbott Deced: was presented into Court by Edward Wyatt the Executor therein Named who made Oath thereto, and it being proved by the Oaths of Paul Jones and Edward Johnson two of the Witnesses thereto is Ordered to be recorded, and on the motion of the sd. Edward Wyatt Certificate is granted him for Obtaining a Probate in Due form.

Volentine Minge, Paul Jones, James Bell and Benjamin Reiks or any three of them being first Sworn by some Majistsrate of this County for that purpose, are Ordered to appraise the Estate of Michal Talbott Deced: and make report of their proceedings to the next Court, when Edward Wyatt the Executor is to return the Inventory.

Thomas Farmar Admr. &c of Francis Rea Deced: returns an Inventory &c of the said Decedts. Estate, which is Ordered to be recorded.

Ordered that Thomas Bilbro an Orphan Boy be bound by the Churchwardens of Martins Brandon Parrish to James Niblet, according to Law and that they Oblige the said James in the Indentures to Learn the sd. Thomas the Trade of a tight Cooper.

John Lett Admr. of Sarah and Roger Drayton Deced: returns into Court Inventorys of the said Decedts. Estates which are Ordered to be recorded.

Mary Potts relict of Thomas Potts Late of this County Deced: came into Court and made Oath the sd. Thomas Potts departed this Life without any Will as farr as She knows or believes, and on her motion and giveing Security according to Law Certificate is granted her for Obtaining a Commission of Administration in Due form.

James Jones, Gilbert Hay, Phill Burrow, and John Smith or any three of them being first Sworn by some Majistrate of this County for that purpose, are Ordered to appraise the Estate of Thomas Potts Deced: and make report of their proceedings therein to the next Court, when Mary Potts the Admx. is to return the Inventory.

The Last Will and Testament of Edward Woodleife Deced: was presented into Court by Sarah Woodleife and Joseph Woodleife the Exrs. therein Named who made Oath thereto, and it being proved by the Oaths of William Stainback, William Ranye and William Stainback Junr. Witnesses thereto is Ordered to be recorded, and on the motion of the said Exrs. Certificate is granted them for Obtaining a Probate in Due form.

[page 231]

Ordered that Sarah Woodleife and Jos. Woodleife Exrs. of Edward Woodleife Deced: return an Inventory of the sd. Decedts. Estate to the next Court.

The action brot. by George Harvie against David Colyshaw the plt. failing to prosecute is Dismist.

The Attachment granted Geo: Harvie agst. John Spain the plt. failing to prosecute is Dismist.

The Attachment granted Drury Bolling agst. John Spain is Continued till the next Court.

The Attachment granted Nathl. Harrison Esqr. agst. John Brewer is Continued till the next Court.

In the action on the case brot. by Timothy Bridges against James Niblet Admr. with the Will annext. of Thomas Bilbro Deced: for three pounds Six Shillings and Eleven pence Due by accot. &c the Deft. moves the plt. may prove his accot. whereupon he makes Oath the same is Justly Due & it's Ordered that the said Defendt. do pay to the said plt. out of the said Decedts. Estate the said Sum & Costs. Als. Exec:

The action of Debt brot. by Sampson Merredeth agst. William Mitchell is continued till the next Court.

In the action on the case brot. by John Berry agst. Francis Epes, the Deft. appears and pleads *Nil Debit*, and the plt. Joining in the Issue the same is referred till the next Court for Tryall.

The action brot. by Thomas Taylor agst. John Sherly the plt. failing to prosecute is Dismist.

In the action on the case brot. by George Harvie agst. John Berry for five hundred Ninety Eight pounds of Tobacco Due by Accot. &c the Deft. being called and not appearing and Richard Smith being returned Security for him on the plts. motion Judgement is granted him against the said Deft. and his said Security for the aforesaid Sum & costs unless the sd. Defendt. Shall appear at the next Court and answer the said Action.

[page 232]

The action brot. by David Crawley agst. Thomas Gregory, neither party appearing is Dismist.

In the action on the case brot. by William Randolph admr. with the Will annext. of Eusebius King Deced: against Edward Simmons for Eight pounds Eighteen Shills. and Tenn pence Due by Accot. &c the Defendt. being called and not appearing and Thomas Simmons Junr. being returned Security for him on the motion of the plts: Attorney Judgement is granted him against the said Defendt. and his said Security for the aforesaid Sum and Costs, unless the said Defendt. shall appear at the next Court and answer the said Action.

In the action on the case brot. by Jos. Irby agst. John Bonner, the Deft. pleads *Nil Debit* and the plt. Joining in the Issue the same is referred till the next Court for Tryall.

In the action brot. by Jos. Irby agst. Mathew Smart, an Imparlance is granted the Defendt. till the next Court.

In the action brot. by Jos. Irby agst. Cornelius Fox, an Imparlance is granted the Defendt. till the next Court.

The action brot. by Danl. Meadows agst. Burrell Green the plt. faililng to prosecute is Dismist.

The action of Debt brot. by Geo. Hunt Exr. &c agst. James Loftin, the plt. failing to prosecute is Dismist.

The action brot. by Francis Mallory agst. Elinor Walpole Admx. of Richard Walpole Deced: is Continued till the next Court.

The Order that Sarah Bishope Exrx. of Wm. Bishope Deced: return an Inventory of the said Decedts. Estate is Continued till the next Court.

The Order that Margery Bowen relict of Cha. Bowen Deced: be Summoned to accept the Admon: of the sd. Decedts. Est. is made Null & Void, and the petition of John Acre for the sd. Admin: is Dismist.

The suit in Chancery brot. by John Bolling agst. Henry Offley and John Bolling is Continued till the next Court.

On the petition of John Lovesay he is Exempt from paying publick and County Leavy for the Future.

[page 233]

In the action on ye Case brot. by George Harvie agst. Thomas Simmons, the plt. failing to file his Declaration in due time, on the Defendts. motion it is Ordered that he be Nonsuit and pay the sd. Defendt. five Shillings with Costs. Als. Exec:

In the action of Debt brot. by Henry Holdcraft agst. Eliza. Epes Exrx. &c of William Epes Deced: for three thousand One hundred Seventy four pounds of Tobacco Due by Bill &c the Deft. being called and not appearing and Francis Epes being returned Security for her on the motion of the plts. Attorney Judgement is granted him agst. the said Deft. and her sd. Security for the aforesaid Sum & Costs unless the said Deft. shall appear at the next Court & answer the said Action.

The action brot. by Timothy Bridges against Henry Gills the plt. failing to prosecute is Dismist.

The Order that Ann Hill Exrx. &c of John Hill Deced: return an Inventory of the said Decedts. Estate is continued till next Court.

The Attachment granted Thomas Spain agst. the Estate of David Colyshaw, the plt. failing to prosecute is Dismist.

The attachment granted Wm. Mitchell agst. the Estate of David Colyshaw, the plt. failing to prosecute is Dismist.

The Attachment granted John Fitzgerrald agst. the Estate of David Colyshaw, the plt. failing to prosecute is Dismist.

The action of Debt brot. by John Nickells agst. John Cotten the plt. failing to prosecute is Dismist.

The action of Debt brot. by John Jackson agst. John Cotten the plt. failing to prosecute is Dismist.

The actoin of Debt brot. by William Webb agst. James Babb the plt. failing to prosecute is Dismist.

The action on the case brot. by David Crawley agst. Edward Murrell, the plt. failing to prosecute is Dismist.

[page 234]

In the action of Trespass on the case brot. by John Hatch agst. John Turner, Majr. Robert Munford became Speciall Bail for the said Defendt. on whose motion an Imparlance is granted him till the next Court.

In the action on the case brot. by Timothy Bridges agst. Thomas Farmar Admr. With the Will annext. of Francis Rea Deced: for One pound Ten Shills. Due by accot. Dated 1718, the Defendt. moves the plt. may prove his accot. whereupon he makes Oath the said Sum is Justly Due, and it is Ordered that the said Defendt. pay to the said plt. out of the said Decedts. Estate the aforesd. sum and Costs. Als. Exec:

The action brot. by John Scott agst. Robert Fellows, the plt. failing to prosecute is Dismist.

The action brot. by Robt. Munford agst. John Berry, the plt. failing to prosecute is Dismist.

In the action of Debt brot. by David Crawley agst. William Taylor for Nine pounds Eleven Shillings and Six pence Due by Bill &c the Deft. being called and not appearing and Titus Creacher being returned Security for him on the motion of the plts. Attorney Judgement is granted him against the said Defendt. and his said Security for the aforesaid sum and Costs, unless the said Defendt. Shall appear at the next Court & answer the said Action.

The action of Debt brot. by David Crawley agst. James Lundy, the plt. failing to prosecute is Dismist.

The action of Debt brot. by Olive Poxson agst. Edmd. Browder, the plt. failing to prosecute is Dismist.

The action of Debt brot. by Thomas Simmons agst. Wm. Floriday the plt. faililng to prosecute is Dismist.

In the action on the case brot. by Elizabeth Jarrard Exrx. of the last Will and Testament of Nicholas Jarrard Deced: agst. James Niblet Admr. with the Will annexe[d] of Thomas Bilbro Deced: for One pound ten Shills. and Seven hundred and fifty pounds of Tobacco Due by accot. &c the deft. moves the plt. may prove the sd. Accot. which she accordingly does by the Oath of William Winkles, and the said Tobacco being Valued by the Court at Six pounds five Shillings, on the plts. motion Judgement is granted her for the same and the aforesaid Sum of One pound Tenn Shillings amounting in the whole to Seven pounds fifteen Shillings, and it is Ordered that the said

[page 235]

Defendt. pay to the said plt. out of the said Decedts. Estate the aforesaid Sum of Seven pounds fifteen Shillings and Costs. Als. Exec:

On the motion of Richard Pigeon it's Ordered that a Lycence Issue for his keeping an Ordinary near the Court house of this County at the usuall place, he haveing given Bond and Security as the Law Directs.

And then the Court Adjourn'd till Court in Course. John Hamlin. Test W: Hamlin, Cl. Cur.

At a Court held at Merchantshope for Prince George County
on the second Tuesday in March being the Tenth Day of the month
Annoq. Dom: 1718[/9].

Present   John Hamlin,   John Poythres,   Randle Platt
                  Robt. Munford,   Robert Hall,   Sampson Merredeth
                  & Lewis Green   Gent. Justices.

James Niblet Administrator &c of Thos. Bilbro Deced: returns a further Inventory of the Estate of the sd. Deced: which is Ordered to be recorded.

The Order of the Last Court that Reba. Spencer Admx. &c of Richard Spencer Deced: return an Inventory of the said Decedts. Estate is Continued.

The Order of the Last Court that Judith Smith Exrx. of Thomas Smith Deced: return an Inventory of the sd. Deceds: Estate, is Continued till the next Court.

The Order of the Last Court that Randle Platt return an Accot. Dr. & Cr. between the sd. Platt and Jos. Greenhill is Continued till the next Court.

Nathaniel Tatum in Open Court acknowledged his Deeds of Lease and Release of Land (Indented and Seald) to Richard Carlile Ordered the said Deeds be recorded.

[page 236]

Nathaniel Tatum in Open Court acknowledged his Deeds of Lease & Release of Land (Indented and Seald) to Samuell Tatum, Ordered the said Deeds be recorded.

The Order that Elizabeth Duke Admx. &c of Henry Duke Deced: return an Inventory of the sd. Decedts. Estate, is Continued till the next Court.

In the action on the case brot. by Randle Platt agst. Henry King for four hundred and Tenn pounds of Tobacco Due by accot. at the Last court time was granted the Defendt. till this Court to reply to the plts. Demurrer, and being now called to do the same did not appear or offer any in Barr of the plts. action thereupon it is Considered by the Court that the plt. recover agst. the sd. Deft. the aforesaid Sum & Costs, unless the said Defendt. shall eppar at the next Court and answer the said action.

In the action of Debt brought by Francis Mallory agst. George Ivie for Two thousand Twenty Six pounds of Tobacco Due by Bill Dated ye Ninth of February 1716, the Defendt. being called and not appearing pursuant to the Conditional Order of the Last Court, on the motion of the plt's. Attorney Judgement is granted & Confirmed agst. the said Defendt., And it is Ordered that the said Defendt. pay to the said plt. the aforesaid Sum of Two thousand twenty Six pounds of Tobacco & Costs. Als. Exec:

Edward Wyatt Executor &c of Michal Talbott Deced: returns an Inventory of the said Decedts. Estate which is Ordered to be recorded.

On the petition of Robert Bolling for an Acre of Land on Tuckers Runn, belonging to David Crawley, for his the sd. Bolling's Convenience to build a Water Mill on, It is Ordered that John Coleman and John Mayes View the said Acre of Land, and if it do not take away any Imediate conveniencys &c to Lay out and Value the same, and upon the sd. Bollings paying the Value thereof to the said Crawley, to put him the sd. Bolling into possession thereof, and report their proceedings thererin to ye Next Court.

Charles Anderson in Open Court acknowledged his Deed for Land (Indented and Seald) With Livery of Seizin thereon, to Cornelius Cargill, and the same is Admitted to Record.

In the action of Debt brot. by Randle Platt agst. David Goodgame for two hundred and Nineteen pounds of Tobacco Due by Bill Dated the Ninth of July 1714, the Deft. being called and not appearing pursuant to the Conditional Order of the Last Court, on the plts: motion Judgement is granted & Confirmed agst. the said Defendt. and it is Ordered that the said Defendt. pay to the said plt. the aforesaid Sum of Two hundred and Nineteen pounds of Tobacco and Costs. Als. Exec:

[page 237]

Elizabeth Whittmore Admx. of Nicholas Whittmore Junr. Deced: returns an accot. Dr. & Cr. of the said Decedts. Estate upon Oath, and the same being Examined and Allowed by the Court is admitted to record.

In the action brot. by Mary Wiggins agst. Richard Winkles, on the Defts. motion time is granted him (by consent of the plt.) till the next court to consider the sd. plts. Declaration.

The Last Will and Testament of John Lanthrop Deced: was Exhibitted into Court by Margaret his Relict, and Joseph ye son of the said Deced: and there being no Executors appointed therein, the said Margaret and Joseph Lanthrop made Oath thereto, and it being proved by the Oaths of Moses Beck, Andrew Beck, and Henry Ledbetter,

Witnesses thereto is Ordered to be recorded, and on the motion of the said Margaret and Joseph Lanthrop and their giveing Security as the Law Directs Certificate is granted them for Obtaining a Commission of Administration with the said Will annext. in Due form.

Ordered that Margaret and Joseph Lanthrop Admrs. &c of John Lanthrop Deced: return an Inventory of the said Decedts. Estate to the next Court.

The action on the case brot. by Nathl. Harrison Esqr. agst. Lydia Clements Exrx. of Francis Clements Deced: the plt. failing to prosecute is Dismist.

The action on the case brot. by James Bell agst. Thomas Clifton the plt. failing to prosecute is Dismist.

The action of Debt Depending between Robert Bolling & George Hamilton is continued till the next Court.

The action of Trespass Depending between John Wilkins and Adam Ivie, the plt. failing to prosecute is Dismist.

the suit in Chancery Depending between Joseph Goffe and Edward Wyatt, is Continued till the next Court.

The Last Will and Testament of Richard Pigeon Deced: was Exhibitted into Court by Nathaniel Harrison Esqr. & Richard Pigeon

[page 238]

the Executor named in the sd. Will, and Elizabeth Pigeon Relict of the sd. Deced: for certain causes thereunto moveing haveing refused to undertake the Burthen of the Execution of the sd. Testament, the said Nathaniel Harrison made oath thereto, and it being proved by the Oaths of Phillip Claud, John Hammersly and John Berry the severall Witnesses thereto, is Ordered to be recorded and upon the motion of the said Nathl. Harrison and his giveing Security as the Law Directs Certificate is granted him for Obtaining a Commission of Administration with the said Will annext in Due form.

George Hamelton, Collingwood Ward, Arthur Biggins and Thomas Booth or any three of them being first Sworn by some Majistrate of this County for that purpose are Nominated and Appointed to appraise the Estate of Richard Pigeon Deced: and make report to their proceedings therein to the next court when Nathaniel Harrison Esqr. the Admr. is Ordered to return the Inventory thereof.

On the motion of Nathaniel Harrison Esqr., Edward Goodrich is Entred his Genrall Attorney in all causes &c: wherein the sd. Harrison is concerned.

The Last Will and Testament of Charles Anderson Late of the County of Charles City Deced: was presented into Court by Frances his relict and Exrx. who made Oath thereto, and it haveing been proved and in Charles Citty County Court by the Oaths of Edward Hill and Sarah Royall (alias Baxter) Witnesses thereto is Ordered to be recorded, and on the motion of the said Francis Anderson and her giveing Security, Certificate is granted her for Obtaining a Probate in Due form.

The action Depending between Randle Platt and John Hardyman is Continued till the next Court.

In the action on the case Depending between Richard Smith and Sampson Merredeth, the Defendt. appears and pleads Nil Debit and the plt. Joining in the Issue the same is referred till the next Court for Tryall.

In the action on the case Depending between William Wallice and Cornelius Fox, the Auditors appointed at the Last Court to Settle and adjust the accots. of the said partys, make the following report, Vizt. In Obedience to an order of Pr: George County Court Dated the 10th of December 1718, we the Subscribers have settled and Adjusted the accots. referred to us between Wm. Wallice plt. and Cornelius Fox Deft: and we find that there is Justly Due to Wm. Wallice forty five Shillings Current money, and further we find that in case John Womack protests a Note this day past by the said Cornelius

[page 239]

Fox payable to the said William Wallice for Twenty Shillings being part of the said accot. now in Dispute, and if the said Wallice produces at Court when this suit is called the said Note protested, that then we find Due to the said William Wallice three pounds five Shillings, Given under my hand this 13th Day of December 1718. [signed] Richard Pigeon, Geo. Hamelton.

And the said William Wallice produceing the said Note protested, on his motion Judgement is granted him agst. the said Deft. for the sd. Sum of three pounds five Shillings, and it is Ordered that the said Defendt. pay to the said plt. the said Sum & Costs. Als. Exec:

In the action of Debt brot. by John Hatch agst. William Coleman for fourteen hundred and forty pounds of porke Due by Bill Dated the Seventh of Aprill 1715: the Defendt. being called and not appearing pursuant to the Conditional order of the Last Court on the plts: motion Judgement is granted and Confirmed agst. the said Defendt. & Bartholomew Crowder his Security for Seven pound Eighteen Shillings and four pence, being the Value of the said porke as Valued by the Court, and it is Ordered that the said Defendt. [(]and the said Crowder or either of them) pay to the said plt. the said Sum of Seven pounds Eighteen Shillings and four pence with Costs. Als. Exec:

The action Depending between Peter Bond and John Hamlin Admr. &c is Continued till the next Court.

In the action Depending between Robert Munford and John Hamlin Admr. &c. for 3883l: Tobacco &c at the Last Court an Imparlance was granted the Defendt: and he being now called to plead did not appear &c: therefore it's considered by the Court that the plt. recover agst. the said Deft. the aforesaid Sum and Costs, unless he shall appear at the next Court and answer the said Action.

In the action Depending between Henry Soane and John Hamlin Admr. &c for 3900l. Tobacco &c: at the Last court [a] time was granted the Deft. till this Court to plead, and he being now called to do the same did not appear &c: therefore it is Considered by the Court that the plt. recover agst. the said Defendt. the aforesaid Sum and Costs unless he shall appear at the next court and answer the said Action.

In the action of Debt Depending between John Hatch and John Hamlin Admr. &c: the Defendt. pleads and the plt. Joining in the Issue the same is referred till the next Court for Tryall.

[page 240]

In the action of Debt brot. by Robert Rogers Agst. John Hamlin Admr. &c: for three pounds Eight Shillings Due by Bill &c at the Last Court time was granted the Deft. till this Court to plead and being now called to do the same did not appear &c: therefore it is Considered by the Court that the plt. recover agst. the said Deft. the said Sum and Costs, unless he shall appear at the next Court and answer the said Action.

The Attachment granted Randle Platt agst. Eliza. Duke Exrx. &c is Continued till the next Court.

In the action of Debt brot. by George Harvie agst. Elizabeth Duke Admx. &c of Henry Duke Deced: for Six hundred Ninety three pounds of Tobacco Due by Bill Dated March 1717/8, the Defendt. by her Attorney moves the plt. may prove his Debt, whereupon he makes Oath the same is Due, and on his motion it is Ordered that the said Defendt. pay to the said plt. the aforesaid Sum and Costs out of the said Decedts. Estate. Als. Exec:

In the action on the case brot. by Robert Honycutt agst. Elizabeth Duke Admx. &c: of Henry Duke Deced: for three pound Seven Shillings, Due by Accot. Dated from the thirtyeth Day of Aprill 1716: to the Nineteenth day of Decembr. 1717 (Inclusive) the Defendt. by her Attorney moves the plt. may prove his accot: whereupon he the sd. plt. (being a Quaker) makes his Affirmation the same is Due, and on his motion is Ordered that the said Defendt. pay to the said plt: the aforesaid Sum and Costs out of the said Decedents Estate. Als. Exec:

Edward Hill Esqr. being Summoned at the suit of William Troughton & the said Troughton failing to prosecute thereupon the said Hill is Dismist. from Attending &c:

The *scire facias* brot. by Geo. Pasmore agst. Charles Williams Admr. &c neither party appearing is Dismist.

In the action brot. by Richard Pace agst. Michal Rosser Junr. an Imparlance is granted the Defendt. till the next court.

The action of Debt brot. by William Saffold agst. James Rivers neither party appearing is Dismist.

The action brot. by Robt. West agst. Charles Chapman, neither party appearing is Dismist.

The action brot. by Henry Ally agst. Thomas Hobby, neither party appearing is Dismist.

[page 241]

The petition of Thomas Mitchell agst. Robert Mitchell is Dismist.

In the action on the case brot. by James Bell agst. James Niblet Adminstrator with the Will annext. of Thomas Bilbro Deced: for five pounds Tenn Shillings Due by account Dated the third of November 1717, the Defendt. moves the plt. may prove his accot. whereupon he makes Oath the same is Justly due and on his motion it is Ordered that the said Defendant pay to the said plt. the said Sum & Costs out of the said Decedts. Estate. Als. Exec:

In the action on the case brot. by Randle Platt agst. Eliza: Duke Admx. &c: of Henry Duke Deced: on the motion of the Defendts. Attorney an Imparlance is granted her till the next Court.

In the action on the case brot. by Robert Gilmore agst. Eliza: Duke Admx. &c: of Henry Duke Deced: Randle Platt enters himselfe Security to pay all costs and Damages that shall be awarded agst. the said Plaintiff, whereupon on the motion of the Defendts. Attorney an Imparlance is granted her till the next Court.

In the action of Debt brot. by James Bell agst. Richard Ingram Admr. with the Will annext. of Richard Hix Deced: for fifteen hundred pounds of Tobacco Due by Bill Dated the fifth of March 1716, the Defendt. makeing no Defence, and the sd. plt. makeing Oath the said Sum is Due to him, thereupon on his motion Judgement is granted him against the said Defendt: for the said Sum, and it is Ordered that the said Deft. pay to the said plt. the said Sum and Costs out of the said Decedts. Estate. Als. Exec:

In the action on the case brot. by Robert Gilmore agst. John Hamlin Admr. &c: of Richard Hamlin Deced: Randle Platt enters himselfe Security to pay all costs and Damages that shall be awarded agst. the said plt: whereupon on the motion of the Defendts. Attorney an Imparlance is granted him till the next Court.

The action brot. by Benja. Foster agst. Robert Abbernathy neither party appearing is Dismist.

The action brot. by Henry Harrison agst. Robert Abbernathy neither party appearing, is Dismist.

The action brot. by John and Robert Bolling Exrs. of Robt. Bolling Deced: agst. Robt. Abbernathy, neither party appearing is Dismist.

[page 242]

In the action on the case brot. by Richard Bland agst. John Pook, on the Defts. motion an Imparlance is granted him till the next Court.

The action brot. by Richard Bland agst. Wm. Anderson, the plt. failing to prosecute is Dismist.

The action brot. by Wm. Bobbit against Instance Hall, the plt. failing to prosecute is Dismist.

The action brot. by Wm. Bobbit agst. Michal Hill, neither party appearing is Dismist.

The action brot. by Wm. Rowlet agst. James Cragg, neither party appearing is Dismist.

In the action on the case brot. by David Crawley agst. William Bobbit for £13:12:0½ Due by accot. &c: the Defendt. being called and not appearing and Robert Bolling being returned Security for him on the motion of the plts: Attorney Judgement is granted him agst. the said Deft. and his sd. Security for the said Sum and Costs, unless the said Defendt. shall appear at the next Court and answer the said Action.

The action brot. by David Crawley agst. Elizabeth Parram, the plt. failing to prosecute, is Dismist.

The action brot. by David Crawley agst. John Stroud, the plt. failing to prosecute, is Dismist.

The action brot. by David Crawley agst. John Brooks, the plt. failing to prosecute, is Dismist.

The Attachment granted Robert Mitchell agst. the Estate of David Collyshaw is continued till the next Court.

Mr. Randle Platt is appointed and Impowered by this Court to receive & to Dispose of the best advantage, the Tobacco Leavied by the Last Assembly in the County's of Isle of Wight and Princess Anne, and Ordered to be paid to this County for Wolves heads &c: who is to account for the same to this Court when he shall be thereto required by the said Court.

Pursuant to the Direction of the Act for regulating Ordinarys &c: Ordered that the rates on Ordinary Liquors, Dyet, Lodgeing &c: be as were formerly set and rated by this Court.

[page 243]

John Peterson made Complaint that David Collyshaw Stands Indebted to him by accot. the sum of four pounds Seven Shillings and Six pence and set forth that the said David hath unlawfully Absconded so that the Ordinary process at Law cannot be Served on him whereupon he by Virtue of an Attachment under the hand of one of his Majestys Justices for this County returnable to this Court hath caused part of the Estate of the said David to be Attacht. for payment thereof, Vizt: One Small bed, One old rugg, One old Sheet, One pillow, Nine Sheep, and the said David being called and failing to appear to replevye the same, and the said plt. makeing Oath the said Sum is Justly Due to him, thereupon Judgement is granted him agst. the sd. Defendt. for the said Sum and Costs, to be Leavied on the Estate Attacht. as aforesaid. Ordered that the Sherr: cause the said Estate to be duly appraised by Henry and William Batte, Edward Mitchell and Thomas Moor or any three of them being first Sworn by some Majistrate of this County for that purpose and Delivered the plt. for and toward the payment of the said Sum and Costs, and make report of their proceedings, and it is further Ordered that the sd. Attachment Continue in full force agst. the Estate of the said David, till the next Court.

And then the Court Adjourn'd till Court in Course. Randle Platt. Test W: Hamlin, Cl. Cur.

At a Court held at Merchantshope for the County of
Prince George on the second Tuesday in Aprill being the fourteenth
Day of the said month, Anno Dom: 1719.

Present   John Hamlin,   Randle Platt,   Robert Hall }
               Sampson Merredeth,   Lewis Green Junr.   & John Peterson }   Gent. Justices

Judith Smith Executrix &c: of Thomas Smith Deced: returns an Inventory of the said Decedts. Estate, which is Ordered to be recorded.

James Anderson in Open Court acknowledged his Deed for Land Indented and Seald, with Livery of Seizin endorst thereon, to Cornelius

[page 244]

Cargill on whose motion the same is Admitted to Record, And then also appeared in Court Mary Anderson Wife of the said James and being first privately Examined freely and Voluntarily relinquisht. to the said Cornelius Cargill her right of Dower of in and to the Lands &c: in the said Deed mentioned, which is Likewise Ordered to be recorded.

John Hamlin in Open Court acknowledged his Deed for Land Indented and Seald, with Livery of Seizin thereon, to Michael Hill on whose motion the same is Admitted to Record.

Peter Jones Junr. in Open Court acknowledged his Deeds of Lease & Release of Land (Indented and Seald) to Robert Munford on whose motion the same are admitted to Record, And then also appeared in Court Mary Jones the wife of the said Peter and being first privately Examined freely and Voluntarily relinquisht. to the said Robert Munford her right of Dower of in and too the Lands &c in the said Deeds mentioned, which is Likewise Ordered to be recorded.

Peter Jones Junr. in Open Court acknowledged his Deeds of Lease & release of Land (Seald) to Richard Smith Junr. on whose motion the same are Admitted to Record, and then also appeared in Court Mary Jones the wife of the said Peter and being first privately Examined freely and Voluntarily relinquisht. to the said Richard Smith her right of Dower of in & too the Lands &c: in the sd. Deeds mentioned which is Likewise Ordered to be recorded.

Peter Jones Junr. in Open Court acknowledged his Deeds of Lease & release of Land (Seald) to Joshua Irby on whose motion the same are Admitted to Record, And then also appeared in Court Mary Jones the Wife of the said Peter and being first privately Examined freely and Voluntarily relinquisht. to the said Joshua Irby her right of Dower of in and too the Lands &c: in the said Deeds mentioned which is Likewise Ordered to be recorded.

Peter Jones Junr. in Open Court acknowledged his Deeds for Land Indented and Seald, with Livery of Seizin thereon, to Abraham Jones on whose motion the same is Admitted to record, And then also appeared in Court Mary Jones the Wife of the said Peter and being first privately Examined freely and Voluntarily relinquisht. to the said Abra. Jones her right of Dower of in and too the Lands &c: in the said Deed mentioned which is Likewise Ordered to be recorded.

William Davis in Open Court acknowledged his Deed for Land, Indented and Seald, with Livery of Seizin thereon, to Robert Munford on whose motion the same is Admitted to Record.

[page 245]

The Last Will and Testament of John Lanier Deced: was Exhibitted into Court by Nicholas Lanier his Exr. who made Oath thereto, and it being Duly proved by William Peebles, Henry Peebles and Thomas Burrow the sevl. Witnesses thereto is Ordered to be recorded, and on the motion of the said Nicholas and his giveing Security according to Law, Certificate is granted him for Obtaining a Probate in Due form.

Ordered that Nicholas Lanier Exr. of John Lanier Deced: return to the next Court an Inventory of the said Decedts. Estate.

John Drayton one of the Orphans of Roger Drayton Deced: came into Court and Chose Capt. John Poythres his Guardian.

Europe a Negro Boy belonging to Richard Bland is Adjudged Eleven years old.

Asia and Africa Negro Boys belonging to Richard Bland are adjudged Ten years old.

America a Negro Boy belonging to Richard Bland is Adjudged Nine years old.

Phebe a Negro Girl belonging to Richard Bland is Adjudged to be twelve years old.

Bella a Negro Girl belonging to Richard Bland is Adjudged Nine years old.

Celia a Negro Girl belonging to Richard Bland is Adjudged to be Seven years old.

Jenny a Negro Girl belonging to William Reves is Adjudged twelve years old.

Beck a Negro Girl belonging to John Cureton is Adjudged fourteen years old.

On the motion of William Savage he is Exempt from paying Leavy for the future.

On the motion of Wm. Hamlin on ye behalfe of Eliza. Hamlin, Tom and Ally Negro's belonging to the said Eliza. Hamlin are Exempt from paying Levey for the future.

[page 246]

A Deed of Release of Land (Seald) from Nicholas Wyatt to Edward Hill Esqr. was proved in Open Court to be the Act and Deed of the said Nicholas by the Oaths of William Braine, John Wyatt and Peter Finney Witnesses thereto and on the motion of the said Edward Hill the same is Admitted to record.

Valentine Minge came into Court and made Oath that John Sherley Deced: Departed this Life Intestate as farr as he knows or believes and on his motion and giveing Security according to Law Certificate is granted him for Obtaining a Commission of Administration in Due form.

Edward Wyatt, Benjamin Reeks, James Bell and Paul Jones or any three of them being first Sworn for the purpose of Some Majistrate of this County are Nominated and appointed to appraise the Estate of John Sherley Deceed: and make report of their proceedings thereunto the next Court when Valentine Minge the Administrator is Ordered to return the Inventory thereof.

In the action of Debt brot. by Sampson Merredeth agst. Silvanus Stokes for thirty one pounds Current money Due by Bill Dated the second Day of January 1718, the sd. partys appearing, the Defendt. moves the plt. may make Oath he has reced: no sattisfaction for the sd. Bill, which he accordingly does, thereupon on the motionof the said plt. it is Ordered that the sd. Defendt. do pay to him the sd. plt. the aforesaid Sum of thirty One pounds Current money and Costs. Als. Exec:

John Coleman and John Mayes who were appointed at the Last Court to View, Lay out and Value One Acre of Land Lying on Tuckers runn and belonging to David Crawley, for Robert Bollings Convenience to Build a Water Mill on according to the said Order make report of their proceedings which is Ordered to be recorded, and is Accordingly truly recorded as follows, Vizt. In Obedience to the above Order whose names are hereunto Subscribed have Laid out for Robert Bolling One Acre of David Crawley's Land on Tuckers Runn bounded, Vizt. beginning upon the said Runn above the old Damm, thence North forty Degrees East Sixteen pole, thence West forty degrees North tenn poles, thence south forty Degrees West Sixteen pole, then East forty Degrees south tenn poles, to the beginning, which we have Valued at Tenn Shillings Current money of Virginia, which we have ready to Deliver the said Crawley on Demand, he haveing failed to attend the Order to have put the said Bolling into possession thereof accordingly, As witness our hands this this [sic] 3d Day of Aprill 1719. [signed] John Coleman, John Mayes. Truly Recorded. Test Wm. Hamlin, Cl. Cur.

[page 247]

The Order that Sarah and Jos: Woodleife Exrs. of Edward Woodleife Deced: return an Inventory of the said Decedts. Estate is Continued till next Court.

The attachment granted Drury Bolling agst. the Estate of John Spain the plt. failing to prosecute is Dismist.

The attachment granted Nathl. Harrison Esqr. agst. the Estate of John Brewer is Continued till next Court.

The action of Debt Depending between Sampson Merredeth and Wm. Mitchell the plt. failing to prosecute is Dismist.

James Vaughn in Open Court acknowledged his Deed for Land Seald, with Livery and Seizin thereon, to Cornelius Fox on whose motion the same is Admitted to Record, And then also appeared in Court Ann Vaughn the Wife of the said James and being first privately Examined freely and Voluntarily relinquisht. to the said Cornelius Fox her right of Dower in and to the Lands &c: in the said Deed mentioned which is Likewise Ordered to be recorded.

In the action of the case brot: by John Berry agst. Fra: Epes for Forty Two Shillings & due by accot. Dated 1716, the Deft. haveing pleaded *Nil Debit* and the Issue being Submitted to the Court for Tryall, the accots. of the said partys were Examined and adjusted, and the Ballance appearing in favour of the Deft. thereupon on his motion the suit is Dismist.

In the action on the case brot. by George Harvie agst. John Berry for five hundred Ninety Eight pounds of Tobacco Due by accot. Dated 1716: the Deft. not appearing pursuant to the Conditional Judgement and Order of the Last Court, on the plts: motion Judgement is granted and Confirmed to him against the said Defendt. and Richard Smith his Security for the said Sum and Costs, and it is Ordered that the said Defendt. and the said Richard Smith or either of them pay to the said plt. the aforesaid Sum and Costs. Als: Exec:

Judgement being this Day past unto George Harvie agst. Richard Smith for five hundred Ninety Eight pounds of Tobacco & costs, by reason of the non appearance of John Berry [with] an Action on the case, at the suit of the said Geo. Harvie, on the motion of the said Richard Smith, an Attachment is granted him against the Estate of the said John Berry for the said Sum and Costs returnable to the next Court for Judgement.

[page 248]

In the action brot. by William Randolph Admr. &c: of Eusebius King Deced: agst. Edward Simmons, on the motion of the plts: Attorney for Special Bail, Thomas Simmons became Special Bail for the said Defendt: who being permitted to plead Severall plea's &c: accordingly files his plea's and a Demr. to the plts. Declaration and on his motion time if granted him till the next Court to Consider the said plea's, and he Joining in the Demurrer the same is referred till the next Court to be argued.

In the action on the case brot. by Joshua Irby against John Bonner for Nine hundred and fifteen pounds of Tobacco Due by accot. Dated 1715, the Defendt. haveing pleaded *Nil Debit*, & the accot. of the plt. being referred (by the Court) to Dr. John Hamersly and Dr. Edmond Irby [words removed] to Examine and Audit [words removed] they accordingly make the the following report, Vizt. We whose names are under written do find for the plaintiff five hundred weight of Tobacco. John Hamersly, Ed. Irby, which on the plts. motion is recorded, and it is Ordered that the said Defendt: pay to the said plt. the sd. Sum of five hundred pounds of Tobacco and Costs. Als. Exec:

In the action of Trespass on the case brot. by Jos. Irby agst. Math. Smart Damage Fivety pounds Current money &c: at the Last Court an Imparlance was granted the Defendt. till this Court to plead and being now called to do the same did not appear &c: thereupon it is considered that the plt. recover agst. the said Deft. the said Sum & Costs unless the said Deft. shall appear at the next Court and answer the said Action.

In the action of Trespass on the case brot. by Jos: Irby agst. Cornelius Fox Damage Twenty pounds Current money &c: at the Last Court an Imparlance was granted the Defendt. till this Court to plead and being now Called to do the same did not appear &c: thereupon it is Considered by the Court that the plt. recover agst. the said Defendt. the said Sum & Costs unless the said Defendt. shall appear at the next Court and answer the said Action.

The action brot. by Francis Mallory agst. Elinor Walpole Admx. of Richard Walpole Deced: neither party appearing is Dismist.

The Order that Sarah Bishope Executrix &c: of William Bishope Deced: return an Inventory of the said Decedts. Estate is Continued till the next Court.

The suit in Chan: brot. by John Bolling agst. Henry Offley and Robert Bolling is Continued till the next Court.

[page 249]

In the action of Debt brot. by Henry Holecroft agst. Elizabeth Epes Executrix of the Last Will and Testament of William Epes deced: for three thousand One hundred Seventy four pounds of Tobacco Due by Bill Dated the twenty fourth Day of July 1717, the Defendt. being called and not appearing pursuant to the Conditional Judgemt. and Order of the Last Court on the motion of the plts: Attorney Judgement is granted and Conrifmed to him agst. the said Deft. and Francis Epes Junr. her Security for the said Sum and it is Ordered that the said Defendt. and the said Frances Epes Junr. or either of them pay to the said plt. the said Sum and Costs. Als. Exec:

The Order that Ann Hill Exrx. of John Hill Deced: return an Inventory of the said Decedts: Estate is Continued till next Court.

In the action of Trespass on the case brot. by John Hatch agst. John Turner Damage Tenn pounds Sterl: at the Last Court on Imparlance was granted the said Defendt. till this Court to plead and being now called to do the same did not appear &c: therefore it is Considered by the Court that the plt. recover agst. the said Defendt. the aforesaid Sum and Costs, unless he shall appear at the next Court & answer the said Action.

In the action of Debt brot. by David Crawley agst. William Taylor for Nine pounds Eleven Shillings and Six pence Due by Bill Dated the 20th Day of May 1717, the Defendt. being called and not appearing pursuant to the Conditional Judgement and Order of the Last Court on the motion of the plts: Attorney Judgemt. is granted and Confirmed to him against the said Defendt. and Titus Creacher his Security for the said Sum, and it is Ordered that the said Defendt. and the said Titus Creacher or either of them pay to the said plt. the aforesaid Sum and Costs. Als. Exec:

On the motion of Francis Coleman Overseer of the Butterwood Road he is Ordered to Turn and Clear the said Road where he shall think fitt for the convenience of the same.

Frances Anderson Executrix of the Last Will and Testament of Charles Anderson Deced: who was One of the Exrs. of the Last Will and Testament of Sarah Boisseau deced: Exhibitts into Court an accot: relatieing to the said Boisseau's Estate, which being referred to and Auditted by Gilbert Hay and Ed: Prince, is on her motion Admitted to record.

[page 250]

Henry Batte came into Court and made Oath that Thomas Harwell Deced: Departed this Life Intestate as far as he knows or believes and on his motion and gieveing Security according to Law Certificate is granted him for Obtaining a Commission of Administration in Due form.

Joshua Poythres, Robert Poythres, John Fitzgerrald and Edward Mitchell or any three of them being first Sworn for that purpose by some Majistrate of this County are Nominated and appointed to appraise the Estate of Thomas Harwell Deced: and make report of their proceedings therein to the next Court when Henry Batte, the Admr. thereof is Ordered to return the Inventory.

And then the Court Adjourn'd till Court in Course. Jno. Hamlin. Test W: Hamlin, Cl. Cur.

Mr. Joseph Greenhill is Dr. to Mr. John Hatch   Cr.

	£ S d	
To. y[r.] Debt on accot. of John Thompson }		pr. Sundry Goods Attached Valued to £ 9.17.0
600 l. Tobacco at 2d pr. l.	5.0.0	
For Sherrs: Fees	0.16.6	
For Clerks Fees	0.17.2	[signed] Gilbert Hay
For 4 Appraisers one Day	1.0.0	Wm. Harrison
To yr. Debt on my Store book	0.7.9	James Harrison
	£8.1.5	James Jones Junr.
The Ballce. attached for Capt. Thos. Goodwyn	1.15.7	
	£9.17.0	Sworn before me John Poythres.

On the Order for the Appraisment of the Estate of Joseph Greenhill Attacht. for John Hatch, the Sherriff made the above report, which is truly Recorded.   pr. Wm. Hamlin, Cl. Cur.

Dr. Joseph Greenhill is to Drury Bolling   Cr.

To Judgement agst. him for	£4.0.0	pr. the Appraisement £6.12.0
To Sherrs: Fees	0.10.8	
To Clerkes Fees	0.17.0	[signed] Wm. Harrison, Gilbert
To 4 Appraisers one Day	1.0.0	Hay, James Harrison, James Jones Junr.
Due to the Estate	0.4.2	
	£6.12.2	Sworn before me John Poythres.

On the Order for the Appraisment of the Estate of Joseph Greenhill Attacht. for Drury Bolling, the Sherriff made the above report which is truly Recorded.   pr. Wm. Hamlin, Cl. Cur.

[page 251]

Mr. Joseph Greenhill is Dr. to John Williamson   Cr.

	£ S d	
To Judgement Obtained agst.		pr. the within Goods Valued to £10.12.9
him for	19.8.6	
To Sheriffs fees	0.16.0	Ball. Due to W. 1.18.11
To Clerks fees	0.17.2	£12.1.8
To the 4 Appraisers one day	1.0.0	[signed] Gilbert Hay, Wm. Harrison
	£12.1.8	James Harrison, James Jones Junr.
		Sworn before me John Poythres.

On the Order for the Appraisment of the Estate of Joseph Greenhill Attacht. for John Williamson, the Sherriff made the above report which is truly Recorded.   pr. Wm. Hamlin, Cl. Cur.

October the 21st 1718.

In Obedience to an Order of Prince George County Court we the Subscribers have Valued the Estate of Jos: Greenhill Attacht. by George Pasmore as follows, Vizt.

A Negro man Named Limbrick at   £30.0.0

The Appraisers sworn by me, John Poythres.   [signed] Gilbert Hay, Wm. Harrison

                                             James Harrison, James Jones Junr.

Joseph Greenhill Dr. 1718   pr. Contra   Cr.

To Pasmores Judgemt. agst. him	£19.0.0	
To Cls: Fees on Do. 106 l. Tobo. is	17.8	By a Negro Attacht. }
To Sherrs. fees and Do.	1.16.8	Valued as above to } £30.0.0
do. the appraisers	1.0.0	
do. paid Goodwynne by the }		
Courts Order	7.5.8	
	£30.0.0	

On the Order for the Appraisement of the Estate of Joseph Greenhill Attacht. for George Pasmore, the Sherriff made the above report which is truly Recorded.   pr. Wm. Hamlin, Cl. Cur.

Dr. Mr. Joseph Greenhill is to Peter Wynne   Cr.

To Judgement Obtained agst. him for	6.14.2	pr. the sundry Goods within
To Sherrs. fees	0.17.2	mentioned Value to £10.10.5

For Cls. fees	0.18.4		
For the 4 Appraisers one Day	1.0.0	[signed] Gilbert Hay, Wm. Harrison	
The Ball. Attached for Capt. }		James Harrison, James Jones Junr.	
Thos. Goodwyne being }	[1].1.1		
	£10.10.5	Sworn before me John Poythres.	

On the Order for the Appraisment of the Estate of Joseph Greenhill Attacht. for Peter Wynne, the Sherriff made the above report, which is truly Recorded.   pr. Wm. Hamlin, Cl. Cur.

[page 252]

Dr. Mr. Joseph Greenhill is to John Dunbarr			Cr.
To Judgement obtained for	£1.19.1½	pr. the Goods within mentioned }	
For Sherrs: Fees	0.11.1	valued to	£4.9.0
For Cls: Fees	0.17.2		
For the 4 Appraisers one day	1.0.0	[signed] Gilbert Hay, Wm. Harrison	
Ball. Due	0.1.7½		
	£4.9.0	Sworn before me John Poythres.	

On the Order for the Apprraisment of the Estate of Joseph Greenhill Attacht. for John Dunbarr, the Sherr: made the Above report which is truly Recorded.   pr. Wm. Hamlin, Cl. Cur.

Joseph Hawks is Dr. to William Troughton			Cr.
To Judgement Obtained agst. him for	£9.1.9½	pr. the within mentioned Goods }	
For Sheriffs Fees	0.15.9	Valued to	9.15.[ ]
For the 4 Apppraizers one Day	1.0.0	Due to Ball: to W.	3.4.4½
	£12.0.2½		£12.0.8½
		[signed] Gilbert Hay, William Harrison	
		James Harrison, James Jones Junr.	
		Sworn before me John Poythres.	

On the Order for the Appraisment of the Estate of Joseph Hawks Attacht. for William Troughton, the Sherriff made the above report which is truly Recorded.   pr. Wm. Hamlin, Cl. Cur.

One small old Bed	}		
One old Rugg, One sheet	}		
One pillow	}	£1.0.0	
Nine Sheep		2.8.0	
		£3.8.0	
Appraised by us	Henry Batte		
	Edm. Batte		
	Thos. [his X mark] Mo[or]		

The above appraisers first Sworn pr. me Lewis Green Junr.

On the Order for the appraisment of the Estate of David Colyshaw Attacht. for John Peterson, the Sherriff made the above report which is Truly Recorded.   pr. Wm. Hamlin, Cl. Cur.

[page 253, faint]

At a Court held at Merchantshope for the County of Prince
George on the Second Tuesday in May being the twelfth Day
of the [sd.] month Anno Dom. 1719:

Present	John Hamlin,	John Poythres, }	
	Robert Hall	& Lewis Green Junr. }	Gent. Justices.

On the petition of Lydia Clements she is Exempt from paying County Leavy for her Negro woman Named Effy.

Valentine Minge Admr. &c: of John Sherley Deced: returns an Inventory of the Estate of the sd. Deced: which is Ordered to be recorded.

Henry Batte Admr. &c of Thomas Harwell Deced: returned an Inventory of the Estate of the sd. Deced: which is Ordered to be recorded.

The Last Will and Testament of James Jones Deced: was Exhibited in Court by James Jones his Executor, who made Oath thereto, and it being proved by the Oaths of Gilbert Hay, Edward Prince & Thomas Sa[mple] [the] witnesses thereto is Ordered to be recorded, and Certificate is granted the said Executor for Obtaining a Probate thereof in Due form the sd. [...] also made Oath that the [...] in the sd. [...] before the [...] and Sealing thereof.

Sarah Jones's Letter to this Court was proved in Open Court by the Oath of Edward Goodrich one of the Witnesses thereto, and on the motion of James Jones is Ordered to be recorded.

Nicholas Lanier Executor &c: of John Lanier Deced: returned an Inventory of the said Decedts. Estate wch. is Ordered to be recorded.

Mr. Sampson Merredeth is appointed to take the List of Tithables in Martins Brandon Parrish on the Tenth Day of June Next.

Capt. John Poythres in Waynoke Parrish

Mr. John Hardyman in Westover Parrish

& Majr. Robt. Bolling in Bristoll Parrish.

Mary Potts, Admx. &c of [Thos.] Potts Deced: returns into Court an Inventory and appraisement of the sd. Decedts. Estate wch. is Ordered to be recorded.

[page 254, faint]

Sampson Merredeth came into Court and made Oath that William Talbott Deced: Departed this Life Intestate as farr as he knows or believes and on his motion and giveing Security for his Just and faithfull Administration of the sd. Decedts. Estate Certificate is granted him for Obtaining a [Commission] of Administraton in Due form.

James Bell, Paul Jones, Richard Ingram and [...] [Buckner] or any three of them being first Sworn by Some Majistrate of this County for that purpose are Nominated and Appointed to appraise the Estate of William Talbott Deced: and make report of their proceedings thereunto the next Court when Sampson Merredeth the Admr. thereof is to [return an] Inventory.

Robert Poythres and Edward Mitchell, who were appointed to Lay out and Value one Acre of Land Lying on Balys Runn and belonging to the heirs of Joseph Holycross Deced: for John Petersons Convenience to build a Water Mill on, make report of their proceedings which is Ordered to be recorded and is accordingly truly recorded as follows, Vizt.

Prince George County ss.

In Obedience to an Order of Court Dated the 13th Day of August 171[ ], We the Subscribers being by Order of Court Appointed to Lay out & Value an Acre of Land belonging to the heirs of Joseph Holycross Deced: for the use of out petitioner John Peterson Senr. have accordingly Laid out one Acre of Land and Valued the same at twelve Shillings [current] money, and possess your petitioner with the same, as Witness our hands this 11th Day of May 1719. [signed] Robert Poythres, Ed [his mark] Mitchell. Truly Recorded pr. Wm. Hamlin, Cl. Cur.

Present Sampson Merredeth & John Peterson, Gent. Justices.

Edward Prince is appointed overseer of the Highways in the room of Randle Platt.

The action of Debt brot. by John Bolling agst. James Lundy neither party appearing is Dismist.

The action of Debt brot: by John and Robert Bolling Exrs. &c: of Colo. Robert Bolling Deced: agst. James Lundy, neither party appearing is Dismist.

The action on the case brot. by Nathaniel [Harrison] Esqr. agst. Richard Harrison the plt. failing to prosecute is Dismist.

The action on the case brot. by Nathaniel Harrison Esqr. agst. Phillip [...] the plt. failing to prosecute is Dismist.

[page 255]

In the action on the case brot. by Nathaniel Harrison Esqr. agst. Richard Whittmore for three hundred thirty three pounds of Tobacco Due accot. &c the Defendt: being called and not appearing and there being no security returned for him on the motion of the plts: Attorney Judgement is granted him agst. the sd. Defendt. and James Thweatt Sherr: of this County for the said Sum and Costs, unless the said Defendt. shall appear at the next Court and answer the sd. Action.

In the action on the case brot. by Nathaniel Harrison Esqr. agst. Henry Bates for four hundred Ninety Seven pounds of Toba: Due by accot. &c: the Defendt. being returned *non est Inventus* & not appearing on the motion of the plts: Attorney an Attachment is granted him against the Estate of the said Defendt. for the said Sum and Costs returnable to the next Court for Judgement.

In the action on the case brot. by George Harvie agst. Thomas Simmons for five hundred and fifteen pounds of Tobacco Due by Accot. the Defendt. appears and pleads *Nil Debit* and the plt. Joining in the Issue the same is referred till the next Court for Tryall.

The Attachment granted Randle Platt agst. the Estate of Allen Tye neither party appearing is Dismist.

In the action of Debt brot. by Moses Beck against Cornelius Fox for five pound five Shillings and Six pence Due by Bill &c: the Defendt. being called and not appearing and there being no Security returned for him, on the plts. motion Judgement is granted him against the said Defendt. and James Thweatt Sherr: of this County for the said Sum and Costs, unless the said Deft. shall appear at the next Court and answer the said Action.

The Order that Rebecca Spencer Admx. of Richard Spencer Deced: return an Inventory of the said Decedts. Estate is Continued till the next Court.

The Order that Randle Platt return an accot. Dr. & Cr. between himselfe and Jos: Greenhill, is made Null & Void.

The Order that Elizabeth Duke Admx. of Henry Duke Deced: return an Inventory of the said Decedts. Estate is Continued till the next Court.

[page 256]

The action on the case brot. by Randle Platt agst. Henry King the plt. failing to prosecute is Dismist.

John Lett Admr. of the Estates of Sarah and Roger Drayton Deced: Exhibitted into Court the Amounts Dr. & Cr. of the said Decedts. Estates upon Oath which being Examined and Allowed by the Court are Order'd to be recorded.

In the action brot. by Mary Wiggins agst. Richard Winkles, the Deft. on his motion has Liberty to plead Several plea's and accordingly files his plea's to the plts: Declaration who has time till the next Court to Consider the same.

The order of the Last Court that Margaret and Jos: Lanthrop Exrs. of John Lanthrop Deced: return an Inventory of the sd. Decedents Estate, is Continued till the next Court.

Elizabeth Jane Relict of Phillip Jane Deced: came into Court and made Oath that the sd. Phillip Jane Departed this Life without makeing any Will as farr as she knows or believes, and upon her motion and giveing Security for her Just and faithfull Administration of the sd. Deceds. Estate, Certificate is granted her for Obtaining Letters of Administration in Due form.

Richard Pace, Thomas Kirkland, Peter Grammer and William Reese or any three of them being first Sworn by Some Majistrate of this County for that purpose are Ordered to appraise the Estate of Phillip Jean Deced: & make report of their proceedings therein to the next Court when Elizabeth Jean the Admx. thereof is to return the Inventory.

Mary Martin Relict of John Martin Deced: came into Court and made Oath that the said John Martin Departed this Life without makeing any Will as farr as She knows or believes, and on her motion and giveing Security for her Just and faithfull Administration of the sd. Deceds: Estate, Certificate is granted her for Obtaining a Commission of Administration in Due form.

John Scoggan, Nicholas Robyson, John Burrow and Nicholas Lanier or any three of them being first Sworn by some Majistrate of this County for that purpose, are Ordered to appraise the Estate of John Martin Deced: and make report of their proceedings therein to the next Court when Mary Martin the Admx. thereof is to return the Inventory.

[page 257]

Pursuant to the Direction of the Act concerning Jurys, a Grandjury was Impannelled and Sworn by Name William Harrison, John Rivers, John Winingham, John Lett, John Wilkins, Saml. Birch, Thomas Weeks, John Cheves, James Harrison, John Patteson, James Moody, Geo: Hamilton, Nicholas Lanier, John Hynes, Richard Cureton, Richard Deardan & Geo. Brewer, who haveing their charge were sent out and soon after make the following return into Court, Vizt. We the Grandjurors are Ignoramus. [signed] Wm. Harrison, foreman.

In the suit in Chancery Brot. by Joseph Goffe agst. Edward Wyatt, the respondent files his answer upon Oath, and on the Complainants motion time is granted him till the next Court to Consider the same.

On the motion of Richard Bland in behalfe of the *Virginia Indian Company*, who set forth that a Sarvant belonging to the said Company Named William Mirick absented himselfe from his Service Nine days and prayed Judgement against him according to Law, and the said William appearing and making no Defence it is thereupon Ordered that he serve the said Indian Company in Leiu thereof Eighteen Days after his time of service by Indenture is Expired, and also one year and four Days over and above, being for the sd. Companys Charge, and Disbursment in takeing up and regaining the sd. Sarvant and for the costs of this Judgement, amounting in the whole to the Value of Eight hundred and fifteen pounds of Tobacco. Provided Nevertheless if the said William shall give Sufficient Security to repay the said Company in Six months their Disbursments, that the same shall be Accepted in Leiu of the said Service.

The Order that Nathaniel Harrison Esqr. Admr. &c: of Richard P[igeon] Deced: return an Inventory of the said Deceds. Estate is Continued till the next Court.

Ann Moor Relict of Thomas Moor Deced: came into Court and made Oath that the said Thomas Moor Departed this Life without any Will as farr as she knows or believes and on her motion and giveing Security for her Just and faithfull Administration of the said Deceds: Estate, Certificate is granted her for Obtaining a Commission of Administration in Due form.

[page 258]
 William Grigg, Edward Mitchell, John Fitzgerrald and John Peterson Junr. or any three of them being first Sworn for that purpose by some Majistrate of this County are Ordered to appraise the Estate of Thomas Moor Deced: and make report of their proceedings therein to the next Court when Ann Moor the Administratrix thereof is to return the Inventory.

 Valentine Minge, William Harrison, Peter Wynne, & Drury Bolling Gent. are recommended by the Court to the Honble. the Leiut. Governor to be added to the Commission of the peace for this County.

 Sarah Wall Exrx. of John Wall Deced: returns a further Inventory of the said Deceds: Estate, which is Ordered to be recorded.

 The action of Debt brot. by Randle Platt agst. John Hardyman the plt. failing to prosecute is Dismist.

 On the motion of Edward Hill Esqr., Edward Goodrich is entred his Attorney in all causes &c: wherein the said Hill is concerned.

 In the action of Debt brot. by Robert Bolling against Geo. Hamilton for 4738: Tobacco Due by Bond &c: the Deft. haveing filed his plea's to the plts: Declaration and he Joining therein A Jury was Impannelled and Sworn to try the matter in Issue by Name William Harrison, James Harrison, John Winningham, Instance Hall, John Pook, Edward Wyatt, Benja. Foster, James Moody, John Wilkason, Thomas Simmons, John Woodleife & John Bonner who haveing heard the Evidence and reced: their charge were sent out and soon after return into Court with their Verdict, which being Imperfect they were again sent out.

 Sarah Woodleife Exrx. &c: of Edward Woodleife Deced: returns an Inventory of the said Deceds: Estate, wch. is Ordered to be recorded.

 In the action brot. by Peter Bond agst. John Hamlin Administrator of the Goods and Chattels of Richard Hamlin Deced: for One thousand Nine hundred and forty pounds of Tobacco, the Deft. haveing pleaded Non Detinet and the plt. Joining in the Issue the same was Submitted to the Court for Tryall, and the accots. of the said partys being Examined in Court and there appearing to be Due to the plt. One thousand Seven hundred fifty four pounds of Tobacco which the plt. made Oath he reced: no sattisfaction for thereupon on the motion of his Attorney it is Ordered that the said Deft. pay to the said plt. out of the said Deceds: Estate the

[page 259]
Sum of F[...]teen hundred twelve Shillings and four pence, being the Value of the sd. Tobacco as Valued by the Court togather with Costs. Als. Exec:

 On the petition of William Stainback senr. he is Exempt from paying County Leavy for the future.

 In the action brot. by Robert Munford agst. John Hamlin Administrator of the Goods and Chattels of Richard Hamlin Deced: for three thousand Eight hundred Eighty three pounds of Tobacco Due by accot. Dated 1717, which the plt. makes Oath is Due to him and which is Valued by the Court at Thirty two pounds, Seven Shillings and two pence, the Defendt. appears and pleads he has remaining in his hands of the said Deceds: Estate only Eight pounds, thereupon on the plts: motion it is Ordered that the sd. Defendt. do pay to the sd. plt. the said Sum of Eight pounds. Als: Exec: and it is also Ordered that the sd. Deft. do pay to the said plt. (out of the said Deceds. Estate) the residue of the sd. Sum of Thirty two pounds Seven Shillings and two pence, being twenty four pounds Seven Shillings and two pence togather with Costs, when assetts of the said Estate shall come to hand &c.

 In the action of Debt brot. by Robert Rogers agst. John Hamlin Admr. of the Goods and Chattels of Richard Hamlin Deced: for three pounds Eight Shillings Due by Bill Dated the 23d day of May 1718, the sd. partys appearing the Defendt. moves the plt. may prove his Debt, whereupon he makes Oath that One pound Eighteen Shillings thereof is Justly Due and on his motion it is Ordered that the said Deft. do pay to the said plt. out of the said Deceds: Estate the said Sum of One pound Eighteen Shillings and Costs. Als. Exec:

 On the Attachment continued at the Last Court of John Peterson against the Estate of David Colysaw, the Sherr: makes the following return, Vizt: more Goods Attacht., Vizt: two ps. of an [...] three old files [...], one old Bellows, One parcell of old I[...]. One Bo[...], Iron, One pr. fire Tongs. It is thereupon

[page 260]
Ordered that the Sherr: cause the said Goods to be duly appraised by Henry and William Batte, Edward Mitchell and Thomas Moor or any three of them being first Sworn by some Majistrate of this County for that purpose and

delivered the plt. for any toward the payment of his Judgement obtained agst. the said David Colyshaw, and make repeort of their proceedings.

The action of Debt brot. by Randle Platt agst. Elizabeth Duke Exrx. &c: of Henry Duke Deced: the plt. failing to prosecute is Dismist.

In the action on the case brot. by Richard Pace against Michal Rosser Junr. the Defendt. pleads *Nil Debit* and the plt. Joining in the Issue the same is referred till the next Court for Tryall.

And then the Court adjourn'd till Court in Course. John Poythres. Test Wm. Hamlin, Cl. Cur.

At a Court held at Merchantshope for the County of Prince George
on the second Tuesday in June being the Ninth Day of the said
month, Anno Dom. 1719:

| Present | John Hamlin, | Robert Munford, | Robt. Hall |
| | Lewis Green Junr. | & John Peterson, | Gent. Justices |

On the petition of John White he is Exempt from paying publick and County Levy for the future.

On the petition of Thomas Sams he is Exempt from paying publick & County Levy for the future.

Ordered that a Road be cleared from Samuel Harwells on Nottoway River, over Stony Creeke near Capt. Jones's, and that all the Inhabitants on that part of Nottoway River and on Bushskin Creek and Sapponee Creeke Assist Samuel Harwell (who is Appointed Overseer of the sd. Road) in Clearing the same.

Deeds of Lease and Release of Land (Indented and Seald) from John Bolling, Francis Epes Junr. & Henry Randolph of the one part, to Thomas Eldridge of the other part, were proved in Court by the Oaths of

[page 261]
Drury Bolling, Francis Epes Junr. and Richard Kennon the severall Witnesses thereto, to be the Act and Deed of the said John Bolling, Francis Epes Junr. and Henry Randolph to the said Thomas Eldridge on whose motion the same are Ordered to be recorded.

Henry Batte Admr. &c: of Thomas Harwell Deced: returns an accot. Dr. & Cr. of the Estate of the said Deced: upon Oath and the same being Examined by the Court is Ordered to be recorded.

Bridget Ward Relict of Collingwood Ward Deced: came into Court and made Oath that the said Collingwood Ward Departed this Life Intestate as farr as she knows or belives and on her motion and giveing Security for her Just & faitnfull Administration of the said Deceds. Estate, Certificate is granted her for Obtaining a Commission of Administration in Due form.

Thomas Booth, Thomas Simmons Junr., Arthur Biggins and John Cureton or any three of them being first Sworn by Some Majistrate of this County for that purpose are Ordered to Appraise the Estate of Collingwood Ward Deced: and make report of their proceedings therein to the next Court when Bridget Ward the Admx. thereof is to return the Inventory.

On the petition of John Collier and Edward Winingham they are Exempt from paying public and County Levy for the future.

The Depositions of Gilbert Hay and Edward Prince relateing to the Last Will and Testament of James Jones Deced: were taken in Court and Ordered to be recorded.

On the motion of William Mattox he is for the furutre Exempt from paying publick and County Levy for his Negro man Jack.

Sampson Merredeth Admr. &c: of William Talbott Deced: returns an Inventory of the Estate of the said Deced: togather with the Appraisment thereof which is Ordered to be recorded.

[page 262]
Henry Harrison appeared in Court and made Oath that John Sherly Deced: Dyed Indebted to him by Accot. the sum of Forty five Shillings & two pence, thereupon by Consent of Valentine Minge Admr. of the said Deced: it is Ordered that he the said Minge pay the said Harrison out of the said Deceds: Estate the aforesaid Sum and Costs. Als. Exec:

Mary Martin Admx. of John Martin Deced: returns an Inventory and Appraisment of the said Deceds: Estate, which is Ordered to be recorded.

The Last Will and Testament of John Butler Deced: was Exhibitted into Court by Mary his Relict and Esexutrix, who (being a Quaker) made her Affirmation thereto, and it being proved by the Oaths of George Crooke and

Elizabeth Crooke Witnesses thereto is Ordered to be recorded, and Certificate is granted the said Mary Butler for Obtaining a Probate of the sd. Will in Due form.

William Hatt Book=keeper for Nathaniel Harrison Esqr. appeared in Court and made Oath that John Sherly Deced: Dyed Indebted to the sd. Harrison by accot. the sum of three pounds Seven Shillings and five pence, thereupon by Consent of Valentine Minge Admr. of the said Deced: it is Ordered that he the said Minge pay the said Harrison out of the said Deceds: Estate, the aforesaid Sum & Costs. Als: Exec:

In the action on the case brot. by Henry Harrison agst. William Heeth Admr. &c: of Adam Heeth Deced: for Eight pounds Eighteen Shillings and five pence three farthings and Eight hundred thirty Eight pounds of Tobacco Due by accot., the Deft. appearing and makeing no plea or Devense and the plt. makeing Oath the sd. Sums are Justly due to him thereupon on his motion it is ordered that the said Defendt. pay to the said plt. the said Sum of Eight pounds Eighteen Shillings and five pence three farthings and Eight hundred thirty pounds of Tobacco out of the said Deceds: Estate, togather with costs. Als. Exec:

The Last Will and Testament of Randle Platt Deced: was Exhibitted into Court by Henry Holdcraft his Executor who made Oath thereto, and it being proved by the Oaths of William Troughton, Peter Finney and James Loftin Witnesses thereto, and also a Codicil to the sd. Will proved by the Oaths of Francis Hardyman, Benjamin Foster and Thomas Eldridge Witnesses thereto, is Ordered to be recorded, And on the motion of the said Henry Holdcraft and his giveing Security according to Law, a Certificate is granted him for Obtaining a Probat[e] of the said Will in Due form.

[page 263]

John Poythres, John Hatch, William Harrison and Gilbert Hay or any three of them being first Sworn for that purpose by some Majistrate of this County, are Ordered to Appraise the Estate of Randle Platt Deced: and make report of their proceedings to the next Court when Henry Holdcraft the Executor is to return the Inventory thereof.

William Davis is appointed Overseer of the Road from Nottoway River, instead of John Wall.

Mary Potts Admx. of Thomas Potts deced: returned upon Oath an Accot. Dr. & Cr. of the said Deceds: Estate, which being Examined by the Court is Ordered to be recorded.

The Last Will and Testament of Henry Chamnis Deced: was Exhibitted into Court by Robert Bolling and Mary Chamnis his Executors who made Oath thereto, and it being proved by the Oaths of Thomas Addison and Hugh Golightly Witnesses thereto is Ordered to be recorded and on the Motion of the said Robert Bolling and Mary Chamnis, and their giveing Security as the Law Directs, Certificate is granted them for Obtaining a Probate in Due form.

Ordered that Robert Bolling and Mary Chamnis Executors of Henry Chamnis Deced: return to the next Court an Inventory of the said Deceds: Estate.

In the action of Debt brot. by John Hatch agst. John Hamlin Admr. of the Goods and Chattels of Richard Hamlin Deced: for Seven pounds Due by Bill and One pound Nineteen Shillings and four pence Due by accot., the sd. partys appearing the Deft. moves the plt. may prove his Debt, whereupon he makes Oath that three pounds fifteen Shillings and two pence of the said Sum is Justly Due, thererupon & on the motion of the said plt. it is Ordered that the said Defendt. do pay to the said plt. out of the sd. Deceds: Estate the aforesaid Sum of three pounds fifteen Shillings and two pence and Costs. Als: Exec:

[page 264]

In the suit brot. by John Allen agst. John Hamlin Admr. of the Goods and Chattels of Richard Hamlin Deced: for the reviveing and renewing a Judgement granted to the said John Allen agst. the said Richard Hamlin in this County Court on the 14th Day of May 1717, for Six hundred and thirty pounds of Tobacco and Costs amounting to One hundred Seventy Six pounds of Tobacco, the said partys appearing the Defendt. proves a Discount or the payment of five hundred thirty two pounds of Tobacco of the sd. Sum and the plt. makeing Oath he hath reced: no further sattisfaction thereupon Judgement is granted and renewed to him for the residue, and it is Ordered that the said Defendt. do pay to the said plt. Forty three shillings and two pence, the Value of the said Tobacco, out of the said Deceds: Estate. Als. Exec:

Ordered that Hugh Golightly be Overseer of the Highways instead of Thomas Addison, who was formerly appointed Overseer of the Road from Worronak to the Extent of the County.

Ann Moor Admx. of Thomas Moor Deced: returns an Inventory and Appraisment of the sd. Deceds: Estate, Ordered it be recorded.

In the Action on the case brot. by Nathaniel Harrison Esqr. agst. Richard Tomlinson and Elinor his Wife Admx. of Richard Walpole Deced: for Eleven hundred Eighty three pounds of Tobacco Due by accot. &c: the sd. partys appearing the Defendts. move the plt. may prove his accot. Whereupon Mr. Hatt book=keeper for the said Harrison makes Oath the same is Sue, and on the motion of the plt. it is Ordered that the said Defts. do pay to the said plts. out of the said Deceds: Estate the sum of Nine pounds Seventeen Shillings and two pence, the Value of the sd. Tobacco, togather wth. Costs. Als. Exec:

Edward Goodrich appears in Court and Assumes to pay to this County and to give Credit to the same at the Laying of the next Levy on the said County, the sum of three thousand pounds of Tobo. in Consideration of three thousand Eight hundred pounds of Tobo. Levied by the Last Assembly for the sd. County and Ordered to be paid in the County of Isle of Wight, Ordered that the Sherriff of the said County of Isle of Wight pay to the sd. Edward Goodrich the aforesaid Sum of three thousand Eight hundred pounds of Tobacco Accordingly.

[page 265]

Sarah Bishope Executrix of William Bishope Deced. returns an Inventory of the said Deceds: Estate, which is Ordered to be recorded.

In the action of the Depending between Robert Bolling and George Hamelton, the Jury that was at the Last Court Impannelled and Sworn to try the matter in Issue between the said partys failing then to return their Verdict and also failing now to appear It's thereupon Ordered on the motion of the Attorneys of the sd. partys that the cause be referred till the next Court and if the Jury do not then appear that the Sherr: Impannell another Jury.

The action brot. by Nathl. Harrison Esqr. agst. Robert Abbernathy the plt. failing to prosecute, is Dismist.

In the action on the case brot. by Nathl. Harrison Esqr. agst. Richard Whittmore for three hundred thirty three pounds of Tobo. Due by accot., Richard Pace appears and enters himselfe Special Bail for the said Defendt. who thereupon appears and Confesses Judgement to the plt. for the said Sum thereupon it is Ordered that the said Deft. pay to the sd. plt. the sd. sum & Costs. Als. Exec:

The action Depending between Richard Smith and Sampson Merredeth is continued till the next Court.

The action Depending between Henry Soane and John Hamlin Admr. &c: is Continued till the next Court.

Randle Platt agst. Elizabeth Duke Admx. of Henry Duke Deced: no appearance, Dismist.

In the action brot. by Robert Gilmore agst. Elizabeth Duke Admx. of Henry Duke Deced., the Deft. failing to appear &c on the motion of the plts: Attorney Judgement is granted him agst. the sd. Deft. pr. *Nihil Dicit*.

Robert Gilmore agst. John Hamlin Admr. of Richd. Hamlin Deced: the Deft. failing to appear &c: on the motion of the plts. Attorney Judgement is granted him agst. the said Deft. pr. *Nihil Dicit*.

[page 266]

The action on the case brot. by Richard Bland agst. John Pook the plt. failing to prosecute is Dismist.

In the action on the case brot. by David Crawley against William Bobbit for thirteen pounds twelve Shillings and a halfe penny Due by Accot. Dated 1718, the Defendt. being called and failing to appear pursuant to the Conditional Judgement and Order of the Last Court, on the motion of the plts: Attorney Judgement is granted and Confirmed to him agst. the said Defendt: and Robert Bolling his security for the said Sum & it is Ordered that the said Defendt. and the said Robert Bolling or either of them pay to the said plt. the aforesaid Sum & Costs. Als: Exec:

The Attachment granted Robert Mitchell against the Estate of David Collyshaw, neither party appearing, is Dismist.

And then the Court adjourn'd till Court in Course. Robt. Munford. Test Wm. Hamlin, Cl. Cur.

More Goods Attacht. of the Estate of David Colyshaw for John Peterson pr. me James Thweatt Sherr:

Vizt. To 50 l. wt. of old Iron	£0.4.2
To 1 beak Iron wt. 15¼	0.5.1
To 5 old files and 3 old broke Gunn Locks	0.3.0
To 2 peices of Anvils, One old bellows,	4.3.0
To 1 pr. Tongs old	0.1.0
To Little Bitts of Iron and Brass	0.0.6
	£1.16.9

Appraised by us this 8th Day of June 1719. [signed] Henry Batte, Wm. Batte.

Pursuant to an Order of the Last Court John Peterson makes the above return of the Appraisment of the Goods Attacht. of the Estate of David Colyshaw, and the same is truly Recorded. Test Wm. Hamlin, Cl. Cur.

[page 267]

At a Court held at Merchantshope for the County of
Prince George on the second Tuesday in July being the
Fourteenth Day of the sd. month, Anno Dom: 1719.

Present John Poythres,   Robt. Munford
      Robt. Hall   & Lewis Green Junr.   Gent. Justices

Roger a Negro Boy, belonging to John Scott Junr. is adjudged five years old.

Dick a Negro Boy, belonging to John Scott Junr. is adjudged three years old.

Hannah a Negro Girl, belonging to John Moor is adjudged Nine years old.

Annica a Negro Girl, belonging to John Lewis Junr. is adjudged Seven years old.

Jenny a Negro Girl, belonging to Thomas Clay is adjudged thirteen years old.

Lewis a Negro Boy, belonging to Daniel Sturdivant is adjudged Tenn years old.

Sue a Negro Girl belonging to James Sturdivant is adjudged Eleven years old.

Stafford a Negro boy belonging to Peter Mitchell is Adjudged Tenn years old.

Frank a Negro boy belonging to Robert West is Adjudged Tenn years old.

Kate a Negro Girl belonging to William Green is Adjudged Tenn years old.

Present John Hamlin, Gent.

Scipio a Negro Boy belonging to Lewis Green Junr. is Adjudged Eleven years old.

Jenny a Negro Girl belonging to Ephraim Parram is Adjudged Nine years old.

John Lewis Junr. in Open Court Acknowledged his Deeds of Lease and Release of Land (Seald) to Richard Bland on whose motion the same are Admitted to Record.

[page 268]

John Lewis Junr. in Open Court acknowledged his bond for performance of Covenants to Richard Bland, on whose motion the same is Admitted to Record.

Bridget Ward Admx. of Collingwood Ward Deced: returns an Inventory and Appraisment of the sd. Deceds: Estate, which is Ordered to be recorded.

Present Robt. Bolling, Gent.

Joseph Lanthrop Exr. of John Lanthrop Deced: returns an Inventory of the sd. Deceds: Estate, which is Ordered to be recorded.

Mary Martin Admx. of John Martin Deced: Exhibitts an accot. Dr. & Cr. of the Estate of the said Deced: which being Examined and allowed by the Court is Admitted to Record.

On the petition of William Davis an Overseer of the Highways &c: It's Ordered that John Wall, Wm. Wall, Jos: Wall, Daniel Wall, John Green, Peter Mitchell, Richard Burch, Robert Glidewell, John Browder and Richard Judson, be summoned to the next Court to answer the said petition.

Michael an Irish Sarvant Boy belonging to John Coleman is Adjudged thirteen years Old.

Ceesar and Martin Negro Boys belonging to Robt. Munford are Adjudged Seven years old each.

John Banister in Open Court acknowledged his Deeds of Lease and Release of Land (Indented and Seald) to Nicholas Vaughn on whose motion the same are Admitted to Record.

The action brot. by David Crawley agst. Richard Westmoreland, the plt: failing to prosecute, is Dismist.

The action brot. by David Crawley agst. William Coleman, the plt: failing to prosecute, is Dismist.

In the action on the case brot. by Thomas Simmons agst. Nicholas Overby, Oyer of the plts: accot. is granted him and time till the next Court to consider the same.

In the suit in Chancery brot. by Fra. Anderson Exrx. &c: agst. Henry Offley and Robert Bolling, the sd. Bolling appears and on his motion time is granted him till the next Court to answer the Complts. Bill.

[page 269]

In the action of Debt brot. by Edward Hill Esqr. against John Brewer, the deft. pleads *Nil Debit* and the plt. Joining in the Issue the same is referred till the next Court for Tryall.

The Attachment granted Nathl. Harrison Esqr. agst. the Estate of John Brewer (the plt. failing to prosecute) is Dismist.

The Attachment granted Richard Smith agst. the Estate of John Berry (the plt. failing to prosecute) is Dismist.

In the action on the case brot. by William Randolph Admr. with the Will annext. of Eusebius King Deced: against Edward Simmons for Eight pounds Eighteen Shillings and Tenn pence Due by account dated May the Ninth 1700, at the Last Court the Defendant being permitted to plead severall pleas, accordingly filed his plea's and a Demurrer to the plts: Declaration [words removed] who had time till this Court to Consider the sd. plea's, and he then Joining in the Demurrer aforesd. the same was referred till this Court to be argued, and the said partys by their Attorneys appearing and the Court haveing heard and Considered their arguments, do adjudge the sd. Demurrer Good, thereupon on the motion of the Defendts. Attorney the suit is Dismist.

From which Judgement the plt. by his Attorny moves for an Appeal to the Sixth day of the next October Genrall Court.

Ordered that the sd. plt. give Security to prosecute the sd. Appeal according to Law, whereupon Thomas Eldridge entred into Bond for the Appellant in the sum of Twenty pounds Sterling with Condition to prosecute the said Appeal on the sd. Sixth day of the next October Genrall Court and to pay Damages according to Law if in the Genrall Court this Court's Judgement shall be Confirmed.

And thereupon pursuant to the plts. prayer an Appeal is granted him to the sixth Day of the next October Genrall Court.

In the action brot. by Joshua Irby agst: Mathew Smart, the Deft. files his plea to the plts: Declaration who has time till the next Court to Consider the same.

In the action brot. by Joshua Irby agst. Cornelius Fox, the Deft. files a plea & Demurrer to the plts: Declaration who has time till the next Court to Consider the same.

The Order that Ann Hill Exrx. of John Hill Deced: return an Inventory of the said Deceds: Estate is Continued till next Court.

[page 270]

Nicholas Vaughn in Open Court acknowledged his Deeds of Lease and Release of Land (Indented and Seald) to Thomas Hardaway on whose motion the same are Admitted to record, And then also appeared in Court Ann the Wife of the said Nicholas Vaughn and being first privately Examined, freely and Voluntarily relinquisht. to the sd. Thomas Hardaway her right of Dower in and to the Lands &c: in the said mentioned which is Likewise Ordered to be Recorded.

In the Suit in Chancery brot. by John Bolling agst. Henry Offley and Robert Bolling, the sd. Bolling appears and on his motion time is granted him till the next court to answer the Complts. Bill.

In the action brot. by John Hatch agst. John Turner, the plt. paying Costs and amending his Declaration, the Defendt. has time till next Court to consider the same.

The action brot. by Nathl. Harrison Esqr. agst. John Pook, the plt. failing to prosecute, is Dismist.

The action brot. by Thomas Goodwynn agst. John Pook and Wm. Mattox, the plt. failing to prosecute is Dismist.

The action brot. by William Woodward agst. Cornelius Fox the plt. failing to prosecute, is Dismist.

In the action on the case brot. by Charles Williams agst. John Hines, on the motion of the Defents. Atto: Oyer of the plts: accot. is granted him and time till the next Court to Consider the same.

In the action on the case brot. by Wm. Hamlin agst. Peter Wynne, on the motion of the Defts. Attorny an Imparlance is granted him till ye next Court.

The action brot. by John Drayton &c: agst. John Lett, the plt. failing to prosecute, is Dismist.

In the action of Debt brot. by Wm. Stroud [Shouds] agst. Valentine Minge Admr. of John Sherley Deced: for five hundred pounds of Tobacco Due by Bill dated the Sixteenth of March 1715/6, the sd. partys appearing, the Defendt. moves the plt. may prove his Debt, whereupon he makes Oath the sd. Sum is Justly due, and on his motion It's Ordered that the sd. Defendt. do pay to the sd. plt. the Sum of four pounds three Shillings and four pence, the Value of the sd. Tobacco, out of the said Deceds. Estate, with Costs. Als. Exec:

In the action on the case brot: by Richard Bodyman agst. Valentine Minge Admr. of John Shereley Deced: for three pounds due by accot. dated 1718, the said partys appearing, the deft. moves the plt: may prove his accot. whereupon he makes Oath the same is Due, and on his motion It's Ordered that the said Defendt. do pay to the said plt. out of the sd. Deceds: Estate the aforesaid Sum & Costs. Als: Exec:

[page 271]

The action on the case brot. by Jeffrey Gray agst. John Selwood the plt. failing to prosecute, is Dismist.

The action of Trespass on the case brot. by Jeffrey Gray agst. John Selwood, the plt. failing to prosecute, is Dismist.

In the action on the case brot. by Richard Pace agst. Samuel Burch and Eliza. his wife &c: the plt. failing to prosecute, on the motion of the Defendts. Attorney it is Ordered that he be Nonsuit and pay the sd. Defendts: five Shillings with Costs. Als. Exec:

In the action on the case brot: by Richard Pace agst. Saml. Burch et Uxor, the plt. failing to prosecute, on the motion of he Defendts. Attorney it is Ordered that he be Nonsuit and pay the sd. Defendts. five Shillings with Costs. Als. Exec:

The action of Debt brot. by Buller Herbert agst. Henry Batte Admr. of Thomas Harwell Deced: the plt. failing to prosecute is Dismist.

In the action brot. by William Byrd Esqr. agst. Nathl. Harrison Esqr. Admr. of Richard Pigeon Deced: an Imparlance is granted the Defents. till the next Court.

In the action on the case brot. by John Berry agst. Nathl. Harrison Esqr. Admr. &c: the plt. failing to prosecute, on the motion of the Defendts. Attorney It's Odered that he be Nonsuit and pay the sd. Defendt. five Shillings with Costs. Als. Exec:

In the action on the case brot. by Edward Burt agst. Nathl. Harrison Esqr. Admr. of Richard Pigeon Deced: an Imparlance is granted him till the next Court.

The Order that Eliza Jane return an Inventory of the Estate of Phillip Jane Deced: is continued till next Court.

The Order that Rebecca Spencer Admx. of Richard Spencer Deced: return an Inventory of the sd. Deceds: Estate is continued till next Court.

Elizabeth Duke Admx. of Henry Duke Deced: returns an Inventory and Appraisment of the said Deceds: Estate which is Ordered to be recorded.

[page 272]

The Order that Nathl. Harrison Esqr. Admr. of Richard Pigeon Deced: return an Inventory of the sd. Deceds: Estate is Continued till the next Court.

The Attachment granted Nathl. Harrison Esqr. agst. the Estate of Hen: Bates, the plt. failing to prosecute, is Dismist.

In The action on the case brot by George Harvie agst. Thomas Simmons, the plt. failing to prosecute on the Defendts. motion it's Ordered that he be Nonsuit and pay the said Defendt. five Shillings with Costs. Als. Exec:

In the action of Debt brot. by Moses Beck agst. Cornelius Fox, the Defendt. by his Attorny pleads payment and the plt. Joining in the Issue the same is referred till the next Court for Tryall.

The suit in Chancery Depending between Joseph Goffe and Edward Wyatt, is referred for Tryall upon Bill and answer, till the next Court.

In the action Depending between Richard Pace and Michael Rosser the Tryall is referred till the next Court, on the motion of the Defts. Attorny he paying the Cost of this reference.

In the Action Depending between Mary Wiggins and Richard Winkles the plt. Joins in the pleas of the Defendt. and the same is referred till the next Court for Tryall.

In the action on the case brot. by John Hamersly agst. Elizabeth Duke Admx. of Henry Duke Deced: an Imparlance is granted the Defendt. till ye next Court.

In the action on the case brot. by John Hamersly agst. Nicholas Brewer Junr. for Six pounds Seven Shillings and Ten pence Due by accot. Dated 1718, John Brewer became Special Bail for the sd. Defendt. who thereupon appears and Confesses Judgement to the plt. for the said Sum, therefore it's Ordered that the said Defendt. pay to the said plt. the said Sum & Costs. Als. Exec:

In the action on the case brot. by John Hamersly agst. Henry Bates for Twenty Eight Shillings and a halfe penny Due by accot. the Defendt. being returned *non est Inventus* and not appearing on the motion of ye plts. Attorny an Attachment is awarded them agst. the sd. Defendts. Estate for the said Sum and Costs returnable to the next Court for Judgement.

[page 273]

Ann Hamlin agst. Jeffrey Gray, no prosecution, Dismist.

John Simmons Assignee of Edward Horskins agst. Richard Harrison pr. *Scire Facias*, Dismist.

John Lett agst. Joseph Peirson, no appearance, Dismist.

In the action on the case brot. by David Crawley agst. Stephen Evans for Nine pounds thirteen Shillings and Seven pence due by Account, the Defendt. being returned arrested and failing to appear and there being no bail returned, on the motion of the plts: Attorny Judgement is granted him agst. the said Defendt. and James Thweatt Sherr: &c: for the said Sum and Costs, unless the said Defendt. shall appear at the next Court and answer the sd. Action.

In the action on the case brot. by James Gretion agst. Robt. Enon, the Deft. pleads *Nil Debit* and the plt. Joining in the Issue the same is referred till next Court for Tryall.

In the action on the case brot. by John Fitzgerrald agst. Stephen Cater for three pounds twelve Shillings and Eleven pence halfe penny Due by accot. the Defendt. being arrested and not appearing and there being no security returned for him, on othe plts: motion Judgement is granted him agst. the said Defendt. and James Thweatt Sherr: &c: for the said Sum and Costs, unless the said Defendt. shall appear at the next Court and answer the said Action.

The action brot. by Henry Cabinis agst. Wm. Woodward, neither party appearing, is Dismist.

The Order that Henry Holdcroft Exr. of Rand. Platt Deced: return in Inventory of the sd. Deceds: Estate, is Continued till next Court.

The Order that Robert Bolling and Mary Chamnis Exrs. of Henry Chamnis Deced: return an Inventory of the sd. Deceds: Estate is Continued till next Court.

The suit Depending between Richard Smith and Sampson Merredeth is referred till next Court, the Defendt. paying the cost of this reference.

[page 274]

In the action brot. by Henry Soane agst. John Hamlin Admr. of Richard Hamlin Deced: for three thousand Nine hundred pounds of Tobacco Due by a Note &c: accepted by the sd. Richard Dated December 1716, the sd. partys appearing, the Defendt. pleads fully Administred, thereupon the plt. makes Oath that thirteen hundred and Sixteen pounds of the said Sum is Justly Due and on his motion it is Ordered that the sd. Defendt. do pay to the said plt. Tenn pounds Nineteen Shillings and four pence, the Value of the said Tobacco, out of the sd. Deceds: Estate, with Costs, When Assetts of the said Deceds: Estate shall come to hands &c:

In the action brot. by Robert Gilmore agst. John Hamlin Admr. of Richard Hamlin Deced: for three pounds Sixteen Shillings and Eight pence three farthings Due by accot. Dated 1717, the defendt. pleads fully Administred and the plt. haveing made an Oath the sd. Sum is Justly Due, thereupon on the motion of his Attorny it is Ordered that the said Defendt. do pay to the said plt. out of the said Deceds: Estate, the aforesaid Sum and Costs when Assetts thereof shall come to hand &c:

In the action brot. by Robert Gilmore agst. Elizabeth Duke Admx. of Henry Duke Deced: for three pounds fifteen Shillings and two pence halfe penny Due by accot. Dated 1717, the Defendt. by her Attorny apearing and makeing no plea or Objection, and the plt. haveing made Oath the said Sum is Justly Due, on the motion of his Attorny It is Ordered that the sd. Defendt. do pay to pay [sic] to the said plt. the said Sum and Costs, out of the said Deceds: Estate. Als: Exec:

In the action brot. by John Hamersly agst. Nathl. Harrison Esqr. Admr. of Richard Pigeon Deced: an Imparlance is granted the Defendt. till the next Court.

In the action brot. by Richard Pigeon agst. Nathl. Harrison Esqr. Admr. &c: an Imparlance is granted the Defendt. till the next Court.

In the Action brot. by Bridget Ward Admx. of Coll. Ward Deced: agst. Nathl. Harrison Esqr. Admr. &c: an Imparlance is granted the sd. Deft. till the next Court.

The action of ye Case brot. by Bridget Ward &c agst. Henry Holdcroft &c the plt. failing to prosecute is Dismist.

The action on the case brot. by Timothy Bridges agst. Sampson Merredeth Adm. &c: is Continued till the next Court.

Sampson Merredeth agst. Geo: Hunt, no appearance, Dismist.

[page 275]

In the action brot. by Thomas Goodwynn agst. John Poythres for thirty four pounds Six Shillings and three pence Due by Accot. the Defendt. being arrested and not appearing nor any Security returned for him on the motion of the plats: Attorny, Judgement is granted him agst. the said Defendt. and James Thweatt Sherr: for the sd. Sum and Costs, unless the said Defendt. shall appear at the next Court and answer the said action.

In the action of Debt brot. by Fra. Wynne agst. Henry Batte Admr. &c: the Defendt. pleads fully Administred, and the plt. Joining in the Issue the same is referred till the next Court for Tryall.

The action brot. by Robert Glidewell agst. John Ellis Junr. the plt. failing to prosecute is Dismist.

The action on ye Case brot. by David Crawley agst. Edward Murrell, the plt. failing to prosecute, is Dismist.

The action of Debt brot. by David Crawley agst. Edwd. Murrell the plt. failing to prosecute, is Dismist.

The action brot. by David Crawley agst. Edmond Browder the plt. failing to prosecute, is Dismist.

Henry Holdcraft Exor. of Rand. Platt Deced: being Summoned to render an accot. of what part of the Estate of Joseph Greenhill he has in his hands or how much he stands Indebted to him as Exr. &c: the same being Attacht. for Charles Chiswell, and he appearing on his motion the same is deferred till the next Court.

And then the Court adjourned till Court in Course. Jno. Hamlin. Test Wm. Hamlin, Cl. Cur.

[page 276]

At a Court held at Merchantshope for the County of Prince George on the
Second Tuesday in August being the Eleventh day of the said Month
Anno Dom. 1719.

Present   John Hamlin,   Robert Hall }
        Sampson Merredeth   & John Peterson}   Gent. Justices

Pursuant to the Direction of the Act of Assembly Entituled An Act for Setting the Titles and bounds of Lands &c It is Ordered that the Vestrys of the Severall Parrishes within this County respectively Divide their Parrishes into so many precincts as to them shall seem most Convenient for processioning every particular persons Land in their severall Parrishes respectively and appoint the particular times between the Last Day of September and the Last Day of March next comeing when such processioning shall be made in every precinct, And also appoint at Least two Intelligent, honest Freeholders of every precinct to see such possessioning [sic] performed, and take and return to the Vestry an Account of every persons Land they shall procession, and of the persons present at the same, and of what Lands in their precincts they shall fail to procession, and of the particular reasons of such failure.

Samuel Eaton in Open Court acknowledged his Deed for Land (Indented & Seald) with Livery of Seizin endorst. thereon, to John Scoggan on whose motion the same is Ordered to be recorded.

Francis Coleman in Open Court acknowledged his Deeds of Lease & Release of Land (Indented and Seald) to William Parsons, and they are Admitted to Record.

Present John Poythres and Lewis Green, Gent. Justs.

A Letter of Attorny from Honor Coleman (the wife of Francis Coleman), to Edward Goodrich was proved in Court by the Oaths of James Thweatt and Richard Smith Witnesses thereto, and Ordered to be recorded.

Edward Goodrich Attorny of Honor Coleman, the Wife of Francis Coleman appears in Court and relinquishes her right of Dower in and to Certain Lands this Day Conveyed & made over by her said Husband, to William Parsons, which is Ordered to be recorded.

Jupiter a Negro Boy belonging to Mr. Robt. Hall is Adjudged Nine years old.

Tony a Negro Boy belonging to Mr. John Hatch is Adjudged Nine years old.

Betty a Negro Girl belonging to Henry Mitchell is Adjudged Tenn years old.

[page 277]

Samuel Eaton in Open Court acknowledged his Deeds of Lease and Release of Land (Indented and Seald) to John Green on whose motion they are Ordered to be recorded.

Samuel Eaton in Open Court acknowledged his Bond for performance of Covenants, to John Green, on whose motion the same is Ordered to be recorded.

John Leonard in Open Court acknowledged his Deed for Land (Indented and Seald) with Livery of Seizin thereon, the Richard Nance on whose motion the same is Ordered to be recorded, And then also appeared in Court Elizabeth the Wife of the sd. John Leonard and being first privately Examined, freely and Voluntarily relinquisht. to the sd. Richard Nance her right of Dower in and to the Lands &c in the said Deed mentioned, which is Likewise Ordered to be recorded.

John Wall, William Wall, Jos: Wall, Daniel Wall, John Green, Peter Mitchell, Richard Burch, Robert Glidewell, John Browder & Richard Hudson being summoned to answer the petition and Complaint of William Davis an Overseer of the Highways, for their Contempt in refuseing to assist in clearing the highways of which the sd. Davis is Overseer, and the sd. persons (Except John Browder) failing to show Just causes for their contempt It's Ordered that they the said John Wall, Willim. Wall, Jos: Wall, Danl. Wall, John Green, Peter Mitchell, Richard Burch, Robt. Glidewell & Richard Hudson, each of them pay to the sd. William Davis five Shillings with Costs. Als. Exec:

Present Majr. Robt. Munford

Elizabeth Griffith Relict of Richard Griffith Deced: came into Court and made Oath that the sd. Richard Griffith dyed without any will as farr as she knows or believes, and on her motion and giveing Security for her Just and faithfull Administration of the sd. Deceds. Estate Certificate is granted her for Obtaining a Commission of Administration in Due form.

Elizabeth Griffith Admx. of Richard Griffith Deced: togather with William Short her security entred into Bond for her Just and faithfull Administration on the sd. Deceds: Estate, and acknowledged the same in Court.

Benjamin Reeks, Peter Talbott, John Smith and Wm. Jackson or any three of them being first Sworn by some Majistrate of this County for that purpose, are Ordered to Appraise the Estate of Richard Griffith Deced: and make report of their proceedings therein to the next Court when Eliza. Griffith the Admx. is to return the Inventory thereof.

[page 278]

On the petition of John Wall, William Wall, Joshua Wall, Danl. Wall, Peter Mitchell, Richard Burch and John Green, It is Ordered that a Road be cleared from the plantation of John Wall into the Road of which Samuel Harwell is Overseer and that they be added to the sd. Road.

The Last Will and Testament of Francis Mallory Deced: was Exhibitted into Court by Elizabeth Mallory, John Hamlin and Edward Goodrich, his Executors who made Oath thereto, and the same being proved by the Oaths of Joshua Irby and Joseph Renn Witnesses thereto, is Ordered to be recorded, and on the motion of the said Executors and their giveing Security according to Law, Certificate is granted them for Obtaining a Probate of the said Will in Due form.

Elizabeth Mallory, John Hamlin and Edward Goodrich Executors of the Last Will and Testament of Francis Mallory Deced: togather with Francis Poythres their Security entred into Bond for their Just and Faithfull Executorship of the sd. Will, and acknowledged the same in Court.

John Hatch, Edmond Irby, Gilbert Hay, and William Harrison, Gent. or any three of them being first Sworn by some Majistrate of this County for that purpose, are Ordered to appraise the Estate of Francis Mallory Deced: and make report of their proceedings to the next Court when Eliza: Mallory, John Hamlin, and Edward Goodrich the Exrs. are to return the Inventory thereof.

On the petition of James Baugh an Overseer of the Highways, It's Ordered that Peter Mitchell senr., John Phillips, William Russell, George Reves & William Eaton with their male Tythes be added to the Roads of which the said Baugh is Overseer.

The petition of Francis Poythres Exr. &c agst. Eliza. Mallory &c Exrs. of Francis Mallory Deced: is referred till the next Court.

Cupit a Negro Boy belonging to Mr. John Hardyman is adjudged Six years old.

Venus a Negro Girl belonging to the sd. Hardyman is adjudged Nine years old.

In the action of Debt Depending between Robert Bolling and George Hamilton, a Jury was Impannelled and Sworn to trye the matter in Issue by Name William Harrison [no other names, blank] who haveing heard the Evidence and reced. their charge were sent out. Ordered that when the Jury have agreed on their Verdict that they seal up the same and Deliver it with the Declaration, plea, and Bond, to the Sherriff.

In the action brot. by Thomas Simmons agst. Nicholas Overby, the Deft. failing to plead, Judgement is granted the plt. agst. him by *Nihil Dicit*.

[page 279]

The suit in Chancery brot. by Frances Anderson Executrix of Charles Anderson Deced: against Henry Offley and Robert Bolling is referred till next Court.

The action of Debt brot. by Edwd. Hill Esqr. agst. John Brewer, is continued till next Court, on the plts: charge.

In the action brot. by Joshua Irby agst. Mathew Smart, the plt. Joins in the Issue tendered by the Defendt: and the same is referred till the next court for Tryall.

In the action brot. by Joshua Irby agst. Cornelius Fox, the plt. Demurrs to the plead of the Defendt. who has time till next Court to Consider the same.

The suit in Chancery brot: by John Bolling agst. Henry Offley and Robert Bolling, is referred till next Court.

In the action Depending between John Hatch and John Turner the Defendt. (being permitted to plead sevll: plea's) files his plea's to the plts: Declaration, who Joins in the Issue tendered by the sd. Defendt. and the same is referred till the next Court for Tryall.

In the action on the case brot: by William Hamlin agst. Peter Wynne for five hundred Sixty three pounds of Tobacco due by accot. Dated 1717, the Defendt. appearing by Edward Goodrich by Attorny and failing to make any plea and moveing the plt. may prove his Accot. thereupon the said plt. makes Oath the same is Due, and it is Ordered that the sd. Defendt. pay to the said plt. the said Sum and Costs. Als: Exec:

In the action on the case brot. by William Byrd Esqr. agst. Nathaniel Harrison Esqr. Admr. with the Will annext of Richard Pigeon Deced: for Six pounds Tenn Shillings and Six pence due by account &c: the Defendt. by his Attorny moves the plt. may prove his accot: and the same haveing been Sworn to by John Braine Bookeeper for the sd. plt: it's thereupon Ordered that the sd. Defendt. pay to the said plt. out of the said Deceds: Estate the sd. Sum and Costs. Als. Exec:

In the action brot. by Edward Burt agst. Nathaniel Harrison Esqr. Admr. with the Will annext. of Richard Pigeon Deced: for three pounds five Shillings and Tenn pence Due by accot. Dated 1718, the Defendt. by his Attorney moves the plt. may prove his accot., and the same haveing been Sworn to, thereupon it is Ordered that the said Defendt. pay to the said plt. out of the said Deceds. Estate the said Sum and Costs. Als: Exec:

141

[page 280]

In the action on ye Case brot. by Charles Williams against John Hines, Judgemt. is granted the plt. against the sd. Defendt. pr. *Nihil Dicit*.

The action of Debt Depending between between Moses Beck and Cornelius Fox is Continued till the next court.

In the suit in Chancery brot. by Joseph Goffe of the City of Boston, in the Province of New England, Merchant, agst. Edward Wyatt, the Complainant Sheweth, that in or about the year One thousand Seven hundred and fourteen, he haveing severall affairs, and Concerns, to negotiate in this Colony, which did require his personal Attendance, and bringing with him a Considerable quantity of Goods, to Trade and merchanedize withall, did therewith purchase, and buy, four hundred, forty five, bushels of Indian corn, more than he Exported out of this Colony, and that he did constitute and appoint this respondent, to receive and for the use of the said Complainant, to dispose of the said Corn, and a true account and due payment to make of the proceeds, to this Complainant or his Attorneys &c when he should be thereunto require, yet hath neither paid or remitted the same, or any part thereof, to the said Complainant or his Attornys as aforesaid, alth' he hath been thereto often requested, as in the Complainants sd. Bill is more particularly set forth, the respondent haveing filed his answer upon Oath to the Complainants said Bill, the cause was referred by Consent to the Attornys till this Court for Tryall, upon Bill and answer, and the sd. partys appearing by their Attornys, and the respondent haveing confest the receipt of three hundred and Twenty Bushells of the said Corn, which is Valued by the Court at Thirty two pounds current money, and also in his answer Exhibitting an account against the said Complainant, for Twenty Nine pounds Tenn Shillings and the Court haveing heard and considered the Arguments of the said Attornys, and it appearing that the sd. respondt. is Indebted to the said Complainant, the sum of Fivety Shillings, do thereupon Decree that the said respondt. pay to the said Complt. the said Sum of Fivety Shillings Current mony with Costs.

And then the Court Adjourn'd till Court in Course. Jno. Hamlin. Test Wm. Hamlin, Cl. Cur.

[page 281]

At a Court held at Merchantshope for the County
of Prince George on the second Tuesday in September, being
the Eighth day of the said month, Annoq. Dom: 1719.

Present   John Poythres,   Robt. Munford }
                    Robt. Hall,   Sampson Merredeth }
                    Lewis Green   & John Peterson }   Gent. Justices

Elizabeth Griffith Admrx. of Richard Griffith Deced: returns an Inventory and Appraisment of the said Deceds: Estate, which is Ordered to be recorded.

James Anderson in Open Court acknowledged his Deeds of Lease & Release of Land (Indented and Seald) to Richard Cureton, on whose motion the same are Ordered to be recorded, and then also appeared in Court Elizabeth the wife of the said James Anderson, and being first privately Examined, freely and Voluntarily relinquisht. to the said Richard Cureton, her right of Dower, in and to the Lands &c: in the said Deeds mentioned, which is Likewise Ordered to be recorded.

Jack, a Negro Boy belonging to Thomas Hardoway, is adjudged Eight years Old.

Cate, a Negro Girl belonging to Thomas Hardoway, is Adjudged Seven years old.

Prince, a Negro boy belonging to Robert Bolling, is Adjudged Seven years Old.

Dolly, a Negro Girl belonging to Robert Bolling, is Adjudged Nine years Old.

The Deposition of George Rives, concerning a Mallatto Man Slave belonging to Samuel Harwood Junr., was taken in Court, and on the motion of the said Harwood, is Ordered to be recorded.

Elizabeth Jane Admx. of Phillip Jane Deced: returns an Inventory and Appraisment of the sd. Deceds: Estate, which is Ordered to be recorded.

Present John Hamlin, Gent.

Robert Rivers, who was Security for Rebecca Spencer, Admx. of Richard Spencer Deced: returns an Inventory and Appraisment of the sd. Deceds: Estate, which is Ordered to be recorded.

Rachell, a Negro Girl belonging to Mrs. Frances Anderson, is Adjudged twelve years old.

[page 282]

On the motion of Richard Bland, in the behalf of the Late *Virginia Indian Company*, who set forth that their Sarvant William Merick absented himselfe from their Service five days, and that in recovering the said Sarvant he Expended Seven pounds Seven Shillings and Six pence, and prayed Judgement agst. him according to Law, the said William being brot. to the Barr, and failing to make any plea &c It's Ordered that he serve the said Company, for the time he was absent, and for their said Disbursments which is Valued in Tobacco at Tenn Shillings pr. Cent, and for the costs of this Judgement after his time of Service by Indenture, or otherwise is Expired, One year Tenn Months and an halfe, And it is further Ordered that if the said Bland Shall think fitt, that he give the said William Twenty Nine Lashes on his bare back well Laid on.

Richard Smith in Open Court acknowledged his Deeds of Lease & Release of Land (Indented and Seld) to John Stith, on whose motion the same are Ordered to be recorded.

Richard Smith in Open Court acknowledged his Bond for performance of Covenants, to John Stith, on whose motion the same is Ordered to be recorded.

In the action brot: by Richard Pace against Michal Rosser Junr. for Eight hundred and forty pounds of Tobacco, Due by amount Dated 1717: the Defendt. haveing pleaded *Nil Debit*, and the plt: Joining in the Issue, the same was submitted to the Court for Tryall, and the Court haveing heard and Considered the arguments and allegations of the said partys, and allowing a Discount to the deft. of four hundred and twenty five pounds of Tobacco, do Order that the said Defendt. do pay to the said plt. the residue of the aforesaid Sum, being four hundred and fifteen pounds of Tobacco, and Costs. Als: Exec:

The Action Depending between Mary Wiggins, and Richard Winkles, the plt. failing to prosecute is Dismist.

In the action on the case, brot: by John Hamersly agst. Elizabeth Duke Admrx. of Henry Duke Deced: the Defendt. pleads *Non Detinet*, and the plt. Joining in the Issue, the same is referred till next Court for Tryall.

In the action on the case brot. by John Hamersly agst. Henry Bates, the Defendt. pleads *Nil Debit*, and the plt. Joining in the Issue, the same is referred till next Court for Tryall.

In the action Depending between David Crawley and Stephen Evans for Nine pounds thirteen Shillings and Seven pence Due by accot. Dated from February the Sixteenth 1716: to June the fifth 1718, Inclusive, the Deft. being called and failing to appear, pursuant to the conditional Judgement and Order of the Last Court, on the motion of the plts: Attorny Judgement is granted and Confirmed to him agst. the said Defendt. and James Thweatt Sherr: &c& for the said Sum, and it is Ordered that the said Defendt. and the said James Thweatt or either of them pay to the said plt. the aforesaid Sum & Costs. Als: Exec:

[page 283]

Judgement being this Day past to David Crawley against James Thweatt Sherr: of Prince George County, for Nine pounds thirteen Shillings & Seven pence, by reason of the Non appearance of Stephen Evans in an Action on the case, at the suit of the sd. Crawley, On the motion of the said James Thweatt an Attachment is granted him agst. the Estate of the said Evans, for the aforesaid Sum and Costs, returnable to the next Court for Judgement.

The action on the case brot: by James Gretion agst. Robt: Enon, the plt: faililng to prosecute, is Dismist.

In the action brot: by John Fitzgerald agst. Stephen Cater, for three pounds twelve Shillings and Eleven pence halfe penny, Due to accot. Dated 1718, the Defendt: being called and not appearing, pursuant to the Conditional Judgement of the Last Court, on the motion of the plts: Attorney Judgement is granted, and Confirmed to him agst. the said Defendt: and James Thweatt Sherr: &c for the said Sum, and it is Ordered that the sd. deft: and the said James Thweatt or either of them, pay to the sd: plt. the aforesaid Sum & Costs. Als: Exec:

Judgement being this day past unto John Fitzgerrald, agst. James Thweatt Sherr: of Prince Geo: County for three pounds, twelve Shillings, and Eleven pence halfe penny, by reason of the non appearance of Stephen Cater in an action on the Case, at the suit of the sd. Fitzgerrald on the motion of the said James Thweatt, an Attachment is granted him agst. the Estate of the said Cater, for the aforesaid Sum & Costs returnable to the next Court for Judgement.

Henry Holdcroft Exr. &c: of Randle Platt Deced: returns an Inventory and Appraisment of the Estate of the sd. Deced: which is Ordered to be recorded.

In the action on the case brot: by Richard Smith agst. Sampson Merredeth, for Seven hundred forty three pounds of Tobacco, Due by Account, Dated October 1716, the Defendt. haveing pleaded *Nil Debit*, and the plt: Joining in the Issue, the same was Submitted to the Court for Tryall, and the Court haveing heard and Considered the Arguments and Allegations of the said partys, gives Judgement to the plt: & Orders that the sd. Defendt. do pay to the said plt: the aforesaid Sum & Costs, Als: Exec: whereupon the Defendt: files a plea in Arrest, of the said Judgement, which is referred till the next Court to be Argued.

Edward Goodrich appeared in Court and Exhibitted an Accot: against the Estate of Randle Platt Deced: and made Oath that the said Randle Platt Dyed Indebted to him by the sd. Amount Two thousand three hundred thirty

143

[page 284]

five pounds of Tobacco, thereupon by Consent of Henry Holdcroft Executor of the Last Will and Testament of the said Deced: It's Ordered that he the said Holdcroft pay to the said Goodrich, out of the said Deceds: Estate, the aforesaid Sum and Costs. Als: Exec:

In the action brot: by Edward Hill agst. John Brewer for five hundred pounds of Tobacco, Due by Bill Dated the fifth day of April 1715, the Defendt. haveing pleaded *Nil Debit* and the plt. Joining in the Issue, the same was Submitted to the Court for Tryall, & the Deft. produceing a Discount, and the Court haveing heard and Considered the Evidence, and Allegations of the said partys, gives Judgement for the Defendt: and on his motion the suit is Dismist.

On the motion of the plt. It's Ordered that it be entred upon Record that he offered the Defendt. the Liberty of Denying on his Oath, that the Tobacco in Dispute was paid on the account of Rent, which he refused to doe.

From the Judgement abovesaid Edward Hill the plt. moves for an Appeal to the Sixth day of the next October Genrall Court.

Ordered that the sd. plt. give Security to prosecute the said Appeal, according to Law, whereupon Edward Goodrich became his Security, and with him entred into Bond, in the sum of Twenty pounds Sterling, with Condition to prosecute the said Appeal on the said Sixth day of the next October Genrall Court, and to pay Damages according to law, if in the Genrall Court this Courts Judgement shall be confirmed.

And therepon an Apeal is granted the sd. Edward Hill, to the Sixth day of the next October Genrall Court.

Ann Hill Exrx. of John Hill Deced: returns an Inventory of the said Deceds: Estate, which is Ordered to be recorded.

Elizabeth Mallory, John Hamlin and Edward Goodrich Exrs. of Francis Mallory Deced: returns an Inventory and Appraisment of the Estate of the said Deced: which is Ordered to be recorded.

On the petition of Mary Burchett, the wife of Robt: Burchett, It's Ordered that the said Robert be Summoned to the next Court to answer the same.

In the action of Debt Depending between Robert Bolling and George Hamelton, the Jury that at the Last Court was Impannelled and Sworn, to trye the matter in Issue, haveing agreed on and returend their Verdict in the following words, Vizt: we find the Interlineation mentioned in the Defents: plea interlined in the said Bond, Yet if the plt. can prove the same to be done by the consent of the Defendt: then we find for the plt: otherwise we find for the Defendt. Wm. Harrison, foreman, the plt. thereupon agreed that if the Defendt. wou'd Declare upon his Oath, that the sd. Interlineation was not made and done with his knowledge, and Consent, that he wou'd discharge him from the said Debt, whereupon the sd. Defendt. came into Court and made Oath Accordingly, and on his motion the suit is Dismist., the said Defendt: assuming to pay the Costs.

And then the Court Adjourn'd till Court in Course. John Hamlin. Test Wm. Hamlin, Cl. Cur.

[page 285]

At a Court held at Merchantshope for the County of Prince George on the second Tuesday in October being the thirteenth day of the said month, Annoq. Dom: 1719.

Present   John Poythres,   Robt. Hall,   Sampson Merredeth,   Lewis Green Junr.,   & John Peterson,   Gent. Justices.

Stepney, a Negro Boy belonging to William Gillam, is Adjudged Seven years old.

The Last Will and Testament of Mathew Marks Deced: was presented into Court by Robert Norden and John Avery his Executors who made Oath thereto, and it being proved by the Oaths of Elizabeth Marks, Mary Jones, and Joseph Thomas, Witnesses thereto, is Ordered to be recorded, And upon ye motion of the said Executors & their giveing Security according to Law, Certificate is granted them for Obtaining a Probate of the sd. Will in Due form.

Robert Norden and John Avery Executors of the Last Will and Testament of Mathew Marks Deced: togather with George Devenport their Security enter into Bond for their Just and fainfull Executorship of the sd. Will & acknowledge the same in Court.

Thomas Adams, Travis Morris, John Bishope and Francis Wilkinson or any three of them being first Sworn by Some Majistrate of this County for that purpose, are Ordered to Appraise the Estate of Mathew Marks Deced: and make report of their proceedings therein to the next Court, when Robert Norden and John Avery Exrs. &c: are to return the Inventory thereof.

Amy, a Negro Girl, belonging to Peter Poythres is Judged Eleven years old.

Tom, a Negro Boy, belonging to Peter Poythres, is Judged Nine years old.

Jenny, a Negro Girl, belonging to Francis Poythres, is Judged Nine years old.

Francis Coleman in Open Court acknowledged his Deeds of Lease & Release of Land (seald) to Adam Sims, on whose motion they are Ordered to be recorded, and then also appeared in Court Mary the Wife of the sd. Francis Coleman, and being first privately Examined acknowledged the sd. Deeds to the sd. Adam Sims, and to him freely & Voluntarily relinquisht. her right of Dower in & to the Lands &c: in the said Deeds mentioned which is Likewise Ordered to be recorded.

In the action on the case brot. by John Hamersly agst. Nathl. Harrison Esqr. Admr. with the Will annext. of Richard Pigeon Deced: for four pounds, One Shilling and five pence halfe penny, due by account dated 1718, the Defendt.

[page 286]

moves the plt. may prove his accot. whereupon the sd. plt. makes Oath that One pound Eighteen Shillings and One penny halfe penny of the sd. Sum is Justly Due, whereupon Judgemt. is granted him agst. the sd. Defendt. for the sd. Sum of Thirty Eight Shillings & three halfe pence to be paid out of the said Deceds: Estate with costs. Als. Exec:

The action on the case brot. by Bridget Ward Admrx. of Collingwood Ward Deced: agst. Nathl. Harrison Esqr. Admr. &c: of Richard Pigeon Deced: the plt. failing to prosecute is Dismist.

In the case brot. by Richard Pigeon agst. Nathl. Harrison Esqr. Admr. with the Will annext of Richard Pigeon Deced: for five pounds Due by accot. Dated 1718, the Defendt. moves the plt. may prove his account, where upon he makes Oath the sd. sum is Justly due, and on his option Judgement is granted him agst. the sd. Defendt. for the sd. Sum and Costs, to be paide out of the said Deceds: Estate. Als. Exec:

George Tillman in Open Court acknowledged his Deeds of Lease and Release of Land (Indented and Seald) to John Kerby, on whose motion the same are Ordered to be recorded, and then also appeared in Court Mary the Wife of the said George, and being first privately Examined, freely and Voluntarily relinquisht. to the said John Kerbey, her right of Dower, in and to, the Lands &c in the said Deeds mentioned, which is Likewise Ordered to be recorded.

John Tillman in Open Court acknowledged his Deeds of Lease & release of Land (Indented and Seald) to Richard Cooke, on whose motion the same are Ordered to be recorded.

In the action on the case brot. by Nathl. Harrison Esq. agst. Elizabeth Mallory, John Hamlin and Edward Goodrich Executors of the Last Will and Testament of Francis Mallory Deced: for twelve Hundred forty Two pounds of Tobacco Due by account dated 1716, the Defendts. move the plt. may prove his accot. whereupon he makes Oath the said Sum is Justly due and on his motion it's Ordered that the sd. Defendts. pay to the said plt. Tenn pounds Seven Shillings, Value of the sd. Tobacco, out of the said Deceds. Estate with Costs, als. Exec:

In the action on the case brot. by Timothy Bridges agst. Sampson Merredeth Admr. of William Talbott Deced: for fifty Shillings and Tenn pence halfe penny due by accot. dated 1718, the Defendt. moves the plt. may prove his accot. whereupon he makes Oath the sd. Sum is Justly due, and on his motion it is Ordered that the sd. Defendt. pay to the said plt. the aforesaid Sum & costs, out of the Deceds: Estate, Als. Exec:

On the petition of Peter Talbott for the Administration of the Estate of William Talbott Deced. It is Ordered that Mary Talbott Relict of the said Deced: be summoned to the next court, to accept or refuse the sd. Admon.

[page 287]

In the action on the case brot. by Edward Hill agst. Elizabeth Mallory, John Hamlin and Edward Goodrich Exrs. of Francis Mallory Deced: Littlebury Epes, John Hardyman and Francis Hardyman or any two of them are appointed to Settle and ajust the accts. of the said partys and make report thereof to the next Court.

Thomas Huddells power of Attorney to William Troughton was produced in Court by the Oaths of John Blaine and William Hamlin & Ordered to be recorded.

On the Complaint of William Troughton that his sarvant John Miller absented himselfe from his service twenty four day's, and that in recovering the said Sarvant he Expended to the Value of three hundred pounds of Tobacco, the sd. John was brot. to the barr and he failing to make any plea &c: On the motion of the sd. Wm. Troughton It is Ordered that the said John Miller do serve him for the time of his absence and for the sd. Disbursments, Six months and three days after his present time of Service by Indenture or otherwise is Expired.

The action on the case brot. by Thomas Goodwynn agst. John Poythres, the plt. failing to prosecute, is Dismist.

A Deed for Land (Indented and Seald) from Richard Harrison to William Blaikley was proved in Court to be the Act and Deed of the sd. Richard Harrison by the Oath of Thomas Harrison and Richard Winkles Witnesses thereto, and Ordered to be recorded.

In the action on the case brot. by Frances Anderson Executrix of the Last Will and Testament of Charles Anderson Deced: agst. Elizabeth Mallory, John Hamlin and Edward Goodrich Executors of the Last Will and Testament of Francis Mallory Deced: for four thousand Eight hundred and twenty pounds of Tobacco due by account dated 1709, the

Defendts. move the plt. may prove her accot. whereupon she makes Oath that three thousand Eight hundred and five pounds and a quarter of Tobacco of the aforesaid Sum is Due, as Appears by accots. under the hand of the sd. Francis Mallory, and on her motion It is Ordered that the said Defendts. pay to the said plt. out of the sd. Deceds. Estate, Thirty One pounds fourteen Shillings and three pence halfe penny, Value of the said Tobacco, togather with Costs. Als. Exec:

In the action of Debt brot. by Frances Wynne agst. Henry Batte Admr. of Thomas Harwell Deced. the Defendt. haveing pleaded *plene Administravit* and the plt. Joining in the Issue the same was Submitted to the Court for Tryall, and the Court haveing considered the Evidence and allegations of the sd. partys, give Judgement for the Defendt. and thereupon the suit is Dismist.

[page 288]

The Order that Henry Holdcraft Exr. of Randle Platt Deced: return an accot. of the Estate of Joseph Greenhill in his hands &c is Continued till next Court.

In the action of Debt Depending between Littlebury Epes plt. and Elizabeth Mallory, John Hamlin and Edward Goodrich Executors of the Last Will & Testamt. of Francis Mallory Deced: Defendts. for fourteen hundred Seventy two pounds of Tobacco and Eight Shillings and Eight pence currt. money due by Bond dated the thirteenth day of September 1714, the defendts. move the plt. may prove his Debt, whereupon he makes Oath the same is Due, and on his motnion It is Ordered that the sd. Defendts. pay him the sd. plt. twelve pounds five Shillings and four pence Value of the said Tobacco, and the said Sum of Eight Shillings and Eight pence amounting in the whole to twelve pounds fourteen Shillings out of the said Decedts: Estate with costs. Als: Exec:

In the action on the case brot. by Timothy Bridges agst. William Heeth Admr. of Adam Heeth Deced: for Forty Six Shillings and four pence due by accot. the Defendt. being called not appearing nor any Security returned for him on the motion of the plts: attorny Judgement is granted him agst. the sd. Deft. and James Thweatt Sherr: &c: for the said Sum and Costs unless the sd. Defendt. shall appear at the nex Court and answer the said action.

In the action on the case brot. by Nathaniel Harrison Esqr. agst. John Pook for twelve hundred and nine pounds of Tobacco due by account dated 1713, the Defendt. came personally into Court and Confest Judgement to the plt. for the sd. Sum, thereupon on the motion of the plts: attorny It's Ordered that the sd. Defendt. pay to the said plt. the aforesaid Sum and Costs. Als. Exec:

In the action of Detinue brot. by William Cooke and Rebecca his Wife against James Jones, the Defendt. pleads *Non Detinet*, and the plts: Joining in the Issue the same was referred till next Court for Tryall.

The action of Debt brot. by John Threweet [sic] agst. Peter Wynne, the plt. failing to prosecute is Dismist.

In the action on the case brot. by Drury Bolling agst. William Jackson for Eight pounds Tenn Shillings due by accot. the Defendt. being called and not appearing, nor any Security returned for him on the motion of the plts: Attorny Judgement is granted him agst. the said Defendt. and James Thweatt Sherr: for the said Sum and Costs, unless the said Defendt. shall appear at the next Court and snwer the said action.

The action of Debt brot. by James Moody agst. John Berry, the plt. failing to prosecute is Dismist.

The action of Trespass brot. by John Leonard agst. James Moody, the plt. failing to prosecute is Dismist.

[page 289]

In the action of Trespass brot. by William Spiller agst. John Whittmore the Defendt. files his plea to the plts: Declaration who has time till next Court to Consider the same.

The action brot. by John Browder agst. William Barbar, neither party appearing, is Dismist.

The attachment granted Joshua Irby agst. the Estates of John Colson, William Stroud, and James Mayo, is Continued till the next Court.

Francis Poythres Surviveing Executor of the Last Will and Testamt. of Jos. Pattison Deced: agst. Elizabeth Mallory, John Hamlin and Edward Goodrich Executors of the Last Will and Testament of Francis Mallory Deced: for two thousand thirty one pounds of Tobacco and Seventeen Shillings Due by accot. to the Estate of the sd. Joseph Pattison Deced: the Defendts. move the plt. may prove the said accot. whereupon he makes Oath the same is due, and on ghis motion it's Ordered that the sd. Defendts. pay to the sd. plt. out of the sd. Mallory's Estate, Seventeen pounds three Shillings and Six pence, Value of the sd. Tobacco, and sd. Sum of Seventeen Shillings, amounting in the whole to Eighteen pounds and Six pence, with Costs. Als: Exec:

The action on the case brot. by Thomas Lawlor agst. John Berry the plt. failing to file his Declaration, the suit is Dismist.

In the action brot. by Thomas Simmons agst. Nicholas Overby the Defendt. files his plea's to the plts. Declaration, who has time till the next Court to Consider the same.

The suit in Chancery brot. by Frances Anderson Exrx. &c: agst. Henry Offley and Robert Bolling, is Continued till next Court.

The suit in Chancery brot: by John Bolling agst. Henry Offley and Robert Bolling, is Continued till next Court.

By consent of the Attornys of Edward Hill and John Brewer the Appeal granted the said Hill at the Last Court is withdrawn.

The action Depending between Joshua Irby and Mathew Smart is Continued till the next Court.

The action Depending between Joshua Irby and Cornelius Fox is Continued till next Court.

In the action of Debt brot. by John Bolling and Robert Bolling Executors of the Last Will and Testament of Robert Bolling Deced: against Elizabeth Mallory, John Hamlin and Edward

[page 290]
Goodrich Executors of the Last Will and Testament of Francis Mallory Deced: for Eight thousand five hundred twenty Seven pounds of Tobacco due by a Judgemt. of Prince George County Court dated the Eighth day of March 1714, the defendts. move the plts. may prove the sd. Debt, whereupon John Bolling one of the plts: makes Oath, Six thousand five hundred fifty two pounds of Tobacco of the aforesaid Sum is Justly Due, and on his motion It is Ordered that the said defts. pay to the said plts: Fivety four pounds twelve Shillings, Value of the sd. Tobo. out of the sd. Francis Mallorys Estate with Costs. Als. Exec:

In the action brot. by John Bolling agst. Elizabeth Mallory, John Hamlin and Edward Goodrich Executors of the Last Will and Testament of Francis Mallory Deced: for Sixteen hundred thirty one pounds of Tobacco and three pounds Eleven Shillings and Eight pence due by accot. the Defendts. move the plt. may prove his account, whereupon he makes Oath the same is due, and on his motion it is Ordered that the said Defendts. pay to the sd. plts. out of the sd. Deceds: Estate, the sum of thirteen pounds, Eleven shillings and Ten pence, Value of the sd. Tobacco, and the sd. Sum of three pds: Eleven Shillings and Eight pence, amounting in the whole to Seventeen pounds, three Shillings and Six pence, with costs. Als. Exec:

In the action of Trespass on the case Depending between John Hatch and John Turner commander of the *Alexander* Brigantine, For that the said John Hatch on the twenty Eighth day of February 1717, in the Parrish of Westover in this County was possessed of a hogshead of Tobacco Numbred Tenn, containing Six hundred, and one pounds weight of neet Tobacco, of the Value of Tenn pounds Sterling as of his own, and the same did ship and put on board the sd. Brigantine, whereof the sd. John Turner was then commander, and the sd. Hogshead of Tobacco so shiped did consign unto Mr. Robert Wise Merchant in London, which said Hogshead of Tobacco the sd. Defendt. took under his care, and gave Bills of Loading for, to be delivered as aforesaid, and altho' he the sd. Defendt. safely arrived with. the sd. Tobacco at the sd. Port of London, and knew the same to belong to the sd. Hatch, yet hath not delivered the same, but hath converted the said Tobacco to his own use, and to the plts: Damage Ten pounds Sterling, as in the sd. plts: Declaration is set forth, The defendt. haveing pleaded in writeing to the plts. Declaration and he Joining therein, a Jury was Impannelled and Sworn to trye the matter in Issue by Name Edmond Irby, Gilbert Hay, James Moody, William Harrison, Timothy Bridges, Cornelius Cargill, George Tillman, John Tillman, James Bell, Richard Reess, John Avery and John Pook, who haveing heard the Evidence and received their charge were sent out and soon after return into Court with their Verdict, We find for the plt. Six pounds Sterling. Edmond Irby, foreman, which on the plts. motion is recorded and it is Considered by the Court that the plt. recover agst. the said

[page 291]
Defendt. the aforesaid Sum of Six pounds Sterling, being his Damages aforesaid by the Jurors in manner aforesaid assessed, togather with costs. Als. Exec:

And it appearing to the Court that the Defendt. did unjustly and Vexatiously delay the plt. on the motion of the sd. plts: Attorny it is Ordered that One Attorneys Fee be Taxed to the Bill of Costs of this suit to be Leavied of the Defendt. for the sd. plt.

Prince a Negro Boy belonging to Joshua Poythres is Judged five years old.

In the action on the case brot. by Robert Honycutt agst. Elizabeth Mallory, John Hamlin and Edward Goodrich Executors of the Last Will and Testament of Francis Mallory Deced: for Tenn pounds Seven Shillings and Two pence due, by accot. dated 1718, the Defendts. move the plt. may prove the said accot. whereupon he (being a Quaker) made his affirmation thereto, and on his motion it is Ordered that the sd. Defendts. pay to the said plt. out of the said Deceds. Estate, the aforesaid Sum and Costs. Als: Exec:

In the action on the case brot. by John Davis agst. Elizabeth Mallory, John Hamlin and Edward Goodrich Executors of the Last Will and Testament of Francis Mallory Deced: for Twenty five pounds Tenn Shillings and four pence, due by accot. dated 1718, the defendts. move the plt. may prove his account, whereupon he makes Oath the sd. Same is Justly due, and on his motion it is Ordered that the said Defendts. pay to the said plt. the aforesaid sum and Costs, out of the said Deceds: Estate. Als: Exec:

The petition of Mary Burchett agst. Robert Burchett is referred till the next Court for the plt. to prove her allegations &c

In the action of Debt brot. by John Peterson agst. Elizabeth Mallory, John Hamlin and Edward Goodrich Executors of the Last Will and Testament of Francis Mallory Deced: for fifteen pounds Currt. mony Due by Bill dated the Seventeen day of February 1715, the defts. move the plt. may prove his Debt, whereupon he makes Oath the sd. Sum is Justly due, and on his motion it is Ordered that the said Defendts. pay to the said Plt. the aforesaid Sum and Costs out of the Deceds. Estate. Als: Exec:

On the petition of Thomas Simmons It is Ordered that a Lycence Issue for his keeping an Ordinary at the usuall palce near the Court house of this County, he with Thomas Simmons Junr. his Security haveing entred into bond according to Law.

[page 292]

On the petition of John Stith it is Ordered that his Ear Marke be recorded, Vizt. both Ears cropt and the right Ear underkeeled.

And then the Court adjourn'd till Court in Course. John Poythres. Test Wm. Hamlin, Cl. Cur.

At a Court held at Merchantshope for the County of Prince George on the
Second Tuesday in November being the Tenth day of the said month, Anno Dom:
1719.

Present   John Poythres,   Robert Munford,   Robert Hall }
    Sampson Merredeth,   John Hardyman   & Lewis Green Junr. }   Gent. Justices

William Coleman in Open Court acknowledged his Deeds of Lease & Release of Land (Seald) to Robert Munford, on whose motion the same are Ordered to be recorded, And then also appeared in Court Faith the Wife of the said William Coleman and being first privately Examined freely and Voluntarily relinquisht to the said Robert Munford her right of Dower in and to the Lands &c: in the said Deeds mentioned which is Likewise Ordered to be Recorded.

On the petition of James Baugh it is Ordered that George Rives, William Eaton, John Thweatt, Henry Thweatt, James Thweatt, Thomas Gregory & Daniel Vaughn be Summoned to the next Court to answer the same.

In the action on the case brot. by Edward Hill against Elizabeth Mallory, John Hamlin and Edward Goodrich Executors of the Last Will and Testament of Francis Mallory Deced. the Auditors appointed at the Last Court to settle & adust the accounts of the said partys, make the following report, Vizt. Pursuant to an Order of Prince George County Court Dated the 13th October Last We the subscribers have inspected, settled and adjusted the severall accots. between Colo. Edward Hill, and the Executors of Capt. Francis Mallory Deced: and do find that there remains due on Ballance thereof to Colo. Hill from the sd. Deceds: Estate fourteen thousand, Seven hundred, Seventy Six pounds of Tobacco, and the Colo. to be accountable to the said Estate for twelve pounds, Eleven Shillings & Eleven pence currt. mony, Given under our hands this 10th November 1719: Littlebury Epes, John Hardyman and the plt. makeing Oath the aforesaid Sum of Tobacco is justly due, and which is Valued by the Court at one hundred twenty three pounds, two Shillings and Eight pence, thereupon on the motion of the plt. and his allowing a Discount the aforesaid Sum of twleve pounds, Eleven Shillings and Eleven pence currt. mony, Judgement is granted him agst. the sd. Defendts. for the Ballance, being One hundred and Tenn pounds Ten Shillings & nine pence, and it is Ordered that the said Defendts. pay to the said plt. out of the said Deceds: Estate the aforesaid Sum of One hundred & Tenn pounds, Tenn Shillings & Nine pence & Costs. Als. Exec:

[page 293]

William Colgill's and Elizabeth Midleton's Deed to Thomas Jeffreys and others was proved in Court by the Oathes of Robert Rogers and Johanah Haly witnesses thereto, and on the motion of the sd. Rogers Attorny of the said Colgill the same is Ordered to be recorded.

Richard Newman an Orphan, Came into Court and chose Edward Scott his Guardian, who togather with John Hamersly his Security entred into Bond according to Law, and acknowledged the same in Court.

In the action on the case Depending between Charles Williams and John Hines, the Defendt. files his plea to the plts. Declaration, who has time till the next Court to Consider the same.

In the action on the case brot. by Francis Lightfoot agst. Elizabeth Mallory, John Hamlin and Edward Goodrich Executors of the Last Will and Testament of Francis Mallory Deced: on the Defendts. motion an Imparlance is granted them till the next Court.

In the action on the case brot. by John Simmons agst. Elizabeth Mallory, John Hamlin & Edward Goodrich Exrs. &c of Francis Mallory deced: an Imparlance is granted the Defendts. till the next Court.

In the action of Debt brot. by Edmond Major agst. Elizabeth Mallory, John Hamlin and Edward Goodrich Exrs. &c: of Francis Mallory Deced: an Imparlance is granted the Defendts. till the next Court.

In the action on the case brot. by George Braxton agst. Elizabeth Mallory, John Hamlin and Edward Goodrich Exrs. &c: of Francis Mallory Deced: an Imparlance is granted the Defendts. till the next Court.

In the action on the case brot. by Thomas Goodwynn agst. Elizabeth Mallory, John Hamlin & Edward Goodrich Exrs. &c: of Francis Mallory Deced: an Imparlance is granted the Defendts. till the next Court.

In the action on the case brot. by Joshua Lizland agst. Elizabeth Mallory, John Hamlin and Edward Goodrich Exrs. &c: of Fra. Mallory Deced. an Imparlance is granted the Defts. till the next Court.

In the action on the case brot. by David Crawley agst. Elizabeth Mallory, John Hamlin & Edward Goodrich Exrs. &c: of Fra. Mallory Deced: an Imparlance is granted the Defendts. till the next Court.

Present John Hamlin, Gent.

In the action of Trespass brot. by Roger Taylor agst. John Berry, John Hardyman became Special Bail for the said Deft. and on the motion of his Attorney an Imparlance is granted him till the next Court.

[page 294]

In the action of Trespass brot. by George Hamilton agst. John Berry, John Hardyman became Special Bail for the said Defendt. and on the motion of his Attorny an Imparlance is granted him till the next Court.

The action on the case brot. by Lydia Clements Executrix of Fra. Clements Deced: agst. Thomas Harrison, the plt. failing to prosecute, is Dismist.

In the action on the case brot. by John Hamersly agst. Abraham Odium for twelve pounds Tenn Shillings and Six pence farthing currt. mony due by accot. the Defendt. being returned *non est Inventus* and not appearing, on the motion of the plts: Attorny an Attachment is awarded him agst. the sd. Defendts. Estate for the said Sum & Costs, returnable to the next Court for Judgement for what shall appear to be due.

The action of Debt brot: by Richard Bland agst. William Ledbetter, the plt. failing to prosecute is Dismist.

In the action on the case brot. by Littlebury Epes agst. Thomas Simmons, on the Defendts. motion an Imparlance is granted him till the next Court.

In the action on the case brot. by John Hamersly agst. Elizabeth Duke Administratrix of the Goods and Chattels of Henry Duke Deced: for three pounds Sixteen Shillings and Six pence due by account Dated from January 1717 to May Following inclusive, the Defendt. by her Attorny moves the plt. may prove his account, whereupon he makes Oath the same is due, and on his motion it is Ordered that the sd. Defendts. pay to the sd. plt. out of the said Deceds: Estate the aforesaid Sum & Costs. Als. Exec:

In the action on the case brot. by John Hamersly agst. Henry Bates for One pound Eight Shillings and a halfe penny due by account Dated the 6th of May 1718, the Defendt. haveing pleaded *Nil Debit* and the plt. Joining in the Issue, the same was Sjbmitted by the Attornys to the Court for Tryall, and the Court haveing heard the allegations of the sd. partys, and it appearing that the Defendt. paid to the plt. the aforesaid Sum Since action brought &c therefore it is Considered by the Court that the sd. plt. recover agst. the Deft. the Costs of suit only. Als: Exec: Whereupon the Defendt. filed his plea in arrest of Judgement, which is referred till the next Court to be argued.

The attachment awarded James Thweatt Sherr: &c: agst. the Estate of Stephen Evans, the plt. failing to prosecute, is Dismist.

The Attachment awarded James Thweatt Sherr: &c: agst. the Estate of Stephen Cater, the plt. failing to prosecute, is Dismist.

The action on the case Depending between Richard Smith and Sampson Merredeth, the plt. failing to prosecute, is Dismist.

In the action of Debt brot. by Edward Hill agst. John Brewer, on the motion of the Defendts. Attorny an Imparlance is granted him till the next Court.

[page 295]

In the action of Debt brot. by George Hamilton agst. Elizabeth Mallory, John Hamlin and Edward Goodrich Exrs. &c: of Francis Mallory Deced: an Imparlance is granted the said Defendts. till the next Court.

In the action on the case brot. by Francis Epes agst. Elizabeth Mallory, John Hamlin and Edward Goodrich Exrs. &c: of Francis Mallory Deced: an Imparlance is granted the said Defendts. till the next Court.

In the action on the case brot. by Humphrey Bell & Henry Dee of London Merchants, agst. Eliza. Mallory, John Hamlin and Edward Goodrich Exrs. &c: of Francis Mallory Deced: Thomas Eldride [sic] entred himselfe Security to pay all costs and Damages that shall be awarded the Defts. agst. the sd. plts. & on the motion of the Defendts. an Imparlance is granted them till the next Court.

In the motion on the case brot. by John Bonner agst. Elizabeth Mallory, John Hamlin and Edward Goodrich Exrs. &c: of Fra. Mallory Deced: an Imparlance is granted the Defendts. till the next Court.

In the action on the case brot. by William Wray agst. Eliza. Mallory, John Hamlin & Edward Goodrich Exrs. &c: of Fra. Mallory Deced: an Imparlance is granted the Defendts. till the next Court.

The action on the case brot. by George Pasmore agst. Elizabeth Mallory, John Hamlin and Edward Goodrich Exrs. &c: of Fra. Mallory Deced: the plt. failing to prosecute, is Dismist.

In the action on the case brot. by Lydia Clements Exrx. &c: of Fra. Clements Deced: agst. Elizabeth Mallory, John Hamlin and Edward Goodrich Exrs. &c: of Francis Mallory Deced: an Imparlance is granted the Defendts. till the next Court.

The Last Will and Testament of Nathaniel Tatum Deced: was presented into Court by Edward Tatum one of his Executors, who made Oath thereto, and it being proved by the Oaths of Stith Bolling, Henry Tatum and Thomas Hood, Witnesses thereto, is Ordered to be recorded and it concerning Lands and Tenements only, therefore no Certificate is granted the sd. Executor for Obtaining a Probate.

On the petition of William Troughton, it is Ordered that Dennis Wright his Sarvant, be added to the List of Tithables of Westover Parrish.

James Greeshon in Open Court acknowledged his Deeds of Lease & Release of Land (Indented and Seald) to Henry Ledbetter on whose motion the same are Ordered to be recorded, and then also appeared in Court Margaret the Wife of the said James, and being first privately Examined freely and Voluntarily relinquisht to the said Henry Ledbetter her right of Dower in & to the Lands &c: in the said Deeds mentioned, which is Likewise Ordered to be recorded.

[page 296]
James Greeshon in Open Court acknowledged his Deed for Land &c: Mortgaged (Indented and Seald) with Livery and Seizin endorst thereon, to Buller Herbert on whose motion the same is Ordered to be recorded.

William Wallice is appointed Overseer of the Blackwater Road & Bridge Instead of James Greeshon.

Elizabeth Hamlin and John Hamlin in Open Court acknowledged their Deed for Land (Indented and Seald) with Livery of Seizin endorst thereon to William Hamlin on whose motion the same is Ordered to be recorded.

Mary Burchet the Wife of Robert Burchet by her petiton set forth that she is frequently beaten, wounded and Evil intreated by her said Husband and denyed the necessarys of Life (as Dyet and clothing) and prayed to be relieved, and the said Robert appearing, and the Court haveing heard and considered the Evidence and allegations of the said partys, do thereupon Order that the Sherriff of this County take the said Robert into his Custody, and him safely to keep and Detain untill he shall give bond with Sufficient Security to the King in the Sum of Twenty pounds Sterling, for his (the sd. Roberts) good behaviour, as well towards the said Mary as all others, for the Term of one whole year and a Day next Comeing.

Pursuant to the Direction of the Act concerning Jurys, a Gandjury was Impannelled and Sworn by Name Henry Thweatt, William Mattox, William Reess, Daniel Meadows, Henry Ledbetter, John Risby, John Bonner, Mathew Smart junr., Edward Scott, John Pook, Richard Cureton, Richard Tomlinson, James Jones, Joseph Woodleife & Henry Tatum who haveing reced: their charge were sent out and soon after returned into Court with the following presentments, Vizt. Wee the Grandjury present Hannah Headworth and Margaret Mattox for haveing Bastard Children. Henry Thweatt, foreman.

On the motion of John Hardyman one of the Churchwardens of Westover Parrish, it is Ordered that Hannah Headworth and Margaret Mattox be Summoned to the next Court to answer the presentment of the Grandjury.

Ordered that Robert Burchet pay the costs and charges that accrued on the petition and complaint made against him by Mary Burchet.

And then the Court adjourned till Tomorrow morning Tenn a Clock. John Poythres. Test. Wm. Hamlin, Cl. Cur.

[page 297]

At a Court held at Merchantshope for the County of Prince
George the 11th day of November 1719, for Laying the County
Levy.

Present   John Hamlin,   John Poythres }
           Robert Hall,   & Lewis Green Junr. }   Gent. Justices

Pr. George County Dr. Nov: the 11th 1719.

For Wolves Killed, Vizt.

To Majr. Robert Munford pr. Sevll. Vizt.	John Evans	4 }	
	Indian Sawny	1 }	
	Henry Embry	1 }	I Tobo.
	Will Matt	2 }	800
To Richard Smith Senr.		1	100
To Francis Coleman Senr.		1	100
To George Stell		1	100
To Peter Jones		1	100
To Joshua Poythres		1	100
		13	1300
To Mr. Lewis Green Junr. for an Inquest &c: and Summoning Jury			183
To James Thweatt Sherr: for the County Service, & Caske			1080
To Wm. Hamlin Clerk for Do. and Caske			1080
To Thomas Simmons for Sweeping the Court house			0250
To Do. for mending the Prison			0050
To John Randolph Cl. of the House of Burgesses for two }			
Copys of the Laws and Levy 1718 }			0650
To Wm. Epes Junr. for Timber for Jos. Swamp Bridge			0100
			Totall 4693

Pr. Geo: County Cr. Nov: 11th 1719.

By James Thweatt Sherr: part of the publick propportion	}	I Tobo.
on this County the Last year	}	4693

     Ordered that James Thweatt Sherriff of this County pay to The Severall persons above mentioned their severall Claims, amounting in the whole to four thousand and Six hundred Ninety three pounds of Tobacco, and that he give bond and Security accordingly, whereupon the said James Thweatt togather with Thomas Simmons his Security enter into Bond, with Condition for his Just and ffaithfull performance and payment of the sd. Severall Sums of Tobacco to whom they are proportioned and Ordered in the above Levy.

     And then the Court Adjourn'd. John Hamlin. Test: Wm. Hamlin, Cl. Cur.

[page 298]

At a Court held at Merchantshope for the County of Prince George
on Wednesday the Eleventh Day of November, Anno Dom: 1719.

Present   John Hamlin,   John Poythres   }
           Robert Hall,   & Lewis Green Junr.   }   Gent. Justices

     In the Ejection Firm[ee] brought by Arthur Law agst. Abell Dunn for One certain Tract of Land Containing One hundred and fifty Acres, Sicutate Lying and being in the Parrish of Waynoke in the County of Prince George, on which is one plantation with one Dwelling house, one Milk house and One Tobacco House with the Appurtenances thereunto belonging wch: Henry Peoples of the County aforesaid Demised, Granted, and to Farm Lett unto the sd. Arthur Law for a Term not yet Expired, on which the said Abell Dunn hath entred and him the said Arthur Law from the same Ejected, and other Enormitys to him did doe, to the Damage of him the said Arthur Law (one hundred pounds Sterling) and agst. the peace of our Soveraign Lord the King that Now is &c: as in the plts: Declaration is Set forth. Oath being made by Thomas Simmons that he delivered a copy of the Declaration in this cause, with an Endorsment thereon in the following words, Vizt. "John Ivy, You may perceive by the within Declaration that I am Sued for the Lands and Plantation of which you are now in possession, these are therefore to give you Notice that unless you or they under whom you claim, appear at the next Court to be held for Prince George and make your selfe or themselves Defendts. thereunto, and by Rule of Court confess Lease entry and Ouster and insist only on the

Title at the Tryall I will Suffer Judgement to goe against me by Default, and you thereupon will be Turned out of possession. Your Friend, Abell Dunn. To John Ivy. Tennant in Possession of the Lands and Premises within mentioned." To John Ivy Tennant in Possession of the Lands in Question, and Informed him of the Contents of the same, he being thereupon the said Land and the said John Ivy being called and failing to appear, it is Ordered that unless the said John Ivy or he or they under whom he claims (haveing Legall Notice of this Order) shall appear at the next Court, and make him or themselves Defendt. or Defendts. in the suit and plead not Guilty, & Confess Lease Entry and Ouster, and insist only on the Title at Tryall, Judgement will be given agst. him by default and His Majestys Writt of *Habere Facias* possession awarded to put the plt. in possession of the premises.

And then the Court Adjourn'd till Court in Course. John Hamlin. Test. Wm. Hamlin, Cl. Cur.

[page 299]

At a Court held at Merchantshope for the County of Prince
George on the second Tuesday in December, being the Eighty day
of the said month, Anno Dom: 1719.

Present	John Hamelin,	Robert Munford	}	
	Robert Hall,	Sampson Merredeth	}	
	Lewis Green Junr.	& John Peterson	}	Gent. Justices

The action of Debt Depending between Moses Beck and Cornelius Fox neither party appearing is Dismist.

Henry Batte Admr. of the Goods & Chattells of Thomas Harrwell deced: returns a further Inventory of the said Deceds: Estate, and (the Goods and Chattels therein mentioned being Valued by the Court) is Ordered to be recorded.

Ordered that the Road of which John Tally is Overseer, be cleared to the Outermost inhabitants.

Tomson Stapley in Open Court acknowledged his Deeds of Lease & Release of Land (Seald) to George Stell, on whose motion they are Admitted to record.

John Nance in Open Court acknowledged his Deeds of Lease and Release of Land (Indented and Seald) to Edward Slaughter, on whose motion they are Admitted to record, and then also appeared in Court Joan the Wife of the sd. John Nance and being first privately Examined freely and Voluntarily relinquisht to the said Edward Slaughter her right of Dower in and to the Lands &c: in the sd. Deeds mentioned which likewise Ordered be recorded.

Henry Mayes's Deed for Land (Indented & Seald) to James Baugh was in Open Court proved by the Oaths of Lewis Green junr., Roger Taylor and Cornelius Fox, Witnesses thereto, and on the motion of the said James Baugh the same is Ordered to be recorded.

Nathaniel Harrison Esqr. Admr. &c: of Richard Pigeon Deced. returns an Inventory &c: of the said Deceds: Estate, which is Ordered to be recorded.

In the action on the case brot. by Isham Randolph agst. Nathl. Harrison Esqr. Admr. &c: of Richard Pigeon Deced: for Two pounds Sixteen Shillings and One penny Due by account Dated 1718, the Deft. by his Attorny moves the plt. prove his account, whereupon he

[page 300]

makes oath the same is Justly Due, and on his motion it's Ordered that the sd. Defendt. pay to the said plt. out of the Deceds. Estate, the aforesaid Sum and Costs. Als. Exec:

The Order that Robert Bolling and Mary Chamnis Executors of Henry Chamnis Deced: return an Inveoty of the said Decedts. Estate is Continued till the next Court.

Edmond Irby haveing filed an Information agst. John Carter, on the motion of his Attorny it is Ordered the said Carter be summoned to the next Court to answer the same.

In the action of Trespass brot. by John Carter agst. Edmond Irby, on the motion of the Defendts. Attorny an Imparlance is granted him till the next Court.

The action of Debt brot. by William Firth agst. William Hatt, neither party appearing, is Dismist.

The action on the case brot. by Benja. Foster agst. John Perks, neither party appearing, is Dismist.

The action on the case brot. by John Hamersly agst. John Lett, the plaint. failing to prosecute, is Dismist.

In the action of Debt brot. by John Minge agst. Andrew Crews, the plt. failing to prosecute, on the motion of the Defendts. Attorny, it is Ordered that he be Nonsuit and pay the Deft. five Shillings with Costs. Als. Exec:

Sarah Jones files a Bill in Chancery agst. James Jones Executor of the Last Will and Testament of James Jones Deced: and on the motion of her Attorny it is Ordered that the sd. James Jones be Summoned to the next Court to answer the said Bill &c.

John Avery and Robert Norden Executors of the Last Will and Testamt. of Mathew Marks Deced: returns an Inventory of the said Deceds: Estate which is Ordered to be recorded.

Peter Talbotts petition for the Administration of the Estate of William Talbott Deced: (on the motion of his Attorney) is Dismist.

The Order that Henry Holdcroft Exr. of Randle Platt Deced: return an accot. of the Estate of Joseph Greenhill in his hands &c: is Continued till next Court.

Sampson Merredeth Admr. of William Talbott Deced: returns a further Inventory of the Deceds. Estate, which is Ordered to be recorded.

[page 301]

In the action on the case brot. by Timothy Bridges agst. William Heath Admr. of the Goods and Chattels of Adam Heath Deced: for Two pounds Six Shillings and four pence Due by accot. Dated 1718, which the plt. makes Oath is Justly Due, and the defendt. failing to make any plea or Objection, on the plts. motion it is Ordered taht the said Deft. pay to the sd. plt. out of the said Deceds. Estate, the aforesaid Sum & Costs. Als. Exec:

In the action on the case Depending between John Hamersly and Henry Bates for twenty Eight Shillings and a halfe penny due by accot. &c the Deft. haveing pleaded *Nil Debit* and the plt. Joining in the Issue the same was submitted to the Last Court for Tryall, and it appearing to the Court that the Deft. paid to the plt. the sd. Sum Since action &c: therefore Judgement was granted the plt. for the Costs of suit only, Whereupon the Defendt. filed a plea in arrest of Judgemt. which was referred till this Court to be argued, and the same being accordingly argued by the Attornys of the said partys is Overruled and the Judgemt. aforesaid is Confirmed.

In the action of Detinue brot. by William Cooke and Rebecca his Wife agst. James Jones, Damage forty pounds Sterling &c: the Defendt. haveing pleaded *Non Detinet* and the plts: Joining in the Issue a Jury was Impannelled and Sworn to trye the Matter in Issue, by Name John Thweatt, Henry Thweatt, Geo: Rives, Cornelius Fox, William Rives, Phillip Burrow, John Hynes, Thomas Poythres, Richard Cureton, John Lessenby, Chichester Sturdevant & James Moody, who haveing heard the Evidence and received their charge were sent out.

Ordered that when the Jury have agreed on their Verdict that they Deliver the same to the Sherr:

In the action on the case brot. by Drury Bolling agst. William Jackson for Eight pounds Tenn Shillings due by account Dated 1718, the Deft. being called and not appearing pursuant to the Conditional Judgement and Order of the Last Court, on the motion of the plaintiffs Attorny Judgemt. is granted him agst. the sd. Defendt. and James Thweatt Sherr: &c for the said Sum, and it is Ordered that the said Deft. and the said James Thweatt or either of them pay to the said plt. the aforesaid Sum & Cost. Als. Exec:

Judgement being this day past unto Drury Bolling agst. James Thweatt Sherr: of this County for Eight pounds Tenn Shillings & Costs, by reason of the Non appearance of William Jackson in an action

[page 302]

on the case at the suit of the said Drury Bolling, on the motion of the sd. James Thweatt an Attachment is granted him agst. the Estate of the said William Jackson for the said Sum & Costs, returnable to the next Court for Judgement.

In the action of Trespass brot. by William Spiller agst. John Whittmore, the plt. files a replication to the Defendts. plea, who has time till next Court to Consider the same.

In the action on the case brot. by William Ackrill agst. Instance Hall for Six pounds and Dix pence halfe penny, due by accot. the Defendt. being called and not appearing, nor any Security returned for him, on the motion of the plts. attorny Judgement is granted him agst. the said Defendt. and James Thweatt Sherr: &c: for the said Sum & Costs, unless the said Defendt. shall appear at the next Court and answer the said action.

The Attachment granted Jos: Irby agst. the Estates of John Colson, William Stroud and James Mayo, is Continued till next Court.

In the action on the case Depending between Thomas Simmons and Nicholas Overby, the plt. files a replication to the Defts. plea, who has time till next Court to Consider the same.

Sarah Pace the Wife of Richard Pace appeared in Court, and being first privately Examined, freely and Voluntarily relinquisht to Thomas Goodwynn her right of Dower in and to certain Lands &c: Conveyed and made over by her said Husband to the said Goodwynn, in this County Court in December Last.

The suit in Chancery brot. by Frances Anderson Exrx. agst. Henry Offley and Robert Bolling, is Continued till next Court.

The suit in Chancery brot. by John Bolling agst. Henry Offley and Robt. Bolling, is Continued till next Court.

In the action Depending between Jos: Irby and Mathew Smart, Majr. Robert Bolling and Maj. Robert Munford are chose by the sd. partys and appointed by the Court to Settle the Difference between them, and Ordered to make report of their proceedings to the next Court, and in case they cannot agree, then they (the said Bolling and Munford) are to Choose a third person &c.

In the action Depending between Jos. Irby and Cornelius Fox, the plt. waves his Demurrer and Joins in the plea's of the Defendt: and the same is referred till the next Court for Tryall.

The action of Debt brot. by George Woodleife agst. Fra. Coleman Junr. neither party appearing, is Dismist.

[page 303]

William Hatt bookkeeper for Nathl. Harrison Esqr. Exhibitted into Court an accot. against William Talbott Deced: and made Oath that there is due to the sd. Harrison by the said accot. Thirty four Shillings and three pence, thereupon by Consent of Sampson Merredeth Admr. of the said Deceds. Estate, it is Ordered that he the sd. Merredeth pay to the sd. Harrison out of the said Deceds. Estate, the aforesaid Sum & Costs. Als. Exec:

And then the Court adjourn'd till Court in Course. R. Hall. Test. Wm. Hamlin, Cl. Cur.

At a Court held at Merchantshope for the County of Prince
George on the second Tuesday in January, being the twelfth day
of the said month, Anno Dom: 1719[/20].

Present   John Hamlin,   John Poythres   }
     Robert Munford,   & John Peterson   }   Gent. Justices

On the motion of Nicholas Robyson he is Exempt from paying Levy to the County & publick for the future.

Adam Sims in Open Court acknowledged his Deed for Land (Indented & Seald) to John Ledbetter, on whose motion the same is Ordered to be recorded.

Present Mr. Robert Hall.

In the action on the case brot. by William Ranye agst. James Gretion for twenty One pounds, tenn Shillings & Six pence due by accot. & the Deft. being called and not appearing, nor any Security returned for him, on the motion of the plts: attorny Judgemt. is granted him agst. the said Deft. and James Thweatt Sherr: &c: for the said Sum & Costs, unless the said Defendt. shall appear at the next Court and answer the sd. Action.

The action on the case brot. by Thomas Grigory agst. John Rackly neither party appearing, is Dismist.

In the action of Trespass brot. by William Anderson agst. Henry Thweatt, on the motion of the Defendts. Attorny an Imparlance is granted him till the next Court.

In the action on the case brot. by John Pook agst. Wm. Spiller for Seven Hundred forty Seven pounds of Tobacco due by accot. &c: the

[page 304]

Defendt. being returned *non est Inventus* and not appearing, on the plts: motion an Attachment is awarded him agst. the sd. Defendts. Estate for the said Sum & Costs, returnable to the next Court for Judgement for what shall appear to be due.

The action on the case brot. by Robert Richardson agst. John Midleton et Uxor, is withdrawn by the plaint.

Present Mr. Robt. Bolling

George Rives, Wm. Eaton, John Thweatt and others being Summoned to answer the petition and complaint of James Baugh an Overseer of the Highways, for their contempt in refuseing to assist in clearing the Highways of which the said Baugh is Overseeer, and the sd. persons appearing and Shewing sufficient reasons for their contempt or reglect, they are thereupon discharged.

In the action on the case brot. by Charles Williams agst. John Hines, the plt. files a replication to the Defendts. plea, who has time till the next Court to Consider the same.

In the action of Detinue brot. by William Cooke and Rebecca his wife against James Jones, the Jury that was Impannelled Y& Sworn at the Last Court to trye the matter in Issue, failed then to return their Verdict and being now called and Thomas Poythres one of the Jurors not appearing the cause is thereupon deferred till the next Court, and it is Ordered that the said Thomas Poythres be Summoned to attend accordingly.

And then the Court Adjourn'd till Court in Course. Jno. Hamlin. Test Wm. Hamlin, Cl. Cur.

At a Court held at Merchantshope for the County of Prince
George on the second Tuesday in February, being the Ninth
Day of the said month, Annoq. Dom: 1719[/20].

Present	John Hamlin,	Robert Munford	}	
	Robert Hall	& Lewis Green Junr.	}	Gent. Justices

John Robyson in Open Court acknowledged his Deed for Land (Indented and Seald) with Livery of Seizin thereon, to William Colgill on whose motion the same are admitted to record.

And then also appeared in Court Mary the Wife of the said John and being first privately Examined freely and Voluntarily relinquisht to the said William Colgill her right of Dower in and to the Lands &c: in the said Deed mentioned, which is Likewise Ordered to be recorded.

[page 305]

John Robyson in Open Court acknowledged his Bond (Seald) for performance of Covenants to William Colgill on whose motion the same is Ordered to be recorded.

George Ivy in Open Court acknowledged his Deed for Land (Indented and Seald) with Livery and Seizin endorst thereon to John Smith, on whose motion the same are Ordered to be recorded.

And then also appeared in Court Ruth the wife of the said George and being first privately Examined freely and Voluntarily relinquisht to the said John Smith her right of Dower in and to the Lands &c: in the said Deed mentioned, which is Likewise Ordered to be recorded.

George Ivy in Open Court acknowledged his Deeds of Lease and Release of Land (Indented and Seald) to William Hobbs, on whose motion the same are admitted to record.

And then also appeared in Court Ruth the wife of the sd. George and being first privately Examined freely and Voluntarily relinquisht to the said William Hobbs her right of Dower in and to the Lands &c: in the said Deeds mentioned, which is Likewise Ordered to be recorded.

William Heath is appointed Overseer of the Highways from Simmons's Mill to Warthens Mill and from Warthens Mill to the said Heath's.

Deeds of Lease and Release of Land (Seald) from John Nickells to Thomas Eldridge, were proved in Court by the Oaths of Thomas Posford, Samuel Chappell & Edmond Silver Witnesses thereto, to be the act and Deed of the said Nickells to the sd. Eldridge on whose motion the same are Ordered to be recorded.

On the petition of Robert Munford it is Ordered that a Smooth crop and Slitt in the right Ear and a Nick under the Left, be recorded the Ear marke of his son Robert.

In the action on the case brot. by Thomas Lawlor agst. John Berry for Thirty two Shillings and four pence halfe penny Due by account Dated 1719, the said partys appearing and the plts: accot. being Examined in Court and the plt. makeing Oath that twenty Eight Shillings and Seven pence halfe penny of the sd. Sum is Justly due thereupon on his motion it is Ordered that the said Deft. pay to the said plt. the said Sum of twenty Eight Shillings and Seven pence halfe penny & costs. Als. Exec:

And then the Court Adjourn'd till Court in Course. Jno. Hamlin. Test Wm. Hamlin, Cl. Cur.

[page 306]

At a Court held at Merchantshope for the County of Prince George on the
Second Tuesday in March, being the Eighth day of the said month, Dom: 1719[/20].

Present	John Hamlin,	Robert Hall	}	
	John Hardyman	& Lewis Green Junr.	}	Gent. Justices

Pursuant to the Direction of the Act for regulating Ordinarys &c it is Ordered that the rates on Ordinary Liquors, Dyet, Lodgeing &c: be as were formerly set & rated by this Court.

Pursuant to the Direction of the Act for Appointing sheriffs, John Poythres, Robert Munford and John Hardyman Gent. Justices, are recommended to the Honble. the Lieut. Governr. as fitt and able to Execute the Office of Sherr: of this County the next ensueing year.

In the action on the case brot. by Francis Lightfoot against Elizabeth Mallory, John Hamlin and Edward Goodrich Executors of Francis Mallory Deced: the defts. appear and plead *plene Adminstravit*, and thereupon the suit is Dismist.

In the action on the case brot. by John Simmons agst. Elizabeth Mallory, John Hamlin and Edward Goodrich Executors of the Last Will and Testament of Francis Mallory deced: the defts. appear and plead *plene Administravit*, and thereupon the suit is Dismist.

In the action of Debt brot. by Edmond Major agst. Eliza: Mallory, John Hamlin and Edward Goodrich Executors of Francis Mallory Deced: the plt. not appearing, the suit is Dismist.

The action on the case brot. by George Braxton agst. Eliza. Mallory, John Hamlin and Edward Goodrich Executors of Fra. Mallory Deced: the plt. not appearing, is Dismist.

The action on the case brot. by Joshua Lizland agst. Eliza. Mallory, John Hamlin and Edward Goodrich Executors of Fra. Mallory Deced: the plt. not appearing, is Dismist.

The action on the case brot. by David Crawley agst. Eliza. Mallory, John Hamlin and Edward Goodrich Executors of Fra. Mallory Deced: the plt. not appearing, is Dismist.

The action of Trespass brot. by George Hamelton agst. Eliza. Mallory, John Hamlin and Edward Goodrich Executors of Fra. Mallory deced: the plt. not appearing, is Dismist.

The action on the case brot. by Francis Epes agst. Eliza. Mallory, John Hamlin and Edward Goodrich Executors of Francis Mallory deced: the plt. not appearing, is Dismist.

The action on the case brot. by John Bonner agst. Eliza. Mallory, John Hamlin and Edward Goodrich Executors of Francis Mallory Deced: the plt. not appearing, is Dismist.

[page 307]

The action on the case brot. by William Wray atst. Eliza: Mallory, John Hamlin and Edward Goodrich Executors of Francis Mallory deced: the plt. not appearig, is dismist.

In the action on the case brot. by Lydia Clements Executrix of Francis Clements Deced: agst. Eliza: Mallory, John Hamlin and Edward Goodrich Executors of Francis Mallory deced: the defendts. plead *plene Administravit*, and the plt. Joining in the Issue, the same is referred till next Court for Tryall.

In the action of Trespass brot. by Roger Taylor agst. John Berry at the Last Court the Defendt. haveing had time given him till this Court to plead, and being now called and not appearing, on the plts. motion Judgemt. is granted him agst. the sd. Deft. by *Nihil dicit*.

In the action of Trespass brot. by George Hamelton agst. John Berry, at the Last Court the defendt. haveing had time given him till this Court to plead, and being now called and not appearing, on the plts: motion Judgemt. is granted him agst. the said Deft. by *Nihil dicit*.

The Attachment awarded John Hamersly agst. the Estate of Abram Odium is continued.

In the action on the case brot. by Littlebury Epes agst. Thomas Simmons, the Defendt. pleads *Nill debit* and the plt. Joining in the Issue the same is referred till ye next Court for Tryall.

In the action of Debt brot. by Edward Hill agst. John Brewer at the Last Court the defendt. haveing had time given him till this Court to plead, and being now called and not appearing, on the plts: motion Judgemt. is granted him agst. the sd. Defendts. by *Nihil dicit*.

The Order that Hannah Headworth and Margaret Mattox be Sumoned to answer the presentments of the Grandjury, is Dismist.

In the action on the case brot. by Thomas Goodwynn agst. Elizabeth Mallory, John Hamlin and Edward Goodrich Executors of the Last Will and Testament of Francis Mallory Deced: for Twenty One pounds Nine Shillings and Seven pence halfe penny due by accot. dated from 1714 to 1718, Inclusive, the Defendts. appear and plead fully Administred, thereupon the plt. makes Oath that fifteen pounds Eleven Shillings and Nine pence halfe penny of the aforesaid Sum

[page 308]

Is Justly Due to him and on his motion it is Ordered that the sd. Defendts. pay to the sd. plts. the aforesaid Sum of Fifteen pounds Eleven Shillings and Nine pence halfe penny & Costs, out of the said Deceds: Estate when Assetts thereof Shall come to hand &c:

The Ejectment brot. by Arthur Law agst. Abell Dunn neither party appearing to prosecute &c: is Dismist.

The action on the case brot. by William Mitchell agst. Charles Chapman, neither party appearing, is Dismist.

The action on the case brot. by Titus Creacher agst. Jonathan Carter neither party appearing, is Dismist.

The action on the case brot. by Henry Thweatt agst. William Mitchell neither party appearing, is Dismist.

The action of Debt brot. by John Peterson agst. William Floriday the plt. failing to prosecute, is Dismist.

In the action on the case brot. by Nathl. Harrison Esqr. agst. John Berry for four pounds Current mony due by accot., the defendt. being called and not appearing and John Lett being returned Security for him, on the motion of the plts: Attorny Judgement is granted him against the said defendt. & his sd. Security for the said Sum & Costs, unless the said Deft. shall appear at the next Court and answer the said action.

The action on the case brot. by Henry Bates agst. Geo: Ivie, neither party appearing, is Dismist.

In the action on the case brot. by Benjamin Foster agst. Elizabeth Mallory, John Hamlin and Edward Goodrich Executors of the Last Will and Testament of Francis Mallory Deced: for Seven pounds, twelve Shillings and Eleven pence due by account &c: the defendts. appear and plead fully Administred, thereupon the plt. makes Oath the said Sum is Justly due to him, and on his motion Judgement is granted him against the said Defendts. for the aforesaid Sum & Costs to be paid out of the said Deceds: Estate when assetts shall come to hand &c:

The Order that Robert Bolling and Mary Chamnis Exrs. of Henry Chamnis Deced: return an Inventory of the said Deceds: Estate is Continued till next Court.

Edmond Irby haveing at the Last Court filed an Information agst. John Carter, it was then Ordered that he shou'd be summoned to appear at this Court to answer the same, and he being accordingly summoned & called and failing to appear, on the motion of the plts. Attorny it is Ordered that the sd. John Carter be taken into Custody of the Sherr: till he shall give bond and Security to appear at the next Court to answer the Information aforesaid.

[page 309]

In the action of Trespass brot. by John Carter agst. Edmond Irby, at the Last Court the defendt. haveing had time given him till this Court to plead and being now called and not appearing on the motion of the plts. Attorny Judgement is granted him agst. the said Defendt. by *Nihil decit.*

Elizabeth Mallory, John Hamlin and Edward Goodrich Executors of Francis Mallory Deced: return a further Inventory of the said Deceds: Estate, which is Ordered to be recorded.

The Last Will and Testament of Elizabeth Ivie deced: was presented into Court by Adam Ivie her Executor, who made Oath thereto, and it being proved by the Oath of Elizabeth Foster a Witness thereto, is Admitted to record, And on the motion of the said Adam Ivie and his giveing Security according to Law, Certificate is granted him for Obtaining a Probate in Due form.

Adam Ivie Executor of the Last Will and Testament of Eliza. Ivie deced: togather with Edward Prince his Security entred into Bond for his faithfull Executorship of the said Deceds: Will and acknowledge the same in Court.

Ordered that Adam Ivie Executor of the Last Will and Testament of Eliza. Ivie deced: return to the next Court an Inventory of the said Deceds. Estate.

Eliza. Mallory, John Hamlin and Edward Goodrich Exrs. of the Last Will and Testament of Francis Mallory Deced: presented into Court an Account Dr. & Cr. of the said Deceds: Estate, and the same being Examined by the Court is Ordered to be recorded.

In the suit in Chancery brot. by Sarah Jones agst. James Jones Executor of the Last Will and Testament of James Jones deced: on the motion of the respondts. Attorney time is granted him till the next Court to answer to ye Complainants Bill.

Sharper, a Negro Boy belonging to John Woodleife, is adjudged Tenn years old.

The order that Henry Holdcroft Executor of Rand: Platt deced: return an accot. of Jos. Greenhills Estate in his hands &c: is Continued till next Court.

The Attachment awarded James Thweatt Sherr: against the Estate of William Jackson, is continued till the next Court.

The action of Trespass brot. by William Spiller agst. John Whittmore the plt. failing to prosecute, is Dismist.

[page 310]

In the action on the case brot. by William Ackrill against Instance Hall for Six pounds and Six pence halfe penny due by accot. dated the 26th of June 1719, the deft. Appearing by his Attorny and failing to make any Legall plea thereupon the plt. (by the oath of Thomas Simmons) proves that four pounds Nine Shillings of the aforesaid Sum is Justly due, and on the motion of his Attorny it is Ordered that the said Deft. pay to the sd. plt. the aforesaid Sum of Four pounds Nine Shillings, with Costs. Als. Exec:

The attachment awarded Joshua Irby agst. the Estate of John Colson is Continued till the next Court.

The attachment awarded Jos. Irby agst. the Estate of Wm. Stroud, is continued till the next Court.

The attachment awarded Jos: Irby agst. the Estate of James Mayo, is continued till next Court.

In the action on the case Depending between Thomas Simons & Nicholas Overby, the Defendt. files a Demurrer &c: and on the plats: motion time is granted him till the next Court to Consider the same.

In the action of Detinue Depending between William Cooke and Rebecca his Wife plts. and James Jones Deft. the Jury that was Impannelled and Sworn to trye the matter in Issue now appear and Declare that they cannot agree on a Verdict, thereupon & on their motion, they are discharged, and it is Ordered that another Jury be Impannell'd to the next Court to Trye the said Issue.

In the action on the case brot. by William Ranye agst. James Gretion, the defendt. by his Attorny pleads *Nil debit* and the plt. Joining in the Issue the same is referred till the next Court for Tryall.

In the action depending between Joshua Irby and Math: Smart, the Last Courts Order is continued.

In the action depending between Joshua Irby and Cornelius Fox, Robert Bolling & Robert Munford Gent. are chose by the sd. partys and appointed by the Court to settle the difference between them, and Ordered to make report of their pcoeedings to the next Court, and in case they cannot agree, then the said Bolling and Munford are to choose a third person &c.

In the action of Trespass brot. by William Anderson agst. Henry Thweatt, at the Last Court time was granted the deft. till this Court to plead, and being now called and not appearing, on the motion of the plts: Attorny Judgement is granted him agst. the said Deft. by *Nihil dicit*.

In the action on the case Depending between Charles Williams and John Hynes, the Defendt. files a Demurrer to the plts. replication, who has time till the next Court to Consider the same.

[page 311]

The attachment awarded John Pook agst. the Estate of William Spiller, is Continued till the next Court.

The suit in Chancery brot. by Fra. Anderson Exrx. &c: agst. Henry Offley and Robert Bolling is Continued till the next Court.

The suit in Chancery brot. by John Bolling agst. Henry Offley and Robert Bolling is Continued till next Court.

The action on the case brot. by David Crawley agst. John Hall neither party appearing, is Dismist.

The action of Debt brot. by William Smith agst. Thos. Colley neither party appearing, is Dismist.

The action on the case brot. by William Batte agst. George Archer, neither party appearing is Dismist.

The action of Debt brot. by Timothy Bridges Assignee of Edward Brady agst. William Jackson, neither party appearing, is Dismist.

In the action of Debt brot. by Robert Bolling against Wm. Hamlin, on the defts. motion Oyer of the plts: Bond is granted him and time till the next Court to consider the same.

In the action of Detinue depending between Sarah Wiggins by Wm. Killegrew her next friend, and Richard Winkles, on the motion of the Defts. attorny Oyer of the plts: Deed is granted him and time till the next court to consider the same.

The action on the case brought by James Loftin agst. Peter Finny neither party appearing, is Dismist.

The action on the case brot. by David Crawley agst. Wm. Bobbit neither party appearing, is Dismist.

The action on the case brot. by David Crawley agst. Thos. Spain neither party appearing, is Dismist.

The action on the case brot. by David Crawley agst. Roger Archer, neither party appearing, is Dismist.

The action on the case brot. by Roger Archer agst. Henry Allin, neither party appearing, is Dismist.

The action on the case brot. by James Moody agst. Joseph Renn Junr., neither party appearing, is Dismist.

[page 312]

In the action of Trespass brot. by William Short agst. Thomas Harrison, on ye motion of the defendts. attorny, an Imparlance is granted him till the next Court.

The action on ye Case brot. by Henry Cabinis agst. John Wicketts, on the motion of the plts: Attorny, is referred till next Court.

In the action of Trespass brot. by Benjamin Foster agst. John Tomlinson Damage three pounds Sterl: &c: the deft. being called and not appearing, nor any security returned for him, on the motion of the plts: Attorny Judgement is granted him against the said Defendt. and James Thweatt Sherr: of this County for the aforesaid Sum & Costs, unless the said Defendt. shall appear at the next court and answer the said action.

In the action on the case brot. by George Carter agst. John Lett, the deft. pleads *Nil debit* and the plt. Joining in the Issue the same is referred till next court for Tryall.

The action on the case brot. by John Lett agst. Richard Fox, is withdrawn by the plt.

The action on the case brot. by Thomas Lawlor agst. Thos. Huddell is withdrawn by the plt.

Sampson Merredeth Admr. of Wm. Talbott deced: returns a further Inventory of the said deceds: Estate, which is Ordered to be recorded.

The acion on the case brot. by David Crawley agst. Stephen Evans, the plt. failing to prosecute, is Dismist.

The action of Trespass brot. by Robert Brown agst. Thos. Willson neither party appearing is Dismist.

In the action of Debt brot. by John Soane agst. John Lett, John Berry became Special Bail for the deft. who thereupon appears & pleads payment, and the plt. Joining in the Issue the same is referred till ye next court for Tryall.

The action of Debt brot. by John Stokes agst. Jos. Partridge, neither party appearing is Dismist.

In the action of Debt brot. by Edmond Irby agst. John Carter, on the motion of the defendts. attorny an Imparlance is granted him till the next court.

Hannah Claud Relict of Phillip Claud Deced: came into Court & Made Oath that the said Phillip Claud departed this Life without makeing any Will as farr as She knows or believes, and on her motion and giveing Security for her Just and faithfull Administration of the sd. Decedts. Estate, Certificate is granted her for Obtaining Letters of Administration in due form.

[page 313]

Hannah Claud Admrx. of Phillip Claud deced: with Thomas Simmons & Michal Rosser Junr. her securitys, entred into Bond for her Just & faithfull Administration on the sd. Deceds. Estate.

George Hamelton, Thomas Simmons Junr., Thomas Booth & Arthur Biggins, or any three of them being first Sworn by some Majistrate of this County for that purpose, are Ordered to Appraise the Estate of Phillip Claud Deced: and make report of their proceedings therein to the next Court when Hannah Claud the Admrx. is to return the Inventory thereof.

Robert Bolling haveing a Commission to be a Corroner of this County, he appears in Court and his sd. Commission being read, he is accordingly Sworn.

John Poythres, John Hardyman & Lewis Green Junr., Gent., are recommended to the Honble. the Lieut: Govr. as fitt and able to Execute the Office of Corroners of this County.

And then the Court Adjourn'd till Court in Course. Jno. Hamlin. Test. Wm. Hamlin, Cl. Cur.

At a Court held at Merchantshope for the County of
Prince George on the second Tuesday in Aprill, being
the twelfth day of the said month, Anno Dom: 1720.

Present   John Hamlin,   Robert Munford,   Robt. Hall,
                Lewis Green junr.   & John Peterson   Gent. Justices

Robert Rivers came into Court and made Oath that Joan Hogwood deced: departed this Life without makeing any Will as farr as he knows or believes, and on his motion and giveing Security for his Just and faitnful Administration of the said Deceds: Estate, Certificate is granted him for Obtaining a Commission of Administration in due form.

Robert Rivers Admr. of Joan Hogwood Deced: with Peter Anderson his Security, entred into bond for his Just and faithfull Administration of the said Deceds. Estate, and acknowledged the same in Court.

[page 314]

James Niblett, Peter Talbott, Edward Avery and John Smith or any three of them being first Sworn by Some Majistrate of this County for that purpose, are Ordered to appraise the Estate of Joan Hogwood decedt. and make report of their proceedings therein to the next Court, when Robert Rivers the Admr. is to return the Inventory thereof.

Present Robert Bolling & John Hardyman, Gent.

Dol, an Indian Girl belonging to William Gent is adjudged Ten years old.

The Order that Robert Bolling and Mary Chamnis Executors of Hen: Chamnis Deced: return an Inventory of the sd. Deceds. Estate is Continued till next Court.

Ordered that Peter Talbott be summoned to appear before Sampson Merredeth Gent. to take the Oath of a Constable &c:

Edward Avery is appointed Overseer of the Highways in Martins brandon instead of William Jackson.

Hannah CLaud [sic] Admrx. of Phillip Claud deced: returns an Inventory of the said Deceds. Estate, which is Ordered to be recorded.

The Last Will and Testament of Richard Bland Deced: was presented into Court by William Randolph and Richard Randolph his Executors who made Oath thereto, and it being proved by the Oath's of John Fitzgerrald, Thomas Burge, and Michal Wallice, withesses thereto, is Admitted to record, and on the motion of the said William Randolph and Richard Randolph and their giveing Security, Certificate is granted them for Obtaining a Probate of the said Will in due form.

William Randolph and Richard Randolph Executors of the Last Will and Testament of Richard Bland Deced: togather with Robert Munford & Thomas Eldridge their Securitys, entred into bond for their faithfull Executorship of the said Deceds: Will, and acknowledged the same in Court.

159

Richard Tomlinson in Open Court acknowledged his Deed for Land (Indented and Seald) with Livery of Seizin therein, to Michal Rosser Junr. & Thomas Rosser, on whose motion the same is Admitted to record.

And then also appeared in Court Ellinor the Wife of the said Richard and being first privately Examined, freely and Voluntarily relinquisht to the sd. Michl. Rosser & Thomas Rosser her right od dower in and to the Lands &c in the said Deed mentioned, which is Likewise Ordered to be recorded.

The action on the case brot. by Lydia Clements Exrx. &c agst. Elizabeth Mallory, John Hamlin and Edward Goodrich Exrs. &c is continued till next court on the Defts. cost.

[page 315]

In the action on the case brought by Nathaniel Harrison Esqr. against John Berry for four pounds due by accot. dated 1719, the Defendt. came personally into court & Confest Judgement to the plt. for three pounds seventeen Shillings and Six pence, being the Ballance due on the sd. Accot. thereupon it is Ordered that the said Defendt. pay to the said plt. the said Sum of three pounds Seventeen Shillings and Six pence, and Costs. Als. Exec:

And it is Ordered that one Attornys Fee be taxed to the Bill of Costs of this Suit.

In the action of Trespass Depending between Roger Taylor and John Berry, the Deft. pleads not Guilty, and the plt. Joining in the Issue, the same is referred till next Court for Tryall.

In the action of Trespass depending between Geo: Hamelton and John Berry, the Defendt. pleads not Guilty, and the plt. Joining in the Issue, the same is referred till next Court for Tryall.

The action on the case brot. by John Hamersly agst. Abram Odium, the plt. failling to prosecute, is Dismist.

In the action on the case brot. by Littlebury Epes agst. Thomas Simmons for five hundred and fifteen pounds of Tobacco due by account dated 1715, the defendt. haveing pleaded *Nil debit* and the plt. Joining in the Issue the same was submitted to the Court for Tryall ,and the Accounts of the sd. partys being Examined & Settled and it appearing that the Deft. is indebted to the plt. two Hundred Thirty two pounds of Tobacco, thereupon on the sd. plts. motion it is Ordered that the said Deft. pay him the aforesaid Sum of two Hundred thirty two pounds of Tobacco & Costs. Als. Exec:

In the action of Detinue broght by William Cooke & Rebecca his Wife against James Jones, for the detainer of a Negro boy Slave called Harry of the Price of thirty pounds Sterling, belonging to the plts: & to their Damage forty pounds Sterling, as in the sd. plats: Declaration is set forth the Defendt. by his Attornys appeared & pleaded non Detinet and for Tryall put himselfe upon the Country & the plts: Likewise, whereupon a Jury was Impannelled and Sworn to trye the matter in Issue by Name Henry Batte, George Hamelton, Thomas Burge, Thomas Booth, Roger Taylor, Nicholas Overby, John Pooke, Robert Rivers, John Carter, William Reess, William Cureton & William Davis, who haveing heard the Evidence and received their charge were

[page 316]

sent out, and soon after returend into Court & brought in their Verdict, We find for the plaintiffs the Negroe sued for, or Twenty five pounds Sterling, the Value of him and three pounds Sterling Damages for the detainer of him. Henry Batte, Foreman, which Verdict on the motion of the plts: Attorney is recorded, and thereupon it is considered by the Court that the said William Cooke and Rebecca his Wife recover against the said James Jones the negro aforesaid, or Twenty five pounds Sterling for the Value of him, and also their Damages aforesaid to the Value of three pounds Sterling, by the Jurors aforesaid in manner aforesaid assessed, togather with Costs. Als. Exec: Whereupon the Defendt. files a plea in arrest of Judgemt. which is referred till next Court to be argued.

And then the Court Adjourn'd till Court in Course. John Hamlin. Test Wm. Hamlin, Cl. Cur.

At a Court held at Merchantshope for the County of Prince
George on the second Tuesday in May, being the Tenth day of the
sd. month, Anno Dom: 1720.

Present	John Hamlin,	Robert Munford	}	
	Robert Hall,	Lewis Green junr.	}	
	& John Peterson		}	Gent. Justices

Pursuant to the Direction of the Act Concerning Tithables, Robert Bolling Gent. is appointed to take the List of Tithables in Bristoll Parrish on the Tenth day of June next.

John Hamlin Gent. in Westover Parrish.

John Poythres Gent. in Waynoke Parrish.

& Sampson Merredeth Gent. in Martins=brandon Parrish.

William Temple Junr. came into Court and made Oath that James Howard Deced: Departed this Life without makeing any Will as farr as he knows or believes, and on his motion and giveing Security for his just and faithfull Administration on the said Deceds: Estate, Certificate is granted him for obtaining a Commission of Administration in Due form.

William Temple Junr. Admr. of James Howard Deced: with George Brewer his Security, entred into bond for his Just and faithfull Administration of the said Deceds: Estate and acknowledged the same in Court.

[page 317]

John Scott, Charles Williams, Thomas Addison & Hugh Golightly or any three of them being first Sworn by Some Majistrate of this County for that purpose are Ordered to appraise the Estate of James Howard Deced: and make report of their proceedings therein to the next Court when William Temple Junr. the Administrator is to return the Inventory.

The Last Will and Testament of Thomas Harrison Deced: was presented into Court by Robert Hall his Executor who made Oath thereto, and it being proved by the Oaths of John Hamersly and Timothy Bridges Witnesses thereto is Admitted to record, & on the motion of the said Robert Hall and his giveing Security according to Law, Certificate is granted him for Obtaining a Probate of the said Will in Due form.

Robert Hall Executor of the Last Will and Testament of Thomas Harrison Deced: with Sampson Merredeth his Security entred into Bond for his fainfull Executorship of the sd. Deceds: Will and acknowledged the same in Court.

Timothy Bridges, Edward Wyatt, Benjamin Reeks & Peter Talbott or any three of them being first sworn by some Majistrate of this County for that purpose, are Ordered to Appraise the Estate of Thomas Harrison Deced: and make report of their proceedings therein, to the next Court, when Robert Hall the Executor is to return the Inventory.

Sarah Adkins Executrix of Richard Adkins Deced: returns a Supplementory Inventory of the said Deceds: Estate, which is Ordered to be recorded.

The Last Will and Testament of John Stevens Deced: was presented into Court by Sampson Merredeth One of his Executors, & Nathl. Harrison Esq. the other Executor haveing refused to take on him the burthen and Execution of the said Will, the said Sampson Merredeth made Oath thereto, and it being proved by the Oath of William Haly a Witness thereto, is Admitted to record, and on the motion of the said Sampson Merredeth and his giveing Security according to Law, Certificate is granted him for Obtaining a Probate in due form.

Sampson Merredeth Executor of the Last Will and Testament of John Stevens Deced: with Robert Richardson his Security entred into Bond for his faithfull Executorship of the said Deceds: Will and acknowledged the same in Court.

[page 318]

Peter Anderson, Peter Talbott, John Smith and William Smith or any three of them being first Sworn by some Majistrate of this County for that purpose, are Ordered to appraise the Estate of John Stevens deced: and make report of their proceedings therein to the next Court when Sampson Merredeth the Executor is to return the Inventory.

The Last Will and Testament of Henry Thompson Deced: was presented into Court by Sarah his Relict and Executrix who made Oath thereto and it being proved by the Oaths or Robert Richardson and Sampson Merredeth Wittnesses thereto is admitted to record, and on the motion of the said Sarah Thompson and her giveing Security according to Law, Certificate is granted her for Obtaaiing a Probate in Due form.

Sarah Thompson Executrix of Henry Thompson Deced: with John Jackson her security, entred into bond for her faithfull Executorship of the said Deceds: Will and acknowledged the same in Court.

Peter Anderson, Peter Talbott, John Smith and Wm. Smith or any three of them being first sworn by some Majistrate of this County for that purpose, are Ordered to appraise the Estate of Henry Thompson deced: and make report of their proceeding's therein to the next Court when Sarah Thompson the Exrx. is to return the Inventory.

The Last Will and Testament of William Jackson deced: was presented into Court by Martha his relict and Executrix who made Oath thereto, and it being proved by the Oath of John Hamersly a Wittness thereto, is admitted to record, and on the motion of the sd. Martha Jackson and her giveing Security according to Law, Certificate is granted her for Obtaining a Probate in Due form.

Martha Jackson Executrix of the Last Will and Testament of William Jackson deced: with John Hamersly & Edward Cocke her security's, entred into bond for her faithfull Executorship of the sd. Deceds. Will, and acknowledged the same in Court.

Peter Anderson, Peter Talbott, Timothy Bridges & Edward Avery or any three of them being first Sworn by some Majistrate of this County for that purpose, are Ordered to appraise the Estate of William Jackson deced: and make report of their proceeding's therein to the next Court, when Martha Jackson the Executrix is to return the Inventory.

Dorcas a Negro Girl belonging to Samuel Chappell is adjudged Nine years old.

[page 319]

Betty a Negro Girl belonging to James Fletcher is adjudged Seven years old.

The Last Will and Testament of John Midleton junr. Deced: was presented into Court by Edward Johnson, and there being no Executor appointed in the said Will, the said Edward made Oath thereto, and it being proved by the Oath's of Gilbert Passover and Richard Newman Wittnesses thereto is admitted to record, and on the sd. Edward Johnsons Motion and his giveing Security, according to Law, Certificate is granted him for Obtaining a Commission of Administration with the sd. Will annext in Due form.

Edward Johnson Admr. with the Will annext of John Midleton junr. Deced: with Edward Wyatt his Security, entred into Bond for his faithfull Administration of the sd. Deceds: Estate and acknowledged the same in Court.

Ordered that Edward Johnson Admr. with the Will annext of John Midleton Junr. Deced: return to the next Court an Inventory of the said Deceds: Estate.

Richard Pigeon in Open Court acknowledged his Deed for Land (Indented and Seald) with Livery of Seizin thereon, to Abram Heeth, on whose motion the same is Ordered to be recorded.

Richard Pigeon and Elizabeth Pigeon in Open Court acknowledged their Deed for Land (Indented and Seald) with Livery of Seizin thereon, to Peter Grammer on whose motion the same is Ordered to be recorded.

Robert Rivers Admr. &c: of Joan Hogwood Deced: returns an Inventory of the said Deceds: Estate, which is Ordered to be recorded.

In the action of Debt depending between Edward Hill and John Brewer, the Defendt. being permitted to plead Severall plea's, accordingly files his plea's to the plets: declaration, on whose motion time is granted him till next court to Consider the same.

The Information made by Edmond Irby agst. John Carter is Continued till next Court.

[page 320]

The action of Trespass Depending between John Carter and Edmd. Irby is Continued till next court.

Henry Holdcroft Exr. of Randall Platt Deced: being summoned to give an account of the Estate of Joseph Greenhill in his hands, the same being attacht. by Charles Chiswell, and he failling to prosecute the sd. Suit or Summons is Dismist.

The attachment granted Joshua Irby agst. the Estate of John Colson the plt. failing to prosecute is Dismist.

The attachment granted Joshua Irby agst. the Estate of William Stroud, the plt. failing to prosecute is Dismist.

The attachment granted Joshua Irby agst. the Estate of James Mayo, the plt. failing to prosecute is Dismist.

In the action on the case Depending between Thomas Simons and Nicholas Overby, the plt. Joins in the defts. demurrer, and the same is referred till next Court for Tryall.

The action on the case Depending between William Ranye & James Gretion, is referred till the next Court on the defts. cost.

Pursuant to the direction of the act concerning Jury's a Grandjury was Impannelled and Sworn, by the Name John Scott, Richard Cureton, George Hamelton, William Wallice, Mathew Smart, Timo: Grammar, John Cureton, Abram Odium, John Pooke, William Reves, Richard Warthen, Benja. Foster, Richard Tomlinson, James Jones, John Smith and Peter Anderson, who haveing reced: their charge were sent out and soon after return into Court with the following presentments, Vizt:

We the Jurors present Eliza. Daniel for bearing a Bastard Child &c

Mary Owen for bearing a Mallatto bastard Child

& Agnis Sheffeill for bearing a bastard Child.

Ordered that the Churchwardens of Waynoke Parrish prosecute Elizabeth Daniel, and Agnis Sheffell on the Grandjurys presentment made agst. them this day for haveing Bastard children.

Ordered that the Churchwardens of Westover Parrish prosecute Mary Owen on the Grandjurys presentment made agst. her this day for bearing a Mallatto Bastard Child.

In the suit in Chan: Depending between Sarah Jones and James Jones Exr. &c: of James Jones deced: the respondt. files a Demurrer to the [Complt.] Bill, on whoe motion time is granted her till next Court to Consider the same.

[page 321]

In the action depending between Joshua Irby and Mathew Smart the Last Courts order is Continued.

In the action Depending between Joshua Irby & Cornelius Fox the Last Courts Order is Continued.

In the action of Trespass depending between William Anderson & Henry Thweatt, the deft. pleads not Guilty and the plt. Joining in the Issue the same is referred till next Court for Tryall.

In the action on ye Case depending between Charles Williams and John Hynes, the plt. Joins in the defendts. demurrer, and the same is referred till next Court for Tryall.

In the action on ye Case depending between John Pook and Wm. Spiller, the deft. by his attorny pleads *nil debit* and the plt. Joining in the issue the same is referred till next Court for Tryall.

In the suit in Chan: depending between Frances Anderson Exrx. &c of Charles Anderson deced: Complt. and Henry Offley & Robt. Bolling respondts. on the sd. Bollings motion the cause is referred till next Court for The Complaint. to prove her accot.

In the suit in Chan: depending between John Bolling Complt. and Henry Offley and Robert Bolling respondts. on the sd. Bollings motion the cause is referred til lthe next Court for the Complt. to prove his accot.

In the action of Debt depending between Robert Bolling and William Hamlin for five hundred pound Sterling due by Bond &c: as in the plts: declaration is set forth, Nathaniel Harrison Esqr., Henry Harrison and Robert Hall Gent. are desired by the Cout (& by the consent of the partys) to settle the difference between the said plt. and Defendt. and make report of their proceedings therein to the next Court.

In the action of Detinue brot. by Sarah Wiggins (by William Killegrew her next Friend) agst. Richard Winkles, at the Last Court time was granted the deft. till this Court to plead, and being now called to do the same did not appear &c: thereupon on the motion of the plts: Attorny Judgement is granted her by *Nihil Dicit*.

The action on the case brot. by Henry Cabinis agst. John Wicketts neither party appearing, is Dismist.

[page 322]

In the action of Trespass brot: by William Short agst. Thomas Harrison the Defendt. files a plea to the plts: declaration, on whose motion time is granted him till next Court to Consider the same.

In the action of Trespass depending between Benjamin Foster and John Tomlinson, the defendt. by his attorny pleads not Guilty and the plt. Joining in the Issue, the same is referred till next Court for Tryall.

The action of Debt depending between Edmond Irby and John Carter is Continued till next Court.

In the action on the case depending between George Carter and John Let for Six pounds Tenn Shillings & Nine pence currt. mony due by account Dated 1718, the defendt. haveing pleaded nil debit and the plt. Joining in the Issue a Jury was Impannelled and Sworn to try the same, by Name Gilbert Hay, Thomas Booth, Thomas Weeks, Peter Anderson, John Pook, John Carter, Peter Gramar, Roger Reess, William Wallice, John Bonner, Edward Prince & Mathew Smart who haveing heard the Evidence and allegations of the said partys reced: their charge and were sent out and soon after return into Court with their Verdict, We find for the plaintiff One pound fifteen Shillings & Seven pence currt. mony. Gil. Hay, Foreman, which on the plts: motion is recorded and it is Considered by the Court that the plt. recover against the said Deft. the sd. Sum of One pound fifteen Shillings and Seven pence currt. mony, with Costs. Als: Exec:

And then the Court adjourn'd till Court in Course. Jno. Hamlin. Test Wm. Hamlin, Cl. Cur.

At a Court held at Merchantshope for Prince George County on the second Tuesday in June, being the fourteenth day of the said month, Anno Dom: 1720.

| Present | John Poythres, | Robert Munford, | Robt. Hall, |
| | Robert Bolling | & Lewis Green junr. | Gent. Justices. |

Griffin, an Indian Boy belonging to David Crawley, is adjudged five years old.

John Hardyman Gent. haveing a Commission from the Honble. the Lieut. Governr. to be Sherriff of this County he accordingly

[page 323]

takes the usuall Oaths of Allegiance &c: signs the Test and is Sworn Sherriff as aforesaid, he haveing first given Bond and Security according to Law.

John Hardyman Sherriff of this County, with John Poythres and Edward Goodrich his Security's, entred into Bond for his faithfull discharge of the said Office and trust of Sherriff &c: and acknowledged the same in Court, which is Ordered to be recorded, and accordingly is truly recorded as followeth.

Know all men by these presents that we John Hardyman, John Poythres and Edward Goodrich of Prince Geo: County are held and firmly do stand bound unto our soeveraign Lord George by the Grace of God of Great Brittain, France and Ireland King defender of the Faith &c: in the sum of One thousand pounds Sterling to which payment well and truly to be made to our said Soveraign Lord the King his heirs and Successors, we bind our Selves and every of us, our and every of our heirs, Executors and Admrs. Jointly and Severally firmly by these presents, In Witness whereof we have hereunto set our hands and Seals this 14th day of June 1720:

The condition of the above obligation is Such that whereof the above bounden John Hardyman by Virtue of a Commission from the Honble. the Lieut. Governor is this day Admitted and Sworn Sherriff of Prince George County. Now if the said John Hardyman shall well and truly Execute the sd. Office of Sherriff & faithfully do and perform all and every ct & Acts thing and things, relateing to and enjoined him in the sd. Office of Sherriff, during his Sherrivalty by Virtue of the Commission aforesaid, then this Obligation to be Void and of None Effect otherways to be and remain full power force and Vertue.

Signed Seald & Acknowledged in }
Open Court the 14. of June 1720.}
Test Wm. Hamlin, Cl. Cur.

[signed] John Hardyman {seal}
John Poythres {seal}
E. Goodrich {seal}

William Hardyman haveing taken the Usuall Oaths of Allegiance &c: signs the Test and is Sworn Under Sherriff of Prince George County.

[page 324]

On the Complaint of Robert Richardson that his Mallatto Sarvant Boy Named Tom, absented himselfe from his service Eight days, and that in recovering the said Sarvant &c: he Expended to the Value of three hundred and thirty pounds of Tobacco, the said boy being brought to the barr and failing to make any plea or defence &c: it is thereupon Ordered tha the sd. Boy Tom Serve his said Master for the time of his absence sixteen days, and for the sd. Disbursments four months and Nineteen days, after his present time of Service by Indenture or otherwise is Expired.

On the petition of Andrew Beck he is permitted to turn the main Road that Leads by his plantation, provided he make the same passable & Convenient.

The Last Will and Testament of Rebecca Limbry deced: was presented into Court by Elizabeth Limbry her Executrix, who made Oath thereto, and it being proved by the Oaths of Thomas Collier, Gilbert Gray & Samuel Magget Wittnesses thereto is admitted to record, and on the motion of the said Elizabeth Limbry and her giveing Security Certificate is granted her for Obtaining a Probate of the sd. Will in due form.

Elizabeth Limbry Executrix of the Last Will and Testament of Rebecca Limbry deced: with Robert Wilkins her security, entred into bond for ther faithfull Executorship of the said deceds: Will and acknowledged the same in Court.

Ordered that Elizabeth Limbry Executrix of the Last Will &c: of Rebecca Limbry deced: return to the next Court an Inventory of the said Deceds: Estate.

The Last Will and Testament of William Savage deced: was presented into Court by John Savage his Executor who made Oath thereto, and it being proved by the Oaths of Robert Hall, Robert Jones and Elizabeth Berryman Witnesses thereto is admitted to record, and on the motion of the said John Savage and his giveing Security according to Law, Certificate is granted him for Obtaining a Probate of the said Will in due form.

John Savage Executor of the Last Will and Testament of Wm. Savage deced: with William Savage and James Fletcher his Securitys, entred into Bond for his faithfull Executorship of the said deceds: Will, and acknowledged the same in Court.

Ordered that John Savage Executor of the Last Will and Testament of Wm. Savage deced: return to the next Court an Inventory of the said Deceds. Estate.

[page 325]

Martha Jackson Executrix of the Last Will and Testament of William Jackson deced: returns an Inventory &c: of the said Deceds: Estate, which is Ordered to be recorded.

John Tillman in Open Court acknowledged his Deeds of Lease and Release of Land (Indented and Seald) to John Kerby on whose motion they are admitted to record.

On the Complaint of James Gretion that his Sarvant boy Mathew Marshall absented himselfe from his Service Seventy days and that in recovering the said Sarvant he Expended two hundred pounds of Tobacco, the said Marshall being brot. to the barr and failing to make any Legall plea or defence, it is thereupon Ordered that the sd. Mathew Marshall do serve the said James Gretion for the time of his absence and Expense as aforesaid, Two hundred & thirty days, after his time by Indenture or otherwise is Expired.

Timothy Bridges came into Court and made Oath that Thomas Read deced: departed this Life intestate as farr as he knows or believes, and on his motion and giveing Security for his Just and faithfull Administration on the said deceds. Estate, Certificate is granted him for Obtaining Letters of Administration in due form.

Timothy Bridges Admr. of Thomas Read deced: with John Hamersly his security, entred into Bond for his faithfull Administration of the sd. Deceds: Estate, and acknowledged the same in Court.

Sarah Thompson Exrx. of Henry Thompson deced: returns an Inventory of the said Deceds: Estate, which is Ordered to be recorded.

The attachment awarded James Thweatt agst. the Estate of Wm. Jackson, neither parth appearing, is Dismist.

On the petition of William Hamlin he is permitted to keep a ferry from Maycocks to Coggans point & Westover. Ordered that he Constantly keep a good boat Sufficient to carry four horses and two able hands to attend the sd. Ferry, and that they be Exempt from paying Levy, whilst they continue to Serve therein, and also that they be Omitted in the List of Tithables of this present year.

[page 326]

In the suit in Chancery brought by Frances Anderson Executrix of the Last Will and Testament of Charles Anderson deced: against Henry Offley Late of London Merchant and Robert Bolling respondents, the said Complainant Sheweth that the said Charles Anderson in the year of our Lord One thousand Seven hundred & Sixteen, did put on board the ship *Josiah* of London whereof one Stephen Robin's was then Master, four hogsheads of Arronoco Tobacco which the said Charles Anderson Consigned unto the aforesaid Henry Offley to be disposed of on ye proper acount and for the sole benefit and advantage of the sd. Charles Anderson, and that she is Credibly Informed that the said Four hogsheads of Tobacco consigned as aforesaid, were Seized in Great Brittain for Debts due from the said Henry Offley to the Crown, and that the sd. four hogsheads of Tobacco (according to the price given for Tobacco in Great Brittain in the year aforesaid) are reasonably worth Twenty eight poungs Sterl: which the said Charles Anderson in his Lifetime never reced: any sattisfaction for, neither hath this Complt. since the decease of the sd. Charles Anderson reced: any sattisfaction for the said Tobacco, and the said Complt. further shwewth that she is informed that the aforesaid Henry Offley hath failed in his Credit and is withdrawn so that she cannot by common Law Obtain payment of what is due and that she is Likewise informed that Robert Bolling of this County is Indebted to the sd. Offley or hath Effects of his Sufficient to discharge the aforesaid debt, as in the sd. Complainants Bill is more particularly set forth, the said Robert Bolling appearing, confesses to have in his hands in Outstanding debts &c: of the said Offleys Estate, sufficient to discharge the said claim, and praying the complt. may prove her accot., She thereupon produces Severall Letters to convince the Court of the Justice thereof and also makeing Oath thereto, the Court do thereupon Value the said Tobacco at Twenty four pounds Sterl: and do desire that uon the said Complainants giveing Security to the said Bolling to Indemnifie him agst. the said Offley for so much, he the said Bolling do sattisfie and pay to the said Complainant out of the said Offleys debts in his hands, the said Sum of Twenty four pounds Sterling, in Tobacco at One penny per pound togather with Costs, and it is Ordered that an Attornys Fee be Taxed to the Bill of Costs of this Suit.

In the suit in Chancery brought by John Bolling agst. Henry Offley Late of London Merchant and Robert Bolling respondts: the said Complainant Sheweth that he in the year of our Lord, One thousand Seven hundred and Sixsteen did put on board the Ship *Josiah* of London, whereof one Stephen Robins was then Master, Eight Hogsheads of Arronoco Tobacco, which he did consign to the aforesaid

[page 327]

Offley, to be disposed of, on the proper account and for the sole benefit and advantage of the sd. John Bolling, and that he is Credibly Informed that the said Eight Hogsheads of Tobacco consigned as aforesaid, were seized in Great Brittain for debts due from the said Offley to the Crown, and that the said Eight Hogsheads of Tobacco (according to the price given for Tobacco in Great Brittain in the year aforesaid) are reasonably worth fifty five pounds Fifteen Shillings Sterl: which the sd. Complt. never reced. any Sattisfaction for, and the sd. Complt. further sheweth that he is inofrmed that the aforesaid Henry Offley hath failed in his Credit and is withdrawn so that by Common Law he cannot Obtain payment of what is due, and that he is Likewise informed that Robert Bolling of this County is Indebted to the said Offley orhath Effects of his sufficient to discharge the aforesaid debt as in the complts. Bill is more particularly set forth ye sd. Robt: Bolling appearing, Confesses to have in his hands in Outstanding debts &c: of the said Offleys Estate, sufficient to discharge the said Claim, and praying the Complt. may prove the same to be Just, he thereupon files his accot. and makes Oath thereto, and on his motion it is decreed by the Court that upon his the sd. Complaints. giveing Security to the said Bolling to Indemnifie him agst. the sd. Offley for soe much, he the sd. Robert Bolling do sattisfie and pay to the said John Bolling out of the said Offleys debts in his hands, the Sum of Forty Eight pounds Sterling in Tobacco at one penny per pound, being the Value of the said Eight hogsheads of Tobacco as Valued by the Court, togather with Costs, and it is Ordered that an Attornys Fee be Taxed to the Bill of Costs of this suit.

On the petition of Robert Enon he is Exempt from paying Levy for the future.

On the motion of Majr. Bolling in Behalfe of Saml. Burch he is Exempt from paying Levy for the future.

In the action of Debt brot. by John Soane agst. John Lett for four pounds due by Bill dated the fifteenth of August 1716, the defendt. came personally into Court and Confest Judgement to the plt. for fifty Six Shillings current mony, being the Ballance due on the said Bill, and on the sd. plts: motion it is Ordered that the sd. deft. pay to the said plt. the sd. Sum of fifty Six Shillings & Costs. Als. Exec:

[page 328]

In the action on the case brot. by James Fontaine agst. Peter Anderson for thirty Seven Shillings and Eight pence halfe penny due by accot. dated 1718, the defendt. appearing, and the sd. accot. being Examined and Settled in Court and the defendt. appearing to be indebted to the plt. thirty One Shillings and Sven pence halfe penny, on the motion of his attorny it is Ordered that the sd. deft. pay to the said plt. the said Sum of Thirty one Shillings and Seven pence halfe penny wth. Costs. Als. Exec:

The action on the case brot. by Henry Harrison agst. George Mallone, the plt. failing to prosecute is Dismist.

In the action of debt brot. by William Bridges agst. Wm. Jackson deft. for Twenty five Shillings due by Bill dated the Tenth of April 1718, Edward Goodrich became Special bail for the sd. deft. and also as his Attorny confest Judgement to the plt. for the sd. Sum, and on the motion of his Attorny it is Ordered that the sd. deft. pay to the said plt. the aforesaid Sum & Costs. Als. Exec:

The action on the case brot. by William Kennon agst. John Reams, the plt. failing to prosecute, is Dismist.

The action of Trespass brot. by Bartholomew Crowder agst. William Mitchell, the plt. failing to prosecute, is dismist.

In the action on the case brot. by Henry Batte Admr. of Thos. Harwell deced: agst. Saml. Harwell Junr. deft., James Gretion became Special Bail for the sd. deft. and on the motion of his attorny an Imparlance is granted him till the next Court.

The action on the case brot. by Richard Bland agst. [Jas.] Hall, neither parth appearing, is dismist.

The acton on the case brot. by Richard Bland agst. Wm. Davis neither party appearing, is dismist.

The action on the case brot. by Thos. Dinkins agst. Hannah Claud Admrx. of Phillip Claud deced: neither party appearing, is dismist.

The action on the case brot. by Lydia Clements Exrx. &c: agst. Eliza: Mallory, Jno. Hamlin and Edward Goodrich Exrs. &c. is Continued till next Court.

The action of Trespass depending between Roger Taylor & John Berry, the plt. failing to prosecute, is Dismist.

[page 329]

The action of Trespass depending between George Hamelton and John Berry, the plt. failing to prosecute, is dismist.

In the action of Detinue brot. by William Cooke and Rebecca his Wife against James Jones, at the Last Court the plts: recovered Judgement agst. the deft. who moved to arrest the same and failed his reasons which were referred till this Court to be argued and the attornys of the said partys appearing and the sd. reasons being accordingly argued are adjudged insufficient to arrest the said Judgemt. whereupon on the motion of the plts: Attorny the Judgement aforesaid is affirmed wth. Costs.

In the action on the case brot. by Humphrey Bell & Henry Dee agst. Elizabeth Mallory, John Hamlin and Edward Goodrich Executors of Francis Mallory deced: Thos. Eldridge entred himself Security to pay all costs and amages that shall be awarded the defts. &c: whereupon an Imparlance is granted the defts. till next Court.

In the action on the case brot. by John Berry agst. Nathl. Harrison Esqr. Admr. of Richard Pigeon deced:, the plt. not appearing on the motion of the defts. attorny it is Ordered that he be Nonsuit & pay the said deft. five Shillings with Costs. Als. Exec: and it is Ordered that an Attornys Fee be taxed to the Bill of Costs of this suit.

Sampson Merredeth Exr. &c: of John Stevens deced: returns an Inventory &c: of the said deceds: Estate, which is Ordered to be recorded.

On the motion of Robert Poythres he is Exempt from paying Levy for his Negro woman Sue.

In the action on the case brot. by Eliza. Mallory, John Hamlin and Edward Goodrich Exrs. of Francis Mallory deced: agst. Jos. Irby, Majr. Robert Munford became Special Bail for the sd. Deft. who thereupon appears, and on his motion Oyer of the plts: accot. is granted him and time till the next Court to consider ye same.

Thomas Taylor haveing attended four days as an Evidence for William Cooke &c: agst. James Jones, it is Ordered that

[page 330]
the said Cooke pay him for the same One hundred and Sixty pounds of Tobacco, with Costs. Als. Exec:

The action on the case brot. by James Loftin agst. Richd. Lewis neither party appearing, is dismist.

The action on the case brot. by Eliza. Mallory, John Hamlin and Edward Goodrich Exrs. of Fra. Mallory deced: agst. Adam Ivie admr. of John Tiller deced: is referred till next Court.

John Poythres, Robert Poythres and John Woodleife, haveing taken the usual Oaths of Allegiance &c: & Signed the Test, are sworn Vestrymen of Westover Parrish.

And then the Court adjourn'd till Court in Course. Jno. Poythres. Test. Wm. Hamlin, Cl. Cur.

On the 12th day of July 1720, John Gill Exhibitted the following Judgement and desired the same might be recorded that Execution might Issue thereon, Vizt.
Pr. Geo. County Ss.

At the Complaint of John Gill against James Moody that the said Moody is Justly in his debt [...] barrell of Corn which was due by a Bill and the Bill was Lost by Misfortune, and the said John Gill, being ready to make Oath that it was still justly due to him from the said Moody and the said Moody refuseing to make Oath that it was not due, and the said Gill made Oath that it was Justly due to him from the said Moody, and it appeared by other Evidence that heard the said Moody say that the debt was Justly due to the said Gill and that he would pay it notwithstanding the Bill was Lost, it is therefore Ordered that James Moody pay John Gill one Barrell of Indian Corn with Cost of Suit Elce Execution, given under my hand the 18th day of May 1720. [signed Samson Merredeth]

The Constables Fees   30 l Tobo.
To John Smith for 2 day's }
attendance as an Evidence}   30 l Tob.

Truly Recorded pr. Wm. Hamlin, Cl. Cur.

[page 331]
At a Court held at Merchantshope for the County of
Prince George, on the Second Tuesday in August, being the
Ninth day of the said month, Anno Dom: 1720.

Present   John Hamlin,   Robt. Munford   }
           Robt. Hall   & Robt. Bolling   } Gent. Justices

Robert Hall, Executor of Thomas Harrison deced: returns an Inventory & Appraisment of the said Deceds: Estate, which is Ordered to be recorded.

Antilla, a Negro Girl belonging to Lewis Green Junr. is adjudged Nine years old.
Dol, a Negro Girl belonging to Hugh Golightly is Adjudged Eight years old.
Jack, a Negro Boy belonging to Lewis Green Senr. is Adjudged Ten years old.
Pegg, a Negro Girl belonging to Charles Williams is Adjudged Nine years old.
Present John Poythres, Gent.
Thomas Brian, a Sarvant Boy belonging to John Coleman, is Adjudged fifteen years old.
Robin, a Negro Boy belonging to Thomas Harrison, is Adjudged Nine years old.
Bob, a Negro Boy belonging to James Harrison, is Adjudged five years old.
Cato, a Negro Boy belonging to David Poythres, is Adjudged twelve years old.
Mingo, a Negro Boy belonging to George Rives, is Adjudged fifteen years old.

On the petition of Hugh Golightly and Others, it is Ordered that the main Road that Leads by Andrew Becks Plantation remain as it formerly was, and that the said Beck be not permitted to turn or alter the same.

William Garvell, a Sarvant Boy belonging to William Parsons, is adjudged Nine years old.

[page 332]

The Last Will and Testament of Henry Cabanis deced: was presented into Court by Francis Epes Junr. one of his Executors and Mary Cabanis the other Executrix haveing refused to take on her the Burthen and Execution of the said Will, the said Francis Epes made Oath thereto, and it being proved by the Oaths of Drury Bolling and John Fitzgerrald Witnesses thererto, is Admitted to record, and on the motion of the said Francis Epes and his Giveing Security according to Law, Certificate is granted him for obtainin a Probate of the said Will in due form.

Francis Epes Junr. Executor of the Last Will and Testament of Henry Cabinis Deced: Drury Bolling his Security entred into Bond for his faithfull Executorship of the said Deceds: Will and Acknowledged the same in Court.

John Fitzgerrald, John Peterson junr., William Epes and Edwd. Epes or any three of them being first Sworn by some Majistrate of this County for that purpose, are Ordered to appraise the Estate of Henry Cabinis Deced: and make report of their proceedings therein to the next Court when Francis Epes Junr. the Executor is to return the Inventory.

The Last Will and Testament of John Livesay deced: was presented into Court by Joan Livesay his Executrix, who made Oath thereto and it being proved by the Oaths of John Scott, Bethyer Scott & John Scott junr. the Wittnesses thereto, is Admitted to record, and on the motion of the sd. Joan Livesay Certificate is granted her for Obtaining a Probate of the said Will in Due form.

Ordered that Joan Livesay Executrix of the Last Will & Testament of John Livesay deced: return to the next Court an Inventory of the said Deceds: Estate.

Ordered that the Sherriff repair the Common Gaol of this County and make the same according to Law, and bring an account of his Disbursement to the next Levy Court for allowance.

Present John Peterson, Gent.

Robert Williamson and Richard Jones, who were taken up and Comitted on Suspicon of being Runaway Sarvants, and being brought to the Barr in Custody and Examined, and they refuseing to declare to whom they belong, and the Court being of Opinion that they are Runaway Sarvants do thereupon Order that they the said Williamson & Jones be convey'd from Constable to Constable, till they come to the Publick Gaol at Williamsburg, there to be kept till they be delivered thence by due course of Law.

[page 333]

William Temple Junr. Admr. of James Howard Deced: returns an Inventory and Appraisment of the said Deceds: Estate, which is Ordered to be recorded.

The Order that Adam Ivie Executor of Eliza. Ivie deced: return an Inventory of the sd. Deceds: Estate, is Continued till next Court.

The Order that Edward Johnson Admr. &c: of John Middleton Deced: return an Inventory of the Deceds: Estate, is Continued till the next Court.

William Temple Junr. Admr. of James Howard Deced: Exhibitted into Court an accot. Dr. & Cr. of the said Deceds: Estate, which being Examined and allowed by the Court, is Ordered bo te recorded.

On the motion of Sampson Merredeth, Thomas Eldridge is Entred his Genrall Attorny in all causes wherein hs is concerned.

An[d] then the Court adjourn'd till Court in Course. John Poythres. Test Wm. Hamlin, Cl. Cur.

At a Court held at Merchantshope for the County of
Prince George on the second Teusday in September
being the thirteenth day of the said month, Anno
Dom: 1720.

Present	John Hamlin,	John Poythres,	Robt. Munford
	Robert Hall	& John Peterson.	Gent. Justices

Charles Howell in Open Court acknowledged his Deeds of Lease and Release of Land (Seald) to John Fitzgerrald on whose motion they are Admitted to record.

[page 334]

Sambo, a Negro boy, belonging to John Hatch, is adjudged Seven years Old.

Jenny, a Negro Girl belonging to John Poythres is adjudged Eleven years Old.

York, a Negro boy belonging to Edward Burchet is Adjudged thirteen years old.

John Savage Executor &c of William Savage deced: returns an Inventory of the said deceds. Estate, which is Ordered to be recorded.

John Hardy, who was taken up and committed on Suspicon of being a runaway Sarvant, and being brought to the barr in custody of the Sherr: & Examined, and he confessing himselfe to belong to Charles Stagg of Williamsburgh, it is thereupon ordered that he be conveyed from Constable to Constable till he be delivered to his said Master.

Sarah Buckner Reliect of Larrance Buckner deced: came into Court and made Oath that the said Larrance Buckner departed this Life without makeing any Will as farr as she knows or believes, and on her motion and giveing Security for her Just and faithfull Administration on the said deceds. Estate, Certificate is granted her for Obtaining a Commission of Administration in Due form.

Sarah Buckner Admrx. &c of Larrance Buckner deced: togather with Thomas Clifton her security entred into bond for her Just and faithfull Administration on the said Deceds. Estate, and acknowledged the same in Court.

Peter Anderson, Benjamin Reeks, Thomas Scarbro, and Peter Talbott or any three of them being first Sworn by Some Majistsrate of this County for that purpose, are Ordered to Appraise the Estate of Larrance Buckner deced: and make report of thier proceedings therein to the next Court, when Sarah Buckner the Admrx. is to return the Inventory.

John Scott in Open Court acknowledged his Deed for Land (seald) to his son John Scott, on whose motion the ame is Ordered to be recorded.

The Last Will and Testament of Elizabeth Hamlin deced: was prosented into Court by John Hamlin and William Hamlin her Executors who made Oath thereto, and it being proved by the Oaths of Gilbert Hay, Elizabeth Troughton and Rebecca Jones Wittnesses thereto, is

[page 335]

Admitted to record, and on the motion of the said John Hamlin and William Hamlin, Certificate is granted them for Obtaining a Probate fo the said Will in due form.

John Hatch, Gilbert Hay, Adam Tapley & William Harrison or any three of them being first sworn by some Majistrate of this County for that purpose, are Ordered to appraise the Estate of Elizabeth Hamlin deced: and make report of their proceedings there[on] to the next Court when John Hamlin and William Hamlin the Exeucotrs are to return the Inventory thereof.

A Deed for Land (Indented and Seald) with Livery of Seizin from Robert Richardson and Mary his Wife to Nathaniel Harrison Esqr. was proved in Court by the Oaths of Edward Shepheard and Nathaniel Edwards Witnesses thereto, to be the Act and Deed of the said Robert Richardson and Mary his Wife to the said Nathaniel Harrison, and is Admitted to record.

Ordered that Mr. John Hardyman's Storehouse be held, deemed & taken to be the Common Gaol of this County, till the County Gaol shall be repaired.

The action of Debt brot. by Robert Bolling agst. William Ham[lin] the plt. failing to prosecute, is dismist.

In the action of Trespass brought by William Short agst. Thomas Harrison, the plt. files a replication to the defendants plea, who Joins in the Issue therein tendered, and the same is referred till next Court for Tryall.

The action of Trespass depending between Benja. Foster and John Tomlinson, the plt. failing to prosecute, is dismist.

The action on the case brot. by Henry Jones agst. Wm. Jackson the plt. failing to prosecute, is dismist.

The action of Trespass brot. by Wm. Anderson junr. agst. Stephen Evans, the plt. failing to prosecute, is dismist.

The action on the case brot. by John Blaine agst. John Lett, the plt. failing to prosecute, is Dismist.

The action on the case brot. by John Epes agst. Edward Epes, the plt. failing to prosecute, is dismist.

[page 336]

The action on the case brot. by John Blaine agst. John Lett, the plt. failing to prosecute, is Dismist.

In the actin on the case brot. by Joshua Irby agst. John Ellis junr. for Tenn pounds current mony due by account dated the 3d of July 1720, the Defendt. being returned *non est Inventus* and not appearing, on the plts. motion an Attachment is awarded him against the said Defendts. Estate for the said Sum & Costs returnable to the next Court for Judgement, for what shall appear to be due.

The action on the case brot. by Adam Ivie agst. Gilbert Ivie, the plt. failing to prosecute, is Dismist.

The action on the case brot. by William Ray agst. Daniel Megirt, the plt. failing to prosecute, is Dismist.

In the action on the case brot. by John Hatch agst. James Lee for two pounds Eighteen Shillings and Ten pence halfe penny due by accot. &c: the defendt. being called and not appearing and Joshua Irby being returned Security for him, on the plts: motion Judgement is granted him agst. the said Defendt. and the aforesaid Joshua Irby for the said Sum & Costs unless the said Deft. shall appear at the next Court and answer the said action.

Thomas Simmons made Complaint that William Jackson stands Indebted to him by account dated 1720, the sum of four pounds twelve Shillings and Seven pence halfe penny, and set forth that the said Jackson hath unlawfully departed this County so that the Ordinary process at Law cannot be served on him, whereupon he by Virtue of an Attachment under the hand of One of His Majestys Justices for this County, returnable to this Court hath ceased part of the Estate of the said Jackson to be Attacht. for payment thereof, Vizt: Two beds and bedsteads, two blanketts, one Sheet, One pillow, One Iron pott, two pails, One small Table, One small Desk, two pewter dishes, One porringer, One chest, One Jug, One plate, One Earthen dish, One small powdering Tubb, Six bottles, the crop of Tobo. and Corn (if any more than the rent, which is five hundred & thirty pounds of Tobacco), One old Anvill, One pair of Bellows, One Vice and other Small things in the shop, And the said Jackson being called and failling to appear to replevye the same, and the said plt. makeing Oath the said Sum is Justly due to him, thereupon Judgement is granted him agst. the said William Jackson for the said Sum & Costs, to be Levyed on the Estate Attacht. as aforesaid. Ordered that the Sherr: cause the said Estate to be duly appraised by Richard Tomlinson, Thomas Weeks, Wm.

[page 337]

Reess and Richard Reess or any three of them, being first Sworn for that purpose by some Majistrate of this County, and delivered the said Thomas Simmons for payment of the above Judgement, and make report of their proceedings.

John Simmons made Complaint that William Jackson stands Indebted to him by account dated 1719, the sum of Forty Two Shillings and Eleven pence, and Set forth that the said William Jackson hath unlawfully departed this County so that the Ordinary process at Law cannot be served on him, whereupon he by Virtue of an Attachment under the hand of One of his Majestys Justices for this County returnable to this Court hath caused part of the Estate of the said William to be Attacht. for payment thereof, Vizt: three head of Cattle, four Hoggs, One Kersey Coat. And the said William being called and failling to appear to replevy the same, and the plt. makeing Oath the said Sum is Justly due to him, thereupon Judgement is granted him against the said Wm. for the said Sun & Costs, to be Levied on the Estate attacht. as aforesaid. Ordered that the Sherr: cause the said Estate to be duly Appraised by Richard Tomlinson, Thomas Weeks, William Reess and Richard Reess, or any three of them being first Sworn for that purpose by some Majistrate of this County, and delivered the said John Simmons for payment of the above Judgement, and make report of their proceedings.

In the action of Debt brot. by John Lett agst. Charles Royall, Geo: Brewer became Special Bail for the deft. who thereupon appears and Confesses Judgement to the plt. for forty Shillings current mony wch. became due to the sd. plt. by Bill dated the fourth day of August 1719. It is thereupon Ordered that the said deft. pay to the said plt. the aforesaid Sum & Costs. Als: Exec:

The attachment awarded Timothy Grammar agst. the Estate of William Jackson, is Continued till the next Court.

The Attachment awarded Richard Cureton agst. the Estate of Wm. Jackson, is Continued till the next Court.

In the action on the case brot. by Buller Herbert against William Anderson junr. for fourteen pounds Eighteen Shillings and Nine pence, due by accot. &c: the defendt. being called & not appearing, nor any Security returned for him on the motion of the plts: Attorny Judgement is granted him agst. the said defendt. and John Hardyman Sherr: &c: for the said Sum & Costs, unless the said defendt. shall appear at the next Court and answer the said Action.

And then the Court Adjourn'd till Court in Course. John Hamlin. Test Wm. Hamlin, Cl. Cur.

[page 338]

At a Court held at Merchantshope in Prince George County
on Monday the thirty first day of October, Anno Dom: 1720, for
proof of Publick Claims, and for receiveing and Certifying to the
Genrall Assembly the Propositions and Grievances of the Inhabitants of this County.

Present	John Hamlin,	John Poythres,	Robert Munford	
	Robert Hall,	Lewis Green junr.	& John Peterson	Gentlemen Justices

Ordered that the Clerke make out a Certificate to the next Session of the Genrall Assembly, that there hath been Levied & paid inthis County for Wolves killed and Destroyed therein, in the years 1718 and 1719, the sum of Seven thousand, Nine hundred pounds of Tobacco, and also Seven hundred and Ninety pounds of Tobacco to the Sherrif for collecting and paying the aforesaid Sum, amounting in the whole to Eight thousand, six hundred and Ninety pounds of Tobacco.

Sundry Proposition's and Grievances of the Inhabitants of this County, written on one Sheet of paper, were presented into Court and Signed by the freeholders and Inhabitants of the said County Subscribed thereto, which are Ordered to be Certified to the next Session of the Genrall Assembly.

And then the Court Adjourn'd. John Hamlin. Test Wm. Hamlin, Cl. Cur.

At a Court held at Merchantshope for the County of
Prince George on the Second Tuesday in December, being
the thirteenth day of the said Month, Anno Dom: 1720.

| Present | Robert Hall, | Sampson Merredeth | } | |
| | Lewis Green junr. | & John Peterson | } | Gent. Justices |

William Hamlin haveing produced a Commission from the Honble. Alexander Spotswood Esq. His Majesty's Lieut. Governor &c of Virga. to be admitted and Continued Clerk of Prince George County Court he accordingly takes the Oaths appointed by Law to be taken, Signs the Test, and is Sworn Clerke of the County Court aforesaid.

[page 339]

Francis Poythres in Open Court acknowledged his Deed for Land (Indented and Seald) with Livery of Seizin endorst. thereon, to John Poythres, on whose motion the same is Ordered to be recorded.

Ned, a Negro Boy belonging to Robert Munford, is adjudged Eleven years old.

Glocester, a Negro Boy belonging to Robert Munford, is adjudged Tenn years old.

Peter, a Negro Boy belonging to Robert Munford, is Adjudged Nine years old.

Venus, a Negro Girl belonging to Robert Munford, is adjudged Nine years old.

Nancy & Belinda, Negro Girls belonging to Robert Munford, are Adjudged Eight years old each.

Adam Sims, his Deeds of Lease and Release of Land (Seald) to John Ledbetter, were proved in Court by the Oaths of Gilbert Hay, William Hardyman and William Hamlin and on the motion of the said John Ledbetter the sd. Deeds are admitted to record.

William Smith came into Court and made Oath that Francis Longmore deced: departed this Life without makeing any Will as farr as heknows or believes, and on his motion and giveing Security for his just & faitnfull Administration on the said Deceds: Estate, Certificate is granted him for Obtaining Letters of Administration in Due form.

William Smith with John Smith his Security entred into Bond for his faithfull Administration on the Estate of Francis Longmore Deced: and acknowledged the same in Court.

Peter Anderson, Peter Talbott, Thos: Scarbro & Robert Rivers or any three of them being first Sworn for that purpose by some Majistrate of this County, are Ordered to Appraise the Estate of Francis Longmore deced: and make report of their proceedings therein to the next Court when William Smith the Administrator is to return the Inventory thereof.

The Last Will and Testament of John Rivers deced: was presented into Court by Mary Rivers his Executrix who made Oath thereto and it being proved by the Oaths of Edmond Onal and John Hollowell Wittnesses thereto is Admitted to record, and On the motion of the said Mary Rivers and her giveing Security according to Law, Certificate is granted her for Obtaining a Probate of the said Will in due form.

[page 340]

Mary Rivers with John Holloway her security entred into Bond for her faithfull Executorship of the Last Will and Testament of John Rivers deced: and acknowledged the same in Court.

John Hynes, John Burrow, William Rives & Michael Rosser junr. or any three of them being first Sworn for that purpose by some Majistsrate of this County, are Ordered to appraise the Estate of John Rivers deced: and make report of their proceedings therein to the next Court, when Mary Rivers the Executrix is to return the Inventory thereof.

The Last Will and Testament of Nicholas Wyatt deced: was presented into Court by Edward Wyatt his Executor, who made Oath thereto, and it being proved the the Oaths of John Hamersly and Richard Cate, Wittnesses thereto, is admitted to record, and on the motion of the said Edward Wyatt and his giveing Security, Certificate is granted him for Obtaining a Probate of the said Will in Due form.

Edward Wyatt Executor of the Last Will and Testament of Nicholas Wyatt deced: with John Hamersley & Timothy Bridges his Securitys, entred into Bond for this faithfull Executorship of the said Deceds: Will, and acknowledged the same in Court.

Present Robert Bolling, Gent.

On the petition of Thomas Raines, John Woodleife, Edward Woodleife, Roger Ranye, John Whittmore, Shan Raines, Peter Leeth, Arthur Leeth, Thos. Burge, John Burge, Richard Tidmarsh, William Livesay & George Brewer, it's Ordered that they clear a road from a branch runing out of Joans Hole Swamp and heading agst. Waurick Swamp and thence along the ridge between the said Swamps to Mockoson=neck road, and that Thomas Raines be Overseer thereof.

Ordered that a Road be cleared from Mockoson=neck Bridge to Stony Creeke Bridge, and that George Tillman be Overseer thereof.

Resolved that the Court will Lay the County Levy, the day after the next Court to be held for this County.

Francis Anderson and Edward Hill in Open Court acknowledged thier Bond to Robert Bolling, Ordered it be recorded.

[page 341]

In the action on the case brought by Henry Holdcroft Executor of the Last Will and Testament of Randle Platt Deced: against Elizabeth Duke Administratrix of the Goods and Chattels of Henry Duke deced: for three pounds Nine Shillings and a penny due by accot. dated the 21st day of April 1718, the defendt. appears & moves the plt. may prove his accot. whereupon he makes Oath thereto and on his motion it is Ordered that the sd. Defendt. pay to the said Plt. out of the Estate of the aforesaid Henry Duke deced: the said Sum of three pounds Nine Shillings and a penny wth. Costs. Als: Exec:

On the petition of John Scott setting forth that he hath Land on the Birchen Swamp above John Hardymans Mill convenient to build a Water Mill on, and praying Liberty of this Court to perform the same, the said Hardyman appears in Court and Opposes the said Petition, whereupon it is deferred till the next Court for better consideration.

And then the Court adjourn'd till Court in Course. R. Hall. Test. Wm. Hamlin, Cl. Cur.

At a Court held at Merchantshope for the County of Prince
George on the second Tuesday in January, being the Tenth day
of the said month, Anno Dom: 1720[/1].

Present	John Hamlin,	John Poythres	}	
	Robt. Hall,	Robt. Bolling	}	
	Lewis Green	& John Peterson	}	Gent. Justices

Francis Epes Exr. of Henry Cabinis Deced: returns an Inventory and Appraisment of the said Deceds: Estate, which is Ordered to be recorded.

Joan Livesay Exrx. of John Livesay deced: returns an Inventory of the sd. Deceds: Estate, which is Ordered to be recorded.

Adam Tapley in Open Court acknowledged his Deeds of Lease & Relase of Land (Indented and Seald) to Alexander Tapley, on whose motion the same are Odered to be recorded.

[page 342]

Adam Tapley in Open Court acknowledged his Deed of Release of Land (Indented and Seald) to Alexander Tapley on whose motion the same is Ordered to be recorded.

Elizabeth Troughton, Relict of William Troughton deced: came into Court and made Oath that the said William Troughton departed this Life without makeing any Will as farr as she knows or believes, and on her motion and giveing Security as the Law directs, Certificate is granted her for Obtaining Letters of Administration in due form.

Elizabeth Troughton, Admrx. of William Troughton deced: wth. John Hamersly and William Harrison her securitys entred into Bond for her Faithfull Administration on the said Deceds: Estate, and acknowledged the same in Court.

John Hamlin, Gilbert Hay, James Harrison & John Wilkins or any three of them being first sworn by some Majistrate of this County for that purpose, are Ordered to appraise the Estate of William Troughton Deced: and make report of their proceedings therein to the next Court when Elizabeth Troughton the Administratrix is to return the Inventory thereof.

John Bolling and Robert Munford in Open Court acknowledged their Bond to Robert Bolling. Ordered it be recorded.

On the motion of Drury Bolling, Thomas Eldridge is Entred his Genrall Attorny in all causes &c: wherein the said Bolling is concerned.

John Hamlin, Robert Hall, John Baird, Edmond Irby, John Hatch, John Woodleife, John Poythres, Timothy Bridges, James Harrison, William Harrison & John Scott, being chose Vestrymen for the Parrish of Martin Brandon, they accordingly appear in Court and take the Oaths appointed by Law, sign the Test, and are sworn Vestrymen of the Parrish aforesaid.

The Last Will and Testament of Edward Goodrich deced: was presented into Court by Margaret Goodrich an Executrix named in the said Will who made Oath thereto; and it being proved by the Oaths of Gilbert Hay, Arthur Biggins and Ephraim Vernon Wittnesses thereto is Ordered to be recorded, and on the motion of the said Margaret Goodrich and her giveing Security according to Law, Certificate is granted her for Obtaining a Probate of the said Will in Due form.

Margaret Goodrich Executrix of the Last Will and Testament of Edward Goodrich deced: with. Nathaniel Harrison Esqr. and John Hatch her Securitys, entered into Bond for her faithfull Executorship of the said Deceds: Will and acknowledged the same in Court.

[page 343]

John Poythres, Edmond Irby, Gilbert Hay and William Harrison or any three of them being first sworn for that purpose by some Majistrate of this County, are Ordered to appraise the Estate of Edward Goodrich deced: and make report of their proceedings therein to the next Court, when Margaret Goodrich the Executrix is to return the Inventory thereof.

Robert Hall in Open Court acknowledged his Deed (Seald) to Ellinor Harrison and Others. Ordered the said Deed be recorded.

And then the Court Admourn'd till Tomorrow Morning Ten a Clock. John Poythres. Test. Wm. Hamlin, Cl. Cur.

At a Court held at Merchantshope for the County of
Prince George on Wednesday the Eleventh day of January
Anno Dom: 1720[/1].

Present   John Hamlin,   John Poythres   }
          Robt. Munford   & Robert Hall   }   Gent. Justices

On the motion of Thomas Simmons, it is Ordered that Lycence Issue for his keeping an Ordinary at the usuall place near the Court house of this County, he haveing given Bond and Security as the Law directs.

Thomas Simmons with Thomas Simmons junr. his Security entred in Bond for his keeping an Ordinary &c: according to Law, and acknowledged the same in Court.

The action of Debt brought by Edward Hill against John Brewer, the plt. failing to prosecute is Dismist.

The Information made by Edmond Irby against John Carter the plt. failing to prosecute is Dismist.

The action of Trespass brought by John Carter agst. Edmond Irby, the plt. failing to prosecute is Dismist.

The action of Debt brot. by Edmond Irby agst. John Carter, the plt. failing to prosecute, is Dismist.

[page 344]

The action on the case brot. by Thomas Simmons agst. Nicholas Overby is referred for Tryall till the next Court & on the plts: costs.

In the suit in chancery brot. by Sarah Jones agst. James Jones Exr. of James Jones deced: the plt. Joins in the Defendts. Demurrer, and the same is referred till next Court for Tryall.

In the action of Trespass upon the case Depending between Joshua Irby and Mathew Smart junr. for breach of covenants &c: the Gentlemen appointed at a former court to settle the difference between then, make their report in writeing, which on the plts: motion is recorded as follows, Vizt:

In obedience to the within Order we the subscribers have settled and Adjusted the difference between the within named Jos. Irby & Mathew Smart, and Order the said Mathew Smart pay the said Jos. Irby the sum of Four pounds two Shillings and three pence wth. Costs &c: [signed] Robt. Bolling, Robt. Munford. June ye 14th 1720.

And on the motion of the said plt. it is Ordered that the said Mathew Smart pay to the said Joshua Irby the said Sum of Four pounds, two Shillings and three pence and costs. Als: Exec:

The action depending between Jos. Irby and Cornelius Fox is referred till the next Court.

The action of Trespass depending between William Anderson and Henry Thweatt, the plt. failing to prosecute, is Dismist.

The action on the case depending between Charles Williams and John Hynes, is referred till next court for Tryall & on the plts: cost.

In the action on the case depending between John Pook and Wm. Spiller the plt. failing to prosecute, on the motion of the defts. attorny, it is Ordered that the sd. plt. be nonsuit and pay the said Defendt. five shillings with Costs. Als. Exec:

The action of Detinue brot. by Sarah Wiggins &c: agst. Richard Winkles, neither party appearing, is Dismist.

In the action of Debt brot. by David Crawley agst. Stephen Evans for twenty Shillings due by Bill &c: the defendt. being called and not appearing, nor any Security returned for him on the plts: motion Judgement is granted him agst. the said Deft. and James Thweatt late Sherr: &c: for the said Sum & Costs, unless the said Defendt. shall appear at the next Court and answer the said action.

Elizabeth Limbry Exrx. of Rebecca Limbry deced: returns an Inventory of the said Deceds: Estate, which is Ordered to be recorded.

[page 345]

In the action of Trespass upon the case brot. by Henry Batte Admr. of Thomas Harwell deced: agsist Samuel Harwell junr. Damage twenty pounds Current mony &c: at the Last Court an Imparlance was granted the defendt. & time till this Court to plead, and being now called to do the same, did not appear &c: thereupon & on the plts. motion Judgemt. is granted him by *Nihil dicit.*

The action on the case brot. by Lydia Clements Exrx. of Francis Clements Deced: agst. Eliza. Mallory, John Hamlin and Edward Goodrich Exrs. of Francis Mallory Deced: is referred till the next Court.

The action on the case brot. by Humphrey Bell & Henry Dee agst. Eliza: Mallory, John Hamlin and Edward Goodrich Exrs. of Fra. Mallory Deced: is referred till next Court.

The action on the case brot. by Eliza: Mallory, John Hamlin and Edward Goodrich Exrs. of Francis Mallory deced: agst. Joshua Irby is referred till the next Court.

The action ont he case brot. by Eliza. Mallory, John Hamlin & Edward Goodrich Exrs. of Francis Mallory Deced: agst. Adam Ivie Admr. of John Tiller deced: is referred till next Court.

The Last Will and Testament of William Hatt deced: was presented into Court by Nathaniel Harrison Esqr. and Sarah Hatt the Executrix named in the said Will haveing Expressly refused to take on her the Burthen & Execution of the said Will, the said Nathaniel Harrison made Oath thereto, and it being proved by the Oath of Thomas Rogers a Wittness thereto, is Admitted to record and on the motion of the said Nathl. Harrison and his giveing Security according to Law, Certificate is granted him for Obtaining a Commission of Administration with the said Will annext in due form.

Nathaniel Harrison Esqr. Admr. &c: of William Hatt deced: with Robert Hall Gent. his Security, entred into Bond for his faithfull Administration on the said Deceds: Estate and acknowledged the same in Court.

Timothy Bridges, Edward Wyatt, Peter Talbott and Thomas Seabro or any three of them being first sworn for that purpose by some Majistrate of this County, are Ordered to appraise the Estate of Wm. Hatt deced: & make report of their proceedings therein to the next Court, when Nathaniel Harrison Esqr. the Admr. is to return the Inventory thereof.

[page 346]

In the action on the case brot. by William Bates agst. John Sale, for Fifteen pounds current mony due by accot. &c: the defendt. being called and not appearing and Timothy Bridges being returned Security for him, on the motion of the plts: Attorny Judgement is granted him agst. the said Defendt. & his said Security for the said Sum & Costs, unless the said Defendt. shall appear the next Court and answer the said action.

John Moor's Deed to Mary Chamnis was proved in Court by the Oaths of Samuel Temple and William Temple junr. and on the motion of the said Mary Chamnis, the same is Ordered to be recorded.

The action on the case brot. by William Ranye agst. James Gretion, is referred for tryall till the next Court & on ye plts. Cost.

The action Depending between Littlebury Epes &c: and John Hatch is referred till the next Court.

In the action on the case brot. by Drury Bolling against James Thweatt, for five pounds Eleven shillings and five pence due by account &c: the defendt. being called and not appearing and John Peterson being returned security for him, on the motion of the plts: Attorny Judgement is granted him agst. the said Defendt. and his said Security for the said Sum & Costs, unless the said Defendt. shall appear at the next Court and snwer the said action.

In the action of Trespass brot. by William Short and Elizabeth his Wife against Thomas Adams, the plts. failing to file their Declaration, on the motion of the plts: attorny it is Ordered that the sd. plts: be nonsuit & pay the said defendt. five shillings with Costs. Als. Exec:

The action of Detinue brot. by Sampson Merredeth agst. Richard Cureton, is referred till the next Court & on the Defts. cost.

The action on the case brot. by John Sale agst. John Moor, neither party appearing, is Dismist.

The action on the case brot. by John Sale agst. Jerrediah Goodward, neither party appearing, is Dismist.

The action on the case brot. by John Edwards agst. Roland Jones neither party appearing, is Dismist.

In the action on the case brot. by John Peterson agst. Francis Epes Exr. of the Last Will and Testament of Henry Cabinis deced: for Eleven pound, Eleven Shillings and two pence due by accot. &c: the defendt. being called and not appearing, nor any Security returned for him, on the motion of the plts: Attorny, Judgement is granted him agst. the said Defendt. and

[page 347]

John Hardyman Sherr: &c: for the said Sum and Costs, unless the said Defendt. shall appear at the next Court and answer the said Action.

The action on the case Depending between William Troughton & Thomas Huddell, the plt. being dead, is Dismist.

The action on the case brot. by Thos. Huddell agst. William Troughton, the deft. being dead, is Dismist.

In the action on the case brot. by David Crawley agst. Roger Archer for Twenty Seven Shillings due by accot. dated the 30th of May 1719, the said partys appearing the defendt. produces a discount of Forty three Shillings [words removed] & Six pence, and makes Oath thereto whereupon it is Considered by the Court tha the plt. hath no cause of Action, and on the motion of the Defendts. Attorny the suit is Dismist with costs, and it is Ordered that an Attornys Fee be Taxed to the Bill of Costs of this suit to be paid by the plt. to the said Defendt.

And then the Court Adjourn'd till Court in Course. John Poythres. Test Wm. Hamlin, Cl. Cur.

At a Court held at Merchantshope for the County of Prince George, the Eleventh day of January 1720[/1], for Laying the County Levy.

Present   John Poythres,   Robert Munford,   Robt. Hall }
    Robt. Bolling,   Lewis Green Junr.   & John Peterson }   Gent. Justices

Pr. George County Dr. Jany. the 11th 1720[/1].
For Wolves killed, Vizt.

		Q Tobo.			Q Tobo.
To Robert Poythres	1	100	Brought on	15	1600
To Joshua Poythres	4	400	To Joseph Tucker	1	100
To John Poythres	1	100	To Robert Tucker	1	100
To John Gillam Junr.	1	100	To Capt. John Evans	1	100
To John Gillam Senr.	2	200	To John Walker	1	100
To Tho. Clay (kill'd Xbr 20 1720)	1	200	To Buller Herbert	1	100
To Pr. Mitchell Senr.	1	100	To Wm. Batt pr. Pr. Lee	2	200
To John Phillips	2	200	To Wm. Spain	1	100
To Richard Pace	1	100	To James Thweatt pr. Jno. Davis	1	100
To William Russell	1	100	To Mathew Anderson	1	100
	15	1600	carried on	25	2600

[page 348]

					Q Tob.
Prince George County Debt Brought on				25	2600
To Major Robt. Bolling pr. Sevll.					
Vizt. John Wall	3	300	Brot. on	34	3400
Robt. Hancocke	2	200	To Majr. Robt. Munford		
John Stroud	1	100	pr. Severall, Vizt.		
Nicholas Overby Junr.	1	100	Thomas Parham	6	600
Mathew Mayes	1	100	Francis Coleman	1	100
John Wall	2	200	John Wall	4	400
William Coleman Sr.	1	100	Thomas Mitchell	5	500

175

William Natt	1	100	Francis Coleman Senr.	2	200
Stephen Evans	2	200		77	7800
Robt. Hancocke	2	200			
Henry Embry	3	300			
Joseph Wall	2	200			
John Ealam	1	100			
Bartholomew Crowder	1	100			
John Wall	9	900			
William Jones	1	100			
Richard Jones junr.	1	100			
carried on	34	3400			

To William Jones 75 and William Davis 60 for takeing up two Vagrants	0135
To Majr. Robert Bolling for a Corroners Inquest & Summoning a Jury	0183
To Mr. John Peterson for Do.	0183
To Henry Bates for takeing up a runaway Negro Woman Slave }	
named Hannah belonging to Mrs. Mary Stith (distant above 5 miles)	0100
To James Jones for Do. twice	0200
To Edward Burchet for Do. (distant above 10 miles)	0200
To Charles Roberts for takeing up a runaway sarvant man named John Hardy, belonging	
to Mr. Charles Stagg of Wmsburgh. (distant 50 miles)	0200
To Thomas Simmons junr. for Disbursments in clearing Powells Creek	0100
To John Hamlin for a Sectys. Fee for a Commission of the peace pd. by him, 1716	0160
To Thomas Simmons Late Sub. Sherr: for three Insolvents	0123
To Do. for Sweeping the Court house	0250
To William Hamlin Clerke for the County Service this year & Caskes	1080
To Do. for a Lock for the Office door	0040
To Mr. Secretary Cock for Writts for Elections of Burgesses & rec: Inquests	0760
To John Hardyman Sherr: for the County service this year, & Caske	1080
To Do. for Disbursments about the Prison and persons committed thereto	1104
To Do. for compleatly Finishing and Tarring the Prison	2313
	19011
To Sallary for Collecting of 12448 at 1 pr. Cent	1245
Prince George County Cr. Jany. 11th 1720.	20256
by Mr. Hardyman Sherr: for Tobacco Levied by the public on this County, and	
Ordered to be paid to the same for Wolves heads [...]	6562
by 1241 Tithables at 11: l Tobacco pr. ple is	13651
Due to the Sherr: to be Levied next year	00043
	-20256

[page 349]

Ordered that John Hardyman Sherriff of this County, Collect and receive of every Tithable person therein (by Distress in case of refusall or non payment) the Sum of Eleven pounds of Tobacco, the same being the County Levy this present year. And that the said John Hardyman pay the same to the severall person's to whom it is proportioned in the above Levy.

And then the Court Adjourn'd. John Poythres. Test Wm. Hamlin, Cl. Cur.

Joseph Gray Exhibitted the following Judgement and desired the Same might be recorded that Execution might Issue thereon.

Prince George County Ss.

Joseph Gray Complains agst. Anthony Dewston, for that the said Dewston is Indebted to him by account Nineteen Shillings and four pence, the deft. appears and Confesses Judgement. Ordered the said Anthony Dewston pay the said Sum of Nineteen shillings and four pence with Costs. Als: Exec: done this 31st of Jany. 1720[/1]. Before me. R. Hall. To the clerk of the abovesaid County. Truly Recorded by Wm. Hamlin, Cl. Cur.

At a Court held at Merchantshope for the County of
Prince George, on the second Tuesday in February, being the
fourteenth day of the said month, Anno Dom: 1720[/1].

Present   Robert Munford,   Robert Hall,   }
                 Lewis Green Junr.,   & John Peterson,   }   Gent. Justices

Sarah Buckner Admrx. of Larrance Buckner deced: returns an Inventory and Appraisment of the said Deceds: Estate, which is Ordered to be recorded.

John Hamlin and William Hamlin Executors of Elizabeth Hamlin [deced:] return an Inventory and Appraisment of the said Deceds: Estate, which is Ordered to be recorded.

Adam Ivie Executor of Elizabeth Ivie deced: returns an Inventory of the said Deceds: Estate, which is Ordered to be recorded

Present John Hamlin, John Poythres & Robt. Bolling, Gent. Justices

Ordered that Arthur Biggins be Overseer of the Highway's from [...] Hardymans Mill to the Cole pitts, and to the Chappell.

[page 350]

Ordered that George Hamilton be Overseer of the Highways from the Cole pitts and the Ferry Landing, to the Clay Bottom.

Ordered that Arthur Biggins and George Hamilton who are appointed Overseers of the Highways in Merchantshope, apply themselves to Capt. Hamlin for persons to assist them in clearing the said Highways.

Ordered that a Road be cleared from Peter Wynne to James Thweatts plantation whereon Edward Birchet deced: formerly Lived, the Antient and most convenient way, and that John Peterson be Overseer thereof.

Ordered that John Ledbetter be Overseer of the Highway from the Double Branch on the south side of Warrick inward to ye Nottoway Road.

Ordered that a Road be cleared from Joans Hole Bridge to Rowanty Road at Butler's Wolfe pitts, and that John Hill be Overseeer thereof.

Mary Chamnis one of the Exrs. of Henry Chamnis Deced: returns an Inventory of the said Deceds: Estate, which is Ordered to be recorded.

Ordered that Martha Jackson Executrix of the Last Will and Testament of Wm. Jackson deced: pay and deliver to Peter Anderson and William Smith, the Estates and Legacys in her hands as Executrix as aforesaid, belonging to Frances Crabb and Agnes Crabb, two of the Orphans of Francis Crabb deced: Ordered that the said Peter Anderson and William Smith give Security for the same accordingly.

George Brewer haveing made Oath that he attended Ten day's as an Evidence for Joshua Irby in his action of Trespass upon the case brot. against Mathew Smart Junr. Ordered that the said Joshua Irby pay the sd. George Brewer for his said Attendance the sum of Four Hundred pounds of Tobacco, with Costs. Als: Exec:

William Smith Admr. of Francis Longmore deced: returns an Inventory and Appraisement of the said Deceds: Estate, which is Ordered to be recorded.

Mary Rivers Executrix of John Rivers deced: returns an Inventory and Appraisment of the said Deceds: Estate, which is Ordered to be recorded.

In the action on the case brot. by Mary Bond Admrx. of John Bond deced: agst. John Hunt for fourteen pounds currt. mony due by accot. dated 1711, Colo. Francis Epes became Special Bail for the said Deft. who thereupon appears and pleads *Nil debit* and the plt. Joining in the Issue the same was Submitted to the Court for Tryall, and the Court haveing heard the allegations of the said partys, and the deft. denying the plts: accot. upon Oath, thereupon Order the suit to be dismist.

[page 351]

In the *Scire Facias* brot. by Peter Wynne Admr. &c: of Joshua Wynne deced: agst. Martin Sheffeild for the reviveing & renewing a Judgement granted the sd. Peter Wynne as admr. as aforesaid, in the County Court the twelfth day of June 1716, against the said Martin for three hundred and Sixty pounds of Tobacco and Costs of suit amounting to fifty pounds of Tobacco, the said Martin Sheffeild being Summoned to appear before this Court to Show cause if any he have why Execution ought not Issue agst. him for the debt and Damges aforesaid, and he failing to appear, on the plts: motion it is Considered by te Court and Ordered that he have Execution against the said Deft. for his Debt and Costs aforesaid amounting in the whole to four hundred and Ten pounds of Tobacco, togather with costs.

The Last Will and Testament of Paul Jones deced: was presented into Court by Mary Jones his Executrix who made oath thereto and it being proved by the Oaths of Thomas Scarbro, Benja. Reeks and Richard Ingram Witnesses thereto, is admitted to record and on the motion of the said Mary Jones and her giveing Security According to Law, Certificate is granted her for Obtaining a Probate in due form.

Mary Jones Executrix &c: of Paul Jones deced: with Edward Wyatt and Richard Ingram her Securitys, entred into Bond [for] Sum of One hundred and fifty pounds Sterling, for her Faithfull Executorship of the said deceds: Will and acknowledged the same in Court.

James Bell, Peter Anderson, William Bleighton & Peter Talbott or any three of them being first Sworn by some Majistrate of this County for that purpose, are appointed and Ordered to Appraise the Estate of Paul Jones deced: and make report of their proceedings therein to the next Court, when Mary Jones the Executrix is to return the Inventory thereof.

In the action of Trespass depending between William Short and Thomas Harrison, For that on the fifteenth day of February 1719, in the Parrish of Waynoke in this County the House and cl[...] of him the said William the said Deft. did break and enter, and five hundred pounds of Tobacco belonging to the plt. of the Value of two pence for each pound, did take and carry away, and other

[page 352]
Enormities to him the sd. William Short, he the said Thomas Harrison then and there did against the peace &c: and to the plts: Damage Ten pounds Current mony as in the plts: declaration is set forth, the deft. by his Attorny appeared and pleaded in writeing, to the plts: Declaration who replying thereto, the deft. by his Attorny Joined in the Issue Tendered by the plt. in his said replication, whereupon a Jury was Impannelled and Sworn to trye the matter in Issue by Name John Ledbetter, William Temple, Mathew Smart junr., James Gretion, Charles Williams, James Jones, William Wallis, Nicholas Overby, Henry Peoples, John Hynes, Peter Gramar and Thomas Simmons Junr., who haveing heard the Evidence and reced: their charge were sent out, and soon after returend into Court & brought in their Verdict, "The Jury find for the Plaintiff Six pound Current mony, with cost." John Ledbetter, Foreman, which Verdict on the motion of the plt. is recorded, whereupon the deft. by his Attorny alledged the damages are Excessive and moved for a new Tryall which was Overruled, the Jury haveing found the said Damages consideration of the defts. haveing the hold hogshead of Tobacco mentioned in the plts: declaration, wth. the sd. plt. promisses & assumes in Court to deliver him accordingly, and on the plts: motion it is Considered by the Court that he the sd. plt. recover agst. the aforesaid deft. the aforesaid Sum of Six pounds Currt. mony, being his Damages aforesaid by the Jurors in maner aforesaid assessed, togather wth. Costs. Als: Exec:

The action on the case brot. by Josha Irby agst. John Ellis junr: the plt. failing to prosecute is dismist.

The action on the case brot. by John Hatch agst. James Lee the plt. failing to prosecute, is dismist.

Edmond Browder in Open Court acknowledged his Deeds of Lease and Release of Land (Seald) to John Phillips, on whose motion they are Admitted to record.

The Attachment granted Timothy Gramar agst. the Estate of Wm. Jackson, the plt. failing to prosecute, is Dismist.

The Attachment granted Richard Cureton agst. the Estate of Wm. Jackson, the plt. failing to prosecute, is Dismist.

The action on the case depending between Buller Herbert & William Anderson Junr. the plt. failing to prosecute, is Dismist.

[page 353]
In the action on the case brot. by George Allen agst. Sarah Thompson Exrx. &c: of Henry Thompson deced: the plt. failing to prosecute, on the motion of the defendts. Attorny it is Ordered that he be nonsuit and pay the said deft. five shillings with Cost. Als. Exec:

The action on the case brot. by Eliza. Mallory, John Hamlin & Edwd. Goodrich Exrs. of Francis Mallory deced: agst. James Lee, the plts: failing to prosecute, is Dismist.

The action of Detinue brot. by Benja. Reeks agst. Nicholas Wyatt, the deft. being since dead, is dismist.

The action on the case brot. by Richard Ingram agst. James Bell, the plt. failed to prosecute, is Dismist.

In the action of Trespass brot. by Danl. Megirt agst. Adam Ivie, an Imparlance is granted the deft. till next Court.

The action on the case brot. by Thomas Simmons against William Spiller neither party appearing, is dismist.

The action on the case brot. by Francis Lightfoot agst. Paul Sears, neither party appearing, is dismist.

The action of Trespass brot. by Robt. Hannah agst. John Anderson, neither party appearing, is dismist.

In the action of Trespass brot. by Richard Warthen agst. Edward Wyatt the deft. appears and pleads not Guilty, and the plt. Joining in the Issue the same is referred till next Court for Tryall.

The action on the case brot. by James Thweatt agst. John Ingles, the plt. failing to prosecute, is dismist.

Edward Wyatt being chose a Vestryman for the Parrish of Martins=Brandon, he accordingly appears in Court, takes the Usual Oaths, signs the Test, and is Sworn a Vestryman of the Parrish aforesaid.

Drury Stith Junr. haveing a Commission to be one of the Surveyors of Brunswick County, he accordingly appears in Court, takes the Usual Oath, Signs the Test, and is sworn a Surveyor of the County aforesaid.

The action on the case brot. by Richard Pace agst. Robert Acock, the plt. failing to prosecute, is dismist.

The action on the case brot. by Bowler Cocke agst. Peter Leeth, the plt. failing to prosecute, is dismist.

In the action of Debt brot. by Cornelius Cargill against John Lewis for five pounds due by Bill, dated the 12th of Nov: 1720, the deft. being returned *non est Inventus*, and not appearing, on the plts: motion an Attachment is awarded him agst. the defendts. Estate for the said Sum & Costs, returnable to the next Court for Judgement.

And then the Court Adjourn'd till Court in Course. John Hamlin. Test. Wm. Hamlin, Cl. Cur.

[page 354]

At the Court House in Prince George County the fourteenth day of
March Anno Dom: 1720[/1].

Pursuant to a Commission of the Peace from the Honble. Alexander Spotswood Esqr. His Majestys Lieut. Governr. &c: bearing Dated the 28th day of February 1720 and De[...] for Swearing the Justices &c: which being read as usual, Buller Herbert and Drury Bolling Administred the Oaths and Test therein mentioned to John Hamlin, Robert Munford, Robert Hall, Robert Bolling, Lewis Green Junr. and John Peterson, who Administred the Like Oaths and Test to the said Buller Herbert & Drury Bolling, and Drury Stith junr., Francis Epes junr., William Harrison, Timothy Bridges, John Beard & John Scott Junr. Test. Wm. Hamlin, Cl. Cur.

At a Court held at Merchantshope for the County of Prince
George on the second Tuesday in March, being the fourteenth
day of the said month, Anno Dom: 1720[/1].

Present			
	John Hamlin,	Robert Munford	}
	Robert Hall,	Robert Bolling	}
	Lewis Green junr.	John Peterson	}
	Buller Herbert	Drury Bolling	} Gent. Justices
	Drury Stith junr.	Francis Epes junr.	}
	& John Scott junr.		}

The Last Will and Testament of Sampson Merredeth deced: was presented into Court by Elizabeth Merredeth his Executrix who made Oath thereto, and it being proved the Oaths of Thomas Rogers and Robert Rivers Wittnesses thereto is Admitted to records, and on the motion of the said Elizabeth Merredeth Certificate is granted her for Obtaining a Probate of the said Will in due form.

On the petition of Peter Wynne setting forth that he hath Land on both sides of the Butterwood Swamp about halfe a Mile above the Occanechy Path in this County Convenient to build a Water Mill on & praying Liberty of this Court to perform the same, the sd. Petition is accordingly granted and the sd. Peter Wynne is permitted to build a Water Mill at the place aforesaid.

On the petition of John Hardyman, he is permitted to built & keep a rolling House at the Head of Powells Creek.

Mary Jones Executrix of Paul Jones Deced: returns an Inventory & Appraisment of the said deceds: Estate, which is Ordered to be recorded.

Benjamin Edwards junr. haveing a Commission to be one of the Surveyors of Brunswick County, he accordingly appears in Court, takes the Usual Oaths, Signs the Test, and is Sworn a Surveyor of the County aforesaid.

Thomas Walke's Letter of Attorny to Francis Lightfoot was proved in Court by the oath of Robert Tucker & Ordered to be recorded.

[page 355]

John Pook in Open Court acknowledged his Deed for Land (Indented and Seald) with Livery of Seizin thereon, to William Mattox, on whose motion the same is Admitted to record.

Nathaniel Harrison Esqr. Admr. with the Will Annext of William Hatt deced: returns an Inventory and Appraisment of the Estate of the said Deced: which is Ordered to be recorded.

Ordered that the Sheriff of Princess Ann County pay to Robert Tucker Two Thousand Two Hundred & Eighty five pounds of Tobacco the same being Levied on the said County by the Genrall Assembly in 1717 and Ordered to be paid to this County for Wolves heads &c. In Consideration whereof Robert Hall, Gent. in behalfe of the said Tucker appears in Court and assumes to pay to this County four shillings pr. Hundred, for the said Tobacco.

On the petition of Thomas Adams Father in Law to Alexander Tapley setting forth that the sd. Tapley is Lunatic and uncapable of takeing care of himselfe & children & Estate &c: it is Ordered that the Church Wardens of Martin Brandon Parrish take care of the said Tapley, his Children & Estate till the next meeting of the Vestry of the said Parrish.

In the action on the case brot. by Henry Holdcroft Exr. of Randle Platt deced: agst. Francis Epes Exr. of Henry Cabinis deced: an Imparlance is granted the deft. till next Court.

In the action of Debt brot. by Henry Holdcroft & Mary his Wife Surviveing Executrix of Alexander Walker deced: against Paul Sears for five hundred pounds Current mony due by Bond &c: the defendt. being called and not appearing and James Banks being returned Security for him, on the motion of the plts: Attorny Judgement is granted them agst. the said Deft. and his sd. Security for the said Sum & Costs, unless the said Defendt. shall appear at the next Court and answer the said Action.

In the action of Trespass brot. by Richard Cureton & Eliza. his Wife against Richard Harrison, for beating, wounding & Evil Intreating the said Elizabeth against the peace &c: and the plts: Damage fifty pounds Sterling &c: the deft. being returned *non est Inventus* and not appearing, on the motion of the plts: Attorny an Attachment is awarded them agst. the said Defendts. Estate for the said Sum and Costs, returnable to the next Court.

[page 356]

On the petition of John Scott setting forth that he hath Land on both sides of Birchen Swamp in this County above John Hardyman's Mill, convenient to build a Water Mill on, and praying Liberty of this Court to perform the same, the sd. Petition is Accordingly granted, and the said John Scott is permitted to build a Water Mill at the place aforesaid.

The action of Trespass brot. by Mathew Williams agst. John Gill (neither parth appearing) is dismist.

The action on the case brot. by Joseph Gray agst. William Smith is Continued till the next Court.

In the action on the case brot. by Timothy Bridges agst. William Smith Admr. &c: of Francis Longmore deced: for three pounds Seven Shillings and four pence halfe penny due by accot., the Defendt. not appearing nor any security returned for him on the motion of the plt. Judgement is granted him agst. the sd. Deft. and John Hardyman Sherr: &c: for the said Sum & Costs, unless the said deft. shall appear at the next Court and answer the said action.

In the action of Debt brot. by John Peterson Assignee of Edward Goodrich against John Pook, for fifteen pounds, three Shillings and two pence current mony, due by Bill dated the Eleventh day of November 1719, the defendt. appears in Custody and Confesses Judgement to the plt. for the said Sum & Costs, and on the motion of the plts: Attorny it is Ordered that the said Defendt. remain in Custody of the Sherriff, till he hath fully paid and discharged the above Judgement and all Costs incident unto the said John Peterson or his Order.

In the action of Detinue brot. by Benjamin Reeks agst. Edward Wyatt Exr. of Nicholas Wyatt deced: an Imparlance is granted the deft. till the next Court.

In the action on the case brot. by Richard Warthen agst. Henry Holdcroft, the plt. failing to file his declaration, on the motion of the defts. Attorny it is Ordered that the sd. plt. be non suit & pay the said Deft. five shillings, with Costs. Als: Exec:

The action brot. by Stephen Evans agst. Christopher Robertson (neither parth appearing) is Dismist.

And then the Court Adjourn'd till Court in Course. John Hamlin. Test. Wm. Hamlin, Cl. Cur.

Finis.
[page 357 blank]
[page 358]

Returns of Executions &c.

On the Attachment awarded Sampson Merredeth Sherr: of this County against the Estate of Richard Pigeon, the Corroner made the following return, Vizt: November 4th 1714. Attached the within mentioned Richard Pigeons Estate as follows:

One saine	}	
three hanks of twine	}	2352
One Quoil of rope	}	
& one Barrell	}	

pr. me James Thweatt, Corroner. John Hatch, Edmd. Irby, Geo. Hamilton. Truly recorded pr. Wm. Hamlin, Cl. Cur.

On the Execution granted Robert Rogers on his Judgemt. against Samuel Lucy Dated the 13 day of Sept. 1715, the following return was made, Vizt: Reced. the Contents. [signed Robert Rogers]. Truly recorded pr. Wm. Hamlin, Cl. Cur.

On the Execution granted Robert Rogers on his Judgemt. agsinst Samuell Lucy Dated the Eighth of November 15, the following return was made, Vizt: Reced. the Contents. [signed Robert Rogers]. Truly recorded pr. Wm. Hamlin, Cl. Cur.

On the Execution granted John Hatch on his Judgement agst. William Spiller Dated the Ninth of October 1716, the following return was made, Vizt: The within Execution shall be paid pr. me. [signed] John Hamlin. Truly recorded pr. Wm. Hamlin, Cl. Cur.

On the Execution granted Robert Rogers on his Judgmt. agst. John Lett dated the Ninth of October 1716, the following return was made, Vizt: Reced. the Contents. [signed Robert Rogers]. Truly recorded pr. Wm. Hamlin, Cl. Cur.

On the Execution granted William Randolph Admr. &c: of Eusebius King Deced: agst. Henry King, Dated the Ninth of October 1716, the following return was made, Vizt: Jany. 14th 1717, in pursuance of the within Writt of *Capias ad Sattisfaciendum* agst. Henry King, I Thomas Simmons sub Sherr: of Prince George County have divers times endeavoured to Execute the same, but the said King being always upon his Gard Defends himself with force and arms. [signed] Thos. Simmons, Sub. Sherr: Truly recorded pr. Wm. Hamlin, Cl. Cur.

[page 359]
On the Execution granted Benjamin Foster on his Judgement against Richard Hamlin Dated the Eighth of Aprill 1718, the following return was made, Vizt: We the subscribers being appointed appraisers of Sundy Goods of Richard Hamlin Deced: Estate being seized by an Execution Dated May the 13, 1718, Granted unto Benjamin Foster, we being first Sworn do appraise the following Goods &c: this 18th June 1718.

Imprimis				
	One Desk at	240		
	Six Leathern chairs at	200		
	One small Looking glass	108		
	One bed, bolster, Vallence }			
	curtains, Posts, rugg & coverlet }	708	Judgement	1915
	One pr. small hand Irons	072	Clks. Fees	090
	two Iron potts, 1 pr. of hooks	169	Do. Serv. Execution	060
	One small Table 60, one Large do. 90	150	Sum. 4 appraisers	040
	One Skillet 48, one brass kettle 90	138	the appraisers 30 l pr.	120
	One heifer, one yearling Steer	246		2225
	One sadle & Bridle old	100		
		2225		

Gilbt. Hay, Thos. Simmons, Wm. Harrison, James Harrison. [signed] Rand. Platt, Corroner Truly recorded pr. Wm. Hamlin, Cl. Cur.

On the Execution granted Cornelius Fox on his Judgement agst. Wm. Wallice Dated the Eighth day of July 1718, the following return was made, Vizt: In Obedience to the within Order have reced: the said Sum with costs incident. [signed] James Thweatt, Sherr: Truly recorded pr. Wm. Hamlin, Cl. Cur.

On the Execution granted Edward Hill on his Judgement agst. Elizabeth Mallory, John Hamlin and Edward Goodrich, Executors &c: of Fra. Mallory Deced: Dated the Tenth day of Nov. 1719, the following return was made, Vizt: Nov. the 16, 1719. By Virtue of this within written Execution I have this day attached five Negro's (to witt) Jack, Ned: Cato, Tom, Sarah & Jupiter, belonging to the Estate of the within Named Fra: Mallory deced: and they being appraized as the Law directs have delivered to the within named Edward Hill. pr. [signed] Thos. Simmons, Sub. Sherr:
Appraised to One hundred and two pounds Current mony, by Edmond Irby, Gilbt. Hay, Geo: Hamilton, John Carter. Truly recorded pr. Wm. Hamlin, Cl. Cur.

[page 360]

On the Execution granted Frances Anderson Executrix &c: of Charles Anderson Deced: on her Judgement agst. Elizabeth Mallory, John Hamlin and Edward Goodrich Executors &c: of Francis Mallory Deced: Dated the 13th of October 1719, the following return was made, Vizt: Nov. 16, 1719. By Virtue of this Execution I have this day attached two Mallatto Girls named Isabell and Ellin, belonging to the Estate of Francis Mallory deced: and the same being Valued as the Law directs have delivered to the within named Frances Anderson. [signed] Thos. Simmons, Sub. Sherr:

Appraised to thirty five pounds Current mony, by Edmond Irby, Gilbt. Hay, Geo: Hamilton, John Carter. Truly recorded pr. Wm. Hamlin, Cl. Cur.

[End of Order Book]

INDEX

Blaikeley: William, 17

Blaikley: William, 145

Blaine: John, 145, 169

Bland: Richard, 29, 31, 41, 42, 51, 53, 59, 62, 65, 66, 69, 72, 79, 100, 110, 113, 115, 124, 125, 131, 135, 136, 142, 149, 166; Richard, dec., 159; Robert, 59

Blawes: Robert, 2

Blaws: Robert, 7, 32

Bleighton: George, 1, 2, 61, 66, 88; George Sr., 66, 88, 108; George, orphan, 61, 108; William, 51, 105, 178

Bleihley's Mill, 51

Bleike: Benjamin, 58

Bobbit: William, 124, 135, 158

Bobbitt: William, 59

Bodyman: Richard, 137

Boisseau: James, 15; Sarah, 8, 13, 15, 127

Bolling: Drury, 90, 94, 100, 102, 103, 105, 106, 107, 111, 126, 128, 132, 133, 146, 153, 168, 173, 174, 179; Drury, justice, 179; Edward, 7; George, 85, 92; John, 10, 14, 15, 21, 42, 56, 57, 59, 61, 89, 104, 105, 113, 115, 119, 124, 127, 130, 133, 137, 141, 147, 153, 158, 163, 165, 173; John, Maj., 16; Maj., 166; Maj., justice, 46, 65; Robert, 7, 10, 14, 15, 16, 17, 19, 21, 22, 26, 28, 33, 34, 37, 40, 42, 43, 44, 48, 50, 51, 52, 53, 55, 57, 59, 60, 62, 64, 74, 78, 79, 81, 84, 87, 89, 92, 94, 96, 100, 101, 103, 104, 105, 106, 107, 109, 115, 117, 121, 122, 124, 126, 127, 130, 132, 134, 135, 136,137, 139, 141, 142, 144, 147, 152, 153, 157, 158, 159, 160, 163, 165, 166, 169, 172, 173, 179; Robert Sr., 105, 124, 147; Robert, Colo., 130; Robert, justice, 21, 22, 24, 25, 29, 30, 36, 41, 44, 49, 67, 70, 76, 79, 82, 85, 88, 91, 105, 106, 109, 111, 114, 115, 117, 136, 154, 159, 163, 167, 172, 175, 177, 179; Robert, Maj., 30, 83, 92, 95, 114, 130, 153, 175, 176; Robert, Maj., justice, 18, 20; Stith, 10, 14, 16, 17, 19, 21, 26, 28, 34, 64, 66, 102, 117, 150; Thomas, 10, 14, 16, 17, 19, 28, 34; Thomas, infant, 16, 21

Bond: John, 177; Mary, 177; Peter, 29, 33, 38, 117, 123, 132

Bonner: John, 23, 24, 34, 46, 65, 72, 85, 89, 90, 95, 100, 101, 113, 119, 126, 132, 150, 156, 163

Booth: Thomas, 1, 33, 47, 65, 77, 122, 133, 159, 160, 163

Boreman: James, 54, 59, 63, 64; Mortella, 91; Mortilla, dec., 88

Boston, Mass., 142

Bowen: Charles, 70, 86, 89, 93, 94, 100, 109, 119; Margery, 109, 119

Boys: Lucy, 39, 41, 43; Samuel, 39, 41, 43

Bradford: Ralph, 49; Richard, 70, 71

Brady: Edward, 158

Braine: Benjamin, 9, 18, 19, 24, 26, 93; John, 141; William, 125

Brandon Church, 100

Brawn: Robert, 73

Braxton: George, 149, 156

Brewer: Edmond, 10, 14; George, 52, 57, 59, 62, 67, 71, 75, 77, 80, 131, 161, 170, 172, 177; John, 93, 100, 105, 119, 126, 136, 138, 141, 144, 147, 149, 156, 162, 173; Nathaniel Jr., 63; Nicholas, 57, 102; Nicholas Jr., 79, 138

Brian: Thomas, 167

bridges: Abernathy's, 36; Blackwater, 50, 98, 100, 102, 150; Carltons Swamp, 76; Joans Hole, 177; Joseph's Swamp, 151; Lower Blackwater, 36; Mayes's, 30; Mockoson=neck, 172; Monksnak, 105; Monksneck, 114; Namounds, 90; Powhiponock, 90; Rowanty, 30, 36, 82; Stony Creeke, 172; Ward's Creek, 58, 68; Ward's Runn, 51; Warrick, 82

Bridges: Timothy, 9, 13, 91, 96, 97, 99, 102, 103, 105, 115, 117, 119, 120, 139, 145, 146, 147, 153, 158, 161, 162, 165, 172, 173, 174, 179, 180; William, 166

Briscoll: Eliza., 9

Bristol: Elizabeth, 5

Bristoll Parish, 21, 34, 89, 113; tithables, 29, 64, 95, 130, 160

Bristow: Kathrine, 75; Robert, 75; Robert Jr., 75

Brockwell: John, 3

Brooks: John, 18, 124

Browder: Edmond, 60, 82, 102, 109, 120, 178; Edward, 139; John, 136, 140, 146

Brown: Robert, 158

Browne: William, 2, 5

Brunswick County, 179

Buckner: Larrance, 169, 177; Larrance, dec., 169; Mr., 130; Sarah, 169, 177

Burbridge: Robert, 8

Burch: Elizabeth, 137; Richard, 49, 82, 114, 136, 140, 141; Samuel, 27, 63, 64, 68, 72, 137, 138, 166

Burchet: Edward, 80, 84, 169, 176; Mary, 150; Robert, 47, 48, 49, 54, 65, 150

Burchett: Edward, 31, 33, 56, 61, 102; Mary, 144, 148; Robert, 47, 54, 55, 56, 59, 60, 68, 144, 148

Burge: John, 172; Thomas, 81, 86, 93, 96, 99, 159, 160, 172; William, 20, 52, 58

Burrow: John, 39, 58, 60, 131, 171; Phill, 119; Phillip, 19, 25, 32, 39, 47, 58, 60, 74, 113, 114, 153; Thomas, 125

Burt: Edward, 138, 141

Bushskin Creek, 133

Buston: John, 87, 91

Butler: John, 5, 7, 9, 78, 91; John, dec., 133; Mary, 5, 9, 133; Mutas, 7; William, 21, 30, 114

Butler's Wolfe pitts, 177

Butterwood Road, 127

Butterwood Runn, 111

Butterwood Swamp, 179

Byrd: Jane, 89; William, 38, 40, 51, 53, 59, 138, 141

Cabanis: Henry, dec., 168; Mary, 168
Cabinis: Henry, 139, 158, 163, 168, 172, 175, 180
Caleb: William, 14, 16, 17
Caratan: William, 45
Cargill: Cornelius, 39, 52, 59, 62, 63, 67, 70, 71, 73, 75, 76, 77, 79, 80, 82, 84, 89, 101, 121, 125, 147, 179; John, 1, 4, 7, 10, 14, 70, 73, 87; Sarah, 1, 14
Carlile: Richard, 11, 22, 96, 113, 121
Carltons Swamp, 76
Carter: George, 57, 90, 158, 163; John, 152, 157, 159, 160, 162, 163, 173, 181, 182; Jonathan, 84, 100, 156; Joseph, 36, 91, 104
Cate: Richard, 171
Cater: Stephen, 139, 143, 149
Chamberlain: Thomas, 53, 58, 66
Chamberlaine: Thomas, 61
Chamblis: Henry, 11
Chamlis: Henry, 47
Chamnis: Henry, 134, 139, 152, 157, 159, 177; Henry, dec., 134; Mary, 134, 139, 152, 157, 159, 174, 177
chapels, 16, 38, 177
Chapman: Charles, 123, 156
Chappell: James, 5; Samuel, 66, 155, 162; Thomas, 5, 25, 87
Charles City County, 122
Cheese: John, 83
Cheves: John, 131
Chiswell: Charles, 110, 112, 139, 162
Church of England, 8
Claud: Hannah, 159, 166; Phillip, 40, 74, 80, 122, 159, 166; Phillip, dec., 159
Clay: Henry, 32; Thomas, 26, 50, 65, 68, 136, 175; Thos., 8
Clay Bottom, 177
Clement: ffrancis, 1
Clements: ffrancis, 1, 2, 6, 88; ffrancis Jr., 2; Francis, 112, 115, 122, 149, 150, 156, 174; Lydia, 2, 88, 108, 115, 122, 129, 149, 150, 156, 160, 166, 174
Clerke: Robert, 81; Samuel, 81
Cleton: John, 80
Clifton: Thomas, 65, 103, 115, 122, 169
Cock: Powell, 70; Secretary, 176
Cocke: Bowler, 179; Edward, 161; Martha, 71; Stephen, 71; Thomas, 40; William, 33, 98, 103
Coggans Point, 165
Cogill: William, 57, 65
Cole pitts, 177
Coleman: Faith, 148; ffrances, 44; ffrancis, 8, 35, 44, 45, 50; ffrancis Jr., 44, 53, 67; Francis, 71, 82, 111, 114, 127, 140, 145, 175; Francis Jr., 71, 154; Francis Sr., 151, 176; Honor, 140; John, 17, 44, 45, 59, 64, 69, 102, 121, 126, 136, 167; Mary, 145; Robert, 76; William, 21, 49, 116, 122, 136, 148; William Sr., 175
Colgill: William, 86, 148, 155
Colleshaw: David, 100

Colley: Thomas, 158
Collier: John, 28, 133; Thomas, 164
Collishaw: David, 94
Collup: Thomas, 18, 20, 27, 34
Collyshaw: David, 32, 105, 115, 124; Savid, 135
Colson: John, 146, 153, 157, 162
Colysaw: David, 132
Colyshaw: David, 44, 52, 57, 90, 119, 120, 129, 133, 135
constables, 26, 87, 88, 94, 113, 159, 169; fees, 167
contables, 96
Cooke: Rebecca, 146, 153, 154, 157, 160, 166; Richard, 145; William, 41, 146, 153, 154, 157, 160, 166, 167
Cooper: Elizabeth, 63, 64; John, 11, 63, 64; William, 118
coroners, 15, 50, 82, 87, 92, 98, 114, 159, 176, 180, 181
Cotten: Elizabeth, 91; John, 120; Richard, 11, 20, 30, 90, 91, 97, 99, 102, 103; Richard, dec., 96; William, 96
county records, 50
courthouses, 7, 15; door lock, 176; sweeping, 50, 82, 114, 151, 176
Crabb: Agnes, 177; Frances, 177; Francis, 177
Crafford: Thomas, 39, 41, 44
Cragg: James, 124
Crawley: Daniel, 93, 103; David, 24, 40, 53, 56, 57, 61, 64, 66, 69, 71, 72, 74, 75, 77, 86, 90, 92, 95, 97, 98, 100, 102, 103, 115, 116, 119, 120, 121, 124, 126, 127, 135, 136, 138, 139, 143, 149, 156, 158, 163, 174, 175; Elizabeth, 93, 103
Crawly: David, 99
Creacher: Titus, 115, 120, 127, 156
Crews: Andrew, 152
Crook: George, 79, 81, 84, 89, 91
Crooke: Elizabeth, 40, 134; George, 40, 133
Cross: John, 43, 52
Crossland: Edward, 94
Crowder: Barth., 79, 81, 89; Bartho:, 116; Barthol:, 84; Bartholomew, 46, 122, 166, 176; Barthow:, 77; Batt:, 20; Elizabeth, 20
Cuerton: John, 77; William, 1, 34, 71, 77, 79, 84
Curatan: James, 45
Curaton: James, 42, 46; John, 51; William, 46, 52
Cureton: Elizabeth, 180; James, dec., 40; John, 4, 8, 23, 24, 40, 89, 125, 133, 162; Richard, 85, 96, 98, 101, 105, 117, 131, 142, 150, 153, 162, 170, 175, 178, 180; William, 9, 23, 24, 34, 160
Daniel: Eliza., 81; Elizabeth, 162; John, 36; Thomas, 46
Daniell: John, 30, 39, 40, 41, 42; Mary, 30, 36, 39, 40, 41, 42; Thomas, 11
Davis: Christopher, 8; Christopher Jr., 69, 72; Christopher Sr., 69, 72; Elizabeth, 75; John, 6, 147, 175; Robert, 18, 32, 37, 40, 60, 75; William, 68, 69, 76, 77, 82, 125, 134, 136, 140, 160, 166, 176

Dayly: Hugh, 7

Deardan: Richard, 131

Dee: Henry, 150, 166, 174

Denton: Edward, 5, 30, 35, 36, 69; Elizabeth, 23; John, 23, 29, 34; Peter, 36

Derden: Richard, 21

Devenport: George, 144

Dew: Elizabeth, 24, 26, 27, 28, 30, 46; John, 24, 26, 27, 28, 30

Dewell: Jane, 57, 60; Jean, 5; Job, 5

Dewston: Anthony, 176

Dickason: William, 16, 17, 19, 25, 32, 37

Diggs: Colo., 4, 10

Dinkins: Thomas, 166

Dittee: William, 82

Doby: John, 1, 69, 72, 75, 77, 78, 80

Double Branch, 177

Drayton: John, 137; John, orphan, 125; Roger, 11, 97, 101, 113, 118, 125, 131; Roger, dec., 97; Sarah, 97, 101, 113, 118, 131; Sarah, dec., 97

droughts, 25

Duffeild: John, 93

Duffin: John, 118

Duglas: John, 47, 48

Duke: David, 47; Elizabeth, 112, 117, 121, 123, 131, 133, 135, 138, 139, 143, 149, 172; Henry, 8, 13, 17, 18, 19, 25, 26, 32, 33, 39, 41, 42, 43, 45, 59, 68, 97, 101, 112, 117, 121, 123, 131, 133, 135, 138, 139, 143, 149, 172; Henry, dec., 112

Dunbarr: John, 108, 129

Dunn: Abell, 151, 152, 156; William, 86

dwelling houses, 27, 151

Ealam: John, 176

ear marks, 29, 51, 64, 148, 155

Eaton: Samuel, 140; William, 81, 141, 148, 154

Edwards: Benjamin Jr., 179; John, 109, 175; Nathaniel, 99, 169

Eldridge: Thomas, 7, 22, 29, 33, 37, 38, 51, 78, 133, 134, 137, 150, 155, 159, 166, 168, 173

Ellington: John, 63, 82, 114

Ellis: John, 11, 116; John Jr., 1, 3, 5, 9, 10, 57, 61, 64, 69, 83, 89, 139, 169, 178

Embro: Henry, 114

Embry: Henry, 21, 69, 151, 176

Enon: Robert, 138, 143, 166

Epes: Edward, 4, 51, 168, 169; Elizabeth, 1, 3, 4, 8, 9, 13, 14, 15, 16, 17, 19, 24, 32, 37, 40, 56, 64, 71, 120, 127; ffrancis, 19, 38, 40, 41, 49, 51, 56, 79, 93, 98; ffrancis Jr., 96; Francis, 82, 119, 120, 126, 150, 156, 172, 175, 180; Francis Jr., 99, 127, 133, 168, 179; Francis Jr., justice, 179; Francis, Colo., 177; Isham, 2, 6, 10; John, 99, 105, 169; John, dec., 99; Lewis, 103; Littlebury, 4, 10, 42, 46, 93, 99, 104, 116, 145, 146, 148, 149, 156, 160, 174; Sarah, 24; Thomas, 81, 99, 105, 109; William, 1, 3, 4, 8, 9, 13,

15, 16, 19, 24, 32, 40, 49, 56, 120, 127, 168; William Jr., 49, 99, 151

Evans: Benjamin, 79; Benjamin, orphan, 105; Benjamn Sr., 105; John, 5, 21, 23, 69, 72, 151; John, Capt., 175; Sarah, 23; Stephen, 21, 31, 37, 40, 50, 51, 53, 57, 61, 65, 79, 82, 83, 84, 86, 89, 91, 114, 138, 143, 149, 158, 169, 174, 176, 180; Stephens, 43

Farmar: Thomas, 108, 109, 118, 120

Farrell: Bryan, 1; Sarah, 102; William, dec., 102

Farrrell: Bryan, 103

Fellows: Robert, 64, 120

ferries, 165

ferry landings, 177

ffarrar: William, 70, 73

ffarrell: Bryan, 4, 7, 10, 14, 29, 44, 46, 93; Bryan, dec., 44; Elizabeth, 44, 46

ffisher: William, 28

fflint: Richard, 10, 11

ffloriday: William, 59, 85

ffoster: Benjamin, 14, 16, 17, 25, 30, 32, 35, 38, 41, 47, 50, 59, 77, 85, 87, 88, 89, 90, 94, 96, 98; Elizabeth, 38

ffowler: Jos., 50; Joseph, 89

ffox: Cornelius, 90, 93, 94, 95, 96, 100, 101

ffrench settlements, 83

Finney: Peter, 125, 134

Finny: Peter, 158

Firth: William, 87, 152

Fitzgerald: John, 143

Fitzgerrald: John, 67, 120, 127, 132, 139, 143, 159, 168

Fletcher: James, 162, 164

Floriday: William, 120, 156

Fontaine: James, 166

Foster: Benjamin, 19, 36, 112, 118, 124, 132, 134, 152, 157, 158, 162, 163, 169, 181; Elizabeth, 112, 118, 157

Fowler: Joseph, 79, 84

Fox: Cornelius, 79, 86, 116, 119, 122, 126, 127, 131, 137, 138, 141, 142, 147, 152, 153, 154, 158, 163, 173, 181; Richard, 158

France, 164

freeholders, 4, 12, 63, 80, 92, 95, 140, 171

Gamlin: William, 114

gaols, 66; repairs, 168, 169; temporary, 169; Williamsburg, 168

Garvell: William, 168

Gary: Sarah, 36, 39; William, 39; William, dec., 36

Gaudey: Peter, 31

Gee: Charles, 50; Hannah, 14

Gent: Thomas, 88, 114; William, 58, 69, 116, 117, 159

Gerrald: John, 72, 99

Gibbs: William, 51

Gibson: Hubbard, 56, 63; Hubbord, 47, 59; John, 56, 61

Giles: Nicholas, 59

Gill: Henry, 9, 13; John, 90, 167, 180

Gillam: Charles, 38, 63; John, 115; John Jr., 175; John Sr., 175; William, 82, 144

Gillmore: John, 87

Gills: Henry, 120

Gilmore: Robert, 87, 101, 103, 123, 124, 135, 139

Glidewell: Robert, 69, 136, 139, 140

Goffe: Joseph, 103, 116, 122, 131, 138, 142

Golightly: Hugh, 1, 11, 47, 113, 134, 161, 167, 168; John, 11, 48, 49, 54, 55, 118

Goodgame: David, 42, 49, 68, 80, 96, 99, 101, 113, 121; Joshua, 49, 68

Goodrich: Capt., 21, 22; Charles, 1, 3, 8, 9, 13, 18, 20, 26, 30, 37, 41, 44, 45, 52, 57, 61, 65; Charles, Maj., 30; Edward, 1, 2, 4, 6, 9, 13, 15, 17, 23, 30, 31, 32, 33, 35, 37, 38, 40, 42, 43, 45, 49, 51, 52, 53, 56, 58, 59, 64, 66, 68, 70, 71, 74, 75, 76, 77, 81, 86, 91, 92, 93, 104, 109, 114, 122, 130, 132, 135, 140, 141, 143, 144, 145, 146, 147, 148, 149, 150, 155, 156, 157, 160, 164, 166, 167, 173, 174, 178, 180, 181, 182; Edward, dec., 173; Margaret, 66, 173

Goodward: Jerrediah, 175

Goodwin: Thomas, 106

Goodwyn: Thomas, 59, 60, 62, 63, 64, 66, 67, 68, 69, 70, 71, 73, 74, 76, 77, 79, 80, 84, 85, 111, 113; Thomas, Capt., 77, 128

Goodwyne: Thomas, 107; Thomas, Capt., 129

Goodwynn: Thomas, 89, 137, 139, 145, 149, 153, 156

Goodwynne: Thomas, 110

Governors, 11, 12, 16, 22, 25, 35, 40, 88, 97, 98, 132, 155, 159, 163, 164, 171, 179

Gower: William, 73

Gramar: Peter, 163, 178; Timothy, 178

Gramer: Peter, 60, 81

Grammar: Timothy, 162, 170

Grammer: Peter, 12, 131, 162; Timothy, 66

Gravelly Runn, 76

Gray: Gilbert, 164; Jeffrey, 137, 138; Joseph, 176, 180

Great Britain, 65, 164; tobacco seized in, 165

Green: Burrell, 52, 119; John, 136, 140, 141; Lewis, 73, 77, 80; Lewis Jr., 26, 80, 81, 114, 129, 136, 151, 152, 159, 179; Lewis Jr., justice, 30, 43, 56, 60, 64, 67, 70, 79, 80, 97, 102, 106, 109, 111, 115, 124, 129, 133, 136, 144, 148, 151, 152, 155, 159, 160, 163, 170, 171, 175, 177, 179; Lewis Sr., 167; Lewis, justice, 7, 11, 12, 16, 20, 21, 51, 54, 85, 88, 91, 118, 121, 140, 142, 172; Thomas Jr., 167; William, 136

Greenhill: Joseph, 100, 103, 106, 107, 108, 110, 111, 112, 115, 121, 128, 129, 131, 139, 146, 153, 157, 162

Greeshon: James, 150; Margaret, 150

Gregory: Thomas, 62, 102, 119, 148

Grenan: James, 4

Gresion: James, 10

Gression: James, 11

Grestion: James, 54, 55

Gretion: Hanes, 166; James, 47, 48, 49, 100, 138, 143, 154, 158, 162, 165, 174, 178

Griffith: Elizabeth, 140, 142; Richard, 53, 58, 140, 142; Richard, dec., 140; Thomas, 85, 86; Thomas, servant, 5

Grigg: Susan, 74; William, 74, 79, 132

Grigory: Thomas, 154

Grove: John, 1

Gunter: John, 16

Hackney: Thomas, 86

Hall: Instance, 5, 17, 33, 38, 41, 43, 51, 53, 69, 103, 124, 132, 153, 157; James, 81, 166; Jas., 69; John, 158; Justain, 64; Prudence, 29; R., 154, 172, 176; Robert, 11, 12, 13, 20, 22, 24, 26, 36, 37, 46, 108, 114, 118, 140, 161, 163, 164, 167, 173, 174, 179, 180; Robert, justice, 5, 7, 11, 12, 14, 16, 18, 20, 21, 22, 24, 25, 26, 29, 30, 36, 41, 43, 46, 49, 51, 54, 56, 60, 64, 67, 76, 91, 94, 95, 97, 99, 102, 106, 111, 114, 115, 117, 118, 121, 129, 133, 136, 140, 142, 144, 148, 151, 152, 154, 155, 159, 160, 163, 167, 168, 170, 171, 172, 173, 175, 177, 179; William, 99

Haly: Johanah, 148; William, 161

Hambleton: George, 31, 74, 76, 77, 84, 96, 103, 104

Hamelin: Capt., 22; John, 5, 7, 12, 16, 18, 20, 21, 22, 24, 25, 27, 29, 31, 35, 37, 39, 40, 53, 56, 61, 64; John, Capt., justice, 36; John, justice, 5, 11, 12, 15, 16, 18, 20, 21, 22, 24, 25, 26, 30, 39, 41, 46, 51, 56, 61, 64, 152; Richard, 1, 2, 3, 7, 10, 11, 12, 22, 25, 29, 32, 33, 35, 37, 40, 42, 43, 45, 52, 53, 56, 58, 59, 61, 63; Richard, justice, 12, 14, 16, 22, 26; Richard, Sheriff, 35, 39, 41, 42, 45, 46, 50, 51, 52, 53, 59, 63; William, 35, 38, 50, 60; William, clerk, 5, 7, 11, 12, 14, 16, 18, 20, 21, 22, 24, 25, 26, 29, 34, 36, 37, 39, 41, 43, 46, 49, 50, 53, 54, 55, 56, 60, 63, 64, 67

Hamelton: George, 115, 116, 122, 135, 144, 156, 159, 160, 162, 166

Hamersley: John, 172

Hamersly: James, 148; John, 106, 138, 139, 143, 145, 149, 152, 153, 156, 160, 161, 165, 171, 172; John, Dr., 126

Hamilton. See Hambleton; George, 122, 131, 132, 141, 149, 177, 180, 181, 182

Hamlin: Ann, 104, 138; Capt., 177; Elizabeth, 69, 72, 75, 125, 150, 169, 177; Elizabeth, dec., 169; John, 36, 50, 60, 67, 70, 76, 80, 82, 83, 85, 88, 91, 93, 94, 95, 97, 101, 103, 104, 106, 111, 114, 117, 118, 120, 123, 124, 125, 127, 132, 134, 135, 139, 141, 142, 144, 145, 146, 147, 148, 149, 150, 151, 152, 154, 155, 156, 157, 159, 160, 163, 166, 167, 169, 170, 171, 172, 173, 174, 176, 177, 178, 179, 180, 181, 182; John, Capt., 64, 95, 112; John, Capt., justice, 67, 91; John, justice, 29, 49, 80, 82, 83, 85, 88, 94, 95, 97, 99, 102, 105, 109, 111, 117, 118, 121, 124, 129, 133, 136, 140, 142, 149, 151, 154, 155, 159, 160, 167, 168, 170, 172, 173, 177, 179; Richard, 6,

7, 36, 66, 69, 74, 83, 88, 89, 94, 100, 104, 111, 114, 117, 124, 132, 134, 135, 139, 181; Richard, dec., 104; Richard, Sheriff, 67, 70, 71, 73, 74, 75, 78, 82, 85, 86, 87, 88, 92, 93, 94, 95, 96; William, 68, 93, 125, 137, 141, 145, 150, 158, 163, 165, 169, 171, 177; William, clerk, 67, 69, 70, 72, 73, 76, 78, 80, 82, 83, 84, 85, 88, 91, 94, 95, 97, 99, 101, 104, 106, 109, 111, 114, 117, 118, 120, 124, 126, 127, 128, 129, 130, 133, 135, 139, 142, 144, 148, 150, 151, 152, 154, 155, 159, 160, 163, 164, 167, 168, 170, 171, 172, 173, 175, 176, 179, 180, 181, 182

Hammersly: John, 122

Hancocke: Robert, 175, 176

Hannah: Robert, 178

Hanoby: Thomas, 29

Hardaway: Thomas, 137

Hardoway: Thomas, 142

Hardwell: Samuel, 43

Hardwick: Daniel, 30

Hardy: John, 169, 176

Hardyman: Francis, 134, 145; John, 7, 8, 13, 15, 17, 19, 21, 22, 23, 24, 28, 29, 30, 36, 38, 41, 42, 44, 46, 52, 63, 67, 71, 72, 75, 76, 85, 89, 94, 100, 103, 104, 106, 107, 112, 115, 116, 117, 122, 130, 132, 141, 145, 148, 149, 150, 155, 159, 163, 164, 169, 172, 179, 180; John Sr., 36, 67; John, justice, 5, 16, 18, 22, 29, 36, 39, 41, 43, 46, 49, 54, 60, 64, 67, 70, 82, 85, 91, 95, 99, 102, 105, 106, 109, 111, 115, 118, 148, 155, 159; John, Sheriff, 164, 170, 175, 176, 180; Mr., justice, 25, 28, 42, 67, 68; ohn, 13; William, 171; William, under Sheriff, 164

Harman: Ann, 58

Harrison: Benjamin, 8, 13; Colo., 50; Elizabeth, 8, 13; Ellinor, 173; Hannah, 4, 29; Henry, 33, 60, 63, 68, 69, 72, 124, 133, 134, 163, 166; Henry, Capt., 76; James, 71, 74, 91, 98, 102, 106, 107, 108, 109, 110, 111, 112, 128, 129, 131, 132, 167, 172, 173, 181; Nathaniel, 1, 14, 21, 31, 37, 42, 51, 56, 59, 61, 62, 66, 80, 81, 85, 88, 91, 93, 94, 99, 100, 105, 115, 119, 122, 126, 130, 131, 134, 135, 136, 137, 138, 139, 141, 145, 146, 152, 154, 156, 160, 161, 163, 167, 169, 173, 174, 179; Nathaniel, Colo., 7; Rebecca, 4, 8, 11, 29; Richard, 3, 19, 28, 35, 42, 45, 52, 58, 59, 115, 138, 145, 180; Thomas, 8, 11, 13, 17, 19, 30, 31, 37, 40, 42, 51, 81, 90, 145, 149, 158, 161, 163, 167, 169, 178; Thomas, dec., 161; William, 1, 8, 11, 12, 29, 72, 74, 91, 97, 98, 102, 104, 106, 107, 108, 109, 110, 111, 128, 129, 131, 132, 134, 141, 144, 147, 169, 172, 173, 179, 181

Harriss: John, 9

Harrwell: Thomas, 152

Harvie: George, 90, 100, 105, 119, 120, 123, 126, 130, 138

Harvy: George, 94

Harwell. See Hardwell; Samuel, 21, 33, 38, 41, 50, 51, 57, 62, 82, 114, 133, 141, 174; Samuel Jr., 166;

Thomas, 44, 52, 98, 127, 129, 133, 138, 146, 166, 174

Harwood: Samuel, 56, 59, 62, 63, 67; Samuel Jr., 67, 142

Hatch: John, 2, 3, 13, 24, 26, 27, 35, 38, 41, 42, 44, 45, 47, 54, 57, 59, 60, 61, 63, 66, 67, 68, 69, 72, 73, 78, 79, 80, 84, 87, 91, 92, 100, 106, 110, 111, 112, 116, 117, 120, 122, 123, 127, 128, 134, 137, 140, 141, 147, 169, 170, 173, 174, 178, 180, 181; Mr., 107

Hatchers Runn, 76

Hatt: Mr., 135; Sarah, 174; William, 134, 152, 154, 174, 179; William, dec., 174

Hausman: Stephen, 86, 87, 92, 104; Stphen, 98

Haven: Stephen, 8, 13

Hawkins: Edward, 42

Hawks: Jeffery, 18; Jeffrey, 63, 85; Joseph, 108, 129

Hay: Gilbert, 4, 10, 11, 28, 35, 37, 71, 74, 84, 91, 102, 104, 106, 107, 108, 109, 110, 111, 112, 116, 119, 127, 128, 129, 133, 134, 141, 147, 163, 169, 171, 172, 173, 181, 182

Haynes: George, 66, 82; George, servant, 65; William, 94

Hays: Gilbert, 7, 98

Headstead: Hannah, 81

Headworth: Hannah, 106, 150, 156

Heath: Abraham, 34; Abram, 28; Adam, 25, 27, 153; Elizabeth, 25; William, 25, 31, 98, 118, 153, 155

Hedger: Thomas, 28

Hedsted: Hanah, 65

Heeth: Abraham, 89; Abram, 90, 95, 100, 162; Adam, 134, 146; William, 51, 134, 146

Hemelin: John, justice, 54

Henrico County, 2

Herbert: Buller, 21, 26, 38, 46, 50, 85, 90, 98, 138, 150, 170, 175, 178, 179; Buller, justice, 179; John, 38; Richard, 82

Higdon: Daniel, 3, 5, 9, 13, 18, 20, 30, 37, 41, 42, 44, 52, 57, 61, 63, 65, 80, 87, 92, 93, 104; Daniell, 1, 3

Hill: Ann, 111, 120, 127, 137, 144; Edward, 122, 123, 125, 132, 136, 141, 144, 145, 147, 148, 149, 156, 162, 172, 173, 181; Edward, Colo., 148; George, 28; John, 16, 22, 38, 111, 120, 127, 137, 144, 177; John Jr., 30, 31; John, dec., 111; Mary, 16; Michael, 45, 60, 63, 67, 125; Michal, 103, 124

Hines: ffrancis, 20; John, 20, 26, 31, 32, 33, 40, 50, 59, 63, 85, 113, 137, 142, 148, 154; William, 90

Hinton: Christopher, 33, 50, 56, 57

Hix: Richard, 123; Robert, 28, 31, 34, 38, 41, 116

Hobbs: James, 14, 102; John, 5, 7, 10, 14, 15, 19, 58, 60, 65, 68, 91; Robert, 50, 68, 74, 102, 109, 116, 118; Robert, dec., 102; Sarah, 27, 102, 116, 118; Thomas, 102; William, 14, 24, 27, 60, 155

Hobby: Thomas, 82, 123

Hoeth: Abram, 84

Hoggwood: William, 11

Hogwood: Joan, 159, 162; Joan, dec., 159

Holdcraft: Henry, 120, 134, 139, 146
Holdcroft: Henry, 139, 143, 144, 153, 157, 162, 172, 180; Mary, 180
Holecroft: Henry, 127
Hollinsworth: Thomas, 59
Holloway: Edward, 39, 41, 47, 52, 96; John, 65, 85, 88, 101, 171
Hollowell: John, 171
Hollycross: Jos:, 36; Joseph, 38, 40, 41
Holycross: Joseph, 30, 38, 71, 74, 130; Martha, 71, 73, 74
Honycutt: Robert, 98, 110, 123, 147
Hood: Thomas, 150
Horskins: Edward, 45, 52, 58, 138
House: Thomas, 20, 26, 45, 52, 58, 61, 65
House of Burgesses, 22, 151
Howard: James, 161, 168; James, dec., 161
Howell: Charles, 168
Huckaby: Thomas, 20
Huddell: Thomas, 145, 158, 175
Hudson: Charles, 38, 41; ffrances, 51; ffrancis, 33, 41, 43; Richard, 5, 19, 21, 53, 93, 96, 101, 113, 140; Richard Jr., 82
Hughs: John, 8
Hulm: William, 23, 24
Hulme: William, 34
Hunnicutt: Robert, 8, 25, 31
Hunobe: Thomas, 24, 28, 29, 34, 35, 38
Hunoby: Thomas, 23, 28, 29
Hunt: George, 119, 139; John, 177
Hutcheson: William, 90
Hyde: Mary, 79; Richard, 79, 105
Hynes: John, 112, 131, 153, 158, 163, 171, 174, 178
Indians, 21; Dol, 159; Griffin, 163; Jack, 35, 37; Peter, 25; Sary, 47, 54; Sawny, 151; Skipper, 47, 54; trade, 83; Will, 114; Will Mott, 57
Ingles: Charles, Sir, 51; John, 179
Ingram: Richard, 123, 130, 178
insolvents, 50, 82, 176
Irby: Duglas, 30, 47, 48, 49, 54, 55, 68, 91, 95, 96, 100, 101, 110; Edmond, 4, 7, 28, 42, 80, 85, 141, 147, 152, 157, 159, 162, 163, 173, 180, 181, 182; Edmond, Dr., 126; Henry, 35; Jos: , Dr., 106; Jos:, 119, 127, 153, 167; Joshua, 1, 5, 6, 10, 14, 15, 16, 17, 19, 21, 26, 27, 29, 33, 49, 52, 57, 58, 61, 65, 68, 69, 71, 72, 75, 86, 90, 93, 94, 95, 100, 125, 126, 137, 141, 146, 147, 157, 158, 162, 163, 169, 170, 173, 174, 177, 178; William, 35, 69
Irish servants, 136
Isle of Wight County, 124, 135
Ivey: Adam, 11, 33, 59; George, 28, 31, 33, 59, 63; Henry, 63
Ivie: Adam, 37, 39, 87, 96, 101, 113, 115, 117, 122, 157, 167, 168, 169, 174, 177, 178; Elizabeth, 157, 168, 177; Elizabeth, dec., 157; George, 69, 72, 93, 96, 101, 121, 156; Gilbert, 169; Henry, 84

Ivy: George, 155; John, 151, 152; Ruth, 155
Ivye: Adam, 92
Jackson: Ann, 46, 51; Elizabeth, 46; John, 120, 161; Martha, 161, 162, 164, 177; Susanna, 18, 20, 27, 34; Susanna, dec., 18; Thomas, 18, 53, 58; William, 46, 80, 84, 90, 97, 100, 105, 109, 140, 146, 153, 157, 158, 159, 161, 162, 164, 165, 166, 169, 170, 177, 178; William, dec., 161
James River, 83
Jane: Eliza, 138; Elizabeth, 131, 142; Phillip, 84, 138, 142; Phillip, dec., 131
Jaquelin: Edward, 46
Jarrard: Elizabeth, 21; Elizabteh, 120; Nicholas, 20, 21, 30, 120
Jarrett: Nicholas, 11
Jean. *See* Jane; Elizabeth, 83, 131; Phillip, 83, 131
Jefferson: Thomas, 38, 39, 41
Jeffreys: Thomas, 148
Joans Hole Bridge, 177
Joans Hole Swamp, 172
John Grove and Co., 1
John Hardyman & Co., 116, 117
Johnson: Edward, 57, 118, 162, 168
Jones: Abraham, 125; Capt., 133; Daniel, 68, 114; David, 79; Eliza., 59; Elizabeth, 62, 66, 72, 73; Henry, 169; James, 13, 32, 52, 98, 102, 104, 106, 107, 108, 109, 110, 111, 112, 119, 133, 146, 150, 152, 153, 157, 160, 162, 166, 167, 173, 176, 178; James Jr., 5, 27, 35, 59, 60, 66, 68, 71, 75, 128, 129; James Sr., 152, 162, 173; James, dec., 129; Mary, 17, 125, 144, 178, 179; Paul, 4, 6, 7, 11, 63, 81, 87, 118, 126, 130, 178, 179; Paul, dec., 178; Peter, 7, 12, 26, 68, 151; Peter Jr., 30, 125; Peter, Capt., 82, 114; Rebecca, 169; Richard, 17, 23, 57, 68, 168; Richard Jr., 4, 8, 176; Robert, 14, 18, 19, 57, 59, 62, 66, 69, 72, 73, 164; Roland, 175; Sarah, 130, 152, 157, 162, 173; Thomas, 21, 82; William, 62, 72, 114, 176
Jordans, 83
Jordans See, 16
Joseph's Swamp Bridge, 151
Judson: Richard, 136
Kavanaugh: Arthur, 105
Kay: ffrancis, 24
Kemp: Ann, 5, 9, 13, 14, 15, 16, 27; John, 5, 9, 13, 14, 15, 16, 27
Kennon: Richard, 133; William, 103, 107, 166
Kerby: John, 145, 165
Killegrew: William, 158, 163
King: Eusebius, 45, 51, 119, 126, 136, 181; Henry, 28, 45, 76, 86, 92, 96, 100, 113, 121, 131, 181
King George, 164
Kings Road, 30
Kirkland: Richard, 4; Thomas, 30, 131
Kirkwood: Adam, 80
Knight: John, 31

Lanier: John, 125, 130; John, dec., 125; Nicholas, 125, 130, 131

Lanthrop: John, 122, 131, 136; John, dec., 121; Joseph, 121, 122, 131, 136; Margaret, 121, 122, 131

Larrance: Ailce, 101; Allice, 96

lashes, 143

Law: Arthur, 151, 156

Lawes: William, 82

Lawlor: Thomas, 146, 155, 158

Lawts. Run, 30

Ledbetter: Henry, 56, 121, 150; John, 5, 30, 38, 56, 65, 109, 154, 171, 177, 178; Richard, 86, 95; William, 44, 149

Lee: Ann, 91; Henry, 91; Hugh, 8, 17, 19, 21, 56, 82, 102; Hugh Sr., 56; James, 170, 178; John, 31; Nathaniel, 116; Peter, 175; Samuel, 5, 82, 106

Leeth: Arthur, 172; Peter, 172, 179

Leonard: Elizabeth, 140; John, 14, 16, 17, 118, 140, 146

Lessenby: John, 153

Let: John, 163

Lett: John, 1, 7, 8, 10, 13, 14, 15, 16, 24, 28, 30, 31, 37, 39, 40, 41, 42, 43, 44, 45, 46, 51, 53, 59, 60, 68, 71, 75, 81, 83, 84, 87, 96, 97, 101, 113, 118, 131, 137, 138, 152, 156, 158, 166, 169, 170, 181

Lewis: John, 4, 51, 77, 81, 89, 99, 109, 115, 117, 179; John Jr., 79, 84, 89, 94, 100, 104, 109, 117, 136; Richard, 167; Thomas, 5, 8, 13, 15, 16, 19, 72, 76

Lieutenants Runn, 111

Lightfoot: Francis, 149, 155, 178, 179

Liles: John, 103, 116

Lilley: John, 32

Lilly: John, 32, 37

Limbrey: Eliza, 3; Elizabeth, 1, 9, 13; John, 1, 3, 9, 13

Limbry: Elizabeth, 164, 174; Rebecca, 164, 174; Rebecca, dec., 164

Littlepage: Richard, 18, 19, 25, 32

Livesay: Joan, 168, 172; John, 80, 172; John, dec., 168; William, 172

Lizland: Joshua, 149, 156

Loftin: James, 1, 9, 10, 13, 14, 31, 60, 119, 134, 158, 167; Mr., 3

London, Eng., 9, 18, 19, 24, 26, 42, 46, 51, 62, 67, 70, 71, 74, 76, 93, 104, 109, 147, 150, 165

Longmore: ffrancis, 83; Francis, 171, 177, 180; Francis, dec., 171

Lovesay: John, 85, 119

Low: William, 90

Lower Blackwater Bridge, 36

Lowry: Issau, 2

Loyd: Jane, 90, 91, 92; Thomas, 9, 31, 60, 90, 92; Thomas, dec., 90

Lucy: Samuel, 14, 16, 18, 57, 181; Samuell, 9

lunatics, 180

Lundy: Elizabeth, 79; James, 79, 85, 92, 96, 100, 113, 120, 130

Mackmehan: Hugh, 90, 92; Hugh, dec., 90

Magget: Samuel, 164

Mainard: John, 55

Maine: Edward, 40; George, 40

Maise: Henry, 50

Major: Edmond, 149, 156

Mallone: Daniell, 67; George, 166; Mary, 68

Mallory: Elizabeth, 141, 144, 145, 146, 147, 148, 149, 150, 155, 156, 157, 160, 166, 167, 174, 178, 181, 182; ffrances, 56, 61; ffrancis, 4, 7, 10, 17, 23, 25, 28, 29, 33, 35, 38, 41, 43, 45, 51, 59, 61, 62, 67, 68, 70, 71, 74, 76, 77, 80, 83, 84, 85, 93, 96, 99, 101, 103; Francis, 36, 57, 73, 76, 77, 110, 113, 116, 119, 121, 127, 141, 144, 145, 146, 147, 148, 149, 150, 155, 156, 157, 166, 167, 174, 178, 181, 182; Francis, Capt., 148; Francis, dec., 141

Marchand: Daniel, 53, 59, 61

Markes: Edward, 6; Israel, 65; Mathew, 8

Marks: Edward, 2, 6; Elizabeth, 102, 105, 144; Israel, 36, 65, 102, 105; Israel, dec., 102; Mathew, 31, 33, 59, 76, 95, 144, 153; Mathew, dec., 144

Marshall: Mathew, 165

Martin: John, 131, 133, 136; John, dec., 131; Mary, 131, 133, 136

Martins Brandon Parish, 2, 5, 30, 159; Churchwardens, 2, 118, 180; storehouses, 40; tithables, 29, 64, 95, 130, 160; vestrymen chosen, 173, 179

Mason: John, 14

Mathews: Thomas, 82; William, 1, 3, 9, 13

Matson: William, 31

Matt: Will, 151

Matta: William, 82

Mattock: Mary, 38, 39

Mattox: Margaret, 150, 156; Mary, 41; William, 47, 48, 54, 64, 99, 110, 111, 133, 137, 150, 179

Maycocks, 165

Maycocks Neck, 111

Mayes: Elizabeth, 20, 53; Henry, 27, 53, 152; John, 30, 59, 62, 66, 67, 69, 73, 95, 100, 121, 126; Mary, 85; Mathew, 20, 21, 114, 175; William, 5, 14, 17, 19, 24, 28, 32, 37, 38, 40, 51, 64, 85

Mayes's Bridge, 30

Maynard: John, 48

Mayo: James, 116, 146, 153, 157, 162

Meadows: Daniel, 119, 150; David, 79

meeting houses: Anabaptists, 8, 11

Megirt: Daniel, 170, 178

Mell: Peter, 31

Melone: John, 1, 6, 10, 14, 15, 17, 19, 21, 27, 101; Robert, 44, 52, 101

Merchants Hope, 51

Merchantshope, 54, 56, 60, 64, 70, 73, 76, 79, 80, 82, 83, 88, 91, 94, 95, 97, 99, 102, 105, 106, 109, 111,

114, 115, 117, 118, 121, 124, 129, 133, 136, 140, 142, 144, 148, 151, 152, 154, 155, 159, 160, 163, 167, 168, 170, 171, 172, 173, 175, 177, 179

Merick: William, 142

Merredeth: Elizabeth, 179; Mr., justice, 43; Sampson, 25, 35, 40, 41, 43, 60, 64, 90, 95, 96, 100, 102, 104, 115, 116, 119, 122, 126, 130, 133, 135, 139, 143, 145, 149, 153, 154, 158, 159, 160, 161, 167, 168, 175; Sampson, Coroner, 15, 114; Sampson, dec., 179; Sampson, justice, 36, 39, 58, 95, 99, 100, 102, 105, 121, 124, 130, 140, 142, 144, 148, 152, 171; Sampson, sheriff, 1, 7, 11, 12; Sampson, Sheriff, 20, 21, 22, 25, 26, 28, 32, 34, 35, 37, 38, 180; Samson, 50, 68, 167; Samson, justice, 106, 109, 111

Middleton: John, 60, 80, 168

Midleton: Elizabeth, 148; John, 84, 154; John Jr., 162; John Jr., dec., 162

Miles: John, 47

milk houses, 151

Miller: John, 145

Millner: Ann, 32, 39, 42, 46; Elizabeth, 117; Isau, 32, 38, 39; Issau, 42, 46

mills, 65; Balys Runn, 74; Bleihley's, 51; Hardyman's, 177; John Hardyman's, 172, 180; Simmons's, 155; Warthen's, 16, 51, 155; Warthin's, 58, 68, 110; water, 46, 71, 121, 126, 130, 172, 179, 180

Millton: Thomas, 32

Minge: John, 152; Valentine, 112, 125, 126, 129, 132, 133, 134, 137; Volentine, 118

Minnett: Robert, 6

Mirick: William, 131

Mitchell: Edward, 7, 30, 47, 63, 75, 124, 127, 130, 132; Henry, 140; Kathrain, 102; Peter, 21, 50, 60, 82, 92, 114, 136, 140, 141; Peter Jr., 114; Peter Sr., 114, 141, 175; Robert, 44, 118, 123, 124, 135; Thomas, 11, 52, 57, 96, 100, 103, 118, 123, 175; Thomas, orphan, 44; William, 86, 92, 100, 102, 113, 116, 119, 120, 126, 156, 166

Mockoson=neck Bridge, 172

Mockoson=neck road, 172

Monksnak Bridge, 105

Monksneck, 76

Monksneck Bridge, 114

Moody: James, 84, 90, 97, 101, 102, 131, 132, 146, 147, 153, 158, 167

Moor: Ann, 131, 132, 134; John, 115, 136, 174, 175; Thomas, 30, 31, 88, 94, 99, 115, 124, 129, 132, 134; Thomas, dec., 131

Moor's ffeild, 38

More: Thomas, 51

Morren: John, 9

Morris: Travis, 20, 44, 111, 144

Moss: Nathaniel, 103

Mott: Will, 57

Moyes: William, 16

Mulattoes, 13, 142, 162, 164; Ellin, 182; Isabell, 182

Munford: Maj., 40; Maj., justice, 28; Major, 76; Munford, 68; Robert, 20, 21, 22, 23, 59, 69, 74, 78, 81, 87, 88, 92, 96, 101, 104, 107, 116, 117, 120, 123, 125, 132, 135, 136, 148, 155, 158, 159, 171, 173, 179; Robert, justice, 5, 7, 12, 14, 16, 21, 22, 24, 25, 30, 36, 39, 43, 46, 49, 51, 54, 58, 61, 76, 79, 80, 82, 83, 88, 91, 95, 97, 105, 106, 109, 111, 115, 117, 118, 121, 133, 136, 142, 148, 152, 154, 155, 159, 160, 163, 167, 168, 170, 173, 175, 177, 179; Robert, Maj., 4, 40, 51, 64, 67, 72, 75, 82, 90, 103, 114, 120, 151, 153, 167, 175; Robert, Maj., justice, 20, 68, 140

Munn: Richard, 96, 98, 101, 113

Munns: Richard, 93

Muns: Richard, 68

Murrell: Edward, 120, 139

Namocends, 90

Namounds Bridge, 90

Nance. *See* Nants; Daniel, 53, 56, 62; Elizabeth, 62; Joan, 152; John, 49, 51, 52, 56, 57, 59, 61, 62, 66, 69, 73, 75, 76, 78, 81, 82, 84, 87, 99, 103, 111, 152; John Sr., 51, 56, 57, 59, 61, 62, 66, 69, 73, 75, 76, 78, 81, 82, 87; John, dec., 49; Richard, 49, 140; Sarah, 49, 52

Nants: John, 43, 44; Sarah, 43

Natt: William, 176

Naylor: Simon, 57, 69, 72, 75, 90; Susan, 103

Negroes, 6, 73, 103, 107, 128, 160; Ally, 125; America, 125; Amy, 144; Annica, 136; Antilla, 167; Asia, 125; Beck, 125; Belinda, 171; Bella, 125; Betty, 140, 162; Bob, 167; Bridget, 100; Cate, 142; Cato, 167, 181; Ceesar, 136; Celia, 125; Cupit, 141; Dena, 36; Dick, 106, 109, 136; Dina, 100; Dol, 167; Dolly, 142; Dorcas, 162; Effy, 129; Europe, 125; Frank, 136; George, 100; Glocester, 171; Hannah, 136, 176; Harry, 106, 160; Isbell, 84; Jack, 36, 99, 100, 133, 142, 167, 181; Janey, 81; Jenny, 106, 125, 136, 144, 169; Jone, 36; Jupiter, 140, 181; Kate, 136; killed, 111; Lewis, 79, 136; Limbrick, 106, 107, 128; Martin, 136; Mingo, 167; Nancy, 171; Ned, 100, 171, 181; Pegg, 167; Peter, 171; Phebe, 125; Pompey, 67; Prince, 142, 147; Rachell, 142; Robin, 13, 100, 167; Roger, 136; runaway, 176; Sambo, 169; Sarah, 181; Scipio, 136; Sharper, 157; shot, 103; Stafford, 136; Stepney, 144; Sue, 136, 167; Tom, 20, 125, 144, 181; Tomazin, 100; Tony, 140; Venus, 141, 171; Wat, 106; West, 98; York, 169

New England, 142

Newman: Richard, 162; Richard, orphan, 148

Niblet: James, 80, 90, 109, 118, 119, 120, 121, 123

Niblett: James, 11, 13, 20, 57, 97, 105, 159

Nicholls: John, 7

Nicholson: Robert, 4, 8, 109

Nickells: John, 86, 120, 155

Nisbett: John, 50

Norden: Robert, 8, 144, 153

Norten: ffrancis, 8, 39, 71, 74, 77; ffrancis, dec., 68; Francis, 64, 77; Mary, 68, 71, 74, 77, 103

Nottoway River, 76, 133, 134

Nottoway River Road, 102

Nottoway Road, 177

Nowlin: Elizabeth, 20, 27, 29; Richard, 27, 29; Richard, dec., 20

Occanechy Path, 179

Odgan: Abra:, 61, 63

Odium: Abraham, 14, 17, 19, 25, 57, 149; Abram, 156, 160, 162

Offley: Henry, 26, 59, 62, 67, 70, 71, 74, 76, 78, 79, 81, 84, 87, 89, 92, 94, 100, 101, 104, 109, 117, 119, 127, 136, 137, 141, 147, 153, 158, 163, 165

Oliver: Thomas, 103, 116

Onal: Edmond, 171

ordinary licenses, 15, 52, 88, 120, 148, 173

ordinary rates, 60, 91, 124, 155

orphans, 11, 23, 44, 47, 61, 66, 68, 71, 72, 75, 88, 92, 105, 118, 125, 148

Osborn: Elias, 36; Elizabeth, 36

Overby: Nathaniel, 47; Nicholas, 19, 46, 76, 77, 82, 89, 111, 114, 136, 141, 146, 153, 157, 160, 162, 173, 178; Nicholas Jr., 70, 74, 175

Owen: David, 32; John, 2, 6, 9, 118; Mary, 162

Pace: George, 25, 53, 64, 90; James, 24; Richard, 30, 89, 113, 123, 131, 133, 135, 137, 138, 143, 153, 175, 179; Sarah, 153

Parham. *See* Parram, *See* Parram; Elizabeth, 70, 73; James, 70; Thomas, 70, 73, 175

parishes divided into precincts, 140

Parke: Graves, 29

Parker: David, 16, 17, 84, 85, 88, 89; David, dec., 85

Parram: Elizabeth, 66, 75, 78, 81, 82, 86, 87, 89, 92, 124; Ephraim, 80, 136; James, 76, 78, 80, 81, 84, 88; Thomas, 18, 52, 81, 84, 86, 89; Thomas, dec., 66

Parsons: William, 140, 168

Partridge: Jos., 159

Pasmore: George, 53, 79, 103, 106, 107, 123, 128, 150

Passover: Gilbert, 162

Patterson: James, 29; Jane, 24, 28, 34; John, justice, 88; Jos:, 23; Josh:, 28; Joshua, 29

Patteson: John, 41, 42, 81, 84, 92, 96, 100, 131; Tillman, 110

Pattison: John, 86, 89, 96, 113; Jos., 146; Joseph, 146

Peebles: Henry, 125; William, 125

Peirson: Joseph, 138

Pellison: Daniel, 31

Peoples: Henry, 53, 59, 63, 82, 87, 151, 178

Perks: John, 152

Perry: John, 65, 68, 69, 72

Peterson: John, 4, 10, 11, 22, 30, 36, 38, 39, 40, 41, 42, 46, 59, 62, 63, 66, 71, 74, 76, 78, 82, 87, 105, 124, 129, 130, 132, 135, 148, 156, 174, 175, 176, 177, 179, 180; John Jr., 132, 168; John Sr., 130;

John, justice, 5, 7, 12, 15, 18, 20, 21, 22, 36, 44, 49, 51, 54, 56, 60, 70, 76, 79, 80, 82, 83, 85, 91, 97, 105, 106, 109, 118, 124, 130, 133, 140, 142, 144, 152, 154, 159, 160, 168, 170, 171, 172, 175, 177, 179; Mr., justice, 25, 26, 65

Pettypool: William Jr., 51

Phillips: John, 21, 141, 175, 178

Pidgeon: Richard, 7, 9, 10, 14, 15, 28, 32, 33, 35, 44

Pigeon: Elizabeth, 60, 122, 162; Richard, 52, 60, 79, 84, 86, 88, 89, 92, 96, 101, 116, 120, 122, 131, 138, 139, 141, 145, 152, 162, 167, 180; Richard Sr., 145; Richard, dec., 122

Plains: Thomas, 42; William Sr., 5

Platt: Henrietta, 75; Mr., justice, 42, 43; Randall, 1, 3, 5, 8, 9, 11, 13, 15, 17, 19, 21, 22, 23, 28, 29, 32, 33, 37, 40, 41, 42, 43, 44, 45, 46, 49, 52, 57, 58, 59, 61, 64, 65, 67, 88, 162; Randall, justice, 5, 7, 11, 12, 14, 16, 18, 21, 22, 25, 26, 39, 41, 43, 46, 49, 51, 54, 64, 67; Randall, sheriff, 9; Randle, 68, 70, 71, 74, 75, 76, 80, 84, 85, 86, 87, 89, 92, 94, 95, 96, 97, 98, 100, 101, 104, 109, 110, 111, 112, 113, 114, 116, 117, 121, 122, 123, 124, 130, 131, 132, 133, 134, 135, 139, 143, 146, 153, 157, 172, 180; Randle, Coroner, 181; Randle, dec., 134, 139; Randle, justice, 71, 79, 80, 82, 83, 85, 88, 91, 94, 95, 102, 105, 106, 111, 115, 121, 124

Pleasant: Joseph, 10, 14, 17, 19, 20, 25, 29, 35, 38

Poake: John, 60, 64

Poke: John, 28, 70

Poland: Richard, 115

Pook: John, 72, 74, 76, 77, 111, 124, 132, 135, 137, 146, 147, 150, 154, 158, 163, 174, 179, 180

Pooke: John, 16, 93, 109, 110, 160, 162

Posford: Thomas, 86, 155; Thomas Jr., 86

Potts: Mary, 119, 130, 134; Thomas, 19, 25, 28, 89, 94, 119, 130, 134; Thomas Sr., 28; Thomas Sr., dec., 25; Thomas, dec., 119

Powell: Edward, 21

Powells Creek, 30, 85, 176, 179

Powhiponock, 90

Powhiponock Bridge, 90

Poxom: Olive, 14, 17

Poxon: Olive, 10, 15

Poxson: Olive, 60, 86, 120

Poythres: David, 167; ffrancis, 1, 11, 23, 28, 29; Francis, 12, 104, 141, 144, 146, 171; Francis Sr., 113; John, 14, 25, 26, 46, 70, 72, 73, 74, 76, 77, 78, 83, 85, 88, 89, 91, 93, 94, 99, 114, 128, 129, 133, 134, 139, 145, 148, 150, 155, 159, 160, 164, 167, 168, 169, 171, 173, 175, 176; John Sr., 70, 74, 76, 83, 89, 94; John, Capt., 60, 95, 112, 125, 130; John, clerk, 151; John, justice, 7, 11, 12, 14, 26, 30, 43, 64, 70, 79, 82, 83, 84, 85, 88, 94, 95, 97, 99, 102, 114, 117, 121, 129, 136, 140, 142, 144, 148, 151, 154, 163, 167, 168, 170, 172, 173, 175, 177; Joshua, 88, 127, 147, 151, 175; Peter, 11, 35, 60,

144; Robert, 33, 47, 63, 66, 74, 127, 130, 167, 175; Thomas, 113, 153, 154; William, 60

Poythress: Robert, 4

Prawtons, 83

precincts determined, 12

Price: John, 5, 101; Thomas, 116

Prince: Edward, 24, 111, 127, 129, 130, 133, 157, 163

Princess Anne County, 124, 179

prisons, 22, 50, 53, 151, 176; repairs, 176

processioning, 12, 140

Protestant subjects, 8

Proux: James, 15

Quakers, 123, 133, 147

Quin: Abraham, 10

Rachell: Ralph, orphan, 118; William, 118; William, orphan, 118

Rackly: John, 154

Raines: Richard, 12, 65; Shan, 172; Thomas, 12, 172; William, 12, 72

Rains: Richard, 38; Thomas, 12; William, 12, 65

Randolph: Henry, 70, 73, 133; Isham, 29, 93, 96, 101, 113, 152; Richard, 159; William, 41, 45, 51, 57, 93, 99, 103, 116, 119, 126, 136, 159, 181

rangers, 12

Ranye: Roger, 172; William, 86, 119, 154, 158, 162, 174

Ray: Benjamin, 69, 72, 75, 77, 78, 80; Sarah, 77, 78, 80; William, 170

Rea: ffrancis, 111; Francis, 109, 118, 120; Francis Sr., 109; Francis, dec., 108; Joseph, 111; Sarah, 109

Read: Harman, 58; Thomas, 165; Thomas, dec., 165

Reams: John, 166

Rease: Roger, 4; William, 5

Ree: Francis, 99

Reece: Richard, 77

Reeks: Benjamin, 63, 87, 90, 112, 126, 140, 161, 169, 178, 180

Reese: Roger, 30; William, 104, 131

Reess: Richard, 147, 170; Roger, 163; William, 150, 160, 170

Reiks: Benjamin, 118

Renn: Joseph, 40, 42, 45, 46, 52, 99, 141; Joseph Jr., 46, 158; Joshua, 9; William, 46

returns of executions, 180

Reves: George, 65, 141; William, 4, 19, 25, 47, 72, 84, 109, 113, 125, 162

Richardson: Joshua, Dr., 51; Robert, 154, 161, 164, 169

Ricks: Benjamin, 72

Risby: John, 71, 150

Rivers: James, 44, 123; John, 31, 131, 171, 177; John, dec., 171; Mary, 171, 177; Robert, 20, 31, 44, 88, 90, 105, 142, 159, 160, 162, 171, 179

Rives: George, 47, 49, 50, 55, 82, 142, 148, 153, 154, 167; William, 153, 171

Rix: Benjamin, 20, 31, 46, 68, 81

roads, 7, 16, 30, 31, 51, 56, 65, 76, 91, 105, 133, 134, 140, 141, 152, 154, 164, 168, 172, 177; Blackwater, 91, 96, 98, 100, 150; Butterwood, 127; Maycocks Neck, 111; Nottoway, 177; Nottoway River, 102; Rowanty, 76, 177; Stony Creek to Monksneck, 76; Warthen's Mill to Brandon Church, 100

Robberds: John, 91, 98

Roberts: Charles, 69, 176; John, 63

Robertson: Christopher, 180; George, 75, 78, 82, 87, 92; Henry, 64, 68, 71, 103, 115; John, 52, 101; Mary, 169; Nicholas, 5, 11; William, 10, 14

Robins: Stephen, 165

Robinson: Christopher, 57, 59, 60

Robyson: John, 155; Mary, 155; Nicholas, 98, 131, 154

Rogers: Robert, 2, 4, 5, 6, 10, 14, 16, 18, 32, 33, 45, 52, 53, 56, 59, 63, 70, 93, 104, 117, 123, 132, 148, 181; Thomas, 174, 179

rolling houses, 179, *See* rowling houses

Rosser: Ann, 47; Michael, 138; Michael Jr., 93, 171; Michal, 160; Michal Jr., 30, 123, 133, 143, 159, 160; Michall, 5, 28; Thomas, 160

Rowanty Bridge, 30, 36, 82

Rowanty Road, 76, 177

Rowlet: William, 124

rowling houses, 83, 85, *See* rolling houses

Royall: Charles, 170; Sarah, als. Baxter, 122

runaway Negroes, 176

runaway servants, 168, 169, 176

Russell: Elizabeth, 60; William, 60, 82, 141, 175

Ruth: Richard, 65

Sadler: Thomas, 58, 61, 78, 80

Sadler's Estate, 69, 72, 78

Saffold: William, 123

Sale: John, 174, 175

Salmon: James, 12

Sambs: Thomas, 21

Sample: Thomas, 45, 129

Sams: Thomas, 133

Sands: Thomas, 64

Santan: William, dec., 65

Sapponee Creek, 133

Savage: John, 164, 169; William, 109, 125, 164, 169; William Jr., 164; William, dec., 164

Scarbro: Thomas, 169, 171, 178

Scarbrough: William, 47

Scoggan: John, 101, 131, 140

Scoggin: John, 53, 59, 61; Richard, 5, 21

Scoging: John, 98

Scott: Bethyer, 168; Edward, 11, 31, 33, 37, 57, 60, 83, 148, 150; John, 35, 38, 41, 44, 65, 68, 81, 82, 120, 161, 162, 169, 172, 173, 180; John Jr., 136, 168, 169, 179; John Jr., justice, 179

Seabro: Thomas, 174

Sears: Paul, 178

Selwood: John, 137

Sentall: Samuel, 4, 8, 13, 15, 53, 59, 69, 72, 75, 78, 95, 100, 103

servants, 5, 13, 29, 75; Dennis Wright, 150; George Haynes, 65; James Westbrook, 26; John Duffin, 118; John Hardy, 169, 176; John Mainard, 55; John Maynard, 48; John Miller, 145; John Thompson, 110; Mathew Marshall, 165; Michael, 136; runaway, 169; runaways, 168; Thomas Brian, 167; Tom, 164; William Garvell, 168; William Merick, 142; William Mirick, 131

Sevakar: James, 68

Sevecar: James, 1, 6, 9, 14, 15, 17, 19, 24; Sarah, als. Vaughn, 15, 24

Sevekar: James, 93

Shaw: Margaret, 9; Margarett, 13

Sheffeild: Francis, 111; Martin, 28, 31, 34, 35, 38, 43, 52, 60, 68, 71, 75, 177

Sheffeill: Agnis, 162

Sheffell: Agnis, 162

Sheffield: Martin, 41

Shepheard: Edward, 169

Shereley: John, 137

Sherley: John, 7, 19, 24, 31, 33, 37, 57, 60, 63, 125, 126, 129, 137

Sherly: John, 119, 133, 134

Sherrly: John, 7

ships: *Alexander*, 147; *Josiah*, 165; of war, 83; Spotswood, 76

Shirley: John, 17, 19

Short: Elizabeth, 20, 175; Robert, 33; William, 3, 4, 5, 7, 10, 16, 20, 32, 36, 37, 40, 42, 43, 44, 47, 58, 65, 68, 77, 91, 96, 98, 99, 102, 104, 111, 140, 158, 163, 169, 175, 178

Silver: Edmond, 155

Simmons: Edward, 119, 126, 136; John, 8, 20, 26, 42, 45, 50, 68, 88, 97, 138, 149, 155, 170; Peter, orphan, 23; Thomas, 1, 21, 22, 28, 33, 37, 41, 49, 50, 51, 53, 56, 57, 58, 61, 63, 64, 66, 68, 69, 74, 75, 78, 81, 82, 93, 95, 97, 99, 103, 109, 113, 114, 120, 126, 130, 132, 136, 138, 141, 146, 148, 149, 151, 153, 156, 157, 159, 160, 170, 173, 176, 178, 181; Thomas Jr., 30, 50, 99, 105, 119, 133, 148, 159, 173, 176, 178; Thomas, Sheriff, 36; Thomas, sub Sheriff, 83, 181, 182

Simmons's Mill, 155

Simons: John, 52, 58; Thomas, 34, 69, 157, 162

Sims: Adam, 145, 154, 171

Sisson: Thomas, 114

Skerrett: Dominick, 20, 26

Skerretts: Dominick, 13

Slaughter: Edward, 152

slaves, 142; Hannah, 176; Harry, 160; Isbell, 84; Jack Mingo, 21; Robin, 13; Tom, 3

Sloan: Margaret, 5

Smart: Mathew, 30, 63, 100, 119, 127, 137, 141, 147, 153, 158, 162, 163, 173; Mathew Jr., 49, 55, 86, 93, 150, 173, 177, 178

Smith: Eliza., 11; John, 7, 10, 11, 14, 19, 25, 47, 57, 74, 80, 84, 89, 94, 105, 119, 140, 155, 159, 161, 162, 167, 171; John Jr., 7, 10; Joseph, 59, 62, 66, 67, 69, 70, 73, 74, 76, 79, 80, 84, 89; Judith, 111, 121, 124; Mary, 11; Richard, 5, 21, 27, 42, 46, 65, 87, 97, 111, 113, 116, 119, 122, 126, 135, 136, 139, 140, 143, 149; Richard Jr., 125; Richard Sr., 82, 109, 114, 151; Susan, 65; Thomas, 12, 17, 19, 24, 27, 111, 121, 124; Thomas, dec., 111; William, 11, 17, 19, 24, 28, 29, 46, 57, 60, 65, 88, 158, 161, 171, 177, 180

Soane: Henry, 60, 95, 100, 117, 123, 135, 139; John, 39, 41, 44, 158, 166

Spain: John, 50, 53, 57, 59, 60, 63, 90, 94, 100, 105, 119, 126; Thomas, 102, 120, 158; William, 57, 114, 175

Spell: Elizabeth, 37; George, 38, 41, 42; George, dec., 37

Spencer: Rebecca, 111, 121, 131, 138, 142; Richard, 31, 111, 121, 131, 138, 142; Richard, dec., 111

Spiller: William, 8, 9, 45, 83, 146, 153, 154, 157, 158, 163, 174, 178, 181

Spotswood: Alexander, Lt. Gov., 171, 179

Stagg: Charles, 169, 176

Stainback: Onah, 22; William, 22, 47, 48, 49, 54, 55, 64, 89, 119; William Jr., 33, 37, 40, 43, 65, 119; William Sr., 132

Standback: William, 16; William Jr., 1

Stapley: Tomson, 152

Steagall: Jean, 1, 9, 13; Joan, 3

Stell: George, 151, 152

Stevens: John, 53, 57, 58, 161, 167; John, dec., 161

Stith: Drury Jr., 179; Drury Jr., justice, 179; John, 33, 143, 148; Mary, 33, 176

Stokes: Jil:, 30; John, 159; Silvanus, 126

Stony Creek, 76, 133

Stony Creeke Bridge, 172

storehouses, 40, 169

stores, 8, 65, 112

Stroud: John, 28, 34, 63, 85, 124, 175; Joseph, 21, 82, 114; William, 137, 146, 153, 157, 162

Sturdevant: Chichester, 153

Sturdivant: Chichester, 44, 47, 65; Daniel, 64, 69, 136; James, 136; John, 56, 61, 94, 100, 101; Mathew, 64

Surry County, 2, 5, 88

surveyors, 8, 11, 30, 60, 179

Sykes: Bernard, 98, 102, 105, 113, 117; Bernard Jr., 98; Bernard Sr., 98, 102, 105, 113, 117; Bernard Sr., dec., 98; John, orphan, 105; Richard, orphan, 105

Talbott: Mary, 145; Michal, 86, 87, 118, 121; Michal, dec., 86, 118; Peter, 86, 140, 145, 153, 159, 161, 162, 169, 171, 174, 178; William, 86, 130, 133, 145, 153, 154, 158

Talbut: Michael, 14, 81; Peter, 81

Talbutt: Michael, 37, 46; Michal, 52, 88; Michall, 31; Peter, 30, 31, 63, 88

Tally: Henry, 18, 30, 56; Henry Jr., 18; John, 50, 57, 90, 111, 152; Mary, 18, 56

Tapley: Adam, 7, 9, 10, 24, 25, 29, 30, 44, 52, 59, 63, 70, 71, 72, 74, 97, 111, 169, 172; Alexander, 24, 172, 180; Elizabeth, 70

Taply: Adam, 59, 75; Alexander, 97

Tatam: Henry, 115

Tatum: Christopher, 22; Edward, 150; Henry, 150; Mary, 22, 29, 34; Mary, dec., 22; Nathaniel, 8, 11, 14, 15, 17, 19, 21, 22, 23, 26, 27, 29, 34, 35, 51, 121; Nathaniel, dec., 150; Samuel, 11, 14, 15, 21, 23, 26, 27, 34, 121; Samuel, dec., 11

Taylor: John, 75; Roger, 4, 36, 40, 52, 57, 89, 106, 149, 152, 156, 160, 166; Thomas, 119, 167; William, 120, 127

Temple: Samuel, 81, 109, 174; William, 17, 19, 21, 39, 81, 168, 178; William Jr., 50, 161, 168, 174

Thomas: Joseph, 144; Rowland, 83, 88, 94, 100

Thompson: Henry, 161, 165, 178; Henry, dec., 161; John, 103, 110, 128; Sarah, 161, 165, 178

Thweatt: Henry, 26, 42, 68, 88, 98, 102, 148, 150, 153, 154, 156, 158, 163, 174; James, 4, 7, 8, 22, 26, 28, 29, 47, 50, 55, 59, 63, 64, 75, 78, 79, 81, 82, 87, 88, 92, 97, 98, 114, 140, 148, 165, 174, 175, 177, 179; James, Capt., 26, 102; James, Capt., Coroner, 82; James, Coroner, 50; James, Coroner, 180; James, justice, 5, 7, 10, 12, 16, 18, 20, 21, 46, 49, 51, 56, 60, 76, 79, 80, 82, 83, 84, 85; James, Sheriff, 97, 114, 116, 130, 131, 135, 138, 139, 143, 146, 149, 151, 153, 154, 157, 158, 181; John, 30, 68, 98, 102, 148, 153, 154; Judith, 7, 8, 81

Tidmarsh: Elizabeth, 110; John, 110; John, dec., 110; Richard, 172

Tiller: John, 8, 11, 16, 17, 19, 25, 32, 167, 174; Susan, als. Smith, 11

Tillman: George, 18, 19, 28, 66, 81, 86, 87, 89, 90, 92, 96, 98, 100, 105, 113, 114, 145, 147, 172; John, 58, 81, 87, 90, 145, 147, 165; Mary, 145; Roger, 81, 87, 90; Susanna, 58, 61, 66, 68, 86; Susanna, dec., 58

tithables, 8, 12, 14, 20, 22, 29, 50, 60, 64, 82, 95, 102, 111, 114, 130, 141, 150, 160, 165, 176

Titmarsh: Elizabeth, 112; John, 112

tobacco houses, 151

Tomkins: John, 31; Richard, 5, 28

Tomlinson: Elinor, 134; Ellinor, 160; Jane, 71, 75; John, 158, 163, 169; Richard, 134, 150, 160, 162, 170; William, 29, 35, 37, 71, 75

Troughton: Elizabeth, 169, 172; William, 85, 86, 92, 99, 108, 118, 123, 129, 134, 145, 150, 172, 175; William, dec., 172

Tucker: Francis, 98; John, 46, 51, 53, 114; John, dec., 46; Joseph, 114, 175; Martha, 29; Martha, orphan, 72, 75; Mary, 98; Robert, 46, 64, 65, 96, 175, 179; William, 82, 114

Tuckers Runn, 121, 126

Turbyfeild: Richard, 45

Turner: Jerre:, 70; Jerremiah, 73, 76; John, 120, 127, 137, 141, 147

Tye: Allen, 130

Upchurch: Michal, 34; Michall, 28

Urvin: Elizabeth, 24; Nathaniel, 24

Varina Parish, 2

Vaughan: Daniel, 8; Samuel, 8

Vaughn: Ann, 126, 137; Daniel, 79, 86, 102, 148; James, 105, 106, 126; John, 1, 5, 6, 9, 14, 15, 17, 19, 24; Nicholas, 19, 86, 136, 137; Richard, 18, 49, 114; Samuel, 1, 6, 9, 14, 15, 17, 19, 24, 105, 109; Samuel Sr., dec., 105; Samuell, 1; Sarah, 15, 24, 105, 109; William, 15, 24

Vernon: Ephraim, 173; Walter, 83, 89, 94

Virginia Indian Co., 131, 142

Walke: Thomas, 179

Walker: Alexander, 180; John, 175

Wall: Daniel, 136, 140, 141; John, 8, 11, 80, 81, 82, 85, 93, 98, 132, 134, 136, 140, 141, 175, 176; John, dec., 80; Joseph, 136, 176; Joshua, 140, 141; Sarah, 80, 85, 93, 98, 132; William, 136, 140, 141

Wall's Runn, 46

Wallbrook: John, 33

Wallice: Michael, 58; Michal, 159; William, 6, 47, 48, 54, 93, 96, 101, 109, 110, 113, 116, 122, 150, 162, 163, 181

Wallices, 111

Wallis: William, 178

Wallpole: Richard, 33

Wallpool: Richard, 28

Wallpoole: Richard, 2

Walpole: Elinor, 91, 96, 117, 119, 127; Ellinor, 98; Richard, 63, 70, 96, 98, 117, 119, 127, 134; Richard, dec., 91

Ward: Bridget, 133, 136, 139, 145; Collingwood, 122, 133, 136, 139, 145; John, 103; Seth, 70

Ward's Creek, 58, 68

Ward's Runn, 51

Warrick, 177

Warrick Bridge, 82

Warthan: Richard, 65

Warthen: Ailce, 40, 97; Richard, 27, 40, 97, 98, 162, 178, 180; William, 111

Warthen's Mill, 16, 51, 155

Warthin's Mill, 58, 68, 110

Watkins: Henry, 33; Rachel, 33

Waurick Swamp, 172

Waynoke Parish, 151, 178; Churchwardens, 162; tithables, 130, 160

Webb: Giles, 69, 73; Thomas, 69, 70, 73; William, 120

Weeks: Thomas, 89, 131, 163, 170

Weiks: Thomas, 81

Wells: William, 1, 105

West: John, 25, 53; Robert, 32, 123, 136

Westbrook, 68; Henry, orphan, 75; James, 26, 29, 75; John, 26, 68, 75; Margarett, orphan, 75; W., 50; William, 82

Westmoreland: Richard, 136

Westopher Parish, 39; Churchwardens, 5, 9, 14, 23, 25, 35, 47; tithables, 29, 64

Westover, 165

Westover Parish, 77, 101, 147; Churchwardens, 150, 162; tithables, 95, 130, 150, 160; vestrymen elected, 167

Wheatley: Thomas, 81, 86, 88; Thomas, dec., 80; William, 1, 2, 6, 9, 10, 13, 15, 32, 35, 38

Wheatly: William, 4

White: Charles, 87; Elizabeth, 106; John, 29, 106, 133

Whitmore: Elizabeth, 99; Nicholas, 28, 42, 99; Nicholas, dec., 99; Richard, 86, 92, 96, 101, 104

Whittimore: Elizabeth, 47

Whittmore: Elizabeth, 102, 103, 117, 121; John, 146, 153, 157, 172; Mary, 104; Nicholas, 102, 103, 104, 117; Nicholas Jr., 117, 121; Nicholas Sr., 105; Nicholas, dec., 104; Richard, 39, 59, 104, 105, 117, 130, 135

Whood: Thomas, 82

Wicketts: John, 158, 163

Wicks: Thomas, 80

Wiggins: Mary, 115, 121, 131, 138, 143; Sarah, 158, 163, 174

Wilkason: John, 132

Wilkins: ffrancis, 71, 102; John, 1, 71, 84, 87, 92, 96, 101, 102, 108, 109, 110, 113, 115, 117, 122, 131, 172; Robert, 164; Thomas, 118

Wilkinson: Francis, 144; John, 37

Willborn: John, 7

Willcox: John, 9, 18, 26

William & Mary, 8

Williams: Ann, 74; Charles, 4, 16, 17, 19, 25, 32, 37, 74, 77, 79, 80, 81, 84, 89, 94, 123, 137, 142, 148, 154, 158, 161, 163, 167, 174, 178; Cuthbert, 89; James, 18, 38, 88, 105, 114; John, 2, 6; Kath:, 74; Kath., 59; Kathrine, 56, 83, 89, 94, 100; Mathew, 180; Rebecca, 6; William, 17, 19, 25, 32, 37, 74, 77, 79, 80, 81, 84, 89, 94; William, dec., 74

Williamsburg, Va., 22, 169, 176; gaol, 66, 168

Williamson: Cuthbert, 92; John, 107, 108, 114, 115, 128; Robert, 168; Valentine, 19; Volentine, 98

Willis: ffrancis, 75

Willkasons Brickhouse, 16

Willkins: ffrances, 44; ffrancis, 31; John, 35

Willkinson: ffrancis, 47; John, 39, 59

Willson: Thomas, 158

Wilson: John, 93

Winingham: Edward, 133; John, 131; Thomas, 44, 52, 57, 61, 91

Winkles: Richard, 109, 115, 118, 121, 131, 138, 143, 145, 158, 163, 174; William, 120

Winningham: Edward, 98; John, 132

Wise: Robert, 147

wolves heads, 21, 124, 176, 180

wolves killed, 49, 82, 114, 151, 170, 175

Womack: John, 8, 59, 60, 63, 67, 106, 122; John Jr., 53, 114; John Sr., 53; Mary, 60, 106; Richard, 14, 18, 19, 57, 60, 73, 114, 116

Womacke: John Jr., 82, 101, 106, 109

Woodlief: Elizabeth, 5, 9; George, 35, 111; John, 8; Joshua, 99

Woodleife: Edward, 47, 93, 100, 119, 126, 132, 172; Edward, dec., 119; Elizabeth, 9; George, 47, 48, 49, 54, 55, 109, 110, 113, 154; John, 48, 65, 72, 76, 83, 98, 132, 157, 167, 172, 173; Joseph, 81, 101, 119, 126, 150; Joshua, 31, 93, 100; Sarah, 119, 126, 132

Woodson: ffrancis, 38; John, 2

Woodward: William, 137, 139

Worronak, 134

Worsham: John Jr., 103; John, Capt., 46; William, 8, 13, 15, 16, 50, 57

Worthin: Richard, 91

Wray: William, 150, 156

Wright: Dennis, 150

Wyanoake Parish, 4; tithables, 64

Wyanoke Parish, 87; tithables, 29, 95

Wyatt: Anthony, 92; Anthony, orphan, 105; Edward, 20, 46, 63, 68, 72, 76, 81, 87, 92, 95, 103, 112, 116, 118, 121, 122, 126, 131, 132, 138, 142, 161, 162, 171, 172, 174, 178, 179, 180; Francis, 105; John, 102, 105, 109, 115, 125; John, orphan, 92; Nicholas, 59, 125, 172, 178, 180; Nicholas, dec., 171; Susan, 105

Wynne: ffrances, 64; ffrancis, 26, 28, 57; Frances, 146; Francis, 38, 63, 139; Joshua, 4, 8, 13, 15, 17, 18, 19, 24, 26, 27, 28, 31, 48, 73, 86, 89, 93, 103, 177; Joshua, Maj., 5; Martha, 96; Peter, 4, 8, 13, 15, 17, 18, 19, 21, 24, 26, 27, 28, 31, 33, 34, 37, 38, 40, 43, 48, 51, 52, 55, 57, 59, 61, 65, 68, 69, 70, 72, 73, 75, 78, 93, 99, 104, 107, 110, 111, 113, 116, 128, 129, 132, 137, 141, 146, 177, 179; Robert, 5, 96; Thomas, 104, 113, 115; William, 5

Young: Dorrell, 91

Heritage Books by Wesley E. Pippenger:

Essex County, Virginia General Index to Deeds No. 2, 1867–1904, Deed Books 52 to 61

Essex County, Virginia Guardianship and Orphans Records, 1707–1888: A Descriptive Index

Essex County, Virginia Index to Court Orders, 1702–1715

Essex County, Virginia Land Tax Lists, 1782–1814

Essex County, Virginia Marriage Bonds, 1804–1850, Annotated

Essex County, Virginia Marriage Records, 1884–1921

Essex County, Virginia Newspaper Notices, 1738–1938

Essex County, Virginia Newspaper Notices, Vol. 2, 1735–1952

Essex County, Virginia Will Abstracts, 1751–1842 and Estate Records Index, 1751–1799
Revised Edition

Georgetown, District of Columbia 1850 Federal Population Census
(Schedule I) and 1853 Directory of Residents of Georgetown

Georgetown, District of Columbia Marriage and Death Notices, 1801–1838

Husbands and Wives Associated with Early Alexandria, Virginia
(and the Surrounding Area), 3rd Edition, Revised

Index to District of Columbia Estates, 1801–1929

Index to District of Columbia Land Records, 1792–1817

Index to Virginia Estates, 1800–1865: Volumes 4, 5 and 6

John Alexander, a Northern Neck Proprietor, His Family, Friends and Kin

King and Queen County, Virginia Land Tax Lists, 1782–1807

King and Queen County, Virginia Marriage Records Index, 1853–1975

King and Queen County, Virginia Personal Property Tax Lists, 1782–1803

Legislative Petitions of Alexandria, 1778–1861

Marriage and Death Notices from Alexandria, Virginia Newspapers, 1784–1852

Pippenger and Pittenger Families

Prince George County, Virginia Order Book, 1714/5–1720/1

Proceedings of the Orphan's Court, Washington County, District of Columbia, 1801–1808

Richmond County, Virginia Deed Abstracts, 1726–1774, Account Book 1 Extracts and Deed Books 9-13

Richmond County, Virginia Marriage Records, 1854–1890, Annotated

Stafford County, Virginia Land Tax Lists, 1782–1805

Tappahannock and Essex County, Virginia in Early Photographs

The Georgetown Courier *Marriage and Death Notices:*
Georgetown, District of Columbia, November 18, 1865 to May 6, 1876

The Georgetown Directory for the Year 1830: to which is appended, a Short Description of the Churches, Public Institutions, and
the Original Charter of Georgetown, and Extracts of the Laws Pertaining to the Chesapeake and Ohio Canal Company

The Virginia Gazette and Alexandria Advertiser: *Volume 1, September 3, 1789 to November 11, 1790*

The Virginia Journal and Alexandria Advertiser:
Volume I (February 5, 1784 to January 27, 1785)

Volume II (February 3, 1785 to January 26, 1786)

Volume III (March 2, 1786 to January 25, 1787)

Volume IV (February 8, 1787 to May 21, 1789)

The Washington and Georgetown Directory of 1853

Tombstone Inscriptions of Alexandria, Volumes 1–5

Virginia's Lost Wills: An Index

Westmoreland County, Virginia Marriage Records, 1850–1880, Annotated

www.ingramcontent.com/pod-product-compliance
Lightning Source LLC
Chambersburg PA
CBHW080238270326
41926CB00020B/4288